Data Warehousing Design and Advanced Engineering Applications:
Methods for Complex Construction

Ladjel Bellatreche
Poitiers University, France

Information Science REFERENCE

INFORMATION SCIENCE REFERENCE

Hershey • New York

Director of Editorial Content:	Kristin Klinger
Senior Managing Editor:	Jamie Snavely
Managing Editor:	Jeff Ash
Assistant Managing Editor:	Michael Brehm
Publishing Assistant:	Sean Woznicki
Typesetter:	Jeff Ash
Cover Design:	Lisa Tosheff
Printed at:	Yurchak Printing Inc.

Published in the United States of America by
Information Science Reference (an imprint of IGI Global)
701 E. Chocolate Avenue
Hershey PA 17033
Tel: 717-533-8845
Fax: 717-533-8661
E-mail: cust@igi-global.com
Web site: http://www.igi-global.com/reference

Library of Congress Cataloging-in-Publication Data

Data warehousing design and advanced engineering applications : methods for complex construction / Ladjel Bellatreche, editor.
       p. cm.

Includes bibliographical references and index.
Summary: "This book covers the process of analyzing data to extract, transform, load, and manage the essential components of a data warehousing system"--Provided by publisher.

ISBN 978-1-60566-756-0 (hardcover) -- ISBN 978-1-60566-757-7 (ebook) 1. Data warehousing. I. Bellatreche, Ladjel, 1968-

QA76.9.D37D4 2009
005.74'5--dc22
                              2009017418

British Cataloguing in Publication Data
A Cataloguing in Publication record for this book is available from the British Library.

All work contributed to this book is new, previously-unpublished material. The views expressed in this book are those of the authors, but not necessarily of the publisher.

Advances in Data Warehousing and Mining (ADWM)

ISBN: 1935-2646

Editor-in-Chief: David Taniar, Monash Univerisy, Australia

Progressive Methods in Data Warehousing and Business Intelligence: Concepts and Competitive Analytics

Edited By: David Taniar, Monash University, Australia

Information Science Reference • copyright 2008 • 390pp • H/C (ISBN: 978-1-60566-232-9) • $195.00

Recent technological advancements in data warehousing have been contributing to the emergence of business intelligence useful for managerial decision making. Progressive Methods in Data Warehousing and Business Intelligence: Concepts and Competitive Analytics presents the latest trends, studies, and developments in business intelligence and data warehousing contributed by experts from around the globe. Consisting of four main sections, this book covers crucial topics within the field such as OLAP and patterns, spatio-temporal data warehousing, and benchmarking of the subject.

Data Mining and Knowledge Discovery Technologies

Edited By: David Taniar; Monash University, Australia

IGI Publishing • copyright 2008 • 379pp • H/C (ISBN: 978-1-59904-960-1) • $99.95

As information technology continues to advance in massive increments, the bank of information available from personal, financial, and business electronic transactions and all other electronic documentation and data storage is growing at an exponential rate. With this wealth of information comes the opportunity and necessity to utilize this information to maintain competitive advantage and process information effectively in real-world situations. Data Mining and Knowledge Discovery Technologies presents researchers and practitioners in fields such as knowledge management, information science, Web engineering, and medical informatics, with comprehensive, innovative research on data mining methods, structures, tools, and methods, the knowledge discovery process, and data marts, among many other cutting-edge topics.

The Advances in Data Warehousing and Mining (ADWM) Book Series aims to publish and disseminate knowledge on an international basis in the areas of data warehousing and data mining. The book series provides a highly regarded outlet for the most emerging research in the field and seeks to bridge underrepresented themes within the data warehousing and mining discipline. The Advances in Data Warehousing and Mining (ADWM) Book Series serves to provide a continuous forum for state-of-the-art developments and research, as well as current innovative activities in data warehousing and mining. In contrast to other book series, the ADWM focuses on the integration between the fields of data warehousing and data mining, with emphasize on the applicability to real world problems. ADWM is targeted at both academic researchers and practicing IT professionals.

Hershey • New York

Order online at www.igi-global.com or call 717-533-8845 x100–
Mon-Fri 8:30 am - 5:00 pm (est) or fax 24 hours a day 717-533-7115

Table of Contents

Section 2
Physical Design and Self Tuning

Section 3
Evolution and Maintenance Management

Section 4
Exploitation of Data Warehouse

Detailed Table of Contents

Section 1
Conceptual Design and Ontology-Based Integration

This chapter gives a nice survey on conceptual design and user requirement analysis in the context of data warehouse environment and shows its importance in guarantying the success of business intelligence projects.

This chapter focuses on the problem of integrating of XML heterogeneous information sources into a data warehouse with data defined. The main characteristic of this integration is that it is guided by an ontology. The authors present an approach supporting the acquisition of data from a set of external sources available for an application of interest including data extraction, data transformation and data integration or reconciliation. The integration middleware that the authors propose extracts data from external XML sources which are relevant according to an RDFS+ ontology, transforms returned XML data into RDF facts conformed to the ontology and reconciles RDF data in order to resolve possible redundancies.

Chapter 3

Hadj Mahboubi, Université de Lyon (ERIC Lyon 2), France
Jean-Christian Ralaivao, Université de Lyon (ERIC Lyon 2), France
Sabine Loudcher, Université de Lyon (ERIC Lyon 2), France
Omar Boussaïd, Université de Lyon (ERIC Lyon 2), France
Fadila Bentayeb, Université de Lyon (ERIC Lyon 2), France
Jérôme Darmont, Université de Lyon (ERIC Lyon 2), France

This chapter proposes a unified XML warehouse reference model that synthesizes and enhances related work, and fits into a global XML warehousing and analysis approach thea uthors have developed. This chapter is validated by a software platform that is based on this model, as well as a case study that illustrates its usage.

Chapter 4

Yasser Hachaichi, Mir@cl Laboratory, Faculté des Sciences Economiques et de Gestion, Tunisia
Jamel Feki, Mir@cl Laboratory, Faculté des Sciences Economiques et de Gestion, Tunisia
Hanene Ben-Abdallah, Mir@cl Laboratory, Faculté des Sciences Economiques et de Gestion, Tunisia

This chapter presents a bottom-up/data-driven method for designing data marts from two types of sources: a relational database and XML documents compliant to a given DTD. This method has three automatic steps: Data source pretreatment, relation classification, and data mart schema construction and one manual step for DM schema adaptation. This method is illustrated an e-ticket DTD used by an online broker and a relational database modeling a hotel room booking system.

Chapter 5

Patrice Buche, INRA, France
Sandrine Contenot, INRA, France
Lydie Soler, INRA, France
Juliette Dibie-Barthélemy, AgroParisTech, France
David Doussot, AgroParisTech, France
Gaelle Hignette, AgroParisTech, France
Liliana Ibanescu, AgroParisTech, France

This chapter presents an application in the field of food safety using an ontology-based data integration approach. The ontology-based data integration approach permits to homogenize data sources which are heterogeneous in terms of structure and vocabulary. This approach is done in the framework of the Semantic Web, an international initiative which proposes annotating data sources using ontologies in order to manage them more efficiently.

This chapter presents a panorama of spatial OLAP (SOLAP) models and an analytical review of research SOLAP tools. It describes a Web-based system: GeWOlap. GeWOlap is an OLAP-GIS integrated solution implementing drill and cut spatio-multidimensional operators, and it supports some new spatio-multidimensional operators which change dynamically the structure of the spatial hypercube thanks to spatial analysis operators.

Section 2
Physical Design and Self Tuning

This chapter presents the problem of materialized view selection and presents algorithms in dynamic environment. A tool called MATUN, build from the ground up to facilitate different view materialization strategies using the proposed algorithms.

This chapter proposes ChunkSim, an event-based simulator for analysis of load and availability balancing in chunk-wise parallel data warehouses. This chapter discusses first how a shared nothing machine can store and process a data warehouse chunk-wise, and uses an efficient on demand processing approach. Then, it presents different parameters used by ChunkSim. Finally, it presents data allocation and replication alternatives that ChunkSim implements and the analysis that ChunkSim is currently able to run on performance and availability features.

This chapter presents QoS-oriented scheduling and distributed data placement strategies for the Grid-based warehouse. It discusses the use of a physically distributed database, in which tables are both partitioned and replicated across sites. The use of facts' table partitioning and replication is particularly relevant as Grid users' queries may follow geographical related access patterns.

This chapter focuses on the problem of maintenance in the data warehouse domain and provides illustrating examples that motivate the need for data warehouse maintenance. It presents some basic terms and definitions for the common understanding and introduces the different aspects of data warehouse maintenance. Several approaches addressing the problem are presented and classified by their capabilities.

This chapter proposes a formal framework which deals with the problem of integrating of heterogeneous data sources from various categories: the structured data, the semi-structured data and unstructured data. This approach is based on the definition of an integration environment.

This chapter presents the MVDWQL query language, for the multiversion data warehouse that allows: (1) query multiple data warehouse versions that differ with respect to their schemas, (2) augment query results with metadata describing changes made to the queried data warehouse versions, and (3) explicitly query metadata on the history of data warehouse changes and visualize their results. Two types of queries on metadata are supported, namely: (1) queries searching for data warehouse versions that include an indicated data warehouse object and (2) queries retrieving the history of the evolution of an indicated data warehouse object.

This chapter presents a nice survey on ontology query languages dedicated to ontology based databases. To compare these languages, a set of requirements for an architecture that extends the traditional ANSI/ SPARC architecture with conceptual and ontological levels is defined. An interesting discussion about two Semantic Web query languages: SPARQL and RQL is given. Two database-oriented ontology query languages: Oracle extension to SQL and OntoQL to fulfill these requirements are given.

This chapter studies the problem of query personalisation in the context of ontology based databases, where OntoDB model is used to validate the proposed work. A preference model is proposed. It is composed of several types of preferences usually addressed in the literature in a separate way.

This chapter presents an important issue in data warehouse which is security. It describes the traditional security models: mandatory access control (MAC), driven mainly by military requirements and role-based access control (RBAC) is the commonly used access control model in commercial databases. Some issues on statistical databases are given.

Preface

For the past fifteen years, data warehousing and on line analysis (OLAP) technologies have shown their effectiveness in managing and analyzing a large amount of disparate data. Today, these technologies are confronted with new applications (mobile environments, data integration, data flow, personalization, stream data, sensor network applications, etc.) and new challenges as shown by the increasing success of the EII technologies (Enterprise Information Integration). These technologies are attracting a lot of attention from the database, data warehousing and data mining research communities.

Two main particularities of this book are: (i) it covers the whole process of designing and using a data warehouse, which includes requirement specification, conceptual design, logical design, physical design, tuning and evolution management and (ii) it shows the contribution of ontologies in designing and exploiting data warehouses.

The primary objective of this book is to give readers in-depth knowledge of data warehouses and their applications. The book is designed to cover a comprehensive range of steps for designing efficient and self administrable data warehouses and managing their evolution. The fact that most of these steps are supported by some commercial DBMS motivates the need for such a book.

There was great response to the call for proposals, but due to the limited space only 15 chapters were accepted and selected. These chapters are authored by an outstanding roster of experts in their respective fields, and tackle various issues from different angles, requirements and interests. Their topics include user requirement specification, conceptual design, ontology driven ETL process, physical design and self tuning (materialized view selection, parallel processing, etc.), evolution and maintenance management, and security. The conceptual design concerns both classical and complex data sources (XML and spatial data).

The fifteen selected chapters cover the majority of steps executed within data warehouse projects. They can be classified into four sections: Conceptual Design and Ontology-based Integration, Physical Design and Self Tuningt, Evolution and Maintenance Management, and Exploitation of Data Warehouse.

The four sections are summarized as follows.

Section 1: Conceptual Design and Ontology–Based Integration

This part contains six chapters summarized as follows:

From User Requirements to Conceptual Design in Data Warehouse Design – a Survey, by Matteo Golfarelli, gives a nice survey on conceptual design and user requirement analysis in the context of data warehouse environment and shows its importance in guaranteeing the success of business intelligence projects. It points out pros and cons of the different conceptual design techniques. Precise and simple examples are given to facilitate the understanding of existing conceptual models. This criticism may help readers and designers to identify crucial choices and possible solutions more consciously when designing data warehouse projects. A particular attention is devoted to emphasizing the relationships between user requirement analysis and conceptual design and showing how they can be jointly and fruitfully used.

Data Extraction, Transformation and Integration guided by an Ontology, by Chantal Reynaud, Nathalie Pernelle, Marie-Christine Rousset, Brigitte Safar and Fatiha Saïs, focuses on the problem of integrating XML heterogeneous information sources into a data warehouse. This integration is guided by an ontology. It presents an approach supporting the acquisition of data from a set of external sources available for an application of interest including data extraction, data transformation and data integration or reconciliation. The proposed integration middleware extracts data from external XML sources which are relevant according to an RDFS+ ontology, transforms returned XML data into RDF facts conformed to the ontology and reconciles RDF data in order to resolve possible redundancies. This chapter is a great exercise for readers and designers to understand the whole steps of the ETL process: extraction, transformation and loading.

X-WACoDa: An XML-based approach for Warehousing and Analyzing Complex Data, by Hadj Mahboubi, Jean-Christian Ralaivao, Sabine Loudcher, Omar Boussaïd, Fadila Bentayeb and Jérôme Darmont, proposes a unified XML warehouse reference model that synthesizes and enhances related work, and fits into a global XML warehousing. This chapter is validated by a software platform that is based on this model, as well as a case study that illustrates its usage.

Designing Data Marts from XML and Relational Data Sources, by Yasser Hachaichi, Jamel Feki and Hanene Ben-Abdallah, presents a bottom-up/data-driven method for designing data marts from two types of sources: relational database and XML documents compliant to a given DTD. This method has three automatic steps: Data source pretreatment, relation classification, and data mart schema construction and one manual step for DM schema adaptation. The different steps of this method are illustrated using an e-ticket DTD used by an online broker and a relational database describing a hotel room booking system.

Ontology-based integration of heterogeneous, incomplete and imprecise data dedicated to a decision support system for food safety, by Patrice Buche, Sandrine Contenot, Lydie Soler, Juliette Dibie-Barthélemy, David Doussot, Liliana Ibanescu and Gaëlle Hignette, presents an application in the field of food safety using an ontology-based data integration approach. This chapter is a real application of the conceptual design part. This chapter motivates the use of ontology to resolve different conflicts found when integrating heterogeneous sources (structural and semantic). This chapter explores three ways to integrate data according to a domain ontology: (1) a semantic annotation process to extend local data with Web data which have been semantically annotated according to a domain ontology, (2) a flexible querying system to query uniformly both local data and Web data and (3) an ontology alignment process to find correspondences between data from two sources indexed by distinct ontologies.

On Modeling and Analysis of Multidimensional Geographic Databases, by Sandro Bimonte, presents a panorama of spatial OLAP (SOLAP) models and an analytical review of SOLAP tools. Spatial data warehouse does not get the same amount of attention by the community as the classical data warehouse. This chapter describes a Web-based system: GeWOlap. GeWOlap is an OLAP-GIS integrated solution implementing drill and cut spatio-multidimensional operators, and it supports some new spatio-multidimensional operators which change dynamically the structure of the spatial hypercube thanks to spatial analysis operators.

Section 2: Physical Design and Self Tuning

This section contains three chapters summarized as follows:

View Selection and Materialization, by Zohra Bellahsene, presents the problem of selecting materialized views to speed up decision support queries in a dynamic environment. It proposes a view selection method for deciding which views to materialize according to statistic metadata. Polynomial algorithms selecting views to materialize are given. This work is validated by a tool, called MATUN, build from the ground up to facilitate different view materialization strategies using the proposed algorithms. This tool can be used by users and data warehouse administrators to select materialized views.

ChunkSim: A Tool and Analysis of Performance and Availability Balancing, by Pedro Furtado, proposes ChunkSim, an event-based simulator for analysis of load and availability balancing in chunk-wise parallel data warehouses. This chapter discusses first how a shared nothing machine can store and process a data warehouse chunk-wise, and uses an efficient on demand processing approach. Then, it presents different parameters used by ChunkSim. Finally, it presents data allocation and replication alternatives that ChunkSim implements and the analysis that ChunkSim is currently able to run on performance and availability features. Intensives experimentations are presented and show the interest of the author's work. This tool mainly contributes in self-tuning of physical parallel data warehouse. The main particularity of this chapter is that it issues a new research direction in data warehouse which is the development of simulators in order to facilitate the deployment of applications.

QoS-Oriented Grid-Enabled Data Warehouses, by Rogério Luís de Carvalho Costa and Pedro Furtado, presents QoS-oriented scheduling and distributed data placement strategies for a Grid-based warehouse. It discusses the use of a physically distributed database, in which tables are both partitioned and replicated across sites. The use of facts' table partitioning and replication is particularly relevant as Grid users' queries may follow geographical related access patterns. Inter-site dimension tables fragmentation and replication are done in order to achieve good performance in query execution but also to reduce data movement across sites, which is a costly operation in Grids.

Section 3: Evolution and Maintenance Management

This section contains two chapters summarized as follows:

Data Warehouse Maintenance, Evolution and Versioning, by Johann Eder and Karl Wiggisser, focuses on the problem of maintenance in the data warehouse domain, since, data warehouse systems are used in a changing environment thus the need for evolving systems is inevitable. This chapter provides illustrating examples that motivate the need for data warehouse maintenance. It also distinguishes between evolution and versioning problems. It presents some basic terms and definitions for the common understanding and introduces the different aspects of data warehouse maintenance. Several approaches addressing the problem are presented and classified by their capabilities.

Construction and Maintenance of Heterogeneous Data Warehouses, by Mohamed Badri, Faouzi Boufarès, Sana Hamdoun, Véronique Heiwy and Kazem Lellahi proposes a formal framework which deals with the problem of integrating of heterogeneous data sources from various categories: the structured data, the semi-structured data and unstructured data. This approach is based on the definition of an integration environment that is seen as a set of data sources associated with a set of "integration relationships" between the sources components. The originality of this work, contrary to various works on integration, lies in the fact of covering the integration of all the categories of data considered at the same time and in the proposition of a theoretical approach of the data integration. The proposed approach is general and is applicable to any type of integration.

Section 4: Exploitation of Data Warehouse

This section contains four chapters summarized as follows:

On Querying Data and Metadata in Multiversion Data Warehouse, by Wojciech Leja, Robert Wrembel and Robert Ziembicki, presents the *MVDWQL* query language, for the multiversion data warehouse that allows: (1) to query multiple data warehouse versions that differ with respect to their schemas, (2) to augment query results with metadata describing changes made to the queried data warehouse versions, and (3) to explicitly query metadata on the history of data warehouse changes and visualize their results. Two types of queries on metadata are supported, namely: (1) queries searching for data warehouse versions that include an indicated data warehouse object and (2) queries retrieving the history of the evolution of an indicated data warehouse object. The *MVDWQL* have been successfully implemented in a multiversion data warehouse prototype system.

Ontology Query Languages for Ontology-Based Databases: A Survey, by Stéphane Jean, Yamine Aït Ameur and Guy Pierra presents a nice survey on ontology query languages developed for ontology based database (OBDB). First of all, this chapter gives a definition and several criteria of ontology and shows that all existing ontologies are not similar. Therefore, it gives three categories of ontologies: *conceptual canonical ontologies*, *non conceptual canonical ontologies* and *linguistic ontologies* that can be combined into a layered model, called the onion model. Based on this model, a general OBDB architecture that extends the traditional ANSI/SPARC database architecture is defined with a set of language requirements for its exploitation. Different ontology query languages are then analysed by studying their capabilities to fulfil this requirements.

Ontology-Based Database Approach for Handling Preferences, by Dilek Tapucu, Gayo Diallo, Yamine Aït Ameur and Murat Osman Ünalir proposes a solution handling preferences in ontology-based databases. It is an extension of the previous chapter. First, a formal and generic model to handle users' preferences is defined. This proposed model is composed of several types of preferences usually addressed in the literature in a separate way. These preferences are independent of any logical model of data. This model is generic thanks to its ability to define a relationship with any ontology model. Then this chapter shows how this model can be integrated into the OntoDB OBDB architecture.

Security in Data Warehouses, by Edgar R. Weippl, presents an important issue in data warehouse which is security. It describes the traditional security models: *mandatory access control* (MAC), driven mainly by military requirements and *role-based access control* (RBAC) that is the commonly used access control model in commercial databases. Some issues on statistical databases are also given.

Section 1
Conceptual Design and Ontology–Based Integration

Chapter 1
From User Requirements to Conceptual Design in Data Warehouse Design
A Survey

Matteo Golfarelli
DEIS - University of Bologna, Italy

ABSTRACT

Conceptual design and requirement analysis are two of the key steps within the data warehouse design process. They are to a great extent responsible for the success of a data warehouse project since, during these two phases, the expressivity of the multidimensional schemata is completely defined. This chapter proposes a survey of the literature related to these design steps and points out pros and cons of the different techniques in order to help the reader to identify crucial choices and possible solutions more consciously. Particular attention will be devoted to emphasizing the relationships between the two steps describing how they can be jointly used fruitfully.

INTRODUCTION

Data Warehouse (DW) systems are used by decision makers to analyze the status and the development of an organization. DWs are based on large amounts of data integrated from heterogeneous sources into multidimensional schemata which are optimized for data access in a way that comes natural to human analysts. Generally speaking, a multidimensional schema is made up of facts, measures and dimensions. Facts are a focus of interest for the decision-making process (e.g. sales,

orders) and can be monitored through measures and dimensions. Measures are numerical KPIs (e.g., quantity of product sold, price of the products, etc.), and dimensions represent the context for analyzing these measures (e.g., time, customer, product, etc.). Owing to their specificities, the development of DWs is particularly complex and requires ad-hoc methodologies and an appropriate life-cycle.

Conceptual design and requirement analysis are two of the key steps within the DW design process. While they were partially neglected in the first era of data warehousing, they have received greater attention in the last ten years.

DOI: 10.4018/978-1-60566-756-0.ch001

The research literature has proposed several original approaches for conceptual modeling in the DW area, some based on extensions of known conceptual formalisms (e.g. E/R, UML), some based on ad hoc ones. Remarkably, a comparison of the different models pointed out that, abstracting from their graphical form, the core expressivity is similar, thus proving that the academic community has reached an informal agreement on the required expressivity.

On the other hand, the proposed solutions are not always coupled with an appropriate technique for requirement analysis to form a methodological approach ensuring that the resulting database will be well-documented and will fully satisfy the user requirements. DW specificities make these two steps even more related than in traditional database systems; in fact the lack of settled user requirements and the existence of operational data sources that fix the set of available information make it hard to develop appropriate multidimensional schemata that, on the one hand, fulfill user requirements and on the other, can be fed from the operational data sources.

This paper proposes a survey of the literature related to these design steps in order to help the reader make crucial choices more consciously. In particular, after a brief description of the DW life-cycle, the specific problems arising during requirement analysis and conceptual design are presented. The approaches to requirement analysis are then surveyed and their strengths and weaknesses are discussed. Afterwards, the literature related to the DW conceptual models is also surveyed and the core expressivity of these models is discussed in order to enable the reader to understand which are the relevant pieces of information to be captured during user-requirements analysis.

BACKGROUND

The DW is acknowledged as one of the most complex information system modules and its de-sign and maintenance is characterized by several complexity factors that determined, in the early stages of this discipline, a high percentage of real project failures. A clear classification of the critical factors of data warehousing projects was already available in 1997 when three different risk categories were identified (Demarest, 1997), namely *socio-technical* i.e. related to the impact a DW has on the decisional processes and political equilibriums, *technological* i.e. related to the usage of new and continuously evolving technologies, and *design-related* i.e. related to the peculiarities of this kind of systems. The awareness of the critical nature of the problems and the experience accumulated by practitioners determined the development of different design methodologies and the adoption of proper life-cycles that can increase the probability of completing the project and fulfill the user requirements.

The choice of a correct life-cycle for the DW must take into account the specificities of this kind of system, that according to Giorgini et al. (2007), are summarized as follows:

a) DWs rely on operational databases that represent the sources of the data.
b) User requirements are difficult to collect and usually change during the project.
c) DW projects are usually huge projects: the average time for their construction is 12 to 36 months and their average cost ranges from 0.5 to 10 million dollars.
d) Managers are demanding users that require reliable results in a time compatible with business needs.

While there is no consensus on how to address points (a) and (b), the DW community has agreed on an approach that cuts down costs and time to make a satisfactory solution available to the final users. Instead of approaching the DW development as a whole in a top-down fashion, it is more convenient to build it bottom-up working on single data marts (Jensen et al., 2004). A *data mart* is part of a DW with a restricted scope of content and support for analytical processing, serving a single department, part of an organization and/ or a particular data analysis problem domain. By adopting a bottom-up approach, the DW will turn out to be the union of all the data marts.

This iterative approach promises to fulfill requirement (c) since it cuts down development costs and time by limiting the design and implementation efforts to get the first results. On the other hand, requirement (d) will be fulfilled if the designer is able to implement first those data marts that are more relevant to the stakeholders.

It should be noted that adopting a pure bottom-up approach presents many risks originating from the partial vision of the business domain that will be available at each design phase. This risk can be limited by first developing the data mart that plays a central role within the DW, so that the following ones can be easily integrated into the existing backbone, this kind of solution is also called *bus architecture* (Kimbal et al., 1998).

Based on these considerations the main phases for the DW life-cycle can be summarized as follows:

1. *DW planning*: this phase is aimed at determining the scope and the goals of the DW, and determines the number and the order in which the data marts are to be implemented according to the business priorities and the technical constraints (Kimbal et al., 1998). At this stage the physical architecture of the system must also be defined: the designer carries out the sizing of the system in order to identify appropriate hardware and software platforms and evaluates the need for a reconciled data level aimed at improving data quality. Finally, during the project planning phase the staffing of the project is carried out.

2. *Data mart design and implementation*: this macro-phase will be repeated for each data mart to be implemented and will be discussed in more detail in the following. At each iteration a new data mart is designed and deployed.

3. *DW maintenance and evolution*: DW maintenance mainly concerns performance optimization that must be periodically carried out due to user requirements that change according to the problems and the opportunities the managers run into. On the other hand, DW evolution (Golfarelli & Rizzi, 2009) concerns keeping the DW schema up-to-date with respect to the business domain and the business requirement changes: a manager requiring a new dimension of analysis for an existing *fact schema* or the inclusion of a new level of classification due to a change in a business process may cause the early obsolescence of the system.

DW design methodologies proposed in the literature mainly concern phase 2 and thus should be better referred to as data mart design methodologies. Though a lot has been written about how a DW should be designed, there is no consensus on a design method yet. Most methods agree on the opportunity of distinguishing between the following phases:

2.1 *Requirement analysis:* identifies which information is relevant to the decisional process by either considering the user needs or the actual availability of data in the operational sources.

2.2 *Conceptual design*: aims at deriving an implementation-independent and expressive conceptual schema for the data mart, according to the conceptual model.

2.3 *Logical design*: takes the conceptual schema and creates a corresponding logical schema on the chosen logical model. While nowadays most of the DW systems are based on the relational logical model (ROLAP), an increasing number of software vendors are proposing also pure or mixed multidimensional solutions (MOLAP/HOLAP).

2.4 ETL process design: designs the mappings and the data transformations necessary to load into the logical schema of the DW the data available at the operational data source level.

2.5 Physical design: addresses all the issues specifically related to the suite of tools chosen for implementation – such as indexing and allocation.

Requirement analysis and conceptual design play a crucial role in handling DW peculiarities (a) and (b) described at the beginning of the present section: the lack of settled user requirements and the existence of operational data sources that fix the set of available information make it hard to develop appropriate multidimensional schemata that, on the one hand, fulfill user requirements and on the other, can be fed from the operational data sources.

REQUIREMENT ANALYSIS TECHNIQUES

In this section we classify the requirement analysis techniques proposed in the literature discussing their strengths and weaknesses in order to help the reader understand when and why they can be successfully adopted in a real project.

First of all it is necessary to distinguish between *functional* and *non-functional* requirements (Mylopoulos et al. 1992, Chung et al. 1999). Informally speaking, in software systems functional requirements answer what the system does and non-functional requirements answer how the system behaves with respect to some observable quality attributes like performance, reusability, reliability, etc. More specifically within DW systems functional requirements are mainly related to *what* information the DW is expected to provide, while non-functional ones answer *how*

this information should be provided for a correct use. Unfortunately, as has already happened in many other software engineering fields, much more work has been done for the first type than for the second one.

As for functional requirements three different design principles can be identified: supply-driven, goal-driven and user-driven. Part of the literature refers to the last two approaches as *demand-driven* since requirements are mainly obtained by interviewing the company personnel. We will use this term when the peculiarities that distinguish the two original ones are not relevant.

The *Supply-driven* approach (also called *data-driven*) is a bottom-up technique that starts with an analysis of operational data sources in order to identify all the available data (Golfarelli et al. 1998, Jensen et al. 2004). Here user involvement is limited to select which chunks of the available data are relevant for the decision-making process. Supply-driven approaches are feasible when all of the following are true: (1) detailed knowledge of data sources is available a priori or easily obtainable; (2) the source schemata exhibit a good degree of normalization; and (3) the complexity of source schemata is not too high. While the supply-driven approach simplifies the design of the ETL because each data in the DW corresponds to one or more attributes of the sources, it gives user requirements a secondary role in determining the information contents for analysis and gives the designer little support in identifying facts, dimensions, and measures. Consequently, the multidimensional schemata obtained could not fit the user requirements. This happens not only when business users are asking for information that is not actually present in the data sources, but also when the desired KPIs are not directly available but could be obtained through some computations. In other words, with the supply-driven approach there is the risk of generating performance information targeting a non-specified user group; such a risk is particularly high when the target users are at the strategic levels where the use of complex and compound KPIs is more common. On the other hand, the supply-driven approach is simpler and cheaper (in terms of both time and money) than other approaches since its duration only depends on the designer skills and on the data sources complexity. A further strength of this approach is the quality of the resulting multidimensional model that will be very stable since it is based on the schema of the operational data sources that do not change as frequently as the personal requirements of the business users.

The *user-driven* approach is a bottom-up technique that starts from determining the information requirements of different business users (Winter & Strauch, 2003). Their points of view are then integrated and made consistent in order to obtain a unique set of multidimensional schemata. The emphasis is on the requirement analysis process and on the approaches for facilitating user participations. The problem of mapping these requirements onto the available data sources is faced only a posteriori, and may fail, thus determining the users' disappointment. Although this approach is highly appreciated by business users that feel involved in the design and can understand the rationale of the choices, it is usually time expansive since the business users at the tactical level rarely have a clear and shared understanding of the business goals, processes and organization. Consequently, this approach usually requires great effort by the project manager, that must have very good moderation and leadership skills, in order to integrate the different points of view. Furthermore, the risk of obsolescence of the resulting schemata is high if requirements are based on the personal points of view of the users and do not express the company culture and the working procedures.

The g*oal-driven approach* focuses on the business strategy that is extrapolated by interviewing the top-management. Different visions are then analyzed and merged in order to obtain a consistent picture and finally translated into quantifiable KPIs. This approach (Boehnlein & Ulbrich vom Ende, 2000) is typically top-down since by starting from the analysis of a few key business processes, their characterizing measurements are derived first and than transformed into a data model that includes a wider set of KPIs that characterize such processes at all the organizational levels. The applicability of this approach strictly depends on the willingness of the top management to participate to the design process and usually require the capability of the project staff in translating the collected high-level requirements into quantifiable KPIs. Goal-oriented approaches maximize the probability of a correct identification of the relevant indicators, thus reducing the risk of obsolescence of the multidimensional schema.

In many real cases the difference between adopting a goal-driven instead of a user-driven approach may become very vague, on the other hand, it should be clear that the goal-driven process is top-down and based on the progressive refinement of a few goals defined by the top-managements, while in the user-driven approach, requirements are obtained by merging several simpler requirements gathered from the business-users in a bottom-up fashion. The result of a goal-driven approach differs from a user-driven one whenever the users do not have a clear understanding of the business strategy and the organization's goals.

Table 1 reports a comparison of the three basic approaches and may be useful to choose the one that is most suited to a given project. The main technical element influencing such a choice concerns the availability and the quality of the schema of the operational data sources, while several non-technical factors are involved in the choice. In particular, the cost and time constraints suggest a reduction of the time devoted to interviews and discussions with the users; similarly when the business users have a limited knowledge of the business process and strategy a user-driven approach should be avoided.

In order to avoid the drawbacks of the single approaches some mixed strategies have been developed. In particular, Bonifati et al. (2001) mix the

Table 1. Comparison of the basic user requirement techniques

	Supply-Driven	User-Driven	Goal-Driven
Basic approach	Bottom-up	Bottom-up	Top-Down
Users involvement	Low: DB Administrators	High: Business users	High: Top management
Constraints	Existence of a reconciled data level	Business users must have a good knowledge of the processes and organization of the company	Willingness of top management to participate in the design process
Strengths	The availability of data is ensured	Raise the acceptance of the system.	Maximize the probability of a correct identification of the relevant KPIs.
Risks	The multidimensional schemata do not fit business user requirements.	Quick obsolescence of the multidimensional schemata due to changes of the business users.	Difficulties in being supported by top management and in translating the business strategy into quantifiable KPIs.
Targeting organizational level	Operational and tactical	Depends on the level of the interviewed users, typically tactical	Strategic and tactical
Skills of project staff	DW designers	Moderators; DW designers	Moderators; Economist; DW designers
Risk of obsolescence	Low	High	Low
Number of source systems	Low	Moderate	High
Cost	Low	High	High

goal-oriented and the supply-driven techniques. They initially carry out a goal-driven step based on the GQM method (Vassiliadis et al. 1999; Basili et al. 1994) in order to identify the business needs the data mart is expected to meet. The outcome of this phase is a set of *ideal* star schemata obtained by a progressive top-down definition of the KPIs necessary to measure the goals. Then, the schema of the operational data sources are examined using a semi-automatic approach; the *candidate* facts, dimension and hierarchies are extracted and modelled using a graph-based representation (i.e. *star join graph*). Finally, the results of the two phases are integrated, thus determining the multidimensional model of the data mart as the set of candidate star join graphs that is most suited to matching the ideal star schemata.

Similarly, in GRAnD, the approach proposed by Giorgini et al. (2006), a goal-oriented step based on the Tropos methodology (Bresciani, 2004) is carried out in order to identify the business goals and the terms relevant to their monitoring. These terms are then mapped onto the operational source schema that is finally explored in a semi-automatic fashion in order to build the final multidimensional schemata.

A third approach coupling a goal-driven step with a supply-driven one has been proposed in (Mazon et al., 2007). The approach builds on a Model Driven Architecture (Mazon & Trujillo, 2008) where information is formalized using UML. In particular, project goals are modelled using a UML profile based on the *i** framework that has been properly adapted and extended to fit the DW specificities. Starting from the collected goals an initial conceptual model is obtained; then its correctness and feasibility is checked against data sources by using the Multidimensional Normal Forms (Lechtenboerger & Vossen, 2003).

The main difference between the three methods is that while in GRAnD the results of the goal-oriented step are used to drive the supply-driven one, in the other ones the goal-driven and the supply-driven steps are almost independent and they are used jointly a posteriori to verify the correctness of the conceptual model obtained.

Although, the formalisms used in the three approaches for the goal-oriented step are different, their expressivity is very close, showing that a core of common information to be captured has been identified. In particular, the second and the third ones are both based on *i** (Yu, 1995; Yu, 1997). In *i** (which stands for "distributed intentionality"), early requirements are assumed to involve social actors who depend on each other for goals to be achieved, tasks to be performed, and resources to be supplied. The *i** framework includes the strategic dependency model for describing the network of relationships among actors, as well as the strategic rationale model for describing and supporting the reasoning that each actor has about its relationships with other actors. These models have been formalized using intentional concepts such as goal, belief, ability, and commitment (Cohen & Levesque, 1990). The framework has been related to different application areas that, beside DW, include requirements engineering (Yu, 1993), business process reengineering (Yu & Mylopoulos, 1996), and software processes (Yu & Mylopoulos, 1994).

A further mixed method is the one proposed in (Guo, 2006) that puts together all the three basic approaches: a goal-oriented step determines the subject area of interest, defines the main KPIs and the target users. This information is exploited in the data- driven step in order to select the source systems and in the user-driven one to select the users to be interviewed. On the other hand, the results of these two steps refine and detail the results of the goal-oriented one and enable a more complete multidimensional model to be delivered.

Till now we considered techniques oriented to capturing *information* (functional) requirements for DWs. On the other hand, the final product of the DW design process is not just a data model but a whole DW system, where users require the information to have some characteristics when it is provided (security, performance tuning,

user configurations, etc.). Here non-functional requirements come into play. Only a few works in the DW literature have specifically addressed this issue. In particular, Paim & Castro (2003) propose the Data Warehouse Requirements Definition (DWARF) approach that adapts a traditional requirements engineering process for requirements definition and management of DWs. DWARF requires particular attention to non-functional requirements that are captured through an ad-hoc extension of the NFR framework. The NFR framework (Chung et al., 1999) is a goal-oriented approach specifically devised for non-functional requirements that are considered as potentially conflicting or synergistic softgoals to be achieved. A softgoal represent a goal that has no clear-cut definition and/or criteria as to whether it is satisfied or not. A softgoal is said to be "satisfied" when there is sufficient positive evidence and little negative evidence against it. The same authors provide a detailed classification of non-functional requirements (Paim & Castro, 2002) that must be addressed in the development of DWs, and guidelines for their operationalization. At the top level requirements are clustered into four classes, namely: performance, security, multidimensionality and user-friendliness.

Soler et al. (2008) investigate the security aspects by integrating a non-functional requirement analysis step into an existing DW approach for information requirements (Mazon & Trujillo, 2008).

CONCEPTUAL MODELS

Conceptual modeling is widely recognized to be the necessary foundation for building a database that is well-documented and fully satisfies the user requirements. In particular, from the designer point of view the availability of a conceptual model provides a higher level of abstraction in describing the warehousing process and its architecture in all its aspects.

In the last few years multidimensional modeling has attracted the attention of several researchers that defined different solutions each focusing on the set of information they considered strictly relevant. Some of these solutions have no (Agrawal et al., 1997; Pedersen & Jensen, 1999) or limited (Cabibbo & Torlone, 1998) graphical support, and are aimed at establishing a formal foundation for representing cubes and hierarchies and an algebra for querying them. On the other hand, we believe that a distinguishing feature of conceptual models is that of providing a graphical support to be easily understood by both designers and users when discussing and validating requirements. So we will classify "strict" conceptual models for DWs according to the graphical formalism they rely on, that could be either E/R, object-oriented or ad hoc. Some claim that E/R extensions should be adopted since:

1. E/R has been tested for years;
2. designers are familiar with E/R;
3. E/R has proved to be flexible and powerful enough to adapt to a variety of application domains
4. several important research results were obtained for the E/R model (Franconi & Kamble, 2004; Sapia et al., 1999; Tryfona et al., 1999).

On the other hand, advocates of object-oriented models argue that:

1. they are more expressive and better represent static and dynamic properties of information systems;
2. they provide powerful mechanisms for expressing requirements and constraints;
3. object-orientation is currently the dominant trend in data modeling;
4. UML, in particular, is a standard and is naturally extensible (Luján-Mora, 2006; Abello, 2006).

Finally, we believe that ad hoc models compensate for designers' lack of familiarity since:

1. they achieve better notational economy;
2. they give proper emphasis to the peculiarities of the multidimensional model;
3. they are more intuitive and readable by non-expert users (Golfarelli, 2008; Hüsemann et al., 2000; Tsois et al. 2001).

Remarkably, a comparison of the different models made by Abello et al. (2006) pointed out that, abstracting from their graphical form, the core expressivity of most of the conceptual models proposed in the literature is similar, thus proving that the academic community has reached an informal agreement on the required expressivity (see Figure 1).

We emphasize that, within the DW field, conceptual models and formal user-requirement techniques are rarely discussed together to form a comprehensive methodology. Furthermore, even in these cases (Bonifati et al., 2001; Giorgini et al., 2007; Guo, 2006; Mazon et al., 2007), non-functional requirements are almost neglected or they have been presented as a second class type of requirement, frequently hidden inside notes. On the other hand, the experiences in the broader area of software engineering show that capturing non-functional requirements without mapping them into the conceptual model may determine an information loss. In (Cysneiros & Sampaio do Prado Leite, 2004) the authors show how to integrate non-functional requirements into the Class, Sequence, and Collaboration UML Diagrams. The elicitation of non-functional requirements at the conceptual level enables a traceability mechanism. This mechanism provides a way of representing in the models, which aspects are there because of a non-functional requirement. This has shown to be quite useful during the model reviewing process. In different situations, the reviewers were surprised by the inclusion of elements in the conceptual models that did not

Figure 1. the SALE fact modeled, from the top to the bottom, using a StarER (Sapia et al., 1999), a UML class diagram (Luján-Mora et al., 2006), and a fact schema (Hüsemann et. al, 2000)

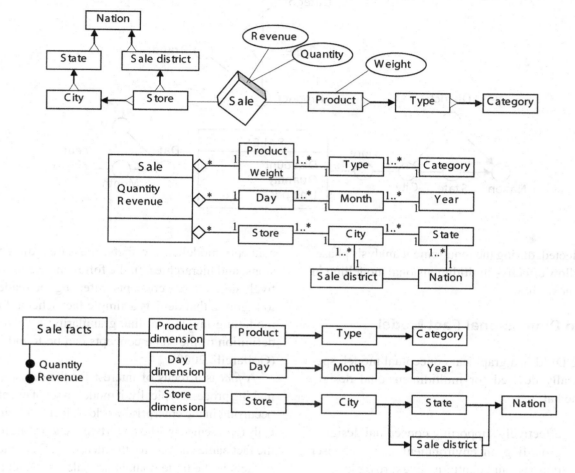

fit their perception of the application; they only became convinced of the necessity by following the traces to the NFR graphs. The traceability mechanism has also proved to be very helpful when evaluating if a non-functional requirement was satisfied or not since it was easier to check the models to see what possible impacts would arise from dropping one non-functional requirement or satisfying another.

To the best of our knowledge the only conceptual model that considers non-functional requirements in the area of DW is the one by Fernández-Medina et al. (2006), that, limitedly to security requirements, set out an Access Control and Audit model that allows the designer to specify access

control and audit considerations when carrying out the conceptual modeling phase.

A different proposal comes from Peralta et al., (2003) that propose modelling the non-functional requirements through guidelines that are not directly related with the conceptual model but are instead exploited during logical design, where most of the choices related to performance (e.g. star vs snowflake schema, view materialization) and security are kept.

In the rest of this section we will present the Dimensional Fact Model (DFM) as a representative in order to give the reader a clear understanding of the required expressiveness and in order to determine the core of information that must be

Figure 2. A basic fact schema for the SALES fact

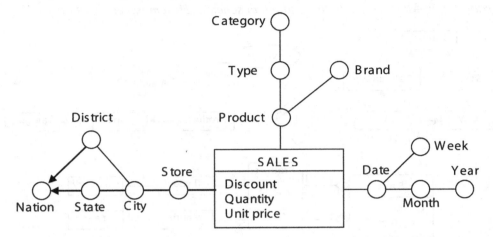

collected, during the requirement analysis phase, to allow effective multidimensional modelling in the next phase.

The Dimensional Fact Model

The DFM is a graphical conceptual model, specifically devised for multidimensional design, aimed at:

- effectively supporting conceptual design;
- providing an environment in which user queries can be intuitively expressed;
- supporting the dialogue between the designer and the end-users to refine the specification of requirements;
- creating a stable platform to ground logical design;
- providing an expressive and non-ambiguous design documentation.

DFM was first proposed in 1998 by Golfarelli and Rizzi and continuously enriched and refined during the following years in order to optimally suit the variety of modeling situations that may be encountered in real projects of small to large complexity.

The representation of reality built using the DFM consists of a set of fact schemata. The basic concepts modelled are facts, measures, dimensions, and hierarchies. In the following we intuitively define these concepts, referring the reader to Figure 2 that depicts a simple fact schema for modelling invoices at line granularity; a formal definition of the same concepts can be found in (Golfarelli, 2008).

A *fact* is a focus of interest for the decision-making process; typically, it models a set of events occurring in the enterprise world. A fact is graphically represented by a box with two sections, one for the fact name and one for the measures. Examples of facts in the trade domain are sales, shipments, purchases; in the financial domain: stock exchange transactions, contracts for insurance policies. It is essential for a fact to have some dynamic aspects, i.e., to evolve somehow across time. The concepts represented in the data source by frequently-updated archives are good candidates for facts; those represented by almost-static archives are not. As a matter of fact, very few things are completely static; even the relationship between cities and regions might change, if some borders were revised. Thus, the choice of facts should be based either on the average periodicity of changes, or on the specific interests of analysis.

A *measure* is a numerical property of a fact, and describes one of its quantitative aspects of interests for analysis. Measures are included in the bottom section of the fact. For instance, each invoice line is measured by the number of units sold, the price per unit, the net amount, etc. The reason why measures should be numerical is that they are used for computations. A fact may also have no measures, if the only interesting thing to be recorded is the occurrence of events; in this case the fact schema is said to be empty and is typically queried to count the events that occurred.

A *dimension* is a fact property with a finite domain, and describes one of its analysis coordinates. The set of dimensions of a fact determine its finest representation granularity. Graphically, dimensions are represented as circles attached to the fact by straight lines. Typical dimensions for the invoice fact are product, customer, agent. Usually one of the dimensions of the fact represents the time (at any granularity) that is necessary to extract time series from the DW data.

The relationship between measures and dimensions is expressed, at the instance level, by the concept of event. A *primary event* is an occurrence of a fact, and is identified by a tuple of values, one for each dimension. Each primary event is described by one value for each measure. Primary events are the elemental information which can be represented (in the cube metaphor, they correspond to the cube cells). In the invoice example they model the invoicing of one product to one customer made by one agent on one day.

Aggregation is the basic OLAP operation, since it allows significant information to be summarized from large amounts of data. From a conceptual point of view, aggregation is carried out on primary events thanks to the definition of dimension attributes and hierarchies. A *dimension attribute* is a property, with a finite domain, of a dimension. Like dimensions, it is represented by a circle. For instance, a product is described by its type, category, and brand; a customer, by its city and its nation.

The relationships between dimension attributes are expressed by hierarchies. A *hierarchy* is a di-

rected graph, rooted in a dimension, whose nodes are all the dimension attributes that describe that dimension, and whose arcs model many-to-one associations between pairs of dimension attributes. Arcs are graphically represented by straight lines. Hierarchies should reproduce the pattern of inter-attribute functional dependencies expressed by the data source. Hierarchies determine how primary events can be aggregated into secondary events and selected significantly for the decision-making process. Given a set of dimension attributes, each tuple of their values identifies a *secondary event* that aggregates all the corresponding primary events. Each secondary event is described by a value for each measure, that summarizes the values taken by the same measure in the corresponding primary events.

The dimension in which a hierarchy is rooted defines its finest aggregation granularity, while the other dimension attributes progressively define coarser ones. For instance, thanks to the existence of a many-to-one association between products and their categories, the invoicing events may be grouped according to the category of the products. When two nodes a_1, a_2 of a hierarchy share the same descendent a_3 (i.e. when two dimension attributes within a hierarchy are connected by two or more alternative paths of many-to-one associations) this is the case of a *convergence*, meaning that for each instance of the hierarchy we can have different values for a_1, a_2, but we will have only one value for a_3. For example, in the geographic hierarchy on dimension customer (Figure 2): customers live in cities, which are grouped into states belonging to nations. Suppose that customers are also grouped into sales districts, and that no inclusion relationships exist between districts and cities/states; on the other hand, sales districts never cross the nation boundaries. In this case, each customer belongs to exactly one nation whichever of the two paths is followed (customer→city→state→nation or customer→sale district→nation).

It should be noted that the existence of apparently equal attributes does not always determine a convergence. If in the invoice fact we had a brand city attribute on the product hierarchy, representing the city where a brand is manufactured, there would be no convergence with attribute (customer) city, since a product manufactured in a city can obviously be sold to customers of other cities as well.

SOLUTIONS AND RECOMMENDATIONS

Requirement analysis and conceptual design are to a great extent responsible for the success of a DW project since, during these two phases, the expressivity of the multidimensional schemata is completely defined. The paper has shown how most of the risk factors can be handled by the adoption of proper methodologies and formalisms. In particular, though some basic approaches to user-requirement analysis are available in the literature the adoption of a "pure" one is not sufficient to protect from its own weaknesses. On the other hand, some authors have proposed, and tested in real projects, mixed techniques proving that the three basic approaches are not mutually exclusive but, as evidenced by (List, 2002), are instead complementary and when used in parallel may overcome many of the problems. In particular, we believe that coupling a data-driven step with a demand-driven one can lead to a design capturing all the specifications and ensuring a higher level of longevity as well as acceptance of the users. Choosing whether the demand-driven step should actually follow the goal-driven or the user-driven approach mainly depends on the project peculiarities that include several factors like budget and time constraints, company environment and culture, goal of the project, etc.

From the analysis of the methodological steps the extent to which the two design phases studied in this paper are related clearly emerges and their synergy can be exploited at best if the two steps share a common and well-structured formalism that facilitates and disambiguates the exchange of information. Whenever a demand-driven step is adopted we recommend the adoption of formalisms that are intuitive and readable by non-expert users in order to facilitate their interaction with the designers. For this reason we believe that ad-hoc formalism should be preferred whenever business-users are involved.

FUTURE TRENDS

While the topic of conceptual modelling in DWing has been widely explored, the subject of user requirement analysis as well as the relationships between these design steps has been only partially studied. In particular, while the way for capturing functional requirements has been paved, techniques for non-functional requirements have been just sketched and still not massively tested in real projects. Thus, we believe that the effort in this area should be twofold: on the one hand, a lot of research is still needed to obtain a comprehensive approach to user requirement analysis, on the other hand, the effectiveness of this step can be exploited at best only if it can be coupled with the conceptual design phase to form a unique framework.

From the practitioners' point of view, we emphasize that the adoption of a structured approach during user requirements analysis and conceptual design is still extremely limited in real projects (Sen & Sinha, 2005), while the need for solutions that reduce the design efforts and that lower, at the same time, the failure risk is strongly felt. This gap is probably due to a lack of commercial design software for DWs. In fact, though most vendors of DW technology propose their own CASE solutions (that are very often just wizards capable of supporting the designer during the most tedious and repetitive phases of design), the only tools that currently promise to effectively automate some phases of design are research prototypes. In particular, (Golfarelli & Rizzi, 2001; Jensen et al. 2004), embracing the supply-driven philosophy, propose two approaches for automatically deriving the conceptual multidimensional schema from the relational data sources. On the contrary the CASE tool proposed in (Trujillo, 2002) follows the demand-driven approach and allows the multidimensional conceptual schemata to be drawn from scratch and to be semi-automatically translated into the target cubes.

CONCLUSION

In this paper we have surveyed the state of the art of the literature related to the first steps of data mart design, namely user requirement analysis and conceptual design. The approaches to requirement analysis have been surveyed and their strengths and weaknesses have been discussed in order to enable the designer to choose the more appropriates for a given project. Similarly, the main conceptual models for DWs have been reported and their basic concepts have been discussed using DFM as a representative.

From our analysis it emerges that although it is evident that the two design steps are strictly related, no comprehensive approach has been devised yet. On the other hand, the research community seems to share some common ideas: the core expressivity of the conceptual models for DW is shared by most of the models discussed regardless of the formalism adopted; furthermore, as for user requirement analysis, several authors chose a mixed method coupling a goal-driven step with a supply-driven one.

REFERENCES

Abello, A., Samos, J., & Saltor, F. (2006). YAM²: A multidimensional conceptual model extending UML. *Information Systems*, *31*(6), 541–567. doi:10.1016/j.is.2004.12.002

Agrawal, R., Gupta, A., & Sarawagi, S. (1997). Modeling multidimensional databases. In *Proceedings of the International Conference on Data Engineering*, Birmingham U.K. (pp. 232-243).

Basili, V. R., Caldiera, G., & Rombaci, H. D. (1994). The goal question metric approach. In *Encyclopedia of software engineering* (pp. 528-532). New York: John Wiley & Sons, Inc.

Boehnlein, M., & Ulbrich vom Ende, A. (2000). Business process oriented development of data warehouse structures. In *Proceedings of Data Warehousing 2000*. Heidelberg, Germany: Physica Verlag.

Bonifati, A., Cattaneo, F., Ceri, S., Fuggetta, A., & Paraboschi, S. (2001). Designing data marts for data warehouses. *ACM Transactions on Software Engineering and Methodology*, *10*(4), 452–483. doi:10.1145/384189.384190

Bresciani, P., Giorgini, P., Giunchiglia, F., Mylopoulos, J., & Perini, A. (2004). Tropos: An agent-oriented software development methodology. *Journal of Autonomous Agents and Multi-Agent Systems*, *8*(3), 203–236. doi:10.1023/B:AGNT.0000018806.20944.ef

Cabibbo, L., & Torlone, R. (1998). A logical approach to multidimensional databases. In *Proceedings of the International Conference on Extending Database Technology*, Valencia, Spain (pp. 183-197).

Chung, L., Nixon, B. A., Yu, E., & Mylopoulos, J. (1999). *Non-functional requirements in software*. Berlin, Germany: Springer.

Cohen, P., & Levesque, H. (1990). Intention is choice with commitment. *Artificial Intelligence*, *42*(2-3), 213–261. doi:10.1016/0004-3702(90)90055-5

Cysneiros, L. M., & Sampaio do Prado Leite, J. C. (2004). Nonfunctional requirements: From elicitation to conceptual models. *IEEE Transactions on Software Engineering, 30*(5), 328–350. doi:10.1109/TSE.2004.10

Demarest, M. (1997). *The politics of data warehousing.* Retrieved August 2008, from http://www.noumenal.com/marc/dwpoly.html

Fernández-Medina, E., Trujillo, J., Villarroel, R., & Piattini, M. (2006). Access control and audit model for the multidimensional modeling of data warehouses. *Decision Support Systems, 42*(3), 1270–1289. doi:10.1016/j.dss.2005.10.008

Franconi, E., & Kamble, A. (2004). A data warehouse conceptual data model. In *Proceedings of the International Conference on Statistical and Scientific Database Management*, Santorini Island, Greece (pp. 435-436).

Giorgini, P., Rizzi, S., & Garzetti, M. (2008). GRAnD: A goal-oriented approach to requirement analysis in data warehouses. *Decision Support Systems, 45*(1), 4–21. doi:10.1016/j.dss.2006.12.001

Golfarelli, M. (2008). The DFM: A conceptual model for data warehouse. In J. Wang (Ed.), *Encyclopedia of data warehousing and mining* (2nd ed.). Hershey, PA: IGI Global.

Golfarelli, M., Maio, D., & Rizzi, S. (1998). The dimensional fact model: A conceptual model for data warehouses. *International Journal of Cooperative Information Systems, 7*(2-3), 215–247. doi:10.1142/S0218843098000118

Golfarelli, M., & Rizzi, S. (2001). WanD: A CASE tool for data warehouse design. In *Demo Proceedings of the 17th International Conference on Data Engineering (ICDE 2001)*, Heidelberg, Germany (pp. 7-9).

Golfarelli, M., & Rizzi, S. (2009). A survey on temporal data warehousing. [IJDWM]. *International Journal of Data Warehousing and Mining, 5*(1), 1–17.

Guo, Y., Tang, S., Tong, Y., & Yang, D. (2006). Triple-driven data modeling methodology in data warehousing: A case study. In *Proceedings of the ACM International Workshop on Data Warehousing and OLAP* (pp. 59-66).

Hüsemann, B., Lechtenbörger, J., & Vossen, G. (2000). Conceptual data warehouse design. In *Proceedings of the International Workshop on Design and Management of Data Warehouses.* Stockholm, Sweden (pp. 3-9).

Jensen, M., Holmgren, T., & Pedersen, T. (2004). Discovering multidimensional structure in relational data. In *Proceedings of the International Conference on Data Warehousing and Knowledge Discovery*, Zaragoza, Spain (pp. 138-148).

Kimbal, R., Reeves, L., Ross, M., & Thornthwaite, W. (1998). *The data warehouse lifecycle toolkit.* New York: John Wiley and Sons, Inc

Lechtenboerger, J., & Vossen, G. (2003). Multidimensional normal forms for data warehouse design. *Information Systems, 28*(5), 415–434. doi:10.1016/S0306-4379(02)00024-8

List, B., Bruckner, R., Machaczek, K., & Schiefer, J. (2002). A comparison of data warehouse development methodologies: Case study of the process warehouse. In *Proceedings of the International Conference on Database and Expert Systems Applications* (pp. 203-215).

Luján-Mora, S., Trujillo, J., & Song, I. Y. (2006). A UML profile for multidimensional modeling in data warehouses. *Data & Knowledge Engineering, 59*(3), 725–769. doi:10.1016/j.datak.2005.11.004

Mazon, J. N., & Trujillo, J. (2008). An MDA approach for the development of data warehouses. *Decision Support Systems, 45*(1), 41–58. doi:10.1016/j.dss.2006.12.003

Mazon, J. N., Trujillo, J., & Lechtenboerger, J. (2007). Reconciling requirement-driven data warehouses with data sources via multidimensional normal forms. *Data & Knowledge Engineering, 63*, 725–751. doi:10.1016/j.datak.2007.04.004

Mylopoulos, J., Chung, L., & Nixon, B. (1992). Representing and using non-functional requirements: A process-oriented approach. *IEEE Transactions on Software Engineering, 18*(6), 483–497. doi:10.1109/32.142871

Paim, F. R. S., & Castro, J. (2002). Enhancing data warehouse design with the NFR framework. In *Proceedings of the Workshop em Engenharia de Requisitos*, Valencia, Spain (pp. 40-57).

Paim, F. R. S., & Castro, J. (2003). DWARF: An approach for requirements definition and management of data warehouse systems. In *Proceedings of the 11ᵗʰ IEEE International Conference on Requirements Engineering*, Monterey Bay, CA, USA (pp. 75-84).

Pedersen, T. B., & Jensen, C. (1999). Multidimensional data modeling for complex data. In *Proceedings of the International Conference on Data Engineering*, Sydney, Australia (pp. 336-345).

Peralta, V., Illarze, A., & Ruggia, R. (2003). On the applicability of rules to automate data warehouse logical design. In *Proceedings of the Decision Systems Engineering Workshop*, Klagenfurt, Austria (pp. 317-328).

Sapia, C., Blaschka, M., Hofling, G., & Dinter, B. (1999). *Extending the E/R model for the multidimensional paradigm* (. LNCS, 1552, 105–116.

Sen, A., & Sinha, A. P. (2005). A comparison of data warehousing methodologies. *Communications of the ACM, 48*(3), 79–84. doi:10.1145/1047671.1047673

Soler, E., Stefanov, V., Mazon, J. N., Trujillo, J., Fernandez-Medina, E., & Piattini, M. (2008). Towards comprehensive requirement analysis for data warehouses: Considering security requirements. In *Proceedings of the Third International Conference on Availability, Reliability and Security - ARES 2008*, Barcelona, Spain (pp. 4-7).

Trujillo, J., Luján-Mora, S., & Medina, E. (2002). The gold model case tool: An environment for designing OLAP applications. In *Proceedings of the International Conference on Enterprise Information Systems*, Ciutad Real, Spain (pp. 699-707).

Tryfona, N., Busborg, F., & Borch Christiansen, J. G. (1999). starER: A conceptual model for data warehouse design. In *Proceedings of the ACM International Workshop on Data Warehousing and OLAP*, Kansas City, USA (pp. 3-8).

Tsois, A., Karayannidis, N., & Sellis, T. (2001). MAC: Conceptual data modeling for OLAP. In *Proceedings of the International Workshop on Design and Management of Data Warehouses*. Interlaken, Switzerland (pp. 5.1-5.11).

Vassiliadis, P., Bouzeghoub, M., & Quix, C. (1999). Towards quality-oriented data warehouse usage and evolution. In *Proceedings of the International Conference on Advanced Information Systems Engineering*, Heidelberg, Germany (pp. 149-163).

Winter, R., & Strauch, B. (2003). A method for demand-driven information requirements analysis in data warehousing. In *Proceedings of the Hawaii International Conference on System Sciences*, Hawaii (pp. 1359-1365).

Yu, E. (1993). Modeling organizations for information systems requirements engineering. In *Proceedings of the First IEEE International Symposium on Requirements Engineering*, San Jose, USA (pp. 34-41).

Yu, E. (1995). *Modelling strategic relationships for process reengineering*. Unpublished doctoral dissertation, Department of Computer Science, University of Toronto.

Yu, E. (1997). Towards modeling and reasoning support for early-phase requirements engineering. In *Proceedings of the 3rd IEEE International Symposium on Requirements Engineering*, Annapolis, USA.

Yu, E., & Mylopoulos, J. (1994). Understanding 'why' in software process modeling, analysis and design. In *Proceedings of the Sixteenth International Conference on Software Engineering*, Sorrento, Italy.

Yu, E., & Mylopoulos, J. (1996). Using goals, rules, and methods to support reasoning in business process reengineering. *International Journal of Intelligent Systems in Accounting Finance & Management*, 5(1), 1–13. doi:10.1002/(SICI)1099-1174(199603)5:1<1::AID-ISAF99>3.0.CO;2-C

KEY TERMS AND DEFINITIONS

Conceptual Model: A formalism, with a given expressivity, suited for describing part of the reality, based on some basic constructs and a set of logical and quantitative relationships between them

Extraction Transformation and Loading (ETL): The process that enables data to be loaded in the DW. It is usually carried out using specialized software and entails extracting data out of the sources, transforming it to fit the business needs and to match the quality requirements, and finally loading it into the end target

Key Performance Indicator (KPI): Are financial and non-financial metrics used to help an organization define and measure progress toward organizational goals

Life-cycle: The set of phases a software system usually goes through from its conception to its retirement.

Multidimensional Model: A data model optimized for data access in a way that comes natural to human analysts. A multidimensional model is centred on a fact that is a focus of interest for the decision-making process and can be monitored through measures and dimensions.

User Requirements: The needs of the of the stakeholders who directly interact with the system

Chapter 2
Data Extraction, Transformation and Integration Guided by an Ontology

Chantal Reynaud
Université Paris-Sud, CNRS (LRI) & INRIA (Saclay – Île-de-France), France

Nathalie Pernelle
Université Paris-Sud, CNRS (LRI) & INRIA (Saclay – Île-de-France), France

Marie-Christine Rousset
LIG – Laboratoire d'Informatique de Grenoble, France

Brigitte Safar
Université Paris-Sud, CNRS (LRI) & INRIA (Saclay – Île-de-France), France

Fatiha Saïs
Université Paris-Sud, CNRS (LRI) & INRIA (Saclay – Île-de-France), France

ABSTRACT

This chapter deals with integration of XML heterogeneous information sources into a data warehouse with data defined in terms of a global abstract schema or ontology. The authors present an approach supporting the acquisition of data from a set of external sources available for an application of interest including data extraction, data transformation and data integration or reconciliation. The integration middleware that the authors propose extracts data from external XML sources which are relevant according to an RDFS+ ontology, transforms returned XML data into RDF facts conformed to the ontology and reconciles RDF data in order to resolve possible redundancies.

INTRODUCTION

A key factor for the success of the Semantic Web is to provide a unified, comprehensive and high-level access to voluminous and heterogeneous data.

Such an access can be provided by an ontology in integrators supporting high-level queries and information interoperation. Our work takes place in the context of a data warehouse with data defined in terms of a global abstract schema or ontology.

DOI: 10.4018/978-1-60566-756-0.ch002

Figure 1. Functional architecture

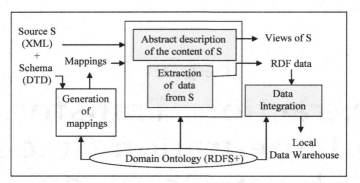

We advocate an information integration approach supporting the acquisition of data from a set of external sources available for an application of interest. This problem is a central issue in several contexts, data warehousing, interoperate systems, multi-database systems, web information systems. Several steps are required for the acquisition of data from a variety of sources to a data warehouse based on an ontology (1) Data extraction: only data corresponding to descriptions in the ontology are relevant. (2) Data transformation: they must be defined in terms of the ontology and in the same format. (3) Data integration and reconciliation: the goal of this task is to resolve possible redundancies.

As a vast majority of sources rely on XML, an important goal is to facilitate the integration of heterogeneous XML data sources. Furthermore, most applications based on the Semantic Web technologies rely on RDF (McBride, 2004), OWL-DL (Mc Guinness & Van Harmelen, 2004) and SWRL (Horrocks et al., 2004). Solutions for data extraction, transformation and integration using these recent proposals must be favoured. Our work takes place in this setting. We propose an integration middleware which extracts data from external XML sources that are relevant according to a RDFS+ ontology (RDFS+ is based on RDFS (McBride, 2004)), transforms them into RDF facts conformed to the ontology, and reconciles redundant RDF data.

Our approach has been designed in the setting of the PICSEL3 project[i] whose aim was to build an information server integrating external sources with a mediator-based architecture and data originated from external sources in a data warehouse. Answers to users' queries should be delivered from the data warehouse. So data have to be passed from (XML) external sources to the (RDF) data warehouse and answers to queries collected from external sources have to be stored in the data warehouse. The proposed approach has to be totally integrated to the PICSEL mediator-based approach. It has to be simple and fast in order to deal with new sources and new content of integrated sources. Finally, it has to be generic, applicable to any XML information source relative to any application domain. In Figure 1 we present the software components designed in the setting of the project to integrate sources and data. This paper focuses on the description of the content of a source, the extraction and the integration of data (grey rectangles in Figure 1). The automatic generation of mappings is out of the scope of the paper.

The extraction and transformation steps rely on correspondences or mappings between local schemas of external sources and the ontology. In a previous work, we proposed techniques to automate the generation of these mappings (Reynaud & Safar, 2009). In this chapter, we present an approach which automates the construction of wrappers given a set of mappings. It starts from the description of the abstract content of an external source and performs data acquisition, i.e. data extraction and transformation in order to conform to a same global schema. The description of the abstract content of an external source is also usable to manage sources with data that remain locally stored, making that way our techniques quite integrated to the PICSEL mediator-based approach. The transformation phase is then followed by a reconciliation step whose aim is to handle several problems: possible mismatches between data referring to the same real world object (different conventions and vocabularies can be used to represent and describe data), possible errors in the data stored in the sources especially frequent when data are automatically extracted from the Web, possible inconsistencies between values representing the properties of the real world objects in different sources. This reconciliation step is essential because the conformity to a same global schema does not indeed prevent variations between data descriptions. For this last step, we propose a knowledge-based and unsupervised approach, based on two methods, a logical one called L2R and a numerical one called N2R. The Logical method for Reference Reconciliation (L2R) is based on the translation in first order logic Horn rules of some of the schema semantics. In order to complement the partial results of L2R, we have designed a Numerical method for Reference Reconciliation (N2R). It exploits the L2R results and allows computing similarity scores for each pair of references.

The paper is organized as follows. In section 2, we present close related work and point out the novel features of the approach presented in this chapter. In section 3, we describe our approach. First, we define the data model used to represent the ontology and the data, the XML sources and the mappings automatically generated used as inputs in the data extraction and transformation process. We present the data extraction and transformation tasks and then the two reconciliation techniques

(L2R and N2R) followed by a summary of the results that we have obtained. In section 4 we briefly describe future research directions. Finally, section 5 concludes the chapter.

BACKGROUND

Many modern applications such as data warehousing, global information systems and electronic commerce need to take existing data with a particular schema, and reuse it in a different form. For a long time data conversion has usually been done in an ad hoc manner by developing non reusable software. Later language-based and declarative approaches have provided tools for the specification and implementation of data and schema translations among heterogeneous data sources (Abiteboul et al.,1997; Cluet et al., 1998). Such rule-based approaches can deal with complex transformations due to the diversity in the data model and to schema matching. In the former case, the approach helps to customize general purpose translation tools. In the latter case, the idea is that the system automatically finds the matching between two schemas, based on a set of rules that specify how to perform the matching. All these works provide tools to design data conversion programs but they do not provide the ability to query external sources. More recently, the Clio system (Popa et al., 2002) has been proposed as a complement and an extension of the language-based approaches. Given value correspondences that describe how to populate a single attribute of a target schema, this system discovers the mapping query needed to transform source data to target data. It produces SQL queries and provides users with data samples to allow them to understand the mappings produced.

Our work can also be compared to data integration systems providing mechanisms for uniformly querying sources through a target schema but avoiding materializing it in advance. These works adopt either the Global-As-View (GAV) approach and describes the target schema in terms of the local schemas, either the Local-As-View (LAV) approach and describes every source schema in terms of the target one. Based on these two approaches, there is a hybrid approach, called Global-Local-As-View (GLAV) and performed in SWIM (Koffina et al., 2006), that allows to specify mappings between elements of the target schema and elements of the source ones, considered one by one. We adopted it also in our work. It simplifies the definition of the mappings and allows a higher automation of extraction and transformation tasks.

Compared with the approaches cited above, the present work shows several interesting features coming both from data conversion and data integration (mediator) work. Given a set of mappings, our approach is entirely automatic. Our solution has to be integrated in the PICSEL mediator-based approach. In PICSEL, queries are rewritten in terms of views which describe the content of the sources. Hence, a solution to data extraction and transformation that generates these views in an automatic way in the same time is a very interesting point. The specification of how to perform the matching between the sources and the data warehouse can then be automatically generated by producing XML queries from the mappings, the views and the ontology. It corresponds to the extraction and transformation steps performed on the source taken as a whole and not attribute per attribute as in the work aiming at converting a relational database in another one. The approach is directed by the ontology. Only data that can be defined in terms of the ontology are extracted. Furthermore XML queries are capable to transform data in order to make them defined in terms of the ontology as well as in the same format. This is a way to handle the transformation task.

The problem of reference reconciliation was introduced by the geneticist Newcombe (1959) and was first formalized by (Fellegi & Sunter, 1969). Since then, several work and various ap-proaches have been proposed. We distinguish these approaches according to the exploitation of the reference description, to how knowledge is acquired and which kind of result is obtained by the methods.

For the reference description we have three cases. The first one is the exploitation of the un-structured description of the text appearing in the attributes (Cohen, 2000; Bilke & Naumann, 2005). In these approaches, the similarity is computed by using only the textual values in the form of a single long string without distinguishing which value corresponds to which attribute. This kind of approaches is useful in order to have a fast similarity computation (Cohen, 2000), to obtain a set of reference pairs that are candidates for the reconciliation (Bilke & Naumann, 2005) or when the attribute-value associations may be incorrect. The second type of approaches consists in considering the reference description as structured in several attributes. A large number of methods have adopted this vision by proposing either probabilistic models (Fellegi & Sunter, 1969), which allow taking decisions of reconciliation after the estimation of the probabilistic model parameters, or by computing a similarity score for the reference pairs (Dey et al., 1998a) by using similarity measures (Cohen et al., 2003). The third one consists in considering, in addition to the reference description structured in a set of attributes, the relations that link the references together (Dong et al., 2005). These global approaches take into account a larger set of information. This allows to improve the results in terms of the number of false positive (Bhattacharya & Getoor, 2006) or in terms of the number of the false negative. Like those approaches, both the logical L2R and the numerical N2R methods are global, since they exploit the structured description composed of attributes and relations. The relations are used both in the propagation of reconciliation decisions by the logical rules (L2R) and in the propagation of similarity scores through the iterative computation of the similarity (N2R).

In order to improve their efficiency, some recent methods exploit knowledge which is either learnt by using supervised algorithms or explicitly specified by a domain expert. For instance, in (Dey et al., 1998b; Dong et al., 2005), knowledge about the impacts of the different attributes or relations are encoded in weights by an expert or learnt on labelled data. However, these methods are time consuming and dependent on the human experience for labelling the training data or to specify declaratively additional knowledge for the reference reconciliation. Both the L2R and N2R methods exploit the semantics on the schema or on the data, expressed by a set of constraints. They are unsupervised methods since no labelled data is needed by either L2R or N2R.

Most of the existing methods infer only reconciliation decisions. However, some methods infer non-reconciliation decisions for reducing the reconciliation space. This is the case for the so-called blocking methods introduced in (Newcombe, 1962) and used in recent approaches such as (Baxter et al., 2003).

THE PICSEL3 DATA EXTRACTION, TRANSFORMATION AND INTEGRATION APPROACH

In this section, we first define the data model used to represent the ontology and the data, the external XML sources and the mappings. In a second sub-section, we present the data extraction and transformation tasks and then the two reconciliation techniques (L2R and N2R) followed by a summary of the results that we have obtained by performing these methods on data sets related to the scientific publications.

Data Model, XML Sources and Mappings

We first describe the data model used to represent the ontology O. This model is called RDFS+

because it extends RDFS with some OWL-DL primitives and SWRL rules, both being used to state constraints that enrich the semantics of the classes and properties declared in RDFS. Then we describe the XML sources we are interested in and the mappings that are automatically generated and then used as inputs of the data extraction and transformation process.

The RDFS+ Data Model

RDFS+ can be viewed as a fragment of the relational model (restricted to unary and binary relations) enriched with typing constraints, inclusion and exclusion between relations and functional dependencies.

The Schema and its Constraints

A RDFS schema consists of a set of classes (unary relations) organized in a taxonomy and a set of typed properties (binary relations). These properties can also be organized in a taxonomy of properties. Two kinds of properties can be distinguished in RDFS: the so-called relations, the domain and the range of which are classes and the so-called attributes, the domain of which is a class and the range of which is a set of basic values (e.g. Integer, Date, Literal). For example, in the RDFS schema presented in Figure 2, we have a relation *located* having as domain the class *CulturalPlace* and as range the class *Address*. We also have an attribute *name* having as domain the class *CulturalPlace* and as range the data type Literal.

We allow the declaration of constraints expressed in OWL-DL or in SWRL in order to enrich the RDFS schema. The constraints that we consider are of the following types:

- Constraints of disjunction between classes: DISJOINT(C,D) is used to declare that the two classes C and D are disjoint, for example: DISJOINT (*CulturalPlace, Artist*).
- Constraints of functionality of properties: PF(P) is used to declare that the property P

Figure 2. Example of a RDFS schema

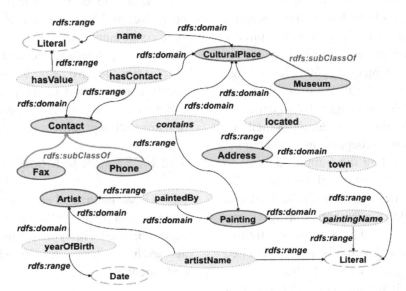

(relation or attribute) is a functional property. For example, PF(*located*) and PF(*name*) express respectively that a cultural place is located in one and only one address and that a cultural place has only one name. These constraints can be generalized to a set $\{P_1,..., P_n\}$ of relations or attributes to state a combined constraint of functionality that we will denote PF($P_1,..., P_n$).

- Constraints of inverse functionality of properties: PFI(P) is used to declare that the property P (relation or attribute) is an inverse functional property. For example, PFI(*contains*) expresses that a painting cannot belong to several cultural places. These constraints can be generalized to a set $\{P_1,..., P_n\}$ of relations or attributes to state a combined constraint of inverse functionality that we will denote PFI($P_1,..., P_n$). For example, PFI(*located, name*) expresses that one address and one name cannot be associated to several cultural places (i.e. both are needed to identify a cultural place).

Data Description and their Constraints

A datum has a reference, which has the form of a URI (e.g. http://www.louvre.fr, NS-S1/painting243), and a description, which is a set of RDF facts involving its reference. A RDF fact can be:

- either a class-fact $C(i)$, where C is a class and i is a reference,
- or a relation-fact $R(i_1, i_2)$, where R is a relation and i_1 and i_2 are references,
- or an attribute-fact $A(i,v)$, where A is an attribute, i a reference and v a basic value (e.g. integer, string, date).

The data description that we consider is composed of the RDF facts coming from the data sources enriched by applying the RDFS entailment rules (Hayes, 2004). We consider that the descriptions of data coming from different sources conform to the same RDFS+ schema (possibly after schema reconciliation). In order to distinguish the data coming from different sources, we use the source identifier as the prefix of the reference of the data coming from that source. Example 1 provides examples of data coming from two RDF data sources S_1 and S_2, which conform to a same RDFS+ schema describing the cultural application previously mentioned.

Example 1: An example of RDF data
Source S1: Museum(r607); name(r607, " Le Louvre "); located(r607, d1e5); Address(d1e5); town(d1e5, "Paris"); contains(r607, p112); paintingName(p112, "La Joconde"); *Source S2:* Museum(r208); name(r208, "musée du Louvre"); located(r208, l6f2); Address(l6f2); town(l6f2, "ville de Paris"); contains(r208, p222) ; paintingName(p222, "Iris "); contains(r208, p232); paintingName(p232, "Joconde");

We consider two kinds of axioms accounting for the Unique Name Assumption (UNA) and the Local Unique Name Assumption (denoted LUNA). The UNA states that two data of the same data source having distinct references refer to two different real world entities (and thus cannot be reconciled). Such an assumption is valid when a data source is clean. The LUNA is weaker than the UNA, and states that all the references related to a same reference by a relation refer to real world entities that are pairwise distinct.

The XML Sources

The XML sources that we are interested in are valid documents, instances of a DTD that defines their structure. We consider DTDs without entities or notations. A DTD can be represented as an acyclic oriented graph with one node for each element definition. The links between two nodes are composition links. The attributes associated to the elements in a DTD are associated to element nodes in the graph representing to the DTD. Because the DTDs are acyclic, their associated graph may be represented as a forest of trees, whose roots correspond to entry points in the graph (nodes without predecessors). Nodes shared in the graph by several trees are duplicated in order to make these trees independent of each other.

Figure 3. Example of a DTD tree

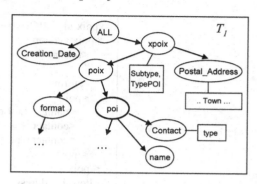

Figure 3 is an example of a DTD of a source to be integrated. It is represented by the tree T_1. A fragment of the XML document conformed to the DTD tree T_1 is presented in Figure 4.

The Mappings

Mappings are computed in a semi-automatic way. They are links between the ontology O and a DTD tree D (elements or attributes). The format of the mappings for the classes and the properties of O is described just below.

When c_1 is a concept of O, the format of the mappings may be:

- $c_1 \leftrightarrow //e$
- $c_1 \leftrightarrow //e/@att$
- $c_1 \leftrightarrow //e/[@att = \text{'val'}]/@att$

When R is a relation between c_1 and c_2 of O such that $\exists\ c_1 \leftrightarrow //a$ and $c_2 \leftrightarrow //b$, the format of the mapping is: $r_1(c_1, c_2) \leftrightarrow r_1(//a, //a/ \ldots/b)$

When A is an attribute of c_1 represented in the ontology O such that $\exists\ c_1 \leftrightarrow //a$ and b being mapped to A in T, the format of the mapping is: A of $c_1 \leftrightarrow A(//a, //a/ \ldots/b)$

In this format, $\leftrightarrow$ indicates a mapping link between entities in O and entities in T defined by their path using XPath (Berglund et al., 2007) in the associated graph. e refers to an element in T, *@att* refers to the attribute *att*.

Figure 4. Example of a XML document conformed to the DTD tree of the Figure 3

```
<xpoix id = 'PCUIDF07721' typePOI ='museum' >
  <poix version = '1' >
    <format >
        ...
    </format >
    <poi>
      <name>  Le Louvre </name>
      <contact type = 'tel'> 01 60 20 11 06</contact>
      <contact type = 'fax'>01 60 20 44 02</contact>
    </poi>
  </poix>
  <Postal_Address>
    <town> Paris </town>
      .....
  </Postal_Address>
</xpoix>
```

Note that we may have conditional mappings when the link with an attribute *att* depends on its value *val* ($C_1 \leftrightarrow$ //e/[@att = 'val']/@att).

Data Extraction and Transformation

Data extraction and transformation are completely automatic tasks usually performed by wrappers. It is a two-step process. First, an abstract description of the content of the external source is built. Second, data is extracted and presented in the format of the data warehouse.

Abstract Description of a Source

The content of an external source is described in terms of views in the language accepted by PIC-SEL (Rousset & Reynaud, 2003) by a set of rules. Each rule links a view $v_i(x)$ with a local name to domain relations $p(x)$ in the ontology. It indicates which kind of data can be found in the source. Our proposal is to build a limited number of views, one view per central concept in a source. A concept is said central if it is mapped to an element in O and if none of its predecessors is mapped.

The construction process of a view is incremental. At first, it is guided by the DTD tree T

of the XML source in order to identify central concepts. A depth-first search is performed on the DTD tree T until an element e_D of T belonging to a mapping is found. This element will necessarily be associated to a class e_O in O representing a central concept. The search of additional central concepts will be pursued later starting from the brother node of e_D. Indeed, all the elements belonging to the sub-tree rooted in e_D and mapped with entities in O should be linked to e_O in O. Second the construction process of a view is guided by the ontology in order to complete the description of the central concepts. We introduce the properties of the classes corresponding in O to the central concepts (relations and attributes) if they are properties with mappings, the classes linked by the introduced relations (called subordinated concepts), their properties with mappings, and so on. Indeed, the same completion process is performed recursively on each subordinated concept. For example, *name*, *located* and *hasContact* are three properties of the class *CulturalPlace* with mappings. *located* and *hasContact* are two relations establishing respectively a link with the classes *Address* and *Contact*. The view under construction corresponding to S_1 will be: $S_1(x,y,z,t) \rightarrow CulturalPlace(x) \wedge name(x,y) \wedge$

$located(x,z) \wedge Address(z) \wedge hasContact(x,t) \wedge Contact(t)...$

Furthermore, we take into account classes that have specializations in O. When specializations correspond to central concepts, we build one view per specialization. For example, *Museum* is a specialization of *CulturalPlace* which is a central concept. We build a new view for *Museum*: S_{12} $(x,y,z,t) \rightarrow Museum(x) \wedge name(x,y) \wedge located(x,z) \wedge Address(z) \wedge hasContact(x,t) \wedge Contact(t)...$

When subordinated concepts have specializations in O, our treatment depends on the cardinality of the relation establishing a link with the subordinated concept. If the cardinality is multiple (non functional property) as the cardinality of the relation *hasContact* in the example just before, we will introduce all the classes that are specializations in the same view. That way, the source S_1 providing instances of *Museum* as it is shown in Figure 4 will be described by a unique view grouping the class *Museum*, its properties and the classes *Address*, *Contact*, *Tel*, *Fax* linked by the relations *located* and *hasContact*: S_{12} $(x,y,z,t, t_1, t_2) \rightarrow Museum(x) \wedge name(x,y) \wedge located(x,z) \wedge Address(z) \wedge hasContact(x,t) \wedge Contact(t) \wedge hasContact(x,t_1) \wedge Tel(t_1) \wedge hasContact(x, t_2) \wedge Fax(t_2)$.

On the opposite, if the relation is a functional property, we build one view per specialization, as it is done for central concepts with specializations.

Data Extraction and Transformation

For each view, we then generate a wrapper which will query the XML source in regard to its language and its vocabulary and transform returned instances into RDF facts conformed to the RDFS+ ontology. Wrappers are associated to queries expressed in XQuery (Boag et al., 2007). The *FLWO* part of a XQuery statement performs the extraction task while the *R* part performs the transformation task from XML to RDF using the terms of the ontology. The construction of wrappers follows the construction process of views. We build one query per view. Queries are built in an incremental way, performing at first the concept, followed by its properties. For each central concept named *conceptC* in O, we look for the instances of its corresponding element (or attribute) *mapC* in D (*FOR* part). For each instance we generate a unique identifier (*generate-Id*). The name of the concept in O is used as a tag in the *Return* part. Thus the initial form of the query is the following:

```
for $x in doc("source.xml")//mapC
let $idcpt:= gi:generate-Id($x1)
return
<p3:conceptC rdf:nodeID="{$idcpt}">
```

$x is associated to *mapC* and contains all the elements belonging to the tree rooted in *mapC* in the XML source. The objective of the query that we want to generate is to extract from *$x* all the elements which are properties in O. For this, we need mappings of these elements. The extraction of attributes in XQuery is made by indicating the path defined in the mapping and by using the primitive *Text()* to obtain the element without tags. The extraction of the relations needs a new identifier for the subordinated concept. A new XML fragment will be added to describe the subordinated concept and its properties. If the considered mappings are conditional, we introduce a Where part in the query in order to specify the condition. An example of a query leading to extract data from S_1 according to the view S_{12} (x,y,z,t) described above is given in Figure 5 (left side) and the extracted data in Figure 5 (right side). S_{12} $(x,y,z,t) \rightarrow Museum(x) \wedge name(x,y) \wedge located(x,z) \wedge Address(z) \wedge Town(z,t)$.

Data Integration

Let S_1 and S_2 be two data sources which conform to the same RDFS+ schema. Let I_1 and I_2 be the two reference sets that correspond respectively

Figure 5. A query (on the left side) and the extracted data (on the right side) from S₁

```
declare namespace gi = "java:pkg.GeneratedId";
declare namespace rdf = "http://www.w3.org/1999/02/22 -rdf-syntax-ns#";
declare namespace p3 ="http://www.lri.fr/picsel3/tourismrdfs#";
for $x in doc("source.xml")//xpoix
  let $idcpt := gi:generate_Id ()
  let $idrel := gi:generate_Id ()
Where @x/@typePOI= "museum"
return
<p3: Museum rdf:nodeID="{ $idcpt} " >
  <p3:name> { $x/poix/poi/name/ text()} </p3:name>
  <p3:located rdf:nodeID="{ $idrel} "/>
</p3: Museum>
<p3: Address rdf:nodeID="{ $idrel} ">
  <p3:town> { $x/Postal_Address/town /text()} </p3:town>
</p3: Address>
```

(a)

```
<p3: Museum rdf:nodeID="r6o7">
  <p3:name> Le Louvre </p3:name>
  <p3:Located rdf:nodeID="d1e5" />
</p3: Museum >

<p3: Address rdf:nodeID="d1e5" >
  <p3:town> Paris </p3:town>
</p3: Address >
```

(b)

to the data of S_1 and S_2. The problem consists in deciding whether references are reconciled or not reconciled. Let *Reconcile* be a binary predicate. *Reconcile(X, Y)* means that the two references denoted by *X* and *Y* refer to the same world entity. The reference reconciliation problem considered in L2R consists in extracting from the set $I_1 \times I_2$ of reference pairs two subsets REC and NREC such that:

$$\begin{cases} REC = \{(i, i') \ / \ Reconcile \ (i, i')\} \\ NREC = \{(i, i'), \emptyset Reconcile(i, i')\} \end{cases}$$

The reference reconciliation problem considered in N2R consists in, given a similarity function $Sim_r{:}I_1 \times I_2 \to [0..1]$, and a threshold T_{rec} (a real value in [0..1] given by an expert, fixed experimentally or learned on a labeled data sample), computing the following set:

$$REC_{N2R} = \{(i,i') \in (I_1 \times I_2) \backslash (REC \cup NREC), tq.Sim_r(i,i') > T_{rec}\}$$

L2R: A Logical Method for Reference Reconciliation

L2R (Saïs et al., 2007) is based on the inference of facts of reconciliation (*Reconcile(i,j)*) and of non-

reconciliation (¬*Reconcile(i',j')*) from a set of facts and a set of rules which transpose the semantics of the data sources and of the schema into logical dependencies between reference reconciliations. Facts of synonymy (*SynVals(v₁, v₂)*) and of no synonymy (¬ *SynVals(u₁, u₂)*) between basic values (strings, dates) are also inferred. For instance, the synonymy *SynVals("JoDS", "Journal of Data Semantics")* may be inferred. The L2R distinguishing features are that it is global and logic-based: every constraint declared on the data and on the schema in RDFS+ is automatically translated into first-order logic Horn rules (rules for short) that express dependencies between reconciliations. The advantage of such a logical approach is that if the data are error-free and if the declared constraints are valid, then the reconciliations and non-reconciliations that are inferred are correct, thus guaranteeing a 100% precision of the results.

We first describe the generation of the reconciliation rules. Then we present the generation of the facts and finally the reasoning, which is performed on the set of rules and facts.

Generation of the Set of Reconciliation Rules
They are automatically generated from the constraints that are declared on the data sources and on their common schema.

- Translation of the constraints on the data sources

The UNA assumption, if it is stated on the sources S_1 and S_2, is translated automatically by four rules. For example, the following rule R1 expresses the fact that two distinct references coming from the same source cannot be reconciled.R1: $Src1(x) \wedge Src1(y) \wedge (x \neq y) \Rightarrow \neg Reconcile(x,y)$ where $Src_i(x)$ means that the reference x is coming from a source S_i.

Analogous rules express that one reference coming from a source S_i can be reconciled with at most one reference coming from a source S_j. Similarly, two rules are generated for translating LUNA semantics.

- Translation of the schema constraints.

For each relation R declared as functional by the constraint PF(R), the following rule R6.1(R) is generated:R6.1(R): $Reconcile(x, y) \wedge R(x, z) \wedge R(y, w) \Rightarrow Reconcile(z, w)$

For example, the following rule is generated concerning the relation *located* which relates references of cultural places to references of addresses and which is declared functional:R6.1(located): $Reconcile(x, y) \wedge located(x, z) \wedge located(y, w) \Rightarrow Reconcile(z, w)$

For each attribute A declared as functional by the axiom PF(A), a similar rule which concludes on *SynVals* is generated.

Likewise, analogous rules are generated for each relation R and each attribute A declared as inverse functional. Rules are also generated for translating combined constraints PF($P_1,..., P_n$) and PFI($P_1,..., P_n$) of (inverse) functionality. For example, the declaration PFI(*paintedBy, paintingName*) states a composed functional dependency which expresses that the artist who painted it jointly with its name functionally determines a painting.

For each pair of classes C and D involved in a DISJOINT(C,D) statement declared in the schema, or such that their disjunction is inferred by inheritance, a rule is generated to express the fact that their references cannot be reconciled. A transitivity rule allows inferring new reconciliation decisions by applying transitivity on the set of already inferred reconciliations.

See (Saïs et al., 2009) for a complete description of the generation process of reconciliation rules.

Reasoning Method for Reference Reconciliation

In order to infer sure reconciliation and non-reconciliation decisions, we apply an automatic reasoning method based on the resolution principle (Robinson, 1965; Chang & Lee, 1997). This method applies to the clausal form of the set of rules R described above and a set of facts F describing the data, which is generated as follows.

- Generation of the set of facts.

The set of RDF facts corresponding to the description of the data in the two sources $S1$ and $S2$ is augmented with the generation of:

- new class-facts, relation-facts and attribute-facts derived from the domain and range constraints that are declared in RDFS for properties, and from the subsumption statements ;
- facts of the form $Src_1(i)$ and $Src_2(j)$;
- synonymy facts of the form $SynVals(v_1, v_2)$ for each pair (v_1, v_2) of basic values that are identical (up to some punctuation or case variations) ;
- non synonymy facts of the form $\neg SynVals(v_1, v_2)$ for each pair (v_1, v_2) of distinct basic values of a functional attribute for which it is known that each possible value has a single form. For instance, $\neg SynVals(\text{"France"}, \text{"Algeria"})$ can be added.
- Resolution-based algorithm for reference reconciliation.

The reasoning is applied to $R \cup F$: the set of rules (put in clausal form) and the set of facts generated as explained before. It aims at inferring all unit facts in the form of *Reconcile(i,j), ¬Reconcile(i,j), SynVals(v₁,v₂)* and *¬SynVals(v₁,v₂)*. Several resolution strategies have been proposed so that the number of computed resolutions to obtain the theorem proof is reduced (for more details about these strategies see (Chang & Lee, 1997)). We have chosen to use the unit resolution (Henschen & Wos, 1974). It is a resolution strategy where at least one of the two clauses involved in the resolution is a unit clause, i.e. reduced to a single literal. The unit resolution is complete for refutation in the case of Horn clauses without functions (Henschen & Wos, 1974). Furthermore, it is linear with respect to the size of clause set (Forbus & de Kleer, 1993). The unit resolution algorithm that we have implemented consists in computing the set of unit instantiated clauses contained in F or inferred by unit resolution on $R \cup F$. Its termination is guaranteed because there are no function symbols in $R \cup F$. Its completeness for deriving all the facts that are logically entailed has been stated in (Saïs et al., 2009).

N2R: A Numerical Method for Reference Reconciliation

N2R has two main distinguishing characteristics. First, it is fully unsupervised: it does not require any training phase from manually labeled data to set up coefficients or parameters. Second, it is based on equations that model the influence between similarities. In the equations, each variable represents the (unknown) similarity between two references while the similarities between values of attributes are constants that are computed by using standard similarity measures on strings or on sets of strings. The functions modeling the influence between similarities are a combination of maximum and average functions in order to take into account the constraints of functionality and inverse functionality declared in the RFDS+ schema in an appropriate way.

Solving this equation system is done by an iterative method inspired from the Jacobi method (Golub & Loan, 1996), which is fast converging on linear equation systems. The point is that the equation system is not linear, due to the use of the max function for the numerical translation of the functionality and inverse functionality axioms declared in the RFDS+ schema. Therefore, we had to prove the convergence of the iterative method for solving the resulting non linear equation system.

N2R can be applied alone or in combination with L2R. In this case, the results of non-reconciliation inferred by L2R are exploited for reducing the reconciliation space, i.e., the size of the equation system to be solved by N2R. In addition, the results of reconciliations and of synonymies or non-synonymies inferred by L2R are used to set the values of the corresponding constants or variables in the equations.

We first use a simple example to illustrate how the equation system is built. Then, we describe how the similarity dependencies between references are modeled in an equation system and we provide the iterative method for solving it.

Example 2

Let us consider the data descriptions of the example 1 and the reference pairs <S1_r607,S2_r208>, <S_d1e5, S2_l6f2>, <S1_p112,S2_p222> and <S1_p112,S2_p232>.

The similarity score *Sim₁(ref, ref')* between the references *ref* and *ref'* of each of those pairs is modeled by a variable: x_1 models *Sim₁ (S1_r607, S2_r208)*, x_2 models *Sim₁ (S1_p112,S2_p222)*, x_3 models *Sim₁ (S1_p112,S2_p232)*, x_4 models *Sim₁ (S_d1e5, S2_l6f2)*

We obtain the following equations that model the dependencies between those variables:
$x_1 = \max(0.68, x_2, x_3, x_4/4)$ $x_2 = \max(0.1, x_1/2)$ $x_3 = \max(0.9, x_1/2)$ $x_4 = \max(0.42, x1)$.

In this equation system, the first equation expresses that the variable x_1 strongly and equally depends on the variables x_2 and x_3, and also on

0.68, which is the similarity score between the two strings "*Le Louvre*" and "*musée du Louvre*" computed by the *Jaro-Winkler* function (Cohen et al., 2003). It also expresses that it weakly depends on x_4.

The reason of the strong dependencies is that *contains* is an inverse functional relation (a painting is contained in only one museum) relating S1_r607 and S2_r208 (the similarity of which is modeled by x_1) to S1_p112 for S1_r607 and S2_p222 for S2_r208, and *name* is a functional attribute (a museum has only one name) relating S1_r607 and S2_r208 respectively to the two strings "*Le Louvre*" and "*musee du Louvre*".

The weak dependency of x_4 onto x_1 is expressed by the term $x_1/4$ in the equation, where the ratio ¼ comes from that there are 4 properties (relations or attributes) involved in the data descriptions of S1_r607 and S2_r208. The dependency of x_4 onto x_1 is weaker than the previous ones because *located* is not an inverse functional relation.

The Equations Modeling the Dependencies between Similarities

For each pair of references, its similarity score is modeled by a variable x_i and the way it depends on other similarity scores is modeled by an equation: $x_i = f_i(X)$, where $i \in [1..n]$ and n is the number of reference pairs for which we apply N2R, and $X = (x_1, x_2, ..., x_n)$. Each equation $x_i = f_i(X)$ is of the form: $f_i(X) = \max(f_{i\text{-df}}(X), f_{i\text{-ndf}}(X))$.

The function $f_{i\text{-df}}(X)$ is the maximum of the similarity scores of the value pairs and the reference pairs of attributes and relations with which the *i*-th reference pair is functionally dependent. The maximum function allows propagating the similarity scores of the values and the references having a strong impact. The function $f_{i\text{-ndf}}(X)$ is defined by a weighted average of the similarity scores of the values pairs (and sets) and the reference pairs (and sets) of attributes and relations with which the *i*-th reference pair is not functionally dependent. Since

we have neither expert knowledge nor training data, the weights are computed in function of the number of the common attributes and relations. See (Saïs et al., 2009) for the detailed definition of $f_{i\text{-df}}(X)$ and $f_{i\text{-ndf}}(X)$.

Iterative Algorithm for Reference Pairs Similarity Computation

To compute the similarity scores, we have implemented an iterative resolution method. At each iteration, the method computes the variables values by using those computed in the precedent iteration.

Starting from an initial vector $X^0 = (x_1^0, x_2^0, ..., x_n^0)$, the value of the vector X at the *k*-th iteration is obtained by the expression: $X^k = F(X^{k-1})$. At each iteration k we compute the value of each $x_i^k : x_i^k = fi(x_1^{k-1}, x_2^{k-1}, ... x_n^{k-1})$ until a fixpoint with precision ε is reached. The fixpoint is reached when: $\forall i, |x_i^k - x_i^{k-1}| \leq \varepsilon$. The more ε value is small the more the set of reconciliations may be large.

The complexity of this method is in (n^2) for each iteration, where n is the number of variables. We have proved its convergence for the resolution of our equation system.

The similarity computation is illustrated by the following equation system obtained from the data descriptions shown in Example 1. The constants correspond to the similarity scores of pairs of basic values computed by using the Jaro-Winkler measure. The constants involved in the value computation of the variables x_1, x_2, x_3 and x_4 are respectively:

- $b11 = Sim_v$ ("*Louvre*", "*musée du Louvre*") $= 0.68$
- $b21 = Sim_v$ ("*La Joconde*", "*Iris*") $= 0.1$
- $b31 = Sim_v$ ("*La Joconde*", "*Joconde*") $= 0.9$
- $b41 = Sim_v$ ("*Paris*", "*Ville de Paris*") $= 0.42$

The weights are computed in function of the number of common attributes and common rela-

Table 1. Example of iterative similarity computation

Iterations	0	1	2	3	4
$x_1 = \max(0.68, x_2, x_3, \frac{1}{4} *_{x4})$	0	0.68	0.9	0.9	0.9
$x_2 = \max(0.1, \frac{1}{2} * x_1)$	0	0.1	0.34	0.45	0.45
$x_3 = \max(0.9, \frac{1}{2} * x_1)$	0	0.9	0.9	0.9	0.9
$x_4 = \max(0.42, x_1)$	0	0.42	0.68	0.9	0.9

tions of the reference pairs. The weights used in the value computation of the variables x_1, x_2, x_3 and x_4 are respectively: $\lambda 11 = \frac{1}{4}$, $\lambda 21 = \frac{1}{2}$, $\lambda 31 = \frac{1}{2}$ and $\lambda 41 = \frac{1}{2}$.

We assume that fixpoint precision ε is equal to 0.005.

The equation system is the one given in Example 2. The different iterations of the resulting similarity computation are provided in Table 1.

The solution of the equation system is $X=(0.9, 0.45, 0.9, 0.9)$. This corresponds to the similarity scores of the four reference pairs. The fixpoint has been reached after four iterations. The error vector is then equal to 0. If we fix the reconciliation threshold T_{rec} at 0.80, then we obtain three reconciliation decisions: two cities, two museums and two paintings.

Experiments

L2R and N2R have been implemented and tested on the benchmark Cora[ii] (used by (Dong et al., 2005; Parag & Domingos, 2005)). It is a collection of 1295 citations of 112 different research papers in computer science. For this data set, the UNA is not stated and the RDF facts describe references, which belong to three different classes (*Article, Conference, Person*). We have designed a simple RDFS schema on the scientific publication domain, which we have enriched with disjunction constraints (e.g. DISJOINT(*Article, Conference*)), a set of functional property constraints (e.g. PF(*published*), PF(*confName*)) and a set of inverse functional property constraints (e.g. PFI(*title, year, type*), PFI(*confName, confYear*)). The re-

call and the precision can be easily obtained by computing the ratio of the reconciliations or non-reconciliations obtained by L2R and N2R among those that are provided in the benchmark.

L2R Results

Since the set of reconciliations and the set of non-reconciliations are obtained by a logical resolution-based algorithm the precision is of 100% by construction. Then, the measure that it is meaningful to evaluate in our experiments is the recall. We focus on the results obtained for the *Article* and *Conference* classes, which contain respectively 1295 references and 1292 references.

As presented in the column named "RDFS+" of the Table 2, the recall is 50.7%. This can be refined in a recall of 52.7% computed on the REC subset and a recall of 50.6% computed on NREC subset.

For this data set, the RDFS+ schema can be easily enriched by the declaration that the property *confYear* is discriminant. When this property is exploited, the recall on NREC subset grows to 94.9%, as it is shown in the "RDFS+ & DP" column. This significant improvement is due to chaining of different rules of reconciliations: the non-reconciliations on references to conferences for which the values of the *confYear* are different entail in turn non-reconciliations of the associated articles by exploiting the constraint PF(*published*).

This recall is comparable to (while a little bit lower than) the recall on the same data set obtained by supervised methods like e.g., (Dong et

Table 2. L2R results on Cora data sets

	RDFS+	RDFS+ & DP
Recall (REC) Recall (NREC)	52.7% 50.6%	52.7% 94.9%
Recall	50.7%	94.4%
Precision	100%	100%

al., 2005). The point is that L2R is not supervised and guarantees a 100% precision.

N2R Results

In the following we presents the results (see Figure 6) obtained by N2R after the application of L2R.

For $T_{rec}=1$, N2R do not obtain more results than L2R. The evolution of the recall and precision values in function of T_{rec} is interesting. Indeed, when the threshold is decreased to 0.85, the recall increases by 33% while the precision only falls by 6%. The best results are obtained when $T_{rec}=0.85$. The F-measure is then at its maximum value of 88%. Besides, when the recall value is almost of 100%, for $T_{rec}=0.5$, the precision value is still about 40%.

The exploitation of the non-reconciliation inferred by L2R allows an important reduction of the reconciliation space handled in N2R. For the Cora data set the size of the reconciliation space is about 37 millions of reference pairs. It has been reduced of 32.8% thanks to the correct no reconciliations inferred by L2R. Moreover, the reconciliations inferred by L2R are not re-computed in N2R.

These experimentations show that good results can be obtained by an automatic and unsupervised method if it exploits knowledge declared in the schema. Furthermore, the method is able to obtain F-Measure which is better than some supervised methods such that (Parag & Domingos, 2005).

FUTURE RESEARCH DIRECTIONS

Work on integration has evolved in recent years to heterogeneous information sources available from the Web or through the intranets and the heterogeneity is becoming more and more important. In the future, we will have to deal with a still larger variety of data structures types (structured, semi-structured or unstructured sources), but also with sources containing both semi-structured and unstructured (or textual) parts. Current wrapper approaches could not be applied with the last kind

Figure 6. N2R results obtained on Cora data set

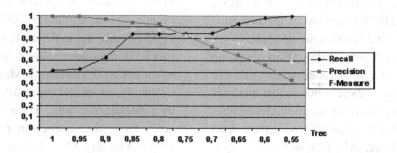

of sources. Suitable data extraction and transformation techniques are required. In fact, the more heterogeneous documents are, the more complex data integration is. The key issue for integrating systems that are more and more heterogeneous is to understand them. Semantic Web techniques will have an increasing role to play in the future in order to facilitate this understanding. Indeed, the concept of ontology which makes possible to add semantic information to the Web and the basic representation languages for the Semantic Web which allow reasoning on the content of sources are the foundations to obtain this understanding.

Reconciliation is an important information integration problem. It arises in other fields such as database area when data from various sources are combined. For example, mailing lists may contain several entries representing the same physical address, each entry containing different spellings. Identifying matching records is challenging because there are no unique identifiers across databases. Satisfactory solutions are not available yet. In all the applications where this problem arises, methods that are efficient while ensuring good results and being not vulnerable to changes of application domain are really required. Furthermore, since sources are more and more accessed from the Internet, additional problems appear and have to be studied: dealing with data freshness in order to store the freshest possible data, dealing with trust into sources which provide data, being capable to consider access rights when querying the most reliable sources.

Generally speaking, automatic methods will be of great importance in the future. Several directions or research can be taken. Unsupervised methods that guarantee a 100% precision of the results if schema and data are error-free are one way to automate reconciliation. Indeed, they allow obtaining reconciliations and non reconciliations that are sure. Capitalization on experience so that methods become more efficient as they are applied is another interesting direction. For example saving the correct (no) synonymies inferred by L2R in a dictionary is

an illustration of capitalization. It allows learning the syntactic variations of an application domain in an automatic and unsupervised way.

Finally, the demand for methods that ensure good results and which can be applied on new data again and again while remaining as efficient as ever will increase. Today there are a lot of difficulties to estimate in advance the precision of a system when it is applied to a new set of data. As a consequence two research objectives should be favored in a near future. A first one is to elaborate generic methods that guarantee sure results (a logical method of the kind of L2R for example). Such methods are very interesting but they can not be used in any case especially when the data is "dirty" or the global schema is an integrated schema resulting from an automatic matching process. Furthermore they must be complemented by others in order to obtain a better recall. A second objective is to propose methods, which reconcile data on the basis of similarity scores (not necessarily 100%) designed together with mechanisms capable to reason on the uncertain reconciliation decisions. That means that uncertainty management will become a major challenge to be taken up. Uncertainty gathered in data warehouses while populating them will have to be exploited by reasoning on tracks of reconciliation decisions.

CONCLUSION

We have presented an information integration approach able to extract, transform and integrate data in a data warehouse guided by an ontology. Whatever the application domain is, the approach can be applied to XML sources that are valid documents and that have to be integrated in a RDF data warehouse with data described in terms of a RDFS ontology. Mappings between the external sources and the ontology are represented in a declarative way. Their definition is made apart from the extraction process. Extraction operates on any XML document given mappings represented in XPath in terms of the ontology. Data transformation consists in converting data in terms of the ontology and in the same format. Both tasks are performed through XML queries associated to views of the sources automatically built beforehand. Through data integration, we addressed the reference reconciliation problem and presented a combination of a logical and numerical approach. Both approaches exploit schema and data knowledge given in a declarative way by a set of constraints and are then generic. The relations between references are exploited either by L2R for propagating (non) reconciliation decisions through logical rules or by N2R for propagating similarity scores thanks to the resolution of the equation system. The two methods are unsupervised because no labeled data set is used. Furthermore, the combined approach is able to capitalize its experience by saving inferred (non) synonymies. The results that are obtained by the logical method are sure. This distinguishes L2R from other existing works. The numerical method complements the results of the logical one. It exploits the schema and data knowledge and expresses the similarity computation in a non linear equation system. The experiments show promising results for recall, and most importantly its significant increasing when constraints are added.

REFERENCES

Abiteboul, S., Cluet, S., & Milo, T. (1997). Correspondence and translation for heterogeneous data. In *Proceedings of the International Conference on DataBase Theory* (pp. 351-363).

Baxter, R., Christen, P., & Churches, T. (2003). A comparison of fast blocking methods for record linkage. In *Proceedings of the ACM SIGKDD '03 Workshop on Data Cleaning Record Linkage and Object Consolidation*, Washington, DC, USA (pp. 25-27).

Berglund, A., Boag, S., Chamberlin, D., Fernandez, M. F., Kay, M., Robie, J., & Simeon, J. (2007). *XML path language (XPath) 2.0*. Retrieved from http://www.w3.org/TR/xpath20/

Bhattacharya, I., & Getoor, L. (2006). Entity resolution in graphs. In L. B. Holder & D. J. Cook (Eds.), *Mining graph data*. New York: John Wiley & Sons.

Bilke, A., & Naumann, F. (2005). Schema matching using duplicates. In *Proceedings of the International Conference on Data Engineering* (pp. 69-80).

Boag, S., Chamberlin, D., Fernandez, M. F., Florescu, D., Robie, J., & Simeon, J. (2007). *XQuery 1.0: An XML query language* (W3C Recommendation). Retrieved from http://www.w3.org/TR/xquery/

Chang, C., & Lee, R. C. (1997). *Symbolic logic and mechanical theorem proving*. New York: Academic Press.

Cluet, S., Delobel, C., Simeon, J., & Smaga, K. (1998). Your mediators need data conversion! In *Proceedings of* the *SIGMOD '98*, Seattle, USA (pp. 177-188).

Cohen, W. W. (2000). Data integration using similarity joins and a word-based information representation language. *ACM Transactions on Information Systems*, *18*(3), 288–321. doi:10.1145/352595.352598

Cohen, W. W., Ravikumar, P., & Fienberg, S. E. (2003). A comparison of string distance metrics for name-matching tasks. In *Proceedings of the Workshop on Information Integration on the Web* (pp. 73-78).

Dey, D., Sarkar, S., & De, P. (1998). Entity matching in heterogeneous databases: A distance based decision model. In *Proceedings of the Thirty-First Hawaii International Conference on System Sciences* (pp. 305-313). Washington, DC: IEEE Computer Society.

Dey, D., Sarkar, S., & De, P. (1998). A probabilistic decision model for entity matching in heterogeneous databases. *Management Science, 44*(10), 1379–1395. doi:10.1287/mnsc.44.10.1379

Dong, X., Halevy, A., & Madhavan, J. (2005). Reference reconciliation in complex information spaces, In *Proceedings of the ACM SIGMOD International Conference on Management of Data* (pp. 85-96). New York: ACM Press.

Fellegi, I. P., & Sunter, A. B. (1969). A theory for record linkage. *Journal of the American Statistical Association, 64*(328), 1183–1210. doi:10.2307/2286061

Forbus, K. D., & De Kleer, J. (1993). *Building problem solvers*. Cambridge, MA: MIT Press.

Golub, G. H., & Loan, C. F. V. (1996). *Matrix computations* (3rd ed.). Baltimore, MD, USA: Johns Hopkins University Press.

Hayes, P. (2004). *RDF semantics*. Retrieved from http://www.w3.org/TR/rdf-mt/

Henschen, L. J., & Wos, L. (1974). Unit refutations and horn sets. [ACM]. *Journal of the Association for Computing Machinery, 21*(4), 590–605.

Horrocks, I., Patel-Schneider, P. F., Boley, H., Tabet, S., Grosof, B., & Dean, M. (2004). *SWRL: A Semantic Web rule language combining OWL and RuleML* (W3C Member Submission). Retrieved from http://www.w3.org/Submission/SWRL

Koffina, I., Serfiotis, G., & Christophides, V. (2006). Mediating RDF/S queries to relational and XML sources. *International Journal on Semantic Web and Information Systems, 2*(4), 78–91.

McBride, B. (2004). The resource description framework (RDF) and its vocabulary description language RDFS. In S. Staab & R. Studer (Eds.), *Handbook on ontologies* (pp. 51-66). Berlin, Germany: Springer.

McGuinness, D. L., & Van Harmelen, F. (2004). *OWL: Web ontology language overview* (W3C recommendation). Retrieved from http://www.w3.org/TR/owl-features

Newcombe, H. B., & Kennedy, J. M. (1962). Record linkage: Making maximum use of the discriminating power of identifying information. *Communications of the ACM, 5*(11), 563–566. doi:10.1145/368996.369026

Newcombe, H. B., Kennedy, J. M., Axford, S. J., & James, A. P. (1959). Automatic linkage of vital records. *Science, 130*, 954–959. doi:10.1126/science.130.3381.954

Parag, S., & Pedro, D. (2004). Multi-relational record linkage. In *Proceedings of the ACM SIGKDD Workshop on Multi-Relational Data Mining* (pp. 31-48).

Popa, L., Velegrakis, Y., Miller, R. J., Hernadez, M. A., & Fagin, R. (2002). Translating Web data. In *Proceedings of the VLDB Conference* (pp. 598-609).

Reynaud, C., & Safar, B. (2009). Construction automatique d'adaptateurs guidée par une ontologie pour l'intégration de sources et de données XML. *Technique et Science Informatiques. Numéro spécial Web Sémantique, 28*(2).

Robinson, A. (1965). A machine-oriented logic based on the resolution principle. *Journal of Association for Computing Machinery, 12*(1), 23–41.

Rousset, M.-C., Bidault, A., Froidevaux, C., Gagliardi, H., Goasdoué, F., Reynaud, C., & Safar, B. (2002). Construction de médiateurs pour intégrer des sources d'information multiples et hétérogènes: Le projet PICSEL. *Revue I3, 2*(1), 9-59.

Rousset, M.-C., & Reynaud, C. (2003). Picsel and Xyleme: Two illustrative information integration agents. In M. Klusch, S. Bergamaschi, P. Petta, & P. Edwards (Eds.), *Intelligent information agents research and development in Europe: An AgentLink perspective* (LNCS State of the Art Surveys, pp. 50-78). Berlin, Germany: Springer Verlag.

Saïs, F., Pernelle, N., & Rousset, M.-C. (2007). L2R: A logical method for reference reconciliation. In *Proceedings of the Twenty-Second AAAI Conference on Artificial Intelligence* (pp. 329-334).

Saïs, F., Pernelle, N., & Rousset, M.-C. (2009). Combining a logical and a numerical method for data reconciliation. *Journal of Data Semantics, LNCS 5480, 12*, 66-94.

ADDITIONAL READINGS

Amann, B., Beeri, C., Fundulaki, I., & Scholl, M. (2002). Querying XML sources using an ontology-based mediator. In R. Meersman & Z. Tari (Eds.), *Proceedings of the Confederated International Conferences Doa, CoopIS and ODBASE* (pp. 429-448). London: Springer-Verlag.

Batini, C., & Scannapieco, M. (2006). *Data quality: Concepts, methodologies and techniques (data-centric systems and applications)*. New York: Springer Verlag.

Benjelloun, O., Garcia-Molina, H., Menestrina, D., Su, Q., Whang, S. E., & Widom, J. (2009). Swoosh: A generic approach to entity resolution. *VLDB Journal*.

Bilenko, M., Mooney, R. J., Cohen, W. W., Ravikumar, P., & Fienberg, S. E. (2003). Adaptive name matching in information integration. *IEEE Intelligent Systems, 18*(5), 16–23. doi:10.1109/MIS.2003.1234765

Calvanese, D., Miller, R., & Mylopoulos, J. (2005). Representing and querying data transformations. In *Proceedings of the International Conference on Data Engineering* (pp. 81-92).

Christophides, V., Karvounarakis, G., Magkanaraki, A., Plexousakis, D., Vouton, V., Box, B., & Tannen, V. (2003). The ICS-FORTH Semantic Web integration middleware (SWIM). *IEEE Data Engineering Bulletin, 26*(4), 11–18.

Cohen, W. W. (1998). Integration of heterogeneous databases without common domains using queries based on textual similarity. In *Proceedings of the SIGMOD Conference* (pp. 201-212).

Doan, A., Lu, Y., Lee, Y., & Han, J. (2003). Profile-based object matching for information integration. *IEEE Intelligent Systems, 18*(5), 54–59. doi:10.1109/MIS.2003.1234770

Hammer, J., Garcia-Molina, H., Nestorov, S., Yerneni, R., Breunig, M., & Vassalov, V. (1997). Template-based wrappers in the TSIMMIS system. In *Proceedings of the ACM SIGMOD International Conference on Management of Data* (pp. 532-535).

Hernandez, M. A., & Stolfo, S. J. (1998). Real-world data is dirty: Data cleansing and the merge/purge problem. *Data Mining and Knowledge Discovery, 2*(1), 9–37. doi:10.1023/A:1009761603038

Herzog, T. N., Scheuren, F. J., & Winkler, W. E. (2007). *Data quality and record linkage techniques*. New York: Springer Verlag.

Kalashnikov, D., Mehrotra, S., & Chen, Z. (2005). Exploiting relationships for domain-independent data cleaning. *SIAM Data Mining*.

Klein, M. (2002). Interpreting XML via an RDF schema. In *Proceedings of the International Workshop on Database and Expert Systems Applications* (pp. 889-893).

Kuhlins, S., & Tredwell, R. (2002). Toolkits for generating wrappers – a survey of software toolkits for automated data extraction from Websites. In M. Aksit, M. Mezini, & R. Unland (Eds.), *Proceedings of the International Conference NetObjectDays* (LNCS 2591, pp. 184-198). Berlin, Germany: Springer.

Laender, H. F., Ribeiro-Neto, B. A., Da Silva, A., & Teixeira, J. S. (2002). A brief survey of Web data extraction tools. *SIGMOD Record*, 84–93. doi:10.1145/565117.565137

Lenzerini, M. (2002). Data integration: A theoretical perspective. In *Proceedings of the ACM SIGMOD-SIGACT-SIGART Symposium on Principles of database systems* (pp. 233-246). New York: ACM Press.

Liu, L., Pu, C., & Han, W. (2000). XWRAP: An XML-enabled wrapper construction system for Web information sources. In *Proceedings of the International Conference on Data Engineering* (pp. 611-621).

Miklos, Z., & Sobernig, S. (2005). Query translation between RDF and XML: A case study in the educational domain. In *Proceedings of the Workshop of the Interoperability of Web-Based Educational Systems*.

Miller, R., Haas, A., & Hernandez, M. (2000). Schema mapping as query discovery. In *Proceedings of the International Conference on VLDB* (pp. 77-88).

Miller, R., Hernandez, M., Haas, A., Yan, L., Howard Ho, C., Fagin, R., & Popa, L. (2001). The clio project: Managing heterogeneity. In *Proceedings of the ACM SIGMOD International Conference on Management of Data* (pp. 78-83).

Milo, T., & Zohar, S. (1998). Using schema matching to simplify heterogeneous data translation. In *Proceedings of the International Conference on VLDB* (pp. 122-133).

Monge, A. E., & Elkan, C. (1997). An efficient domain-independent algorithm for detecting approximately duplicate database records. *ACM SIGMOD Workshop on Research Issues on Data Mining and Knowledge Discovery* (pp. 23-29).

Saïs, F., & Thomopoulos, R. (2008). Reference fusion and flexible querying. In *Proceedings of the Conference on Ontologies, DataBases, and Applications of Semantics (ODBASE)* (pp. 1541-1549).

Velegrakis, Y., De Giacomo, G., Lenzerini, M., Nardo, M., & Riccardo, R. (2001). Data integration in data warehousing. *International Journal of Cooperative Information Systems, 10*(3), 237–271. doi:10.1142/S0218843001000345

Velegrakis, Y., Millar, R., & Mylopoulos, J. (2005). Representing and querying data transformations. In *Proceedings of the International Conference on Data Engineering* (pp. 81-92).

Verykios, V. S., Moustakides, G. V., & Elfeky, M. G. (2003). A Bayesian decision model for cost optimal record matching. *The VLDB Journal, 12*(1), 28–40. doi:10.1007/s00778-002-0072-y

KEY TERMS AND DEFINITIONS

Data Integration: In this chapter, data integration means data reconciliation.

Data Warehouse: It contains data defined in terms of an ontology. These data come from different heterogeneous sources, are transformed according to the ontology of the data warehouse and then reconciled.

Mappings: correspondence relations between a global schema or ontology and the schemas of data sources.

Mediator-Based Approach: An approach integrating multiple data sources which can be syntactically or semantically heterogeneous while related to a same domain (e.g., tourism, culture). It provides a uniform interface for querying collections of pre-existing data sources that were created independently. Mediator systems are based on a single mediated schema in terms of which users' queries are issued and the information sources to integrate are described. The descriptions specify semantic relationships between the contents of the sources and the mediated schema. A user query that is formulated on a mediated schema is translated into a query against local schemas using views. Query plans are computed and executed through wrappers in order to get the answers to the user query. The goal is to give users the illusion that they interrogate a centralized and homogeneous system.

Ontology: A model of the objects of an application domain composed of concepts, attributes of concepts and relations between concepts.

Reference Reconciliation: The reference reconciliation problem consists in deciding whether different identifiers refer to the same data: i.e., correspond to the same world entity

Unsupervised Approach: An approach where the program is not trained by some *data* that are labeled with the desired output and which are provided by human experts.

Wrapper: Systems that aim at accessing a source, extracting the relevant data and presenting such data in a specified format.

ENDNOTES

[i] A research project funded by France Telecom R&D (2005-2008)

[ii] Another version of Cora is available at http://www.cs.umass.edu/~mccallum/data/cora-refs.tar.gz

Chapter 3
X–WACoDa
An XML–Based Approach for Warehousing and Analyzing Complex Data

Hadj Mahboubi
Université de Lyon (ERIC Lyon 2), France

Jean-Christian Ralaivao
Université de Lyon (ERIC Lyon 2), France

Sabine Loudcher
Université de Lyon (ERIC Lyon 2), France

Omar Boussaïd
Université de Lyon (ERIC Lyon 2), France

Fadila Bentayeb
Université de Lyon (ERIC Lyon 2), France

Jérôme Darmont
Université de Lyon (ERIC Lyon 2), France

ABSTRACT

Data warehousing and OLAP applications must nowadays handle complex data that are not only numerical or symbolic. The XML language is well-suited to logically and physically represent complex data. However, its usage induces new theoretical and practical challenges at the modeling, storage and analysis levels; and a new trend toward XML warehousing has been emerging for a couple of years. Unfortunately, no standard XML data warehouse architecture emerges. In this chapter, the authors propose a unified XML warehouse reference model that synthesizes and enhances related work, and fits into a global XML warehousing and analysis approach we have developed. They also present a software platform that is based on this model, as well as a case study that illustrates its usage.

DOI: 10.4018/978-1-60566-756-0.ch003

INTRODUCTION

Data warehouses form the basis of decision-support systems (DSSs). They help integrate production data and support On-Line Analytical Processing (OLAP) or data mining. These technologies are nowadays mature. However, in most cases, the studied activity is materialized by numeric and symbolic data, whereas data exploited in decision processes are more and more diverse and heterogeneous. The development of the Web and the proliferation of multimedia documents have indeed greatly contributed to the emergence of data that can:

- Be represented in various formats (databases, texts, images, sounds, videos...);
- Be diversely structured (relational databases, XML documents...);
- Originate from several different sources;
- Be described through several channels or points of view (a video and a text that describe the same meteorological phenomenon, data expressed in different scales or languages...);
- Change in terms of definition or value over time (temporal databases, periodical surveys...).

We term data that fall in several of the above categories *complex data* (Darmont *et al.*, 2005). For example, analyzing medical data regarding high-level athletes has lead us to jointly exploit information under various forms: patient records (classical database), medical history (text), radiographies and echographies (multimedia documents), physician diagnoses (texts or audio recordings), etc. (Darmont & Olivier, 2006; Darmont & Olivier, 2008)

Managing such data involves lots of different issues regarding their structure, storage and processing (Darmont & Boussaïd, 2006); and classical data warehouse architectures must be reconsidered to handle them. The XML language

(Bray *et al.*, 2006) bears many interesting features for representing complex data (Boussaïd *et al.*, 2007; Boussaïd *et al.*, 2008; Darmont *et al.*, 2003; Darmont *et al.*, 2005). First, it allows embedding data and their schema, either implicitly, or explicitly through schema definition. This type of metadata representation suits data warehouses very well. Furthermore, we can benefit from the semi-structured data model's flexibility, extensibility and richness. XML document storage may be achieved either in relational, XML-compatible Database Management Systems (DBMSs) or in XML-native DBMSs. Finally, XML query languages such as XQuery (Boag *et al.*, 2007) help formulate analytical queries that would be difficult to express in a relational system (Beyer *et al.* 2004; Beyer *et al.*, 2005). In consequence, there has been a clear trend toward XML warehousing for a couple of years (Baril & Bellahsène, 2003; Hümmer *et al.*, 2003; Nassis *et al.*, 2005; Park *et al.*, 2005; Pkorný, 2002; Vrdoljak *et al.*, 2003; Zhang *et al.*,2005).

Our own motivation is to handle complex data into a complete decision-support process, which requires their integration and representation under a form processable by on-line analysis and/or data mining techniques (Darmont *et al.*, 2003). We have already proposed a full, generic data warehousing and on-line analysis process that includes two broad axes (Boussaïd *et al.*, 2008):

- Data warehousing, including complex data integration and modeling;
- Complex data analysis.

More precisely, the approach we propose consists in representing complex data as XML documents. Then, we recommend an additional layer to prepare them for analysis. Complex data under the form of XML documents are thus multidimensionally modeled to obtain an XML data warehouse. Finally, complex data analysis can take place from this warehouse, with on-line analysis, data mining or a combination of the two approaches.

Unfortunately, in this context, though XML and XQuery are normalized, XML DBMSs and data warehouse architectures are not. The XML warehouse models and approaches proposed in the literature share a lot of concepts (originating from classical data warehousing), but they are nonetheless all different. In this paper, we aim at addressing this issue. We first quite exhaustively present and discuss related work regarding XML warehousing and OLAP. Then, we motivate and recall our XML warehousing methodology, where XML is used for integrating and warehousing complex data for analysis. Our main contribution is a unified, reference XML data warehouse architecture that synthesizes and enhances existing models. We also present an XML warehousing software platform that is architectured around our reference model and illustrate its usage with a case study. Finally, we conclude this paper and provide future research directions.

RELATED WORK

In this section, we first recall a couple of fundamental definitions before detailing literature work related to XML data warehousing and OLAP.

Definitions

A *data warehouse* is a copy of transaction data specifically structured for query and analysis (Kimball, 2002). More formally, a data warehouse is a subject-oriented, integrated, time-variant and non-volatile collection of data in support of management's decision making process (Inmon, 2005). A single-subject data warehouse is typically referred to as a *datamart*, while data warehouses are generally enterprise in scope (Reed *et al.*, 2007).

A *star schema* is the simplest data warehouse schema. Shaped like a star, it consists of a single, central *fact table* linked to peripheral *dimensions*. A *fact* represents a business measurement (Kimball, 2002) and is constituted of references to its descriptive dimensions and a set of usually numeric and additive *measures* (such as sale amounts, for instance). Dimensions contain textual descriptors (*members*) of the studied business (Kimball, 2002). Star-like schema including hierarchies in dimensions (e.g., town, region and country granularity levels in a geographical dimension) are termed *snowflake schemas*. Star-modeled data warehouses with several fact tables are termed *constellation schemas*.

Finally, *On-Line Analytical Processing* or *OLAP* (Codd *et al.*, 1994) is an approach for efficiently processing decision-support, analytical queries that are multidimensional by nature. Data are stored in multidimensional arrays called *data cubes* that are typically extracted from data warehouses. Data cubes are then manipulated with the help of OLAP operators.

XML Data Warehousing

Several studies address the issue of designing and building XML data warehouses. They propose to use XML documents to manage or represent facts and dimensions. The main objective of these approaches is to enable a native storage of the warehouse and its easy interrogation with XML query languages.

Research in this area may be subdivided into three families. The first family particularly focuses on Web data integration for decision-support purposes. However, actual XML warehouse models are not very elaborate. The second family of XML warehousing approaches is explicitly based on classical warehouse logical models (star-like schemas). They are used when dimensions are dynamic and they allow the support of end-user analytical tools. Finally, the third family we identify relates to document warehousing. It is based on user-driven approaches that are applied when an organization has fixed warehousing requirements. Such requirements correspond to typical or predictable results expected from an XML document warehouse or frequent user-query patterns.

XML Web Warehouses

The objective of these approaches is to gather XMLWeb sources and integrate them into a Web warehouse. Vrdoljak *et al.* (2003) introduce the design of aWeb warehouse that originates from XML Schemas describing operational sources. This method consists in preprocessing XML Schemas, in creating and transforming the schema graph, in selecting facts and in creating a logical schema that validates a data warehouse.

Golfareli *et al.* (2001) also propose a semi-automatic approach for building a datamart conceptual schema from XML sources. The authors show how data warehouse multidimensional design may be carried out starting directly from XML sources. They also propose an algorithm that solves the problem of correctly inferring the information needed for data warehousing.

Finally, the designers of the Xyleme system propose a dynamic warehouse for XML data from the Web that supports query evaluation, change control and data integration (Xyleme, 2001). No particular warehouse model is proposed, though.

XML Data Warehouses

In his XML-star schema, Pokorný (2002) models a star schema in XML by defining dimension hierarchies as sets of logically connected collections of XML data, and facts as XML data elements.

Hümmer *et al.* (2003) propose a family of templates enabling the description of a multidimensional structure (dimension and fact data) for integrating several data warehouses into a virtual or federated warehouse. These templates, collectively named XCube, consist of three kinds of XML documents with respect to specific schemas: *XCubeSchema* stores metadata; *XCubeDimension* describes dimensions and their hierarchical levels; and *XCubeFact* stores facts, i.e., measures and the corresponding dimension references. These federated templates are not actually directly related

to XML warehousing, but they can definitely be used for representing XML star schemas.

Rusu *et al.* (2005) propose a methodology, based on the XQuery technology, for building XML data warehouses. This methodology covers processes such as data cleaning, summarization, intermediating XML documents, updating/linking existing documents and creating fact tables. Facts and dimensions are represented by XML documents built with XQueries.

Park *et al.* (2005) introduce a framework for the multidimensional analysis of XML documents, named XML-OLAP. XML-OLAP is based on an XML warehouse where every fact and dimension is stored as an XML document. The proposed model features a single repository of XML documents for facts and multiple repositories of XML documents for dimensions (one repository per dimension).

Eventually, Boussaïd *et al.* (2006) propose an XML-based methodology, named XWarehousing, for warehousing complex data. They use XML Schema as a modelling language to represent user analysis needs. These needs are then compared to complex data stored in heterogeneous XML sources. Information needed for building an XML cube is extracted from these sources and transformed into OLAP facts.

Note that all these studies, though all different, more or less converge toward a unified XML warehouse model. They mostly differ in the way dimensions are handled and the number of XML documents that are used to store facts and dimensions.

XML Document Warehouses

Nassis *et al.* (2005) propose a conceptual approach for designing and building an XML repository, named xFACT. They exploit object-oriented concepts and propose to select dimensions based on user requirements. To enhance the XML data warehouse's expressiveness, these dimensions are represented by XML virtual views. In this approach, the authors assume that all dimensions are part of fact data and that each fact is described in a single XML document.

Rajugan *et al.* (2005) also propose a view-driven approach for modeling and designing an XML fact repository, named GxFact. GxFact gathers xFACTs (distributed XML warehouses and datamarts) in a global company setting. The authors also provide three design strategies for building and managing GxFact to model further hierarchical dimensions and/or global document warehouses.

Baril and Bellahsène (2003) envisage XML data warehouses as collections of views represented by XML documents. Views, defined in the warehouse, allow to filter and to restructure XML sources. A warehouse is defined as a set of materialized views and provides a mediated schema that constitutes a uniform interface for querying the XML data warehouse. Following this approach, Baril and Bellahsène have developed a system named DAWAX.

Finally, Zhang *et al.* (2005) propose an approach to materialize XML data warehouses based on frequent query patterns discovered from historical queries. The authors apply a hierarchical clustering technique to merge these queries and therefore build the warehouse.

Multidimensional Analysis over XML Data

Though several studies from the literature address the issue of XML data warehousing, fewer actually push through the whole decision-support process and address the multidimensional analysis of XML data. To query XML cubes, Park et *al.* (2005) propose a multidimensional expression language, XML-MDX. The authors supplement the Microsoft multidimensional expression language, MDX, with two additional statements: CREATE XQ-CUBE to create XML cubes, and SELECT to query them. In addition, the authors define seven aggregation operators: ADD, LIST, COUNT, SUMMARY, TOPIC, TOP KEYWORD and CLUSTER. Some operators are inherited from the relational context, while others are designed for non-additive data and exploit text mining techniques.

Beyer et *al.* (2005) argue that analytical queries written in XQuery are difficult to read, write, and process efficiently. To address these issues, the authors propose to extend XQuery FLWOR expressions with an explicit syntax for grouping and numbering query results. They also present solutions dealing with the homogeneous and hierarchical aspect of XML data for explicit grouping problems.

In the same context, Wang et *al.* (2005) present concepts for XOLAP (OLAP on XML data). The authors define a general XML aggregation operator, GXaggregation. This operator permits property extraction from dimensions and measures through their XPath expression. Hence, computing statistics over XML data becomes more flexible. This process is performed with functions that aggregate heterogeneous data over hierarchies. The authors also envisage to embed GXaggregation in an XML query language such as XQuery.

Finally, Ben Messaoud et *al.* (2006a) propose an OLAP aggregation operator that is based on an automatic clustering method: OpAC. The authors' proposal enables precise analyses and provides semantic aggregates for complex data represented by XML documents. OpAC has been applied onto XML cubes output by the XWarehousing approach (Boussaïd *et al.*, 2006).

XML WAREHOUSING AND ANALYSIS METHODOLOGY

In a data warehousing process, the data integration phase is crucial. Data integration is a hard task that involves reconciliation at various levels (data models, data schemas, data instances, semantics). Nowadays, in most organizations, XML documents are becoming a casual way to represent

Figure 1. XML data warehousing and analysis process

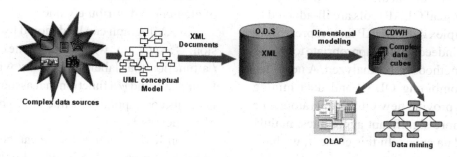

and store data. Therefore, new efforts are needed to integrate XML in classical business applications. Integrating heterogeneous and complex information in DSSs requires special consideration. Existing ETL (Extract, Transform, Load) tools that organize data into a common syntax are indeed ill-adapted to complex data. Furthermore, if XML documents must be prepared for future OLAP analyses, storing them in a data repository is not enough. Through these documents, a more interesting abstraction level, completely oriented toward analysis objectives, must be expressed. It is thus necessary to structure XML data with respect to a data warehouse multidimensional reference model.

Though feeding data warehouses with XML documents is getting increasingly common, methodological issues arise. The multidimensional organization of data warehouses is indeed quite different from the semi-structured organization of XML documents. A data warehouse architecture is subject-oriented, integrated, consistent, and data are regularly refreshed to represent temporal evolutions. Then, how can multidimensional design be carried out with a semi-structured formalism such as XML?

XML may be characterized by two aspects. On one hand, it helps store and exchange data through XML documents. On the other hand, XML Schemas are relevant for describing data. Multidimensional modeling helps structure data for query and analysis. An XML formalism can thus be used to describe the various elements of a multidimensional model (Boussaïd *et al.*, 2006). But XML can only be considered as a logical and physical description tool for future analysis tasks on complex data. The reference conceptual model remains the star schema and its derivatives.

One challenge we address in our approach is to propose a multidimensional model (thus oriented for analysis) that is described in XML, to derive a physical organization of XML documents that contributes to performance enhancement. To support this choice, we propose a modeling process (Figure 1) that achieves complex data integration (Boussaïd *et al.*, 2003; Boussaïd *et al.*, 2007; Boussaïd *et al.*, 2008).

We first design a conceptual UML model for a complex object. This UML model is then directly translated into an XML Schema, which we view as a logical model. At the physical level, XML documents that are valid against this logical model may be mapped into a relational, object-relational or XML-native database. In this paper, we focus on the latter family of DBMSs. After representing complex data as XML documents, we physically integrate them into an Operational Data Store (ODS), which is a buffer ahead of the actual warehouse.

At this stage, it is already possible to mine the stored XML documents directly, e.g., with XML structure mining techniques. In addition, to further analyze these documents' contents efficiently, it is interesting to warehouse them, i.e., devise a multidimensional model that allows OLAP analyses. However, classical OLAP tools are ill-adapted to deal with complex data. OLAP facts representing complex data indeed require appropriate tools and aggregation methods to be analyzed. A new idea consists in combining OLAP and data mining algorithms to provide new OLAP operators able to compute more significant aggregates, mainly on complex data cubes. In this context, we have proposed three approaches.

1. *Sparse data visualization:* with multiple correspondence analysis, we have reduced the negative effect of sparsity by reorganizing cube cells (BenMessaoud *et al.*, 2006).
2. *Complex fact aggregation:* with agglomerative hierarchical clustering, we obtain aggregates that are semantically richer than those provided by traditional multidimensional structures (BenMessaoud *et al.*, 2006a).
3. *Explanation of possible relationships in multidimensional data:* we have designed a new algorithm for guided association rule mining in data cubes (BenMessaoud *et al.*, 2007).

MODELING XML DATA WAREHOUSES

In this section, we mainly present our analysis of related work and our proposal to unify and enhance existing XML warehouse models. Our reference model notably exploits the concept of virtual key reference we define previously.

Preliminary Definitions

An XML document is defined as a labeled graph (an *XML graph*) whose nodes represent document elements or attributes, and whose edges represent the element-subelement (or parent-child) relationship. Edges are labeled with element or attribute names. Let E be the set of distinct element names, A the set of distinct attribute names and V the set of element and attribute values.

An XML graph can be denoted by the expression: $G := \langle t, l, \psi \rangle$, where t is an finite ordered tree, l a function that labels a node in t with symbols from $E \cup A$, and ψ a function that associates a node in t to its corresponding value in V. The root node of t is denoted $root_t$.

In an XML graph, a node e can be referenced by another node e'. Let a and a' be two attribute nodes that are children of e et e', respectively. Then, e references e' if and only if $\psi(a) = \psi(a')$ and $l(a)$ *unequals* $l(a')$. Such a link is referred to as a *virtual key reference*.

XML Data Warehouse Reference Model

Previous XML data warehouse architectures converge toward a unified model. They mostly differ in the way dimensions are handled and in the number of XML documents that are used to store facts and dimensions. We may distinguish four different families of physical architectures:

1. One XML document for storing facts and another for storing all dimension related information (XCube);
2. A collection of XML documents that each embed one fact and its related dimensions (X-Warehousing);
3. A collection of XML documents where facts and dimensions are each stored in one separate document (XML-OLAP);
4. One XML document for storing facts and one XML document for storing each dimension (analogous to relational star-like schemas).

A performance evaluation study of these different representations has been performed by Boukraa *et al.* (2006). The authors have built four XML mammographic warehouses with respect

Figure 2. XML data warehouse model

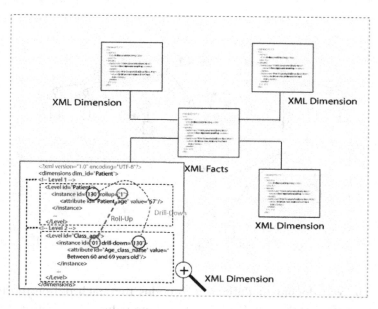

to the four architectures we have enumerated. These XML warehouses have been stored on the eXist XML-native DBMS (Meier, 2002). Then, the authors measured the response time of a fixed XQuery workload over these warehouses and showed that representing facts in one single XML document and each dimension in one XML document allowed the best performance. They especially conclude that storing facts in one single XML document helps decrease their scanning cost.

Moreover, this representation also allows to model constellation schemas without duplicating dimension information. Several fact documents can indeed share the same dimensions. Also, since each dimension and its hierarchical levels are stored in one XML document, dimension updates are more easily and efficiently performed than if dimensions were either embedded with the facts or all stored in one single document.

Hence, we adopt the architecture model from Figure 2 to represent our XML data warehouse. It is actually the translation of a classical snowflake schema from the relational model to the XML model, i.e., tables become XML documents. Note,

however, that XML warehouses can bear irregular structures that are not possible in relational warehouses. On the physical level, our reference data warehouse is composed of the following XML documents:

- *DW-model.xml* represents the warehouse-metadata, basically the warehouse schema: fact document(s) structure (related dimensions, numeric measures), dimension documents structure (including any hierarchical level information, each level being characterized by descriptive member attributes);
- A set of *facts$_f$.xml* documents that each help store information related to set of facts f, i.e., dimension references and measure values;
- A set of *dimension$_d$.xml* documents that each help store a given dimension d's member values.

Figure 3 represents the *dw-model.xml* document's graph structure. The equivalent XML Schema definition we actually use in practice is available on-line to accommodate space con-

Figure 3. DW-model.xml graph structure

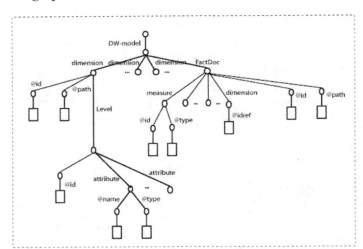

straints[1]. The *dw-model.xml* document defines the multidimensional structure of the warehouse. Its root node, *DW-model*, is composed of two types of nodes: *dimension* and *FactDoc* nodes. A *dimension* node defines one dimension, its possible hierarchical levels (*Level* elements) and attributes (including their types), as well as the path to the corresponding *dimension$_d$.xml* document. A *FactDoc* element defines a fact, i.e., its measures, virtual key references to the corresponding dimensions, and the path to the corresponding *facts$_f$.xml* document.

Figure 4(a) represents the *facts$_f$.xml* documents' graph structure. Its equivalent XML Schema is available on-line[2]. A *facts$_f$.xml* document stores facts. The document root node, *FactDoc*, is composed of *fact* subelements that each instantiate a fact, i.e., measure values and dimension virtual key references. These identifier-based references support the fact-to-dimension relationship.

Finally, Figure 4(b) represents the *dimension$_d$.xml* documents' graph structure. Its equivalent XML Schema is available on-line[3]. A *dimension$_d$.xml* document helps instantiate one dimension, including any hierarchical level. Its root node, *dimension*, is composed of *Level* nodes. Each one defines a hierarchy level composed of *instance* nodes that each define the level's member attribute values. In addition, an *instance* element contains *Roll-up* and *Drill-Down* attributes that define the hierarchical relationship within dimension *d*. More precisely, these multivalued virtual key references help link sets of instances of a given dimension hierarchy level to their aggregate in the next level (*Roll-up*), and vice-versa (*Drill-Down*).

SOFTWARE PLATFORM

In order to support experimentations and projects that validate our XML complex data warehousing approach (X-WACoDa), we have developed a software platform we also named X-WACoDa by extension. We detail in this section its architecture, as well as a case study that illustrates our whole approach and exploits the software platform.

X-WACoDa's architecture is represented in Figure 5. It consists of three components that are further detailed in the following sections:

1.   An ETL component that allows to extract complex data representations in an homogeneous XML format and to integrate them into

Figure 4. Facts$_f$.xml (a) and dimension$_d$.xml (b) graph structure

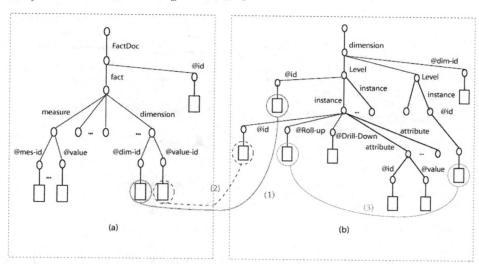

the XML data warehouse. This component is based on user requirements;

2. An actual warehouse component that manages XML data with respect to our XML data warehouse reference model;

3. An analysis component that permits various analyses (OLAP, data mining...) over the data warehouse.

ETL Component

The ETL component in X-WACoDa is actually a set of tools that form a chain of data extraction, transformation and loading into the XML data warehouse.

First, SMAIDoC is a multi-agent system that allows complex data extraction and transformation into a predefined XML format (Boussaïd *et al.*, 2003). SMAIDoC (Figure 6) consists of a set

Figure 5. X-WACoDa software platform architecture

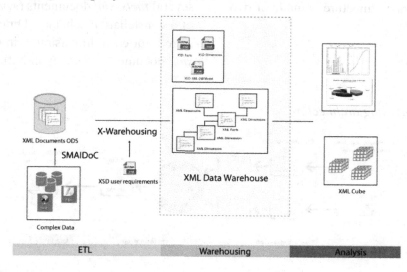

Figure 6. SMAIDoC architecture

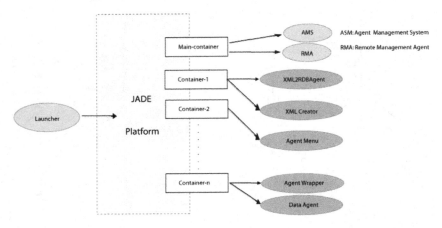

of agents that collect or extract data (*DataAgent*), structure and model them (*WrapperAgent*), translate them and generate the corresponding XML documents (*XML Creator*), and finally store the obtained XML documents into a database (*XML2RDBAgent*).

Then, UML2XML is a graphical interface that helps users express their analysis requirements in UML and outputs an XML document representing the warehouse schema: *dw-model.xml*.

Finally, X-Warehousing generates the warehouse's XML documents (Boussaïd *et al.*, 2006). XWarehousing inputs the complex data that have been formated in XML by SMAIDoC, as well as the user analysis requirements produced by UML2XML. Its architecture is made of two modules (Figure 7):

1. A *loader module* that loads user requirements and XML data source schemas, and then transforms them into attributes trees (Golfarelli *et al.*, 2001);
2. A *merger module* that merges these attribute trees into one final attribute tree representing the warehouse schema. The merging process operates through the application of fusion functions (pruning and grafting).

Data Warehouse

X-Warehousing directly outputs XML documents that form an XML data warehouse with respect to our reference model. Fact data are stored in one or several *facts_f.xml* documents (several in the case of a constellation schema). Dimension data are stored, for each dimension d, in the *dimension_d.xml* document. Data exploitation is achieved

Figure 7. X-Warehousing architecture

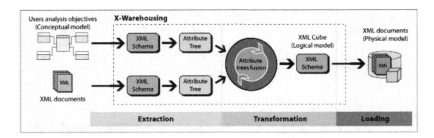

through a DBMS. Two types of DBMSs currently support XML data storage, management, and query processing and optimization: relational, XML-enabled systems that map XML data into relational tables, and XML-native DBMSs.

In our approach, we focus on XML-native systems. They indeed consider XML documents as the fundamental unit of storage. They define a specific XML storage schema for XML documents, and store and retrieve them according to this model, which includes elements, attributes, their contents and order. Moreover, many XML databases provide a logical model for grouping XML documents, called collections or libraries. XML-native DBMSs also implement XML query engines supporting XPath and XQuery. In addition, some XML-native DBMSs support the XML:DB Application Programming Interface (API) that features a form of implementation independent access to XML data.

Query engine performance is the primary criterion when selecting an XML native DBMS. A good candidate system must be capable to perform complex queries in reasonable response times and to store a large volumes of data. This may currently be seen as a weak point in our choice, since XML-native DBMSs are not mature yet, but we are also working in parallel on optimizing their performances (Mahboubi *et al.*, 2006; Mahboubi *et al.*, 2008; Mahboubi *et al.*, 2008a).

Analysis Component

X-WACoDa's analysis component is constituted of two subcomponents. First, an *ad hoc* reporting application helps users create specific and customized decision support queries. This application is based on XML:DB and allows database connection, sending and saving XML query results in XML format. Analytical queries are expressed in XQuery. We selected XQuery because it allows performing complex queries over multiple XML documents. In addition, we extended XQuery's FLWOR clauses with an explicit grouping con-

struct comparable to the SQL group by clause, in order to allow common business analysis (i.e., OLAP-like) queries (Mahboubi *et al.*, 2006).

The second analysis subcomponent, Mining-Cubes, is a Web-based application that includes a set of on-line analysis and mining components (BenMessaoud *et al.*, 2006a). Analysis components aim at loading data and performing multidimensional explorations (through two or three-dimension views). Data mining components implement methods such as agglomerative hierarchical clustering or frequent itemset mining. From a user's point of view, MiningCubes integrates these components in a transparent way. For instance, a factorial approach can be used to represent and reorganize relevant OLAP facts, association rules may be mined from an OLAP cube, or clustering may be exploited to aggregate non-additive dimension members in roll-up/drill-down operations.

Case Study

Let us now apply the X-WACoDa approach onto a real-world application domain and consider complex data from the Digital Database for ScreeningMammography[4] (DDSM). DDSM gathers 2604 medical history cases of anonymous patients. Each case contains an ASCII text file representing general information about a patient and four LJPEG radiography image files. These data are issued from multiple sources and encoded through different file types, and may thus be considered complex.

The first step in our approach is to transform DDSM data in XML format to guarantee an homogeneous representation and to allow data integration into an XML data warehouse. Such XML documents individually describe one whole medical case by gathering study information (date, examination...), patient information, and radiography image descriptors (file name, url, scanner resolution...). All documents bear the same structure and are valid against an XML Schema.

Figure 8. Sample XQuery over the DDSM XML warehouse

```
for $x in //FactDoc/fact
$y in //dimenion/Level[@id='Patient']/instance
let $q := $x/measure[@mes-id='Number_of_regions']/@value
where $y/attribute/@id='Patient_age'
and $a/attribute/@value='58'
and $x/dimension/@value-id=$y/@id
and $x/dimension/@dim-id='Patient'
return fn:sum($q)
```

In this case study, we selected and processed 1406 XML documents.

The second step in our approach is to design a *dw-model.xml* document representing user analysis requirements, with the help of the UML2XML software. In the present case study, this document represents a star schema composed of *Suspicious region* facts (suspected cancerous regions) characterized by the *Region length* and *Number of regions* measures. *dw-model.xml* also describes dimensions and their hierarchies. We obtain ten dimensions: *Patient, Lesion type, Assessment, Subtlety, Pathology, Date of study, Date of digitization, Digitizer, Scanner image* and *Boundary*.

In a third step, both the XML documents representing complex medical data and *dw-model.xml* are submitted to the X-warehousing software to actually build an XML data warehouse. X-warehousing outputs ten XML documents representing dimensions: *Patient.xml, Lesion_type.xml, Assessment.xml, Subtlety.xml, Pathology.xml, Date_of_study.xml, Date_of_digitization.xml, Digitizer.xml, Scanner image.xml* and *Boundary.xml*; and one XML documents containing facts: *facts.xml*. These documents constitute the XML data warehouse. We chose to store this warehouse within the X-Hive XML-native DBMS[5]. X-Hive allows the native storage of large documents and supports XQuery. It also provides APIs for storing, querying, retrieving, transforming and publishing XML data.

Finally, our analysis application exploits a set of decision-support queries expressed in XQuery. Figure 8 provides an example of analytical query that returns the total number of suspicious regions for fifty-eight-year-old patients. It performs one join operation between the *Patient* dimension and facts, a selection and an aggregation operation. Variable *q* stores the *Number of regions* measure values used by the aggregation function.

CONCLUSION AND PERSPECTIVES

Nowadays, data processed by DSSs tend to be more and more complex and pose new challenges to the data warehousing community. To efficiently manage and analyze complex data, we propose a full, generic, XML-based data warehousing and on-line analysis approach: X-WACoDa. This approach includes complex data integration, multidimensional modeling and analysis. In this paper, we identified some substantial heterogeneity in XML warehouse models from the literature, and thus focused on proposing a unified reference XML data warehouse architecture. We also presented a software platform, also named X-WACoDa, which implements our ideas.

Research perspectives in the young field of XML warehousing are numerous. Regarding complex data integration, we aim at extracting useful knowledge for warehousing from data themselves, by applying data mining techniques. We plan to study a metadata representation of data mining results in mixed structures combining XML Schema and the Resource Description Framework (RDF). These description languages are indeed well-suited for expressing semantic properties and relationships between metadata.

On a technical level, SMAIDoC could also be extended to converse with on-line search engines (including some semantic Web tools) and exploit their answers to identify and qualify Web data sources.

Our choice of an "all-XML" architecture also leads to address performance problems. Our research in this area shows that using indexes and/or materialized views significantly improves response time for typical analytical queries expressed in XQuery (Mahboubi *et al.*, 2006; Mahboubi *et al.*, 2008; Mahboubi *et al.*, 2008a). Further gains in performance can be achieved, though. For instance, it is widely acknowledged that indexes and materialized views are mutually beneficial to each other. We have designed a method for simultaneously selecting indexes and materialized views in the relational context, which we aim at adapting to the XML context. Finally, our performance optimization strategies could be better integrated in a host XML-native DBMS. In particular, the mechanism for rewriting queries exploiting materialized views would be more efficient if it was part of the system.

We finally have a couple of perspectives regarding complex data analysis. First, since the structure of XML documents carries some relevant information, we plan to exploit XML structure mining to, e.g., discover tag relevance. Relevant tags may then be selected as measures or dimensions in our multidimensional modeling process. Second, we have underlined with the MiningCubes software the benefit of associating OLAP and data mining to enhance on-line analysis power. We are currently working on extending on-line analysis with new capabilities such as explanation and prediction, with the aim of better handling data complexity.

REFERENCES

Baril, X., & Bellahsène, Z. (2003). Designing and managing an XML warehouse. In *XML Data Management: Native XML and XML-enabled Database Systems* (pp. 455-473). Reading, MA: Addison Wesley.

BenMessaoud, R., Boussaïd, O., & Loudcher-Rabaséda, S. (2006). Efficient multidimensional data representation based on multiple correspondence analysis. In *Proceedings of the ACM SIGKDD International Conference on Knowledge Discovery and Data Mining (KDD'06)*, Philadelphia, USA (pp. 662-667) New York: ACM Press.

BenMessaoud, R., Boussaïd, O., & Loudcher-Rabaséda, S. (2007). A multiple correspondence analysis to organize data cubes. In *Vol. 155(1) of Databases and Information Systems IV – Frontiers in Artificial Intelligence and Applications* (pp. 133-146). Amsterdam: IOS Press.

BenMessaoud, R., Loudcher-Rabaséda, S., & Boussaïd, O. (2006a). A data mining-based OLAP aggregation of complex data: Application on XML DOCUMent. *International Journal of Data Warehousing and Mining, 2*(4), 1–26.

Beyer, K. S., Chamberlin, D. D., Colby, L. S., Ozcan, F., Pirahesh, H., & Xu, Y. (2005). Extending XQuery for analytics. In *Proceedings of the ACM SIGMOD International Conference on Management of Data (SIGMOD'05)*, Baltimore, USA (pp. 503-514). New York: ACM Press.

Beyer, K. S., Cochrane, R., Colby, L. S., Ozcan, F., & Pirahesh, H. (2004). XQuery for analytics: Challenges and requirements. In *Proceedings of the First InternationalWorkshop on XQuery Implementation, Experience and Perspectives <XIME-P/>*, Paris, France (pp. 3-8).

Boag, S., Chamberlin, D., Fernandez, M., Florescu, D., Robie, J., & Simeon, J. (2007). *XQuery 1.0: An XML query language* (W3C Recommendation). Retrieved from http://www.w3.org/TR/xquery/

Boukraa, D., BenMessaoud, R., & Boussaïd, O. (2006). Proposition d'un modèle physique pour les entrepôts XML. In *Proceedings of the Atelier Systèmes Décisionnels (ASD'06), 9th Maghrebian Conference on Information Technologies (MC-SEAI'06)*, Agadir, Morocco.

Boussaïd, O., BenMessaoud, R., Choquet, R., & Anthoard, S. (2006). X-warehousing: An XML-based approach for warehousing complex data. In *Proceedings of the 10th East-European Conference on Advances in Databases and Information Systems (ADBIS'06)*, Thessaloniki, Greece (LNCS 4152, pp. 39-54). Berlin, Germany: Springer.

Boussaïd, O., Bentayeb, F., & Darmont, J. (2003). A multi-agent system-based ETL approach for complex data. In *Proceedings of the 10th ISPE International Conference on Concurrent Engineering: Research and Applications (CE'03)*, Madeira, Portugal (pp. 49-52).

Boussaïd, O., Darmont, J., Bentayeb, F., & Loudcher-Rabaseda, S. (2008). Warehousing complex data from the Web. *International Journal of Web Engineering and Technology, 4*(4), 408–433. doi:10.1504/IJWET.2008.019942

Boussaïd, O., Tanasescu, A., Bentayeb, F., & Darmont, J. (2007). Integration and dimensional modelling approaches for complex data warehousing. *Journal of Global Optimization, 37*(4), 571–591. doi:10.1007/s10898-006-9064-6

Bray, T., Paoli, J., Sperberg-McQueen, C., Maler, E., Yergeau, F., & Cowan, J. (2006). *Extensible markup language (XML) 1.1* (W3C Recommendation). Retrieved from http://www.w3.org/TR/2006/REC-xml11-20060816/

Codd, E., Codd, S., & Salley, C. (1994). *Providing OLAP (on-line analytical processing) to user-analysts: An IT mandate* [white paper]. E.F. Codd Associates.

Darmont, J., & Boussaïd, O. (Eds.). (2006). *Managing and processing complex data for decision support*. Hershey, PA: Idea Group Publishing.

Darmont, J., Boussaïd, O., Bentayeb, F., & Sabine Loudcher-Rabaseda, Y. Z. (2003). Web multiform data structuring for warehousing. In *Vol. 22 of Multimedia Systems and Applications* (pp. 179-194). Amsterdam: Kluwer Academic Publishers.

Darmont, J., Boussaïd, O., Ralaivao, J.-C., & Aouiche, K. (2005). An architecture framework for complex data warehouses. In *Proceedings of the 7th International Conference on Enterprise Information Systems (ICEIS'05)*, Miami, USA (pp. 370-373).

Darmont, J., & Olivier, E. (2006). A complex data warehouse for personalized, anticipative medicine. In *Proceedings of the 17th Information Resources Management Association International Conference (IRMA'06)*, Washington, USA (pp. 685-687). Hershey, PA: Idea Group Publishing.

Darmont, J., & Olivier, E. (2008). Biomedical data warehouses. In *Encyclopaedia of healthcare information systems*. Hershey, PA: IGI Global.

Golfarelli, M., Rizzi, S., & Vrdoljak, B. (2001). Data warehouse design from XML sources. In *Proceedings of the 4th International Workshop on Data Warehousing and OLAP (DOLAP'01)*, Atlanta, USA (pp. 40-47). New York: ACM Press.

Hümmer, W., Bauer, A., & Harde, G. (2003). XCube: XML for data warehouses. In *Proceedings of the 6th International Workshop on Data Warehousing and OLAP (DOLAP'03)*, New Orleans, USA (pp. 33-40). New York: ACM Press.

Inmon, W. (2005). *Building the data warehouse* (4th ed.). New York: John Wiley & Sons.

Kimball, R., & Ross, M. (2002). *The data warehouse toolkit* (2nd ed.). New York: John Wiley & Sons.

Mahboubi, H., Aouiche, K., & Darmont, J. (2006). Materialized view selection by query clustering in XML data warehouses. In *Proceedings of the 4th International Multiconference on Computer Science and Information Technology (CSIT'06)*, Amman, Jordan (pp. 68-77).

Mahboubi, H., Aouiche, K., & Darmont, J. (2008). A join index for XML data warehouses. In *Proceedings of the 2008 International Conference on Information Resources Management (Conf-IRM'08)*, Niagara Falls, Canada.

Mahboubi, H., & Darmont, J. (2007). Indices in XML databases. In *Encyclopedia of database technologies and applications, second edition*. Hershey, PA: IGI Global.

Meier, W. (2002). eXist: An open source native XML database. In *Proceedings of the Web, Web-services, and database systems, NODe 2002 Web and Database-Related Workshops*, Erfurt, Germany (LNCS 2593, pp. 169-183). Berlin, Germany: Springer.

Nassis, V., Rajugan, R., Dillon, T. S., & Rahayu, J. W. (2004). Conceptual design of XML document warehouses. In *Proceedings of the 6th International Conference on Data Warehousing and Knowledge Discovery (DaWaK'04)*, Zaragoza, Spain (LNCS 3181, pp. 1-14). Berlin, Germany: Springer.

Nassis, V., Rajugan, R., Dillon, T. S., & Rahayu, J. W. (2005). A requirement engineering approach for designing XML-view driven, XML document warehouses. In *Proceedings of the 29th International Conference on Computer Software and Applications (COMPSAC'05)*, Edinburgh, UK (pp. 388-395). Washington, DC: IEEE Computer Society.

Nassis, V., Rajugan, R., Dillon, T. S., & Rahayu, J. W. (2005). Conceptual and systematic design approach for XML document warehouses. *International Journal of Data Warehousing and Mining, 1*(3), 63–86.

Park, B.-K., Han, H., & Song, I.-Y. (2005). XML-OLAP: A multidimensional analysis framework for XML warehouses. In *Proceedings of the 7th International Conference on Data Warehousing and Knowledge Discovery (DaWaK'05)*, Copenhagen, Denmark (LNCS 3589, pp. 32-42). Berlin, Germany: Springer.

Pokorný, J. (2002). XML data warehouse: Modelling and querying. In *Proceedings of the 5th International Baltic Conference (BalticDB&IS'06)*, Tallin, Estonia (pp. 267-280). Institute of Cybernetics at Tallin Technical University.

Rajugan, R., Chang, E., & Dillon, T. S. (2005). Conceptual design of an XML FACT repository for dispersed XML document warehouses and XML marts. In *Proceedings of the 20th International Conference on Computer and Information Technology (CIT'05)*, Shanghai, China (pp. 141-149). Washington, DC: IEEE Computer Society.

Reed, M. (2007). A definition of data warehousing. *Intranet Journal*. Retrieved from http://www.intranetjournal.com/features/datawarehousing.html

Rusu, L. I., Rahayu, J. W., & Taniar, D. (2005). A methodology for building XML data warehouse. *International Journal of Data Warehousing and Mining, 1*(2), 67–92.

Vrdoljak, B., Banek, M., & Rizzi, S. (2003). Designing Web warehouses from XML schemas. In *Proceedings of the 5th International Conference on Data Warehousing and Knowledge Discovery (DaWaK'03)*, Prague, Czech Republic (LNCS 2737, pp. 89-98). Berlin Germany: Springer.

Wang, H., Li, J., He, Z., & Gao, H. (2005). OLAP for XML data. In *Proceedings of the 1ˢᵗ International Conference on Computer and Information Technology (CIT'05)*, Shanghai, China (pp. 233-237). Washington, DC: IEEE Computer Society.

Xyleme, L. (2001). Xyleme: A dynamic warehouse for XML data of the Web. In *Proceedings of the International Database Engineering & Applications Symposium (IDEAS'01)*, Grenoble, France (pp. 3-7). Washington, DC: IEEE Computer Society.

Zhang, J., Wang, W., Liu, H., & Zhang, S. (2005). X-warehouse: Building query pattern-driven data. In *Proceedings of the 14ᵗʰ international conference on World Wide Web (WWW'05)*, Chiba, Japan (pp. 896-897). New York: ACM Press.

KEY TERMS AND DEFINITIONS

Complex Data: Data that present several axes of complexity for analysis, e.g., data represented in various formats, diversely structured, from several sources, described through several points of view, and/or versioned.

Database Management System (DBMS): Software set that handles structuring, storage, maintenance, update and querying of data stored in a database.

Web Warehouse: "A shared information repository. A web warehouse acts as an information server that supports information gathering and provides value added services, such as transcoding, personalization." (Cheng et al., 2000)

XML-Enabled DBMS: Database system in which XML data may be stored and queried from relational tables. Such a DBMS must either map XML data into relations and translate queries into SQL, or implement a middleware layer allowing native XML storing and querying.

XML-Native DBMS (NXD): Database system in which XML data are natively stored and queried as XML documents. An NXD provides XML schema storage and implements an XML query engine (typically supporting XPath and XQuery). eXist (Meier, 2002) and X-Hive (X-Hive Corporation, 2007) are examples of NXDs.

XML Data Warehouse: XML database that is specifically modeled (i.e., multidimensionally, with a star-like schema) to support XML decision-support and analytic queries.

XML Document Warehouse: An XML document repository dedicated to e-business and Web data analysis.

ENDNOTES

[1]	http://eric.univ-lyon2.fr/~hmahboubi/X-WACoDa/Schemas/dw-model.xsd
[2]	http://eric.univ-lyon2.fr/~hmahboubi/X-WACoDa/Schemas/facts.xsd
[3]	http://eric.univ-lyon2.fr/~hmahboubi/X-WACoDa/Schemas/dimension.xsd
[4]	http://marathon.csee.usf.edu/Mammography/Database.html
[5]	http://www.x-hive.com/products/db/

Chapter 4
Designing Data Marts from XML and Relational Data Sources

Yasser Hachaichi
Mir@cl Laboratory, Faculté des Sciences Economiques et de Gestion, Tunisia

Jamel Feki
Mir@cl Laboratory, Faculté des Sciences Economiques et de Gestion, Tunisia

Hanene Ben-Abdallah
Mir@cl Laboratory, Faculté des Sciences Economiques et de Gestion, Tunisia

ABSTRACT

Due to the international economic competition, enterprises are ever looking for efficient methods to build data marts/warehouses to analyze the large data volume in their decision making process. On the other hand, even though the relational data model is the most commonly used model, any data mart/warehouse construction method must now deal with other data types and in particular XML documents which represent the dominant type of data exchanged between partners and retrieved from the Web. This chapter presents a data mart design method that starts from both a relational database source and XML documents compliant to a given DTD. Besides considering these two types of data structures, the originality of our method lies in its being decision maker centered, its automatic extraction of loadable data mart schemas and its genericity.

INTRODUCTION

Faced with the ever increasing economic competition, today's enterprises are hard-pressed to rely on decision support systems (DSS) to assist them in the analysis of very large data volumes. As a response to this constraint, data warehousing technologies have been proposed as a means to extract pertinent data from information systems and present it as historical snapshots used for *ad hoc* analytical queries and scheduled reporting. Indeed, a data warehouse (DW) is organized in such a way that relevant data is clustered together for an easy access. In addition, a DW can be used as a source for building data marts (DM) that are oriented to specific subjects of analyses.

Traditionally, the data loaded into a DW/DM is mainly issued from the enterprise's own operational information system. Thus, most currently proposed DW/DM construction approaches sup-

DOI: 10.4018/978-1-60566-756-0.ch004

pose a single, often relational data source; *cf.,* (List, Bruckner, Machacze, & Schiefer, 2002), (Golfarelli, Maio, & Rizz, 1998), (Cabibbo, L., & Torlone, R. 1998), (Moody , & Kortnik, 2000), (Prat, Akoka , & Comyn-Wattiau, 2006), (Zribi, & feki, 2007), (Golfarelli, Rizzi, & Vrdoljak, 2001), (Vrdoljak, Banek, & Rizzi, 2003), (Jensen, Møller, & Pedersen, 2001). However, due to the international competition, enterprises are increasingly forced to enrich their own data repository with data coming from external sources. Besides data received from partners, the web constitutes the main external data source for all enterprises. For instance, an enterprise may need to retrieve from the web data about the exchange rates in order to analyze the variation of the quantities of its sold products with respect to the exchange rates during a period of time.

To deal with such an open data source, a DW/ DM construction approach must, hence, overcome the main difficulty behind the use of multiple data sources: the structural and semantic heterogeneities of the sources. In fact, even though the relational data model is the most commonly used model (Wikipedia encyclopedia, 2008), a DW construction approach must now deal with other data types and in particular XML documents which represent the dominant data type on the web. On the other hand, the semantic data heterogeneity comes into play when the internal and external data sources are complementary, *e.g.,* the case of transactional data between partners. This type of heterogeneity remains a challenging problem that can be treated either at the data source level or the DW/DM level (Boufares, & Hamdoun, 2005).

This chapter deals with the structural data heterogeneity when designing a data mart. More precisely, it presents a DM design method that starts from both a relational database source and XML documents compliant to a given DTD. Besides considering these two types of data structures, our method has three additional advantages. First, it provides for a DSS development centered on decision makers: it assists them in defining their analytical needs by proposing all analytical subjects that could be automatically extracted from their data sources; the *automatic* extraction of DM schemas distinguishes our method from currently proposed ones. Secondly, it guarantees that the extracted subjects are loadable from the enterprise information system and/or the external data sources. The third advantage of our design method is its genericity: It is domain independent since it relies on the structural properties of the data sources independently of their semantics. It automatically applies a set of rules to extract, from the relational database and XML documents, all possible facts with their dimensions and hierarchies.

To achieve these advantages, our method operates in four steps. First, it structurally homogenizes the two types of data sources by converting the DTD into a relational model. Secondly, it classifies the set of relations issued from both the converted DTD and the repository of the source relational DBMS. This classification is then used to identify automatically the facts, measures, dimensions and their attributes organized into hierarchies; these identified multidimensional elements are modeled as star DM schemas. Finally, the resulting DM schemas can be manually adapted by the decision makers/designers to specify their particular analytical needs. The automatic steps of our design method allowed us to incorporate it into a CASE toolset that interactively provides for DM schema adaptation.

The remainder of this chapter is organized as follows. First we overview current DW design approaches for relational and XML data sources. Then, we illustrate our four-step DM design method through a relational data source and a set of XML documents extracted from the web. Finally, we summarize the presented work and outline our ongoing research efforts.

CURRENT DATA WAREHOUSE DESIGN APPROACHES

Data-driven (or bottom-up) development approaches rely on the analysis of the corporate data model and relevant transactions (List, Bruckner, Machacze, & Schiefer, 2002), *cf.,* (Golfarelli, Maio, & Rizz, 1998), (Cabibbo, L., & Torlone, R. 1998), (Moody , & Kortnik, 2000), (Prat, Akoka , & Comyn-Wattiau, 2006), (Zribi, & feki, 2007), (Golfarelli, Rizzi, & Vrdoljak, 2001), (Vrdoljak, Banek, & Rizzi, 2003), (Jensen, Møller, & Pedersen, 2001). Data-driven approaches were justified by Bill Inmon (Inmon, 1996) by the fact that unlike transactional systems whose development lifecycle is requirements-driven, decision support systems (DSS) have data-driven development lifecycle. In addition, Inmon argues that requirements are the last thing to be considered in a DSS development; they are understood after the data warehouse is populated with data and query results are analyzed by the decision makers. Hence, data-driven approaches enjoy a double advantage: they reduce the task of decision makers by proposing potential analytical needs and they guarantee that the enterprise's information system can feed the selected needs with pertinent data.

Considering the advantages of data-driven approaches, we elected to propose a data mart design method within this category. Hence, we next limit ourselves to over viewing works pertinent to data-driven approaches where the majority starts from conceptual schemas modelled through E/R, XML models, or UML *cf.* (Prat, Akoka, & Comyn-Wattiau, 2006) and (Zribi, & feki, 2007). We focus on those works that start from E/R and XML models since they are more pertinent to our method.

E/R Diagram-Based Design Approaches

(Golfarelli, Maio, & Rizz, 1998) propose a semi-automated method to carry out a DM conceptual modeling from an E/R diagram. Their method produces a fact schema by: 1) defining facts from relationships or from frequently updated entities; 2) building an attribute tree for each fact, useful to construct a fact schema; 3) pruning and grafting the attribute tree in order to eliminate unnecessary levels of detail; 4) defining dimensions; 5) defining measures; and 6) defining hierarchies. The third, fourth and fifth steps are supported by the preliminary workload declared by decisional users.

Also starting from a given E/R diagram, (Cabibbo, & Torlone, 1998) propose a method to build a multidimensional database in four steps: 1) identifying facts, dimensions and measures through a thorough, manual analysis of the given E/R diagram; 2) restructuring the E/R diagram to describe facts and dimensions in a more explicit way. The produced version of the E/R diagram can be directly mapped onto the source data model; 3) deriving a dimensional graph that succinctly represents facts and dimensions from the restructured E/R diagram; and finally, 4) translating the dimensional graph into the multidimensional model. In this method, the first step which is the most crucial is manually done. In this method, the designer must have domain expertise to correctly identify all potentially needed multidimensional elements.

(Moody, & Kortnik, 2000) propose a three-step method to design a DM/DW also from an E/R data model: 1) entity classification which classifies entities into three categories: transaction entity (describes an event that happens at a point in time), component entity (directly related to a transaction entity via a one-to-many relationship) and classification entity (related to component entities by a chain of one-to-many relationships) 2) hierarchy identification using to-many relationship and 3) data mart schema development for each transaction entity. Each schema is a star schema represented through a fact table and a number of dimension and sub-dimension tables. Separates star schemas can be combined to form constellations or galaxies.

XML-Based Design Approaches

(Golfarelli, Rizzi, & Vrdoljak, 2001) propose a method for the design of an XML DW from XML sources. Their method relies on two assumptions: the existence of a DTD for the XML documents, and the conformity of these documents to their corresponding DTD. This method designs a DW in three steps: 1) DTD simplification mainly to flatten nested elements; 2) DTD graph creation in order to represent graphically the source structure and simplify the manual fact selection; and 3) construction of an attribute tree for each fact in the graph; within the attribute tree dimensions and measures are found among the nodes immediately linked to the chosen fact. In this method, the selection of facts and measures is manual and requires the intervention of an expert in the domain of the XML documents that will load the future data warehouse.

In an attempt to improve their method, (Vrdoljak, Banek, & Rizzi, 2003) developed a semi-automated process to design XML data warehouses from XML schemas. Once again, in this process, facts and measures are chosen manually. For each selected fact, they 1) build the dependency graph from the XML schema graph; 2) rearrange the dependency graph to define dimensions and measures; and then 3) create a logical schema. One main drawback of this method is that it requires an intensive intervention of the designer. In addition to manually identifying the fact, dimensions and measures, the designer must also identify the many-to-many relationships among elements; these relationships are needed to construct the dependency graph.

On the other hand, the authors of (Rusu, Rahayu, & Taniar, 2004) and (Rusu, Rahayu, & Taniar, 2005) also propose a generic method for building an XML DW for XML documents. Their method first applies a set of cleaning and integration operations in order to minimize the number of occurrences of dirty data, XML structural errors, duplications or inconsistencies. Secondly, it summarizes data in XML documents to extract only useful and valuable information in order to create other XML document(s) used for the construction of the dimensions. Thirdly, the method creates intermediate XML documents from the initial documents; this step focuses on determining the main activity data (data involved in queries, calculations etc.). Thus, each intermediate document linked to other documents represents a fact document. Finally, the method updates/links all intermediate XML documents (fact and dimension documents), in such a way that relationships between keys are established, and an XML DW is created. In this method, several sub-steps have to be accomplished manually by an expert in the XML document domain.

Furthermore, (Jensen, Møller, & Pedersen, 2001) studied how an OLAP cube can be obtained from XML data. To build a cube, the DTD of the XML documents is transformed into a UML class diagram using a set of transformation rules. Once the class diagram is obtained, the designer uses it to specify an OLAP DB model (named a UML snowflake diagram) through a graphical user interface. Finally, the UML snowflake diagram is transformed into relational structures to prepare the implementation of the OLAP cube. This approach is also used by (Ouaret, Z., Bellatreche, L., and Boussaid, O., 2007) who starts from XML schemas instead of the DTD.

In summary, we notice that:

1. although data-driven approaches for multi-dimensional design proceed automatically from either E/R or UML, they are based on conceptual models that companies either do not always have, or detain obsolete versions;

2. the few proposed approaches for the design of XML-based DM/DW suppose that the designer is able to *manually* identify the interesting facts to be analyzed. However, this identification requires a high expertise both in OLAP domain and, the XML document domain;

Figure 1. Designing data mart schemas from XML and relational data sources

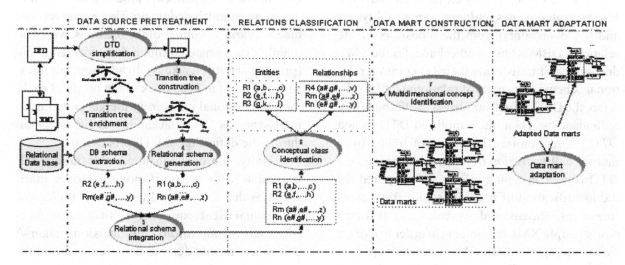

3. all methods consider that the candidate DM built are of the same pertinence whereas some of these DM may not be useful for the decisional process; and

4. the proposed approaches try to represent the main DM properties at a conceptual level by abstracting away details of an envisaged DW implementation platform. *"Unfortunately, none of these approaches defines a set of formal transformations in order to: (i) univocally and automatically derive every possible logical representation from the conceptual model; or (ii) help the designer to obtain the most suitable logical representation of the developed conceptual model"* (Mazón, & Trujillo, 2008).

To overcome these problems, we propose a bi-source method that builds DM schemas from data sources either modeled as relational databases or structured as XML documents compliant to a given DTD. This method enjoys four main advantages: 1) It overcomes the problem of absence/obsoleteness of conventional documentation (*i.e.*, E/A diagram, UML class diagram). In fact, it exploits the recent version of the data source extracted from the DBMS repository or described

by XML documents in use; 2) it automates the main design steps; 3) it assists the designer in the choice of relevant multidimensional concepts among those extracted by assigning to each one a relevance level reflecting its analytical potential for the decision-making; and 4) it keeps track of the origin of each component in the generated DM schema. This traceability is fundamental both to automatically derive logical representations and to define ETL processes.

DATA MART DESIGN FOR RELATIONAL AND XML SOURCES

Our design method is a bottom-up method for DM that starts from a relational database source and XML documents compliant to a given DTD. Unlike existing approaches, ours is composed of four steps (Figure 1) among which only the last is manually conducted by the decision makers; in this step, they adapt the automatically constructed DM schemas for their particular needs.

As illustrated in Figure 1, our design method starts with a *data source pretreatment* step to resolve the structural heterogeneity of the two types of data sources. For the relational database, this step is trivial since it only extracts the database schema (table names, column names and types, and key constraints) from the repository of the relational DBMS. On the other hand, for the XML documents, it transforms their DTD into a relational schema (*i.e.,* a set of relational tables). To do so, the DTD is first simplified to eliminate any redundancies. Then, the simplified DTD (noted *DTD^s*) is reorganized into a set of linked trees that we call *transition trees*. In addition, since a DTD is poor in typing information required for the identification of multidimensional concepts (measures, dimensional attributes ...), this step scans sample XML documents in order to extract richer typing information; the extracted types are assigned to the attributes and packed data elements in the transition trees. Based on the existing links among the typed transition trees, these latter are transformed into a relational schema. This step is concluded by a schema integration phase that merges the two source schemas to produce one semantically coherent schema; it applies existing propositions for relational database schema integration, *cf.*, (Bright, Hurson, & Pakzad, 1994), (Sheth, & Larson, 1990), (Ceri, Widom, 1993), (Hull, 1997) and (Zhang, & Yang, 2008).

Once the data source pretreatment produces the integrated relational schema, the design continues with the *relation classification* step. This latter performs a reverse engineering task by examining the structure of the relations in the source schemas obtained from the first step. It automatically determines the conceptual class of each relation: A relation conceptually either models a relationship or an entity. This classification optimizes the automatic fact and dimension identification and improves its results.

The third step of our design method (*data mart schema construction*) extracts the multidimensional concepts (facts and their measures, dimensions and attributes organized into hierarchies) from the classified relations and produces star models. To automate this step, we define for each multidimensional concept a set of extraction rules.

Our rules are independent of the semantics of the data sources and their domain. They rather rely on the *structural semantics* of the relations, which is mainly disseminated through the key constraints (primary and foreign keys). In addition, our rules have the merit to keep track of the origin of each multidimensional concept in the generated data mart schemas. This traceability is fundamental during the definition of ETL processes.

Finally, the decision makers/designers are presented with a set of potential data mart schemas that they can adjust to meet their particular analytical requirements. In this final step (*data mart adaptation*), the decision makers/designers can add derived data, remove, and/or rename DM schema elements. The application of these adaptation operations is constrained to ensure that the resulting schemas are well-formed (Schneider, 2003) (Salem, Ghozzi, & Ben-Abdallah, 2008), *e.g.,* a fact must have at least two dimensions.

Before explaining in detail the above four steps, in the remainder of this section, we overview the concepts of XML structures and the relational model.

Basic XML Structural Concepts

An XML document has two types of information: the *document structure* and *data content*; XML provides a means for separating one from the other in the electronic document. The document structure is given by opening and closing, matching tag pairs (each called an *element*) and the data content is given by the information between matching tags. In addition, an element can have *attributes* whose values are assigned in the opening tag of the element.

To define the structure of a set of XML documents, a DTD document can be used. A DTD is a context free grammar specifying all allowable elements, their attributes, and the element nesting structure. Given one DTD, it can be verified whether an XML document is *conforming* to/

respects the DTD, and if so, the XML document is said to be *valid*.

Note that there exist other formalisms for describing XML document structures, *e.g.*, XML Schema and DCD (Document Content Description). However, the DTD is a formalism recommended by the World Wide Web Consortium (W3C) (W3C, 2008). For this, we assume in our method that the structure of an XML document is described by a DTD and that the XML source documents are valid.

A DTD is composed of element types, sub-element types, attributes, and terminal strings such as ENTITY, PCDATA and CDATA. The DTD types are however very limited since all of the types are considered as strings. In addition, a DTD can constrain the occurrences of an element and a sub-element type through the symbols: "*" (a set with zero or more elements), "+" (a set with one or more elements), "?" (an optional element), and "|" (alternative elements). For more details about DTD, the reader is referred to (Sahuguet, 2000) and (W3C, 2008).

Figure 2 depicts an example of a DTD describing e-Ticket documents. An e-Ticket document describes the booking in a hotel that a consumer can do and/or the list of concerts that a consumer can attend. Such documents can be used by an online broker that deals with a particular hotel and offers entertainment services (in this case, concert ticket purchase).

Basic Relational Model Concepts

In the relational model (Codd, 1970), a database is modeled by a set of relations (also called tables) that forms a relational schema. A *relation*, denoted $R((A_1, A_2, ..., A_n))$, has a name (R) and a list of attributes $(A_1, A_2, ..., A_n)$ each of which is associated with one domain representing the set of its possible values. Each attribute Ai is the name of a role played by its domain D in the relation R. Thus, a relation R represents a set of tuples $t_1, t_2, ... t_m$. If for any two distinct tuples t_i and t_j in R

there exists an attribute K such that $t_i(K) \neq t_j(K)$_, then such an attribute (set of attributes) is called a candidate *key*. It is common to choose one of the candidate keys as the *primary key* used to uniquely identify tuples in the relation.

Furthermore, a set of attributes FK in a relation R_1 is a *foreign key* if the two following rules are satisfied: (1) the attributes in FK have the same domain as the primary key PK of another relation R_2, and (2) every value of FK in any tuple t_1 in R_1 either occurs as a value of PK for some tuple t_2 in R_2 or it is null.

Figure 3 shows an example of a relational database modeling a hotel room booking system. This example is adapted from the one presented in (Databasedev.co.uk, 2008). In our schema, the primary keys are underlined and the foreign keys are followed by the sharp sign (#) and the name of the referenced relation.

DATA SOURCE PRETREATMENT

This first step of our design method aims at structurally homogenizing the data sources by transforming the source DTD into a set of relations (*i.e.*, tables). It is conducted through an automatic process composed of four stages: *DTD simplification, transition tree construction, transition tree enrichment* and *relational schema generation*.

DTD Simplification

The simplification of a DTD removes empty elements, substitutes and transforms other elements. The empty element removal is applied to every element that is tagged EMPTY and that does not declare an ATTLIST. Such an element has no content in valid XML documents. Thus, it is not useful for the decision process. On the other hand, the element substitution first replaces each reference to an ENTITY type with the text corresponding to that entity, and secondly it removes the corresponding ENTITY declaration.

Figure 2. An example of DTD for e-Ticket documents

```
<?xml version="1.0" encoding="UTF-8"?>
<!ELEMENT e-Ticket (Bookings | Buy)+>
<!ATTLIST eTicket DocID ID #REQUIRED>
<!ELEMENT Bookings (Customer, DateBookingMade, TimebookingMade,
(BookedStartDate, BookedEndDate, Room )+, TotalPayementDueAmount)>
<!ELEMENT TotalPayementDueAmount (#PCDATA)>
<!ELEMENT DateBookingMade (#PCDATA)>
<!ELEMENT TimebookingMade (#PCDATA)>
<!ELEMENT BookedStartDate (#PCDATA)>
<!ELEMENT BookedEndDate (#PCDATA)>
<!ELEMENT Room  (RoomTypes, RoomFacilities) >
<!ELEMENT RoomTypes EMPTY>
<!ATTLIST Room RoomID ID #REQUIRED>
<!ATTLIST RoomTypes RoomtypeID ID #REQUIRED
            TypeDesc CDATA #IMPLIED >
<!ELEMENT RoomFacilities EMPTY>
<!ATTLIST RoomFacilities RoomFacilityID ID #REQUIRED
                          FacilityDesc CDATA #IMPLIED >
<!ELEMENT Customer (City)>
<!ATTLIST Customer CustomerID ID #REQUIRED
            CustomerForenames CDATA #IMPLIED
            CustomerSurnames CDATA #IMPLIED
            CustomerEmail CDATA #IMPLIED >
<!ELEMENT City (State)>
<!ATTLIST City CityID ID #REQUIRED
            CityName CDATA #IMPLIED>
<!ELEMENT State (County)>
<!ATTLIST State StateID ID #REQUIRED
            StateName CDATA #IMPLIED>
<!ELEMENT County (Empty)>
<!ATTLIST County CountyID ID #REQUIRED
            CountyName CDATA #IMPLIED>
<!ELEMENT Buy (BuyDate, Customer, (ConcertDate,
Concert+)*,TotalPayementB)>
<!ELEMENT BuyDate (#PCDATA)>
<!ELEMENT ConcertDate (#PCDATA)>
<!ELEMENT TotalPayementB (#PCDATA)>
<!ELEMENT Concert (Singer, City)>
<!ATTLIST Concert  ConcertID ID #REQUIRED
            ConcertName CDATA #IMPLIED>
<!ELEMENT  Singer EMPTY>
<!ATTLIST Singer SingerID ID #REQUIRED
            SingerForenames CDATA #IMPLIED
            SingerSurnames CDATA #IMPLIED>
```

Recall that an ENTITY is a variable used to define shortcuts for either commonly used text, or text that is difficult to type.

Finally, the third simplification step applies a set of transformations to the DTD to reduce the components of its ELEMENT declarations.

Our transformations slightly differ from those presented in (Shanmugasundarma, Tufte, Zhang, DeWitt, & Naughton, 1999) and (Yan, & ADA, 2001) and resemble the transformations in (Jensen, Møller, & Pedersen, 2001). They are of the three types depicted in Figure 4:

Figure 3. Relational database schema for hotel room booking system

```
Room (RoomID, RoomTypeID#: RoomTypes, RoomBandID#: RoomBand,
RoomFacilityID #: RoomFacilities, Price, Floor, AdditionalNotes)
RoomTypes (RoomTypeID, TypeDesc)
RoomBands (RoomBandID, BrandDesc)
RoomFacilities (RoomFaciliyID, FacilityDesc)
Payments (PaymentID, CustomerID#: Customer, PaymentMethodID#:
PaymentMethods, PaymentAmount, PaymentComments)
PaymentMethods (PaymentMethodID, PaymentMethod)
Bookings (CustomerID#: Customer, DateBookingMade, TimebookingMade,
RoomID#: Room, BookedStartDate, BookedEndDate, TotalPayementDueDate,
TotalPayementDueAmount, BookingComments)
Customer (CustomerID, CustomerForenames, CustomerSurnames, CustomerDOB,
CustomerHomePhone, CustomerWorkPhone, CustomerMobilePhone, CustomerEmail,
CityID #: City).
County (CountyID, CountyName)
State (StateID, StateName, CountyID#: County)
City (CityID, CityName, StateID#: State)
```

1. *Flattening* which converts a nested definition into a flat representation where the binary operators "," and "|" do not appear inside any parentheses;
2. *Reduction* which reduces several consecutive unary operators to a single one; and
3. *Grouping* which replaces multiple occurrences of one sub-element with a single occurrence having the most generic operator.

All of these transformations are iteratively applied to the DTD until no more transformations could be applied. Note that when applying the third transformation, we may lose the initial order of elements; however, this will not affect the final result (*i.e.*, the candidate multidimensional schemas).

To illustrate these transformations, let us consider the two following XML element declarations extracted from the example of Figure 2:<!ELEMENT Buy (BuyDate, Customer, (ConcertDate, Concert+)*,TotalPayementB)> <!ELEMENT Bookings (Customer, DateBookingMade,TimebookingMade,(BookedStartDate, BookedEndDate, Room)+, TotalPayement-DueAmount)>

These elements will be simplified into:<!ELEMENT Buy (BuyDate, Customer, ConcertDate*, Concert*,TotalPayementB) ><!ELEMENT Bookings (Customer, Date-BookingMade, TimebookingMade, Booked-StartDate+, BookedEndDate+, Room+, TotalPayementDueAmount)>where the inner parentheses are dropped and each element has at most one operator.

Transition Tree Construction

As shown in Figure 1, the DTD simplification step is followed by the construction of transition trees for the simplified DTD. In this step, a simplified DTD is split into substructures reorganized as trees that we call *transitiontrees*. These latter facilitate the relational schema generation from the initial DTD.

Each transition tree has a root node, intermediate nodes, terminal nodes (leaves) all of which are connected by directed arcs. The root node and intermediate nodes refer to one element in the simplified DTD (noted DTD^S). On the other hand, a leaf denotes either a PCDATA element, an attribute, or an element identified as the root

Figure 4. Transformations to simplify a DTD

(a) Flattening	(b) Reducing	(c) Grouping
$(e1, e2)* \rightarrow e1*, e2*$	$e1** \rightarrow e1*$	$...,e1*,...,e1*, ... \rightarrow e1*,...$
$(e1, e2)? \rightarrow e1?, e2?$	$e1?? \rightarrow e1?$	$...,e1*,...,e1?, ... \rightarrow e1*,...$
$(e1|e2) \rightarrow e1?, e2?$	$e1++ \rightarrow e1+$	$...,e1?, ...,e1*, ... \rightarrow e1*,...$
$(e1, e2)+ \rightarrow e1+, e2+$	$e1*? \rightarrow e1*$	$...,e1?,...,e1?, ... \rightarrow e1*,...$
	$e1?* \rightarrow e1*$	$..., e1, ..., e1, ... \rightarrow e1+,...$
	$e1*+ \rightarrow e1*$	$...,e1+,...,e1+, ... \rightarrow e1+,...$
	$e1+* \rightarrow e1*$	$...,e1+,...,e1?, ... \rightarrow e1+,...$
	$e1?+ \rightarrow e1+$	$...,e1?,...,e1+, ... \rightarrow e1+,...$
	$e1+? \rightarrow e1+$	$...,e1+, ...,e1*, ... \rightarrow e1+,...$

node of a transition tree (the same tree if the DTD contains a recursion). In addition, the arcs of the transition tree can be labeled with the attribute type (ID, IDREF).

Root Determination

We determine the root node of a transition tree by one of the following four rules that we have developed in (Hachaichi, Feki, & Ben-Abdallah, 2008-a):

R1. Each DTD element that does not appear in the declaration of any other element is a root of a transition tree.

In general, each XML document can be seen as one root element that contains all the elements in the document. Thus, rule *R1* will extract this topmost element as a root of one transition tree. The application of *R1* must however exclude recursive DTD where all elements are sub-elements of other elements (Yan, & ADA, 2001). We treat the case of a recursive DTD in the rule *R4*.

R2. Each element that contains at least one non PCDATA element is a root for a transition tree.

Rule *R2* excludes transition trees composed of the root connected to only leaf nodes (PCDATA). Such a tree, in the XML document, can be considered as a *basic* data entity, in the sense that it cannot represent a relationship. In addition, by imposing that a transition tree contains at least one complex element, *R2* ensures that the transition tree represents a relationship.

R3. Each element contained in the declaration of *n* elements $(n \geq 2)$ is the root of a transition tree.

This rule avoids the redundancy of elements in a transition tree and identifies the elements shared by several trees as one transition tree.

R4. Each element directly or transitively containing its own declaration is the root of a transition tree.

This rule treats the case of recursive DTD. Informally, if an element refers to itself in its declaration (directly or indirectly), then this element contains a non PCDATA element, and thus, in accordance with rule *R2*, this element should be the root of a transition tree.

For our running example (Figure 2), the above four rules identifies eight roots: *e-Ticket, Bookings, Consumer, Room, Buy, Concert, City* and *State*.

Transition Tree Construction

For each identified root, this step constructs a corresponding transition tree. This requires a fine scan of the simplified DTD^S by applying the algorithm *Create_tree (E, DTD^S)* starting from a root *E* (Hachaichi, Feki, & Ben-Abdallah, 2008-b):

```
Algorithm Create_tree (E, DTDˢ)
    // E is the current node in DTDˢ
{
1.foreach element e in the declara-
tion of Edo {
1.1         AddChildNode(E, e)
//add a child e to the node E
1.2             if ( e is deter-
mined as a root) then   //e identi-
fied by rules 1 to 4
1.2.1       AnnotateNode(e, #)
1.3         elseif (e contains
other elements or attributes) then
1.3.1                 CreateTree(e,
DTDˢ)
    }
2. for each attribute a in the dec-
laration of Edo {
2.1         AddChildNode(E, a)
2.2         MarkArcType(E, a)
//mark arc from E to a by ID or
IDREF
    }
}
{
```

In the transition tree construction algorithm, the function AnnotateNode(*e*, #) marks any sub-element that is the root of a transition tree with the symbol #. This annotation is borrowed from the concept of foreign keys in relational databases; it is useful to link transition trees of the same DTD^S and to construct parameter hierarchies. Note that with this annotation, the constructed transition trees will have at most a depth of four. Such a limited depth accelerates the traversal during the DM schema construction step. On the other hand, the function MarkArcType(*E, a*) annotates the arc from *E* to *a* with the type (ID or IDREF) if the attribute is a unique identifier or an attribute that points to an *ID* attribute. Figure 5 shows the transition trees constructed by this algorithm for the e-Ticket DTD example.

Transition Tree Enrichment

To build a relational database schema from transition trees, we need the attribute types (*e.g.*, number, date...). However, such typing information is totally absent in the DTD and XML documents. In fact, a DTD schema declares all data as strings.

To assign a data type to the attributes and PCDATA elements in a transition tree, we query a sample set of XML documents valid with respect to the source DTD. For each leaf not marked with # (*i.e.*, each attribute and PCDATA element), we consult the data contained in its corresponding XML tag. Then, we determine a type by scanning its text value and cast it into one of three appropriate types: date, number or string. To assist us with this analysis of the XML documents, there are several semi-structured query languages for XML documents, including XML-QL, Lorel, UnQL, XQL (from Microsoft), and XQuery (from W3C). All these languages have the notion of path expressions to navigate the nested structures of XML documents. The application of the enrichment step on the transition trees of our running example (Figure 5) adds the data types to the leaf nodes not annotated with the symbol # as shown in Figure 6.

Figure 5. Transition trees for the e-Ticket DTD

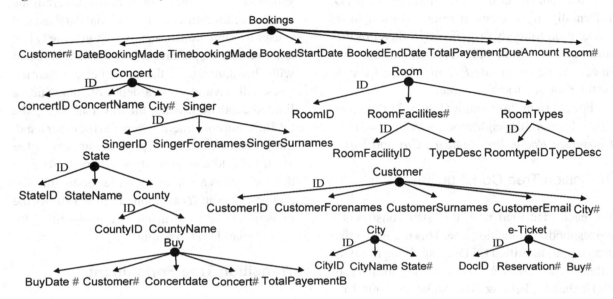

Relational Schema Generation for the XML Source

In this stage, the typed transition trees are transformed into relational schemas based on the links among the transition trees. This transformation is conducted through the algorithm *XML2R* which uses the following notation:

- Ref$_n$: the set of nodes that can be foreign keys in the relation R$_n$ (constructed on node *n*)
- Build_R (n): a function that builds on node *n* a relation called R$_n$
- ID (R$_n$): a function that returns the primary key of a relation R$_n$
- Add_attribute (a, R$_n$): Adds attribute *a* as a column to the relation R$_n$
- Mark_PK (pk, R$_n$): Marks the *pk* list of attributes as the primary key of the relation R$_n$
- Mark_FK (a, R$_n$): Marks the *a* attribute as a foreign key in the relation R$_n$
- ADD_ID (R$_n$): adds an artificial primary key to the relation R$_n$. The primary key

name is *nID*: the concatenation of node name *n* to the string '*ID*'.

Algorithm XML2R( )

```
1.  Nᴿ = the set of transition
trees reduced to roots, i.e., with-
out any descendant.
2.  Nᵀ= the set of nodes all of
whose children are leaves not an-
notated with #.3. For each node n □
Nᴿdo {
3.1         Rₙ = Build_R (n);
3.2         Add_attribute(n, Rₙ);
3.3         Mark_PK({n}, Rₙ);
     }
4. For each node n ∈ Nᵀdo {   // n
has only leave children not anno-
tated with #
4.1         Rₙ = Build_R (n);
4.2         ID_found = False;
4.3         For each child a of n
do {
4.3.1         Add_attribute(a, Rₙ);
4.3.2         If (arc(n, a) = ID)
then {
4.3.2.1                 Mark_
```

Figure 6. Transition trees of Figure 5 enriched with data types

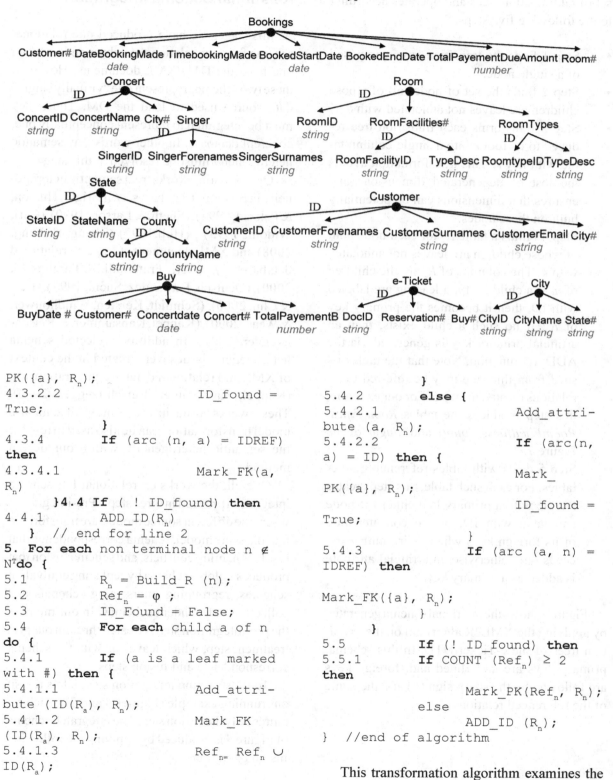

PK({a}, R_n);
4.3.2.2   ID_found =
True;
                    }
4.3.4   **If** (arc (n, a) = IDREF)
then
4.3.4.1   Mark_FK(a,
R_n)
        }4.4 **If** (! ID_found) **then**
4.4.1   ADD_ID(R_n)
    } // end for line 2
5. For each non terminal node n ∉
N^T**do** {
5.1   R_n = Build_R (n);
5.2   Ref_n = φ ;
5.3   ID_Found = False;
5.4   **For each** child a of n
do {
5.4.1   **If** (a is a leaf marked
with #) **then** {
5.4.1.1   Add_attri-
bute (ID(R_a), R_n);
5.4.1.2   Mark_FK
(ID(R_a), R_n);
5.4.1.3   Ref_n= Ref_n ∪
ID(R_a);

        }
5.4.2   **else** {
5.4.2.1   Add_attri-
bute (a, R_n);
5.4.2.2   **If** (arc(n,
a) = ID) **then** {
                    Mark_
PK({a}, R_n);
                    ID_found =
True;
                    }
5.4.3   **If** (arc (a, n) =
IDREF) **then**

Mark_FK({a}, R_n);
        }
    }
5.5   **If** (! ID_found) **then**
5.5.1   **If** COUNT (Ref_n) ≥ 2
then
            Mark_PK(Ref_n, R_n);
        else
            ADD_ID (R_n);
} //end of algorithm

This transformation algorithm examines the

set of all transition trees and operates according to the following five steps:

- Step 1 finds the transition trees composed of a single node.
- Step 2 finds the set of nodes all of whose children are leaves not annotated with #.
- Step 3 transforms each transition tree reduced to its root r into a single-column table with key r. This transformation avoids the lost of degenerated dimensions and ensures that dimensions can be potentially built on these nodes.
- Step 4 builds a table R_n for each node n all of whose children are leaves not annotated with #. The columns of R_n are the children of n. If a child a of n a leading arc labeled with ID, then it becomes the primary key of R_n; if no such a child exists, then an artificial primary key is generated via the ADD_ID function. Note that the tables issued from this step may be referred to by relations created in step 5. For our example, this step produces the tables *RoomTypes*, *RoomFacilities*, *County* and *Singer* of the Figure 7.
- Step 5 deals with tables referencing other tables. For each such table, this step creates a table with a primary key either the node annotated with ID, or the concatenation of its foreign keys when their number exceeds one, otherwise an artificial attribute is added as a primary key.

Figure 7 shows the relational schema generated by applying the XML2R algorithm on the transition trees of the e-Ticket DTD. In this schema, primary keys are underlined and, foreign keys are followed by the sharp sign (#) and the name of the referenced relation.

Relational Schema Integration

At this stage, we have produced one relational schema from the relational database and a second one from the DTD/XML documents. However, these two schemas represent one "virtually single" data source used to load the DM. Thus, they must be integrated to represent conceptually one, coherent database. In other words, any semantic heterogeneity must be resolved at this stage.

Quite existing works treat semantic heterogeneity in relational databases, *cf.*, (Bright, Hurson, & Pakzad, 1994), (Sheth, & Larson, 1990), (Ceri, Widom, 1993) , (Hull,1997) (Zhang, & Yang, 2008) and XML document storage as relational databases, *cf.*, (Ceri, Fraternali, & Paraboschi, 2000), (Deutsch, Fernandez, Suciu, 1999), (Lee, & Chu, 2000), (Schmidt, Kersten, Windhouwer, & Waas, 2000), (Kappel, Kapsammer, & Retschitzegger, 2001). In addition, selected schema heterogeneity issues were treated in the context of XML and relational database integration, *cf.*, (Kappel, Kapsammer, Retschitzegger, 2000). These works, used in the context of database model transformation, can be also used to resolve the semantic heterogeneity within our design method.

Overall, the works on relational DB schema integration proceed in three steps: Pre-integration where the different source models are transformed into the same model, schema correspondence that resolves naming conflicts; and schema fusion that produces a global schema by replacing equivalent schemas, regrouping intersecting schemas and collecting independent schemas. In our method, the pre-integration step is treated through our pre-treatment step, which leaves us with the schema correspondence and fusion steps.

To illustrate the integration step, let us revisit our running example (Figures 3 and 7) which requires only the fusion step. The integrated schema of Figure 8 is produced by applying the following fusion operations:

Figure 7. Relational schema derived from e-Ticket DTD

```
RoomTypes (RoomTypeID, TypeDesc)
RoomFacilities (RoomFaciliyID, FacilityDesc)
County (CountyID, CountyName)
Singer (SingerID, SingerForenames, SingerSurnames)
City (CityID, CityName, StateID#: State)
State (StateID, StateName, CountyID#: County)
Customer (CustomerID, CustomerForenames, CustomerSurnames, CustomerEmail,
CityID #: City).
Room (RoomID, RoomTypeID#: RoomTypes, RoomFacilitiesID #: RoomFacilities)
Bookings (CustomerID#: Customer, RoomID#: Room, DateBookingMade,
TimebookingMade, BookedStartDate, BookedEndDate, TotalPayementDueAmount)
Concert (ConcertID, ConcertName, CityID#: City, SingerID: Singer)
Buy (CustomerID#: Customer, ConcertID# : Concert, BuyDate, ConcertDate,
TotalPayementB)
```

- Import the relations *Payments*, *PaymentMethods* and *RoomBands* from *hotel room booking* relational schema.
- Import the relations *SingerBuy* and *Concert* from the *e-Ticket* relational schema.
- Import the relations *Room*, *RoomTypes*, *RoomBands*, *RoomFacilities*, *Bookings*, *Customer*, *County*, *State* and *City* from *e-Ticket* and *hotel room booking* schemas and integrate them using the union operator.

RELATION CLASSIFICATION

In current data-driven DW/DM development methods, entities and relationships are the keystone of the conceptual design. More precisely, dimensions are often built from entities and date dimensions from temporal attributes; whereas facts are mainly built from *n*-ary relationships linking entities and, rarely on entities. However, this distinction is not explicitly present in the relational model where one single concept is used to model both entities and relationships, namely the relational table (or table for short).

Hence, in order to define a design process that correctly identifies facts and dimensions from a relational schema (*i.e.,* a set of relational tables) we must first determine the conceptual class of each table. To do so, we perform a reverse engineering task by precisely examining the structure of the tables in the sources. In fact, this leads to a scan of the set of attributes composing the primary and foreign keys of the source tables.

We have presented in our previous work (Feki, & Hachaichi, 2007-a) how to partition a set of tables, issued from an operational information system, into two subsets: A subset of tables modeling relationships and another subset modeling entities. Briefly, a table representing a relationship is characterized by its primary key being composed of one or several foreign keys, whereas a table representing an entity generally has its primary key not containing foreign keys. This classification should well form the two subsets of tables by satisfying three basic properties: *Disjointness, Completeness* and *Correctness*. The first property imposes that the two subsets share *no common table*; this ensures that each table is uniquely classified. The completeness property ensures that every table has a class. The correctness property recommends that each table is correctly identified, *i.e.,* as a relationship if it originally models a relationship and as an entity if it models an entity. Correctness is less trivial than the two first properties and it is not satisfied in the two following situations: 1) when the primary key of

Figure 8. Integrated relational schema issued from e-Ticket and hotel room booking

```
Room (RoomID, RoomTypeID#: RoomTypes, RoomBandID#: RoomBand,
RoomFacilityID #: RoomFacilities, Price, Floor, AdditionalNotes)
RoomTypes (RoomTypeID, TypeDesc)
RoomBands (RoomBandID, BrandDesc)
RoomFacilities (RoomFaciliyID, FacilityDesc)
Payments (PaymentID, CustomerID#: Customer, PaymentMethodID#:
PaymentMethods, PaymentAmount, PaymentComments)
PaymentMethods (PaymentMethodID, PaymentMethod)
Bookings (CustomerID#: Customer, DateBookingMade, TimebookingMade,
RoomID#: Room, BookedStartDate, BookedEndDate, TotalPayementDueDate,
TotalPayementDueAmount, BookingComments)
Customer (CustomerID, CustomerForenames, CustomerSurnames, CustomerDOB,
CustomerHomePhone, CustomerWorkPhone, CustomerMobilePhone, CustomerEmail,
CityID #: City).
County (CountyID, CountyName)
State (StateID, StateName, CountyID#: County)
City (CityID, CityName, StateID#: State)
Singer (SingerID, SingerForenames, SingerSurnames)
Concert (ConcertID, ConcertName, CityID#: City, SingerID: Singer)
Buy (CustomerID#: Customer, ConcertID# : Concert, BuyDate, ConcertDate,
TotalPayementB)
```

a relationship is not the concatenation of all its foreign keys, that is, this primary key can be an artificial attribute such as a sequential number; or 2) when the primary key of a relationship is the concatenation of attributes coming from empty entities. Such attributes are never foreign keys since an empty entity (*i.e.*, entity reduced to its key) never transforms into a relation. For more details about empty entities, the reader is referred to (Feki, & Hachaichi, 2007-b) where an illustrative example is given. Table 1 shows the classification of the relations presented in Figure 8.

DM SCHEMA CONSTRUCTION

This third design step builds DM schemas modeled as stars through the application of a set of extraction rules defined for each multidimensional concept. Our rules have the merit to be independent of the semantics of the data source.

In addition, they keep track of the origin (table name, column name, data type and length…) of each multidimensional concept in the generated DM schemas. This traceability is fundamental as we intend to help automating the generation of ETL (Extract Transform and Load) procedures to load the designed DM.

Fact Identification

To identify facts, we exploit our previous table classification and build a set of facts of first-relevance level from tables representing relationships and then, a set of facts of second-relevance level issued from tables representing entities. This distinction in analysis relevance levels is very useful; it assists the DW designer during the selection from several generated facts those facts that have a higher analysis potentiality.

In fact, in all DW design approaches it has been unanimously accepted that a business ac-

Table 1. Source relations classified into entities and relationships

Relational Tables	Conceptual Class
Room	Entity
RoomTypes	Entity
RoomBands	Entity
RoomFacilities	Entity
Payments	Entity
PaymentMethods	Entity
Bookings	Relationship
Customer	Entity
County	Entity
State	Entity
City	Entity
Singer	Entity
Concert	Entity
Buy	Relationship

tivity (*e.g.*, Sales, Bill) is generally modeled as a relationship. This observation incites to limit the construction of facts mainly on relationships (Golfarelli, Maio, & Rizz, 1998), (Cabibbo, L., & Torlone, R. 1998), (Feki, Nabli, Ben-Abdallah, & Gargouri, 2008) and rarely on entities (Moody, & Kortnik, 2000), (Phipps, & Davis, 2002), (Feki, Nabli, Ben-Abdallah, & Gargouri, 2008). On the other hand, in practice, not all relationships are useful to build facts; so we limit the set of facts at the first-relevance level to those containing a non key numeric attribute. For the integrated schema of our running example *e-Ticket* and *hotel room booking*, we obtain the facts depicted in Table 2 where a fact built on a table T is conventionally named F-T.

To complete this fact identification step, we consider that each table representing an entity and containing a numeric, non key attribute is a fact at the second-relevance level (*cf.*, Table 2). Note that the numeric non key attribute condition excludes facts without measures, which are considered as infrequent facts.

Measure Identification

A fact contains a finite set of measures. In most cases, measures serve to compute summarized results (*e.g.*, total amount of sales by month and year, by mart…) using aggregate functions; hence, measures have numeric values. Therefore, we extract measures mainly from *fact-tables* (*i.e.*, table on which the fact is built). Furthermore, rarely few additional measures could be extracted not from a fact-table itself but from tables parallel to it. Below, we informally explain how we extract measures in each of these cases.

Measure Identified from a Fact-Table

To construct a significant set of candidate measures for a fact F-T built on a table T, we exclude key-attributes from the set of numeric attributes of T because keys are generally artificial and redundant data, and they do not trace/record the enterprise business activity. Moreover, we have shown in (Feki, & Hachaichi, 2007-b) that we must exclude from T its "non key attributes belonging to other tables" because these attributes

Table 2. Facts and measures for the integrated schema issued from hotel room booking and e-Ticket of Figure 8

Fact	Relevance level	Measure
F-Room	Second	Price
F-Payments	Second	PaymentAmount
F-Bookings	First	TotalPayementDueAmount TotalPayementDueDate
F-Buy	First	TotalPayementB

really represent keys issued from empty entities. Table 2 shows all measures extracted from each extracted fact-table.

Measure Identified from Parallel Tables

As mentioned above, a second origin of measures is *parallel* tables. We adapted the definition of parallel tables from the concept of parallel relationships which is specific to the E/R model (Seba, 2003). In an E/R diagram, a relationship *R1* connected to *m* entities is said to be parallel to a relationship *R2* connected to *n* entities ($m \leq n$) if the *m* entities linked to *R1* are also linked to *R2*. By analogy, we define the concept of parallel tables as follows:

Let *T1* and *T2* be two relationship tables such as *T1* and *T2* are connected to *m* and *n* ($m \leq n$) tables respectively; *T1* is said to be *parallel* to *T2* (noted *T1//T2*) if and only if the primary key of *T1* is included in or equal to the primary key of *T2* (Feki & Hachaichi, 2007-c). Note that, in this definition, *T1* and *T2* are assumed to be relationships because entities could not be parallel; this optimizes the search of parallel tables (Feki, & Hachaichi, 2007-c). In our running example, there are no parallel tables.

Let *T1* and *T2* be already identified as two fact-tables and let *T1* be parallel to *T2*. The fact *F-T1* (built on *T1*) can receive other measures coming from the fact *F-T2* (built on *T2*) by aggregating measures of *F-T2* before moving them to *F-T1*. Since the measures in *F-T2* are more detailed than those in *F-T1* (i.e., *F-T2* has *n-m>0* dimensions more than *F-T1*), then to move them to *F-T1*, they must be aggregated on the set of their uncommon dimensions. Note that if the dimension set of *F-T1* is equal to the dimension set of *F-T2*, then the set of uncommon dimensions between *F-T1* and *F-T2* is empty; therefore, *T1* is parallel to *T2* and reciprocally. Consequently, the measures of both facts *F-T1* and *F-T2* have the same granularity level and could be seen as two halves of the same fact; hence, we recommend merging them into a single fact conventionally called *F-R1-R2*.

In our design method, aggregated measures as well as dimensions used in their calculation are automatically identified. However, the designer must intervene to define the necessary aggregation functions which are semantics dependent.

Dimension Identification

A dimension is generally made up of a finite set of attributes that define various levels of details (hierarchies), whereas others are less significant but used, for instance, to label results or to restrict data processed in queries. These latter are called weak (or non dimensional) attributes. The set of candidate dimensions for a given fact can be built either on tables modeling entities or attributes.

Given a fact *F-T* (i.e., fact build on table *T*), we consider every table *T1* that represents an entity and that is directly referred by the table *T* as a candidate dimension for *F-T*. Conventionally, the name of this dimension is *D-T1* and its identifier is the primary key of *T1*.

In addition to dimensions built on tables, we can build a dimension both on an attribute of a special data type (Boolean, temporal) as well as on an attribute issued from an empty entity. Such a dimension is known in data warehousing as a degenerated dimension. For instance, a Boolean column splits data-rows of its table into two subsets; thus, such an attribute can be an axis of analysis. In practice, a degenerated dimension is integrated inside the fact.

A Boolean column *b* pertinent to a fact-table *T* produces for *T* a candidate, degenerated dimension named *D-b* and identified by *b*. For instance, a *Gender* column in a *Client* database table can build a dimension *D-Gender*.

Furthermore, the data warehouse community assumes a DW as a chronological collection of data (Kimball, Reeves, Ross, & Thornthwaite, 1998). Consequently, the time dimension appears in all data warehouses. For this reason, we propose to build dimensions on temporal attributes as follows: A temporal attribute *(date or time)* belonging to a fact-table *T* timestamps the occurrences of the fact built on *T*; it generates a candidate dimension for *T* where it is the identifier. For the relational schema issued from *e-Ticket* and *Hotel room booking*, the above rules produce the dimensions shown in Table 3.

Hierarchy Identification

The attributes of a dimension are organized into one or several hierarchies. These attributes are ordered from the finest towards the coarsest granularity. In order to distinguish them, we call these attributes parameters. In addition, any hierarchy of a dimension *d* has the identifier of *d* as its finest parameter (*i.e.*, at the level one) already extracted with *d*. The remaining parameters (*i.e.*, those of level higher than one) forming candidate hierarchies for *d* will be extracted in two steps.

First, we extract the parameters located immediately after the dimension identifier; each ob-

tained parameter constitutes a hierarchy. Secondly, for each one, we extract its successor parameters. Thus, a parameter of level two is either:

a) the primary key of a table of class Entity directly referred by a dimension-table *d*;
b) a Boolean or temporal attribute belonging to a dimension table *d*; or
c) a non (primary or foreign)-key attribute belonging to a dimension-table *d* and to other tables.

The recursive application of the above two steps on the tables obtained in step *a)* produces parameters of level higher than two. Table 4 presents the hierarchy parameters of each dimension in Table 3.

A parameter may functionally determine some attributes within its origin table; these attributes describe the parameter and, therefore, are called descriptive (also non-dimensional or weak) attributes. Descriptive attributes for a parameter *p* are non-key textual or numerical attributes belonging to a table supplying *p* and not belonging to other tables. Among these attributes, those textual are more significant than numerical ones (Feki, & Hachaichi, 2007-a). Table 5 presents for each parameter of Table 4 its associated descriptive attributes.

CASE TOOLSET

To support our design method, we have implemented the CAME (*"Conception Assistée de Magasins et d'Entrepôts de données"*) case toolset. CAME carries out the design of conceptual DM schemes starting from either the relational database schemas of an operational database, or from a set of XML documents compliant to a given DTD. Its main functions cover our DM design method steps: 1) *Acquisition and pretreatment of a DTD* using a DTD parser and the XQuery language to extract typing information; 2) *Conversion of XML*

Table 3. Dimensions for the extracted facts

Fact	Dimension	Identifier
F-Room	D-RoomTypes	RoomTypeID
	D-RoomBands	RoomBandID
	D-Facilities	RoomFaciliyID
F-Payments	D-Customer	CustomerID
	D-PaymentMethods	PaymentMethodID
F-Bookings	D-Customer	CustomerID
	D-DateBookingMade	DateBookingMade
	D-TimebookingMade	TimebookingMade
	D-Room	RoomID
	D-BookedStartDate	BookedStartDate
	D-BookedEndDate	BookedEndDate
F-Buy	D-Customer	CustomerID
	D-Concert	CustomerID
	D-BuyDate	BuyDate
	D-ConcertDate	ConcertDate

structure to relational scheme; 3) *Acquisition of the relational schema;* 4) *Schema integration* by applying the fusion approach presented in (Hull, 1997); 5) *Conceptual class identification;* 6) *DM Conceptual design* whose result can be seen both in a tabular format (as illustrated in Figure 9 through the running example) and in a graphical representation (Figure 10); and 7) *Adaptation of the obtained DM* when the designer adjusts the constructed DM schemas to the analytical require-

Table 4. Parameters for the dimensions of Table 3

Dimension	Hierarchy parameters		
	(From finest to coarsest)		
D-Customer	CityID	StateID	CountyID
	CustomerDOB		
D-Room	RoomTypeID		
	RoomBandID		
	RoomFaciliyID		
D-Concert	SingerID		
	CityID	StateID	CountyID

ments of decisional users. In this step, CAME is linked to our case tool MPI-EDITOR (Ben Abdallah, Feki, & Ben-Abdallah, 2006) which allows the designer to graphically manipulate the built DM schemas and adapt them to produce well-formed schemas (Figure 10).

CONCLUSION

In this chapter, we have presented a bottom-up/ data-driven design method for DM schemas from two types of sources: a relational database and XML documents compliant to a given DTD. Our method operates in three automatic steps (Data source pretreatment, relation classification, and DM schema construction) followed by a manual step for DM schema adaptation. It exploits the recent schema/DTD version of a data source to automatically apply a set of rules that extract all candidate facts with their measures, dimensions and hierarchies. In addition, being automatic, our design method is supported by a CASE toolset that allowed us to evaluate it through several

Table 5. Descriptive attributes for the parameters of Table 4

Hierarchy parameters	Descriptive attributes
RoomTypeID	TypeDesc
RoomBandID	BandDesc
RoomFaciliyID	FacilityDesc
RoomID	Price, Floor, AdditionalNotes
PaymentMethodID	PaymentMethod
CountyID	CountyName
StateID	StateName
CityID	CityName
CustomerID	CustomerForenames
	CustomerSurnames
	CustomerHomePhone
	CustomerWorkPhone
	CustomerMobilePhone
	CustomerEmail
SingerID	SingerForenames
	SingerSurnames
ConcertID	ConcertName

Figure 9. Candidate DM schema for the integrated schema

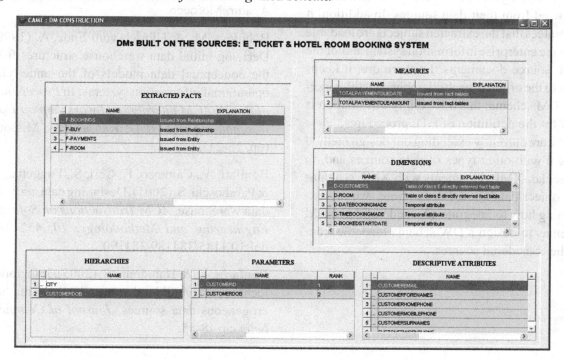

Figure 10. GUI for DM schema adaptation

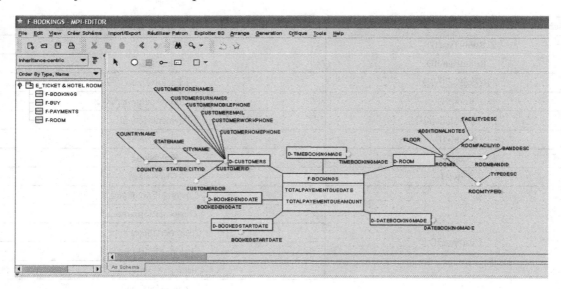

examples. In this paper, we illustrated the method through an e-Ticket DTD used by an online broker and a relational database modeling a hotel room booking system.

Our design method assists decision makers in defining their analytical needs by proposing all analytical subjects that could be automatically extracted from their data sources. In addition, it guarantees that the extracted subjects are loadable from the enterprise information system and/or the XML source documents. Furthermore, it keeps track of the origin of each component of the generated DM schema; this traceability information is vital for the definition of ETL procedures.

We are currently extending our design method to deal with other types of data sources and, in particular, XML documents with XML schemas and object databases. Furthermore, we are examining how to integrate adjusted/validated DM schemas to design a DW schema loadable from all the considered sources.

REFERENCES

Ben Abdallah, M., Feki, J., & Ben-Abdallah, H. (2006). MPI-EDITOR : Un outil de spécification de besoins OLAP par réutilisation logique de patrons multidimensionnels. In *Proceedings of the Atelier des Systèmes Décisionnels (ASD '06)*, Agadir, Morocco.

Böhnlein, M., & Ulbrich-vom Ende, A. (1999). Deriving initial data warehouse structures from the conceptual data models of the underlying operational information systems. In *Proceedings of the 2nd ACM international workshop on Data warehousing and OLAP,* Kansas City, Missouri (pp. 15-21).

Bonifati, A., Cattaneo, F., Ceri, S., Fuggetta, A., & Paraboschi, S. (2001). Designing data marts for data warehouse. *ACM Transactions on Software Engineering and Methodology, 10,* 452–483. doi:10.1145/384189.384190

Boufares, F., & Hamdoun, S. (2005). Integration techniques to build a data warehouse using heterogeneous data sources. *Journal of Computer Science,* 48-55.

Bright, M. W., Hurson, A. R., & Pakzad, S. (1994). Automated resolution of semantic heterogeneity in multidatabases. [TODS]. *ACM Transactions on Database Systems*, *19*(2), 212–253. doi:10.1145/176567.176569

Bruckner, R., List, B., & Schiefer, J. (2001). Developing requirements for data warehouse systems with use cases. In *Proceedings of the 7th Americas Conf. on Information Systems* (pp. 329-335).

Cabibbo, L., & Torlone, R. (1998). A logical approach to multidimensional databases. In *Proceedings of the Conference on Extended Database Technology*, Valencia, Spain (pp. 187-197).

Ceri, S., Fraternali, P., & Paraboschi, S. (2000). XML: Current developments and future challenges for the database community. In *Proceedings of the 7th Int. Conf. on Extending Database Technology (EDBT)*, (LNCS 1777). Berlin, Germany: Springer.

Ceri, S., & Widom, J. (1993). Managing semantic heterogeneity with production rules and persistent queues source. In *Proceedings of the 19th International Conference on Very Large Data Bases* (pp. 108-119).

Codd, E. F. (1970). A relational model of data for large data banks. *ACM Communications*, *13*(6), 377–387. doi:10.1145/362384.362685

Databasedev.co.uk. (2008). *Sample data models for relational database design*. Retrieved July 30, 2008, from http://www.databasedev.co.uk/data_models.html

Deutsch, A., Fernandez, M., & Suciu, D. (1999). Storing semi structured data in relations. In *Proceedings of the Workshop on Query Processing for Semi structured Data and Non-Standard Data Formats*.

Feki, J., & Ben-Abdallah, H. (2007). Multidimensional pattern construction and logical reuse for the design of data marts. *International Review on Computers and Software*, *2*(2), 124–134.

Feki, J., & Hachaichi, Y. (2007). Du relationnel au multidimensionnel: Conception de magasins de données. In *Proceedings of the Revue des Nouvelles Technologies de l'Information: Entrepôts de données et analyse en ligne (EDA 2007)* (Vol. B-3, pp. 5-19).

Feki, J., & Hachaichi, Y. (2007). Conception assistée de MD: Une démarche et un outil. *Journal of Decision Systems*, *16*(3), 303–333. doi:10.3166/jds.16.303-333

Feki, J., & Hachaichi, Y. (2007). Constellation discovery from OLTP parallel-relations. In *Proceedings of the 8th International Arab Conference on Information Technology ACIT 07*, Lattakia, Syria.

Feki, J., Nabli, A., Ben-Abdallah, H., & Gargouri, F. (2008). An automatic data warehouse conceptual design approach. In *Encyclopedia of data warehousing and mining* (2nd ed.). Hershey, PA: IGI Global.

Giorgini, P., Rizzi, S., & Maddalena, G. (2005). Goal-oriented requirement analysis for data warehouse design. In *Proceedings of the ACM Eighth International Workshop on Data Warehousing and OLAP*, Bremen, Germany (pp 47-56).

Golfarelli, M., Maio, D., & Rizzi, S. (1998). Conceptual design of data warehouses from E/R schemas. In Proceedings of the *Conference on System Sciences*, Kona, Hawaii. Washington, DC, USA: IEEE Computer Society.

Golfarelli, M., Rizzi, S., & Vrdoljak, B. (2001). Data warehouse design from XML sources. In *Proceedings of the Fourth ACM International Workshop on Data Warehousing and OLAP* Atlanta, GA, USA (pp. 40-47).

Hachaichi, Y., & Feki, J. (2007). Patron multidimensionnel et MDA pour les entrepôts de données. In *Proceedings of the 2nd Workshop on Decisional Systems*, Sousse-Tunisia.

Hachaichi, Y., Feki, J., & Ben-Abdallah, H. (2008). XML source preparation for building data warehouses. In *Proceedings of the International Conference on Enterprise Information Systems and Web Technologies EISWT-08,* Orlando, Florida, USA (pp. 61-67).

Hachaichi, Y., Feki, J., & Ben-Abdallah, H. (2008). Du XML au multidimensionnel: Conception de magasins de données. In *Proceedings of the 4èmes journées francophones sur les Entrepôts de Données et l'Analyse en ligne (EDA 2008), Toulouse, RNTI,* Toulouse, France (Vol. B-4. pp. 45-59).

Hull, R. (1997). Managing semantic heterogeneity in databases: A theoretical prospective. In *Proceedings of the sixteenth ACM SIGACT-SIGMOD-SIGART symposium on Principles of database systems,* Tucson, AZ, USA (pp. 51-61).

Inmon, W. H. (1996). *Building the data warehouse.* New York: John Wiley & Sons.

Jensen, M., Møller, T., & Pedersen, T. B. (2001). Specifying OLAP cubes on XML data. *Journal of Intelligent Information Systems.*

Kappel, G., Kapsammer, E., Rausch-Schott, S., & Retschitzegger, W. (2000). X-ray - towards integrating XML and relational database systems. In *Proceedings of the 19th Int. Conf. on Conceptual Modeling (ER),* Salt Lake City, USA (LNCS 1920). Berlin, Germany: Springer.

Kappel, G., Kapsammer, E., & Retschitzegger, W. (2001). XML and relational database systems - a comparison of concepts. In *Proceedings of the International Conference on Internet Computing (1)* (pp. 199-205).

Kimball, R., Reeves, L., Ross, M., & Thornthwaite, W. (1998). *The data warehouse lifecycle toolkit.* New York: John Wiley & Sons.

Lee, D., & Chu, W. (2000). Constraints-preserving transformation from XML document type definition to relational schema. In *Proceedings of the 19th Int. Conf. on Conceptual Modeling (ER),* Salt Lake City, USA (LNCS 1920). Berlin, Germany: Springer.

List, B., Bruckner, R. M., Machacze, K., & Schiefer, J. (2002). A comparison of data warehouse development methodologies case study of the process warehouse. In *Proceedings of the International Conference on Database and Expert Systems Applications DEXA*

Mazón, J.-N., & Trujillo, J. (2008). An MDA approach for the development of data warehouses. *Decision Support Systems, 45*(1), 41–58. doi:10.1016/j.dss.2006.12.003

Moody, D., & Kortnik, M. (2000). From enterprise models to dimensional models: A methodology for data warehouse and data mart design. In *Proceedings of the DMDW'00,* Suede.

Ouaret, Z., Bellatreche, L., & Boussaid, O. (2007). XUML star: Conception d'un entrepôt de données XML. In *Proceedings of the Atelier des Systèmes d'Information Décisionnels,* Sousse, Tunisie (pp. 19-20).

Paim, F. R. S., & Castro, J. B. (2003). DWARF: An approach for requirements definition and management of data warehouse systems. In *Proceedings of the Int. Conf. on Requirements Engineering,* Monterey Bay, CA.

Phipps, C., & Davis, K. (2002). Automating data warehouse conceptual schema design and evaluation. *In Proceedings of the 4th Int. Workshop on Design and Management of Data Warehouses* (Vol. 58, pp. 23-32).

Prakash, N., & Gosain, A. (2003). Requirements driven data warehouse development. In *Proceedings of the 15th Conference on Advanced Information Systems Engineering Short Paper Proc.,* Velden, Austria.

Prat, N., Akoka, J., & Comyn-Wattiau, I. (2006). A UML-based data warehouse design method. *Decision Support Systems*, *42*, 1449–1473. doi:10.1016/j.dss.2005.12.001

Rusu, L. I., Rahayu, W., & Taniar, D. (2004). On data cleaning in building XML data warehouses. In *Proceedings of the 6th Intl. Conference on Information Integration and Web-based Applications & Services (iiWAS2004),* Jakarta, Indonesia (pp. 797-807).

Rusu, L. I., Rahayu, W., & Taniar, D. (2005). A methodology for building XML data warehouses. *International Journal of Data Warehousing and Mining*, *1*(2), 67–92.

Sahuguet, A. (2000). Everything you ever wanted to know about DTDs, but were afraid to ask. In *Proceedings of the International Workshop on the Web and Databases WebDB 2000* (pp. 171-183).

Salem, A., Ghozzi, F., & Ben-Abdallah, H. (2008). Multi-dimensional modeling - formal specification and verification of the hierarchy concept. In . *Proceedings of the ICEIS, 2008*(1), 317–322.

Schmidt, A. R., Kersten, M. L., Windhouwer, M. A., & Waas, F. (2000). Efficient relational storage and retrieval of XML documents. In *Proceedings of the Workshop on the Web and Databases (WebDB)*, Dallas, USA.

Schneider, M. (2003). Well-formed data warehouse structures. In *Proceedings of the 5th International Workshop at VLDB'03 on Design and Management of Data Warehouses (DMDW'2003)*, Berlin, Germany.

Seba, D. (2003). *Merise - concepts et mise en œuvre*. France: Eni.

Shanmugasundarma, J., Tufte, K., He, G., Zhang, C., DeWitt, D., & Naughton, J. (1999). Relational database for querying XML documents: Limitation and opportunities. *Proceedings of the 25th VLDB Conferences*, Scotland.

Sheth, A. P., & Larson, J. A. (1990). Federated database systems for managing distributed, heterogeneous, and autonoumous databases. *ACM Computing Surveys*, *22*(3), 183–236. doi:10.1145/96602.96604

Vrdoljak, B., Banek, M., & Rizzi, S. (2003). Designing Web warehouses from XML schema. In *Proceedings of the 5th International Conference Data Warehousing and Knowledge Discovery: DaWak*, Prague Czech.

Widom, J. (1999). Data management for XML - research directions. *IEEE Data Engineering Bulletin, Special Issue on XML*, *22*(3).

Wikipedia Encyclopedia. (2008). *Database*. Retrieved August 1, 2008, from http://en.wikipedia.org/wiki/Database

World Wide Web Consortium XML Schema. (2008). *W3C candidate recommendation*. Retrieved August 1, 2008, from http://www.w3.org/XML/Schema.html

Yan, M. H., & Ada, W. C. F. (2001). From XML to relational database. In *Proceedings of the CEUR Workshop*.

Zhang, L., & Yang, X. (2008). An approach to semantic annotation for metadata in relational databases. In *Proceedings of the International Symposiums on Information Processing (ISIP)* (pp. 635-639).

KEY TERMS AND DEFINITIONS

Data Mart: Data marts are analytical data stores designed to focus on specific business functions for a specific community within an organization. A data mart is designed according to a specific model, namely the multidimensional model that highlights the axes of data analyses. Data marts are often derived from subsets of a data warehouse data, though in the bottom-up data warehouse design methodology the data warehouse is created from the union of data marts.

Document Type Definition (DTD): A DTD defines the tags and attributes that can be used in an XML document. It indicates which tags can appear within other tags. XML documents are described using a subset of DTD which imposes a number of restrictions on the document's structure, as required per the XML standard.

DTD Simplification: The simplification of a DTD removes empty elements, replaces each reference to an ENTITY type with the text corresponding to that entity, and then it removes the corresponding ENTITY declaration, and apply Flattening, Reduction and Grouping transformations.

eXtensible Markup Language (XML): XML is a general-purpose specification for creating custom markup languages. It is classified as an extensible language because it allows the user to define the mark-up elements. The main purpose of XML is to aid information systems in sharing data, especially via the Internet.

Model Integration: Model integration produces a single model that combines two or more input models. The produced model can be represented in the same definitional formalism as the input models (or in one of the definitional formalisms used by the heterogeneous input models). The expression of the new model must be formally correct within the definitional formalism used.

Relational Data Model: The relational data model was introduced by E.F. Codd in 1970. It is particularly well suited for modeling business data. In this model, data are organized in tables. The set of names of the columns is called the "schema" of the table. The relational model is the model in most common use today.

Star Schema: The star schema (sometimes referenced as star join schema) is the simplest model of multidimensional schema. The star

Chapter 5

Ontology–Based Integration of Heterogeneous, Incomplete and Imprecise Data Dedicated to a Decision Support System for Food Safety

Patrice Buche
INRA, France

Sandrine Contenot
INRA, France

Lydie Soler
INRA, France

Juliette Dibie-Barthélemy
AgroParisTech, France

David Doussot
AgroParisTech, France

Gaelle Hignette
AgroParisTech, France

Liliana Ibanescu
AgroParisTech, France

ABSTRACT

This chapter presents an application in the field of food safety using an ontology-based data integration approach. An ontology is a vocabulary used to express the knowledge in a given domain of application. In this chapter, the ontology-based data integration approach permits to homogenize data sources which are heterogeneous in terms of structure and vocabulary. This approach is done in the framework of the

DOI: 10.4018/978-1-60566-756-0.ch005

Semantic Web, an international initiative which proposes annotating data sources using ontologies in order to manage them more efficiently. In this chapter, the authors explore three ways to integrate data according to a domain ontology: (1) a semantic annotation process to extend local data with Web data which have been semantically annotated according to a domain ontology, (2) a flexible querying system to query uniformly both local data and Web data and (3) an ontology alignment process to find correspondences between data from two sources indexed by distinct ontologies.

INTRODUCTION

The aim of the data integration systems is to put together a large amount of data coming from multiple and independent sources. One of the main problems of the data integration is the data heterogeneity. It can come from the structure of the data, the vocabulary used to index the data and the format of the data. These characteristics are in general specific to each source of data. Their harmonization is necessary to integrate the data. Another problem of the data integration is the data rarity. Although this problem can seem paradoxical, it can be explained by the fact that the numerous available data are not necessarily pertinent for a given application domain (in food safety for instance). A third problem may also occur in data integration: the imprecision of data. This imprecision can be intrinsic to the data (for instance an interval of pH values) or can correspond to a pertinence degree associated with the

data according to the application domain.

We have developed a system, called CARAT (Chronic & Acute Risk Assessment), to estimate the exposure of a given population of consumers to chemical contaminants which relies on two distinct data sources. Both sources contain information about food products. The first one, called CONTA source, contains measures of the level of chemical contamination for food products. The second one, called CONSO source, stores household purchases of food products. Both sources have been indexed using their own domain ontology, the CONTA ontology and the CONSO ontology, an ontology representing a vocabulary used to express the knowledge in a given application domain. The CARAT system is composed of two sub-systems (see Figure 1): a decision support system that uses statistical methods to compute the exposure of a given population of consumers to chemical contaminants (Buche, Soler & Tressou, 2006) and an ontology-based data integration system which

Figure 1. The CARAT system

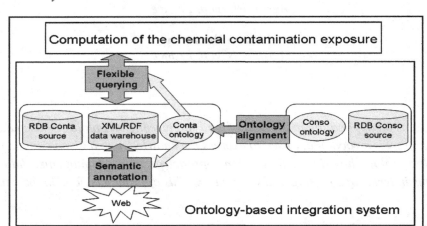

feeds the decision support system with data about the chemical contamination and the consumption of food products. The data integration system is managed using a data warehouse approach: data sources provided by external partners are replicated locally and standardized using ETL (Extract, Transform, Load) technology.

In this chapter, we present the ontology-based data integration system which takes into account the three data integration problems presented above: data heterogeneity, data rarity and data imprecision. The ontology-based data integration system proposes three different ways to integrate data according to a domain ontology. The first one is a semantic annotation process which allows a local database (the CONTA local database), indexed by a domain ontology, to be extended with data that have been extracted from the Web and semantically annotated according to this domain ontology. The second one, which is an original contribution of this chapter, is a querying system which allows the semantically annotated Web data to be integrated with the local data through a uniform flexible querying system relying on a domain ontology (the CONTA ontology). The third one is an ontology alignment method relying on rules which allow correspondences to be found between objects of a source ontology (the CONSO ontology) and objects of a target ontology (the CONTA ontology) according to their characteristics and associated values. Those three ways to integrate data have been designed using the Semantic web approach, an international initiative, which proposes annotating data sources using ontologies in order to manage them more efficiently.

In this chapter, we first present the ontology-based data integration system. We then provide some background on the topic. Third, current projects and future trends are presented. We conclude this chapter in the last section.

THE ONTOLOGY-BASED DATA INTEGRATION SYSTEM

This section describes the different construction steps of the ontology-based data integration system of the CARAT system. In the first section, we present the filling of its data sources. In the second section, we present its querying system. In the third section, we present the alignment between objects of its two data sources which are indexed by distinct ontologies.

Filling the Data Warehouse

There are two types of data available in the CARAT system: contamination data and consumption data. Both types of data concern food products but their content and their treatment are not the same. The contamination data are measures of level of chemical contamination for food products whereas the consumption data are about household purchases of food products during a year.

The contamination data are stored in a relational database, called CONTA local database, which has been defined and filled by our research team from different sources. It is indexed by the CONTA ontology. The consumption data are stored in a relational database, called CONSO database, which is filled from the TNS WORLD PANEL source, a private source of household purchases. It is indexed by the CONSO ontology. Both databases are filled using ETL technology.

In this section, we make a focus on two original characteristics of the contamination data which must be taken into account during their storage: their imprecision and their rarity. On the one hand, we propose to use the fuzzy set theory in order to represent imprecise data. On the other hand, we propose to search and annotate data from the Web using the CONTA ontology in order to extend the CONTA local database. We first present the structure of the CONTA ontology. We then present the fuzzy set theory used to treat the imprecise data. Finally, we detail our semantic annotation process which allows the CONTA local database to be enriched with Web data.

The Structure of the CONTA Ontology

The CONTA ontology is composed of datatypes -numeric types and symbolic types- and of relations that allow one to link datatypes.

Numeric types are used to define the numeric data. A numeric type is described by the name of the type, the units in which data of this type is usually expressed, and the interval of possible values for this type. For example, the type Contamination Level can be expressed in the units μg/g, μg/kg, ng/g, μg/l and has a range of [0, 1000].

Symbolic types are used when the data of interest are represented as a string. A symbolic type is described by the name of the type and the type hierarchy (which is the set of possible values for the type, partially ordered by the subsumption relation). For example, FoodProduct and Contaminant are symbolic types.

Relations are used to represent semantic links between datatypes. A relation is described by the name of the relation and its signature. For example, the relation ContaminationRange represents the average level of contamination of a food product by a contaminant for a given number of samples. This relation has for domain the symbolic types FoodProduct, Contaminant and Samples Total Number and for range the numeric type Contamination Level. Figure 2 shows the structure of an excerpt of the CONTA ontology.

This ontology has been expressed in OWL distinguishing two types of knowledge: (i) generic knowledge which define the structure of the ontology: for instance, the class numericalType (resp. the class Relation) which is the superclass of all numerical types (resp. relations); (ii) domain-dependant knowledge: for instance, the class ContaminationRange is a subclass of the class Relation and the class ContaminationLevel is a subclass of the class numericalType.

Example 1

Figure 2 gives an excerpt of the CONTA ontology.

Figure 2. A simplified excerpt of the CONTA ontology

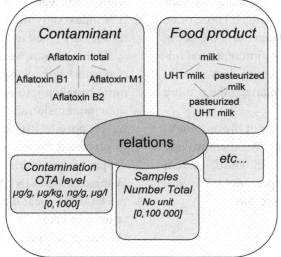

Figure 3. Examples of fuzzy sets

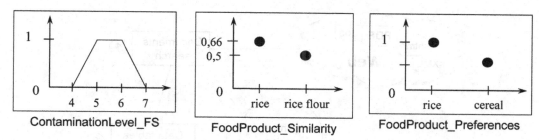

The Fuzzy Set Theory

We propose to use the fuzzy set theory to represent imprecise data. In this chapter, we use the representation of fuzzy sets proposed in (Zadeh, 1965).

Definition A fuzzy set f on a definition domain D(f) is defined by a membership function μ from D(f) to [0,1] that associates the degree to which x belongs to f with each element x of D(f). We call support of f the subset of D(f) such that support(f)= {a ∈ D(f) | $\mu_f(a) > 0$}. We call kernel of f the subset of D(f) such that kernel(f) = {a ∈ D(f) | $\mu_f(a) = 1$}.

We distinguish two kinds of fuzzy sets: (i) discrete fuzzy sets and (ii) continuous fuzzy sets.

Definition A discrete fuzzy set f is a fuzzy set associated with a symbolic type of the ontology. Its definition domain is the type hierarchy.

Definition A continuous fuzzy set f is a trapezoidal fuzzy set associated with a numeric type of the ontology. A trapezoidal fuzzy set is defined by its four characteristic points which correspond to min(support(f)), min(kernel(f)), max(kernel(f)) and max(support(f)). Its definition domain is the interval of possible values of the type.

The fuzzy set formalism can be used in three different ways as defined in (Dubois & Prade, 1988): (i) in the database, in order to represent imprecise data as an ordered disjunction of exclusive possible values, (ii) in the database as a result of the semantic annotation process, in order to represent the similarity between a value from the web and

values from the ontology or (iii) in the queries, in order to represent fuzzy selection criteria which express the preferences of the end-user.

Example 2
The fuzzy set *ContaminationLevel_FS* of Figure 3 is a continuous fuzzy set denoted [4,5,6,7]. It represents the possible values of a level of contamination. The fuzzy set *FoodProduct_Similarity* is a discrete fuzzy set denoted (0.66/rice + 0.5/rice flour). It represents the set of terms of the ontology that are similar with different degrees to the term Basmati rice found in a document retrieved from the Web. The fuzzy set *FoodProduct_Preferences* is a discrete one denoted (1/rice + 0.5/cereal). Used in a query, it means that the end-user is interested by information about rice but also with a lowest interest about cereal.

The Semantic Annotation Process

In order to deal with the data rarity problem of the CONTA local database, we propose to extend the local database with data extracted from the Web. We have designed for that purpose a semi-automatic acquisition tool, called @WEB (Annotating Tables from the WEB). This tool relies on three steps as described in Figure 4. In the first step, relevant documents for the application domain are retrieved using the domain ontology thanks to crawlers and RSS feeds. We focus on documents which contain data tables. This may be seen as a restriction

Figure 4. @WEB architecture

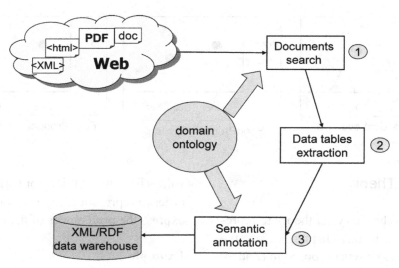

of our approach. But, in a lot of application domains, especially in the scientific field, data tables are often a source of relevant, reliable and synthetic data. Moreover, their tabular structure is obviously easier to automatically parse than natural language. In the second step, the Web documents in html or most usually in pdf are translated into a generic XML format, which allows the representation of data tables in a classical and generic way -- a table is a set of lines, each line being a set of cells. In the third step, the tables are semantically annotated according to the domain ontology.

The semantic annotation process of a table extracted from the web consists in identifying which semantic relations from the domain ontology are represented in the table. The different steps of our semantic annotation process are detailed in Hignette & al. (2007).

The semantic annotation process generates RDF descriptions which represent the semantic relations of the ontology recognized in each row of the Web data table. Some of these RDF descriptions include values expressed as fuzzy sets. The fuzzy values used to annotate Web data tables may express similarity or imprecision. A fuzzy set having a semantic of similarity is associated with each cell belonging to a symbolic column. It represents the ordered list of the most similar values of the ontology associated with the value present in the cell. A fuzzy set having a semantic of imprecision may be associated with cells belonging to numerical columns. It represents an ordered disjunction of exclusive possible values.

Example 3

Table 1 presents an example of a Web data table in which the semantic relation *ContaminationRange*

Table 1. A Web data table

Food	Contaminant	Contaminant Level (ng/g)
Basmati rice	OTA	1.65-1.95
Chili powder	OTA	2.34-4.91
Grape raisins	OTA	0.93-1.20

Figure 5. RDF annotations of the first row of the Web data table presented in Table 1

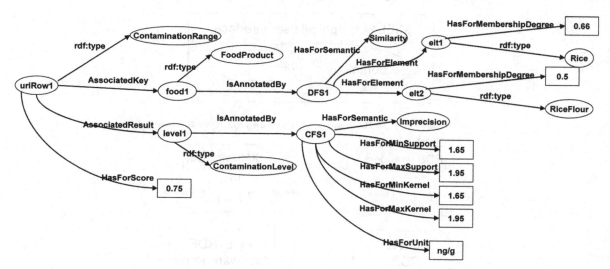

of domain the symbolic types *FoodProduct*, *Contaminant* and *Samples Total Number* and of range the numeric type *Contamination Level* has been identified.

Figure 5 presents a part of the RDF descriptions corresponding to the recognition of the relation *ContaminationRange* in the first row of Table 1. The first row (having the URI *uriRow1* in the XML document) is an instance of the *Contamination-Range* relation recognized with a pertinence score of 0.75. This pertinence score is computed by the semantic annotation process as the proportion of recognized types of the relation. It expresses the degree of "certainty" associated with the relation recognition. A part of the domain of the relation presented in the example (typed by the OWL class *AssociatedKey*) is an instance of the symbolic type *FoodProduct (food1)* and is annotated by a discrete fuzzy set (*DFS1*) which has a semantic of similarity. It indicates the list of closest values of the ontology (*Rice* and *Rice Flour*) compared to the value *Basmati Rice*. The range of the relation (typed by the OWL class *AssociatedResult*) is an instance of the numeric type *ContaminationLevel* and is annotated by a continuous fuzzy set (*CFS1*) which has a semantic of imprecision. It indicates the possible contamination limits ([1.65, 1.95])

represented as the support and the kernel of the fuzzy set.

The output of the @WEB system is an XML/RDF data warehouse composed of a set of XML documents which represent data tables and contain their RDF annotations.

The Flexible Querying System

In order to deal with the data heterogeneity in the CONTA sources, we propose to the end-user a unified querying system, called MIEL++, which permits to query simultaneously the CONTA local relational database and the CONTA XML/RDF data warehouse in a transparent way. The MIEL++ system is a flexible querying system relying on a given domain ontology, the CONTA ontology. It allows the end-user to retrieve the nearest data stored in both sources corresponding to his/her selection criteria: the CONTA ontology -more precisely the type hierarchies- is used in order to assess which data can be considered as "near" to the user's selection criteria.

Figure 6 gives an overview of the MIEL++ architecture. When a query is asked to the MIEL++ system, that query is asked through a single graphical user interface, which relies on the domain

Figure 6. MIEL++ architecture

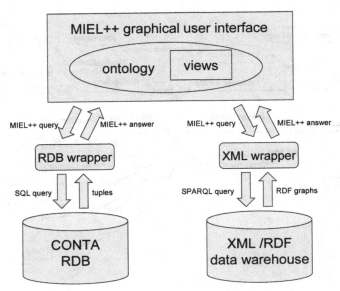

ontology. The query is translated by each subsystem's wrapper into a query expressed in the query language of the subsystem: an SQL query in the relational subsystem (see Buche & al. (2005) for more details about the SQL subsystem), a SPARQL query in the XML/RDF subsystem (SPARQL is a query language recommended by the W3C to query RDF data sources http://www.w3.org/TR/rdf-sparql-query/). Finally, the global answer to the query is the union of the local results of the two subsystems, which are ordered according to their relevance to the query selection criteria.

In this section, we are interested in the XML/RDF subsystem which allows the end-user to query RDF annotations of Web data tables represented in XML documents. A MIEL++ query is asked in a view which corresponds to a given relation of the ontology. A view is characterized by its set of queryable attributes and by its actual definition. Each queryable attribute corresponds to a type of the relation represented by the view. The concept of view must be understood with the meaning of the relational database model: it permits to hide the complexity of the querying in a given subsystem to the end-user. The end-user uses a view to build

his query. In the XML/RDF subsystem, a view is defined by means of a SPARQL generic query where the SELECT clause contains the queryable attributes and the WHERE clause contains the definition of the view.

Example 4

Let us consider the view V associated with the relation ContaminationRange of domain FoodProduct, Contaminant, SamplesNumberTotal and of range ContaminationLevel. The SPARQL query associated with V is presented in Figure 7, the where part of the query being shown graphically for readability reasons.

A MIEL++ query is an instance of a given view specified by the end-user, by choosing, among the set of queryable attributes of the view, which are the conjunctive selection attributes and their corresponding searched values, which are the projection attributes and which is the minimal threshold on the pertinence score associated with the relation represented by the view. In a MIEL++ query, the end-user can express preferences in

Figure 7. The SPARQL query associated with a view

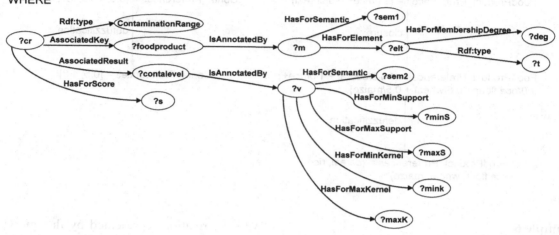

V = {FoodProduct, Contaminant, SamplesNumberTotal, ContaminationLevel | ContaminationRange (FoodProduct, Contaminant, SamplesNumberTotal, ContaminationLevel)}

SELECT ?foodproduct ?contaminant ?samplesnumbertotal ?contaminationlevel
WHERE

his/her selection criteria. These preferences are expressed by fuzzy sets as presented in Subsection "The fuzzy set theory". Since fuzzy sets are not supported in a standard SPARQL query, we propose to "defuzzify" the MIEL++ query before translating it into SPARQL. This defuzzification is performed in two steps.

When the fuzzy value of a selection criterion has a hierarchized symbolic definition domain, it is represented by a fuzzy set defined on a subset of its definition domain. Such a fuzzy set defines degrees implicitly on the whole definition domain of the selection attribute. In order to take those implicit degrees into account, we propose to perform a closure of the fuzzy set as defined in Thomopoulos & al. (2006). Intuitively, the closure propagates the degrees to more specific values of the hierarchy. Then, for each selection criterion represented by a fuzzy set, we can perform the defuzzification of the fuzzy set which consists in deleting the degrees in the case of a DFS and in only keeping the interval which corresponds to the support in the case of a CFS.

Example 5

Let us consider the following MIEL++ query Q where FoodProduct, Contaminant, ContaminationLevel are the projection attributes and where FoodProduct and ContaminationLevel are the selection attributes. Figure 8 presents (i) on the left, the closure and the defuzzification of the fuzzy value FoodProduct_Preferences={1.0/rice + 0.5/cereal} associated with the selection criterion FoodProduct according to the type hierarchy of the type FoodProduct of Figure 2 and (ii) on the right, the defuzzification of the fuzzy value Conta_Preferences={0.5, 0.75, 1.7, 1.8} associated with the selection criterion ContaminationLevel.

The defuzzified MIEL++ query can now be translated into a SPARQL query where the CONSTRUCT clause allows the answers of the query to be built according to the projection attributes of the MIEL++ query and the SELECT clause contains the selection criteria and the threshold of the MIEL++ query. All the selection criteria are represented into the FILTER clause of the SELECT clause.

Figure 8. Defuzzification of a MIEL++ query

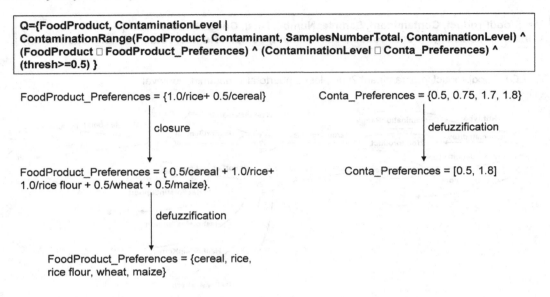

Example 6

The defuzzified MIEL++ query of example 5 can be translated into the SPARQL query of Figure 9 in which, for readability reasons, we do not detail the where part of the query already given in Figure 7.

An answer to a MIEL++ query must (1) satisfy the minimal acceptable pertinence score associated with the relation represented by the query; (2) satisfy all the selection criteria of the query and (3) associate a constant value with each projection attribute of the query. The answer to a MIEL++ query in the XML/RDF subsystem is computed in two steps. First the corresponding SPARQL query is generated and executed into the XML/

Figure 9. The SPARQL query associated with the defuzzified MIEL++ query of example 5

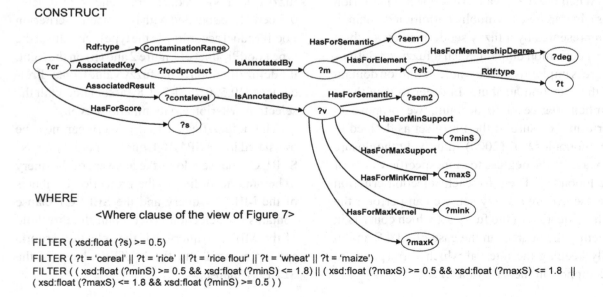

RDF data warehouse. Then, the answer to this SPARL query must be "refuzzified" in order to be able to measure how it satisfies the selection criteria.

To measure the satisfaction of a selection criterium, we have to consider the two semantics -imprecision and similarity- associated with fuzzy values of the XML/RDF data warehouse. On the one hand, two classical measures (Dubois & Prade, 1988) have been proposed to compare a fuzzy set representing preferences to a fuzzy set having a semantic of imprecision: a possibility degree of matching denoted $\prod$ and a necessity degree of matching denoted N. On the other hand, we propose to use the adequation degree as proposed in (Baziz & al., 2006) to compare a fuzzy set representing preferences to a fuzzy set having a semantic of similarity. The comparison results of fuzzy sets having the same semantic (similarity or imprecision) are aggregated using the min operator (which is classically used to interpret the conjunction).

Therefore, an answer is a set of tuples composed of the pertinence score *ps* associated with the relation, three comparison scores associated with the selection criteria in the data warehouse: a global adequation score *ad* associated with the comparison results having a semantic of similarity and two global matching scores $\prod$ and *N* associated with the comparison results having a semantic of imprecision, and, the values associated with each projection attribute. Based on those scores, we propose to define a total order on the answers which gives greater importance to the most pertinent answers compared with the ontology. Thus, the answers are successively sorted according to firstly ps, then *ad* and thirdly a total order defined on $\prod$ and *N* where *N* is considered as of greater importance than $\prod$.

Example 7

The answer to the query of Example 6 compared with the first row of the table presented in Table 1Table 1 A Web data table and annotated

in Figure 4 is given below:Result = {ps= 0.75, ad=0.66, N= 0.0, $\prod$ = 1.0, FoodProduct=(0.66/ Rice + 0.5/Rice Flour), ContaminationLevel=[1.65,1.65,1.95,1.95]}.

The Ontology Alignment

As already said, the CARAT system is composed of contamination data indexed by the CONTA ontology and consumption data indexed by the CONSO ontology. Both types of data concern food products: the contamination data are measures of chemical contamination for food products and the consumption data are about household purchases of food products. Therefore, the decision support system of the CARAT system needs correspondences to be found between food products of the CONTA ontology and food products of the CONSO in order to estimate the exposure of a given population of consumers to chemical contaminants.

Since the CONSO ontology is updated every year by the company which provides the TNS WORLD PANEL data and, on the contrary, the CONTA ontology remains stable, the CONSO ontology is considered as the source ontology in the alignment process and the CONTA ontology as the target ontology. A simple mapping between food product names of the CONSO ontology and food product names of the CONTA ontology is not efficient because only a little set of names have words in common. Therefore we have used an additional knowledge to map food products: the food product description available in both ontologies. For this purpose, the content of the CONTA ontology presented in Subsection "The structure of the CONTA ontology" is extended with an international food description vocabulary called Langual (Ireland & Moller, 2000). Langual is composed of predefined characteristics and of predefined associated values partially order by the subsumption relation. Figure 10 gives an excerpt of the extended version of the CONTA ontology expressed in RDFS: the symbolic type

Figure 10. An excerpt of the extended version of the CONTA ontology

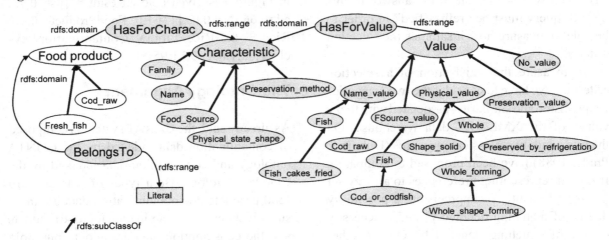

Food product presented in Figure 2 is extended with the Langual vocabulary (colored in grey) which permits to describe the food product.

The CONSO ontology has the same structure. It is restricted to the symbolic type FoodProduct and associated vocabulary used to describe the food product. This food description vocabulary is extracted from the TNS WORLD PANEL data source. As for the Langual vocabulary, it is composed of a food characterization list and predefined associated values.

Our ontology alignment process consists in considering the ontology alignment problem as a rule application problem in which the food descriptions of the CONSO ontology and the food descriptions of the CONTA ontology are put together into a fact base and in which rules are defined from the food descriptions of the CONTA ontology. The different steps of our ontology alignment process are detailed in Buche & al. (2008). At the end of our ontology alignment process, food products of the CONSO ontology are annotated by sets of food products of the CONTA ontology that are candidates for the alignment.

BACKGROUND

The contribution of our system can be evaluated as an application in the field of food safety or as methods in semantic annotation, flexible querying and ontology alignment.

In the field of food safety, a lot of sources of information are available on the Web (see McMeekin & al. (2006) for a recent review). Many efforts have been done to standardize and to classify the food product names used to index the data in those sources at an international level (see Ireland & Moller (2000) for a review). Recent works have also proposed to build ontologies using Semantic Web languages (Soergel & al., 2004). But, for the best of our knowledge, we think that our approach, which permits to semi-automatically integrate data extracted from heterogeneous sources using semantic annotation and ontology alignment methods, is an original contribution.

We have chosen to build an unsupervised annotation system which recognizes predefined relations in tables: first, the ontology can be easily built from explicit metadata associated with relational local databases, which correspond to the relational schemas of the databases and their attributes with their associated domains. This approach has been experimentally tested on three different domains (microbial risk in food, chemical risk in food and aeronautics): three OWL ontologies have been created within a couple of hours thanks to preexisting information retrieved from local databases and a very simple tool which translates automatically csv files containing the metadata into an OWL ontology; second, the structure of data tables is highly variable (even tables in the same paper don't have the same structure) and terms appear in tables with no linguistic context, that invalidates the annotation techniques that learn wrappers based on structure and/or textual context such as Lixto (Baumgartner & al., 2001) or BWI (Freitag & Kushmerick, 2000). Our approach can be compared to the construction of frames from tables described in Pivk & al. (2004) but they use a generic ontology and create new relations according to the table signature, whereas we want to recognize predefined relations in an ontology specific to the target domain.

In the framework of XML database flexible querying, different approaches have been proposed to extend either XPATH or SPARQL. (Campi & al., 2006) proposes FUZZYXPATH, a fuzzy extension of XPATH to query XML documents. Extensions are of two kinds: (i) the 'deep-similar' function permits a relaxed comparison in term of structure between the query tree and the data tree; (ii) the 'close' and 'similar' predicates extend the equality comparison to a similarity comparison between the content of a node and a given value expressed in the query. (Hutardo & al., 2006) proposes an extension of the SPARQL 'Optional' clause (called Relax). This clause permits to compute a set of generalizations of the RDF triplets involved in the SPARQL query using especially declarations done in the RDF Schema. (Corby & al., 2004) also proposes the same kind of extension of the SPARQL query using a distance function applied to the classes and properties of the RDF Schema. The originality of our approach in flexible querying is that we propose a complete and integrated solution which permits (1) to annotate data tables

with the vocabulary defined in an OWL ontology, (2) to execute a flexible query of the annotated tables using the same vocabulary and taking into account the pertinence degrees generated by the annotation system.

Finally, the ontology alignment problem has been widely investigated in the literature (Castano & al., 2007; Euzenat & Shvaiko, 2007; Kalfoglou & Schorlemmer, 2003; Noy, 2004). Our originality is to treat that problem as a rule application problem where a source ontology, considered as a fact base, is aligned with a target one, considered as a rule base.

FUTURE RESEARCH DIRECTIONS

The domain ontology is the central element of our data integration system. In the future, we want to carry on our work on data integration based on ontology.

First, we intend enhancing the performance of the annotation system using machine learning techniques (Doan & al., 2003) on the knowledge of the ontology but without manual training on a subset of the corpus. By example, a new classifier for symbolic types can be added to the existing one and trained using the domain of values associated with the symbolic type in the ontology. Second, we want to integrate the user's opinion on the query result in order to improve the underlying semantic annotation process and consequently to enrich the ontology. Third, since our flexible querying system allows the user to query uniformly several sources indexed by the same ontology, we want to extend our system in order to be able to query several sources relying on distinct ontologies which have been previously aligned. Fourth, one important feature which must be added to @ Web is to be able to detect that data included in tables retrieved from different documents of the Web are redundant. We want to use reference reconciliation methods (Sais & al., 2007) to deal with this problem.

CONCLUSION

In this chapter, we have presented an ontology-based data integration system in the field of food safety. This system allows data of different nature (contamination data and consumption data) and of different sources (filled manually, coming from existing databases or extracted from the Web) to feed together a decision support system to compute the exposure of a given population of consumers to chemical contaminants.

The essential point to retain from this chapter is that the ontology is the core of our data integration system. We have proposed three original processes to integrate data according to a domain ontology. First, the semantic annotation process proposes an unsupervised aggregation approach from cells to relations to annotate Web data tables according to a domain ontology. Second, the querying process relies on a flexible querying system which takes into account the pertinence degrees generated by the semantic annotation process. Third, the ontology alignment process proposes to find correspondences between objects of a source ontology and objects of a target ontology by means of rules which exploit the characteristics and their values associated with each objects of both ontologies.

REFERENCES

Baumgartner, R., Flesca, S., & Gottlob, G. (2001). Visual Web information extraction with Lixto. In *Proceedings of the 27th International Conference on Very Large Data Bases* (pp. 119-128).

Baziz, M., Boughanem, M., Prade, H., & Pasi, G. (2006). A fuzzy logic approach to information retrieval using a ontology-based representation of documents. In E. Sanchez (Ed.), *Fuzzy logic and the Semantic Web* (pp. 363-377). Amsterdam: Elsevier.

Buche, P., Dervin, C., Haemmerlé, O., & Thomopoulos, R. (2005). Fuzzy querying of incomplete, imprecise, and heterogeneously structured data in the relational model using ontologies and rules. *IEEE transactions on Fuzzy Systems, 13*(3), 373–383. doi:10.1109/TFUZZ.2004.841736

Buche, P., Dibie-Barthélemy, J., & Ibanescu, L. (2008). Ontology Mapping using fuzzy conceptual graphs and rules. In P. Eklund & O. Haemmerlé (Eds.), *Supplementary Proceedings of the 16th International Conference on Conceptual Structures* (pp. 17-24).

Buche, P., Soler, L., & Tressou, J. (2006). Le logiciel CARAT. In P. Bertail, M. Feinberg, J. Tressou. & P. Verger (Eds.), *Analyse des risques alimentaires* (pp. 305-333). Lavoisier Tech&Doc.

Campi, A., Damiani, E., Guinea, S., Marrara, S., Pasi, G., & Spoletini, P. (2006). A fuzzy extension for the Xpath query language. In *Flexible Query Answering Systems* (LNCS 4027, pp. 210-221). Berlin, Germany: Springer.

Castano, S., Ferrara, A., Montanelli, S., Hess, G. N., & Bruno, S. (2007). *BOEMIE (bootstrapping ontology evolution with multimedia information extraction). State of the art on ontology coordination and matching* (FP6-027538 Delivrable 4.4). Università degli Studi di Milano.

Corby, O., Dieng-Kuntz, R., & Faron-Zucker, C. (2004). Querying the Semantic Web with corese search engine. In *Proceedings of the 16th European Conference on Artificial Intelligence. Subconference PAIS'2004* (pp. 705-709). Amsterdam: IOS Press.

Doan, A., Domingos, P., & Halevy, A. Y. (2003). Learning to match the schemas of data sources: A multistrategy approach. *Machine Learning, 50*(3), 279–301. doi:10.1023/A:1021765902788

Dubois, D., & Prade, H. (1988). *Possibility theory: An approach to computerized processing of uncertainty*. New York: Plenum Press.

Euzenat, J., & Shvaiko, P. (2007). *Ontology matching*. Berlin, Germany: Springer.

Freitag, D., & Kushmerick, N. (2000). Boosted wrapper induction. In *Proceedings of the 17th National Conference on Artificial Intelligence and 20th Conference on Innovative Applications of Artificial Intelligence* (pp. 577-583). Menlo Park, CA: AAAI Press.

Hignette, G., Buche, P., Dibie-Barthélemy, J., & Haemmerlé, O. (2007). An ontology-driven annotation of data tables. In *Proceedings of the Web Information Systems Engineering – WISE 2007 Workshops* (LNCS 4832, pp. 29-40). Berlin, Germany: Springer.

Hutardo, C. A., Poulovassilis, A., & Wood, P. T. (2006). A relaxed approach to RDF querying. In *Proceedings of the 5th International Semantic Web Conference* (LNCS 4273, pp. 314-328). Berlin, Germany: Springer.

Ireland, J. D., & Moller, A. (2000). Review of international food classification and description. *Journal of food composition and analysis, 13*, 529-538.

Kalfoglou, Y., & Schorlemmer, M. (2003). Ontology mapping: The state of the art. *The Knowledge Engineering Review, 18*(1), 1–31. doi:10.1017/S0269888903000651

Mc Meekin, T. A., Baranyi, J., Bowman, J., Dalgaard, P., Kirk, M., & Ross, T. (2006). Information systems in food safety management. *International Journal of Food Microbiology, 112*(3), 181–194. doi:10.1016/j.ijfoodmicro.2006.04.048

Noy, N. F. (2004). Semantic integration: A survey of ontology-based approaches. *SIGMOD Record, 33*(4), 65–70. doi:10.1145/1041410.1041421

Pivk, A., Cimiano, P., & Sure, Y. (2004). From tables to frames. In *Proceedings of the International Semantic Web Conference* (LNCS 3298, pp. 116-181). Berlin, Germany: Springer.

Saïs, F., Pernelle, N., & Rousset, M. C. (2007). L2R: A logical method for reference reconciliation. In [Menlo Park, CA: AAAI Press.]. *Proceedings of the AAAI, 2007*, 329–334.

Soergel, D., Lauser, B., Liang, A., Fisseha, F., Keizer, J., & Katz, S. (2004). Reengineering thesauri for new applications: The AGROVOC example. *Journal of Digital Information, 4*(4). Retrieved from http://www.informatik.uni-trier.de/~ley/db/journals/jodi/jodi4.html

Thomopoulos, R., Buche, B., & Haemmerle, O. (2006). Fuzzy sets defined on a hierarchical domain. *IEEE Transactions on Knowledge and Data Engineering, 18*(10), 1397–1410. doi:10.1109/TKDE.2006.161

Van Rijsbergen, C. J. (1979). *Information retrieval* (2nd ed.)., Department of computer science, University of Glasgow, Scotland: Butterworth-Heinemann.

Zadeh, L. A. (1965). Fuzzy sets. *Information and Control, 8*, 338–353. doi:10.1016/S0019-9958(65)90241-X

Chapter 6
On Modeling and Analysis of Multidimensional Geographic Databases

Sandro Bimonte
LIRIS (Laboratoire d'InfoRmatique en Images et Systèmes d'information), France

ABSTRACT

Data warehouse and OLAP systems are tools to support decision-making. Geographic information systems (GISs) allow memorizing, analyzing and visualizing geographic data. In order to exploit the complex nature of geographic data, a new kind of decision support system has been developed: spatial OLAP (SOLAP). Spatial OLAP redefines main OLAP concepts: dimension, measure and multidimensional operators. SOLAP systems integrate OLAP and GIS functionalities into a unique interactive and flexible framework. Several research tools have been proposed to explore and the analyze spatio-multidimensional databases. This chapter presents a panorama of SOLAP models and an analytical review of research SOLAP tools. Moreover, the authors describe their Web-based system: GeWOlap. GeWOlap is an OLAP-GIS integrated solution implementing drill and cut spatio-multidimensional operators, and it supports some new spatio-multidimensional operators which change dynamically the structure of the spatial hypercube thanks to spatial analysis operators.

INTRODUCTION

A Data Warehouse is a centralized repository of data acquired from external data sources and organized following a multidimensional model (Inmon, 1996) in order to be analyzed by On-Line Analytical Processing (OLAP) applications. OLAP tools provide the ability to interactively explore multidimensional data presenting detailed and aggregated data. The results of analyses are the basis of strategic business decisions.

It has been estimated that about 80% of data in databases contains geo-referenced information (Franklin, 1992). Geographic Information Systems (GISs) allow memorizing, analyzing and visualizing geographic data.

OLAP systems reduce geographic data to simple textual data. Therefore, they do not present any car-

DOI: 10.4018/978-1-60566-756-0.ch006

tographic representation of geographic data. On the contrary, maps are fundamental for the spatial decision making process because they stimulate user's cognitive process, and reveal hidden precious geospatial information. Therefore, some solutions, called Spatial OLAP, which integrate GIS cartographic visualization and interaction functionalities into OLAP systems, have been developed. Spatial OLAP (SOLAP) is "a visual platform built especially to support rapid and easy spatio-temporal analysis and exploration of data following a multidimensional approach comprised of aggregation levels available in cartographic displays as well as in tabular and diagram displays" (Bédard, 1997). Spatial OLAP systems integrate advanced OLAP and GIS functionalities (Rivest et al., 2005; Kouba et al., 2000). They visualize measures on maps at different spatial granularities revealing relations between facts and dimensions (Bédard, et al., 2001). Moreover, maps allow triggering spatio-multidimensional operators through simple mouse clicks, also. Different SOLAP models have been proposed. They address various aspects of geographic information allowing to model different spatio-multidimensional applications. SOLAP applications can address several and different domains: environmental studies, marketing, archaeology, epidemiology, etc.. SOLAP models define the concepts of spatial/geographic dimension, spatial/geographic measure, and spatio-multidimensional operators.

The integration of spatial data into multidimensional models and systems rises several theoretical and implementation issues. Therefore, in this chapter, we introduce main OLAP and GIS concepts. Then, a detailed review of SOLAP models, architectures and research SOLAP tools is presented. The chapter describes our Web-based prototype for the analysis of spatio-multidimensional databases (GeWOlap) (Bimonte et al., 2006; Bimonte et al., 2007a, Bimonte et al., 2007b). We describe main architectural features, and we present spatio-multidimensional and GIS operators using a study case concerning pollution

in French cities. Main outcome and limits of our approach as regards to existing SOLAP tools are detailed, also. Finally, future research directions in spatio-multidimensional visualization and interaction are discussed.

BACKGROUND

Data Warehouse and OLAP Systems

Data warehouse and OLAP systems are business intelligence tools intended to support multidimensional analysis of huge datasets. Data are modelled according to the multidimensional model, which is based on the concepts of dimensions and facts (Inmon, 1996). Dimensions represent analysis axes. They are organized in hierarchies' schemas. Facts, described by numerical values (measures), are subjects of analysis. Measures are analyzed at different granularities corresponding to dimension hierarchies' levels, and they are aggregated by means of SQL aggregation functions. The instance of a multidimensional model is the hypercube. It is a set of cells representing measures at all combinations of dimensions' levels. OLAP operators permit to navigate into the hypercube. Most common operators are drill and cut operators. Drill operators (i.e., Roll-Up and Drill-Down) let navigating into dimension hierarchies aggregating measures. Cut operators (i.e. Slice and Dice) permit to reduce the analysis space, by selecting a sub-set of dimensions members.

Usually, data warehouse and OLAP systems are based on a three-tier architecture. The first tier is the data warehouse, where data, coming from external heterogeneous sources, are uniformed and stored according to the multidimensional model. The second tier is the OLAP Server. It implements OLAP operators and pre-computes a set of multidimensional queries to grant effective query response times. The OLAP server implements other advanced functionalities also, such as control accesses, multidimensional calculation engine,

Figure 1. Spatial SQL a) Spatial table creation b) Spatial query c) Geographic object creation d) Tabular and cartographic representations

```
CREATE TABLE DEPT (
NOM VARCHAR2 (30),
AREA NUMBER,
POP NUMBER,
GEOM SDO_GEOMETRY);
```

(a)

```
SELECT NOM, POP
FROM DEPT
WHERE
SDO_GEOM.SDO_AREA(GEOM,0.005)> 5000;
```

(b)

```
INSERT   INTO DEPT VALUES (
'AIN',
50000,
154,
SDO_GEOMETRY(2003, NULL, NULL
SDO_ELEM_INFO_ARRAY(1,1003,1),
SDO_ORDINATE_ARRAY(3.3,6.5,4.5,
3.3))
);
```

(c)

NOM	AREA	POP	GEOM
AIN	50000	15.	...
RHONE	60000	250	...

(d)

etc. Finally, the OLAP client allows visualizing and formulating OLAP queries in a unique, interactive and user-friendly visual interface composed of graphic displays and pivot tables.

Geographic Information Systems

A Geographic Information System encompasses a set of tools for organizing, memorizing, analyzing and visualizing geographic information (Longley et al., 2001).

Geographic information is the representation of geo-referenced real phenomena. It is described by a spatial component (the shape and the position on earth surface) and a set of alphanumerical attributes and (spatial) relationships.

Main GIS functionality is the integration and memorization of geographic data. Data are organized in layers. A layer represents a set of geographic data of the same type (i.e. roads, buildings, departments, etc.). Each element of the layer (geographic object or feature) is described by geometry and some alphanumeric attributes. Layers are stored in GIS using Spatial DBMSs, which extend classical DBMS with spatial types (i.e. point, line, etc.) and spatial functions (i.e. overlap, etc.). As an example, the spatial table representing French departments, and a spatial query selecting departments with an area greater than 5000 Km2, using Oracle's Spatial SQL, are shown on figure 1a and figure 1b, respectively. A tuple creation and its cartographic representation are shown in figure 1c and figure 1d, respectively.

GIS's geographic data can be analyzed by means of spatial analysis methods. They allow estimating, predicting and understanding spatial data and phenomena by means of (spatial) statistic (i.e. centroid, etc.), transformation (i.e. buffer, etc.) and querying techniques. These methods are supported by visual representation of maps' features. Indeed, visualization plays a central role for the spatial analysis process. Map feature's geometries are represented using a two dimensional space. Alphanumeric attributes are visualized with graphic displays (i.e. bars, pies charts, etc.), coded using visual variables (size, value, colour, shape, orientation and grain) (Bertin & Bonin, 1992). GISs make possible to change map's scale, reduce visualized features, access to alphanumeric information using the map, etc. Sometimes, maps provide also an interface to advanced (visual) analysis techniques. Users can explore alphanumeric data, perform complex analysis methods, and obtain personalized and complex visual representations of data by simply interacting with map's features (interactive maps). Interactive maps are the basis of geovisualization systems (MacEachren, et al., 2004). Such systems integrate scientific visualization and image analysis techniques, and GIS tools into an interactive, flexible and user-friendly framework in order to explore and analyze spatial data. Interactive capabilities are mandatory for spatial decision-making process (MacEachren & Kraak, 1997).

SPATIO-MULTIDIMENSIONAL DATABASES: MODELS AND TOOLS

Spatio-Multidimensional Models

The more natural and common manner to integrate spatial information into multidimensional models, is to use it as a dimension. As defined in Bédard et al. (2001), a spatial dimension can be "spatial non geometric" (i.e. with text only members), "spatial geometric" (i.e. with members with a cartographic representation) or "mixed spatial" (i.e. combining cartographic and textual members). Malinowsky & Zimányi (2005) define a spatial dimension as a set of spatial hierarchies. A "spatial hierarchy" is a hierarchy with at least one level with the spatial attribute (spatial level). Topological intersection or inclusion relationships exist between members of different spatial levels. Bimonte (2008) proposes the concept of "Geographic Dimension" enriching spatial dimensions with "Map Generalization Hierarchies". "Map Generalization Hierarchy" represents geographic information at different scales or according secondary themes where the members of a level are the result of map generalization operators applied to the members of the lower

level. Map generalization is the process used to derive data and maps for secondary scales and/or themes, preserving a good and clear representation focused on the goal of the map (Weibel & Dutton, 2001). Map generalization provides a simplified vision of the spatial phenomenon enriching spatio-multidimensional analysis capabilities and improving SOLAP clients' visualization.

An example of SOLAP application using a spatial dimension is a study for pollution supervision in French cities. This multidimensional application presents three dimensions: "Time", "Pollutants", and "Location" (spatial dimension), and a numerical fact, "Pollution". This fact is depicted by three measures giving minimum, maximum and average pollution values (see Figure 2) (Bimonte et al., 2007a). This multidimensional application answers questions like "What are the average, min and max values per month, and pollutant for departments with population above 2M?"

A very different way to introduce spatial information in data warehouses is using it as an analysis subject, i.e. as a fact. Different definitions of the spatial measure can be found in literature: a collection of geometries (spatial objects) (Stefanovic et al., 2000; Rivest et al. 2001), geometries or numerical values resulting from spatial (i.e. topological and metric) operators (Malinowsky & Zimányi, 2004), and/or spatial members (Marchand et al., 2003). Spatial aggregations (i.e. union, intersection, etc.) replace SQL SUM, MIN, MAX, AVG, and COUNT functions. Maps, then, are the cells of the hypercube.

Let us take the spatio-multidimensional model given in figure 3a. The spatial attribute of the "City" level of application of figure 2 is now used as spatial measure. The spatial measure is aggregated using the topological union. Pollution values grouped by 5mg/l are used as analysis dimension. This model analyzes polluted French cities according to time, pollutants and pollution values. In this model, the user should be able to deduce information about the influence of geographical location of cities in the pollution problem.

Figure 2. Multidimensional model with spatial dimension

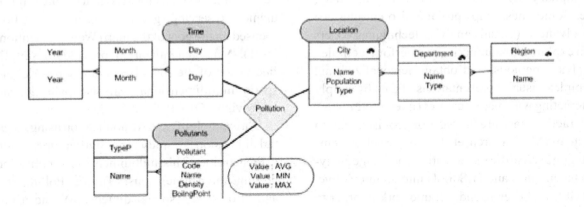

Descriptive attributes of geographic data could be useful to the spatio-multidimensional decisional process. Thus, Bimonte (2008) introduces the concept of "Geographic Measure". A "Geographic Measure" is a geographic object described by alphanumeric and spatial attributes. Moreover, it could belong to one or many hierarchy schemas. This establishes a complete symmetry of geographic measures and geographic dimensions.

Replacing the spatial measure of the multidimensional application in the previous example with the geographic measure representing cities (see Figure 3b), it should be possible to answer queries like: "What cities, their population, and their socio-economic types, are polluted by CO2 per month?" Indeed, a city is a geographic object described by geometry and two alphanumeric attributes: population and socio-economic type. Note that a (spatial) aggregation function is applied to each (spatial) attribute of the geographic measure (i.e. topological union for geometry, list for name, sum for population and a ratio for socio-economic type).

Spatio-multidimensional operators extend drill and cut OLAP operators. "Spatial Roll-up" and "Spatial Drill-down" authorize to navigate into spatial dimensions by the simple interaction with the map component of the SOLAP user-interface (Rivest et al., 2005). "Spatial Slice"

makes possible cutting the spatial hypercube by selecting directly spatial members through SO-LAP user-interface (Rivest et al., 2005), using spatial/alphanumeric predicates (Sampaio et al., 2006) or spatial analysis operators such as buffer (Scotch & Parmanto, 2006). Exploiting the symmetrical representation of geographic dimensions and measures, Bimonte (2008) proposes two operators, "Permute" and "Measure navigation". "Permute" allows exchanging dimension and geographic measure. This operator dynamically modifies the structure of the spatial hypercube. "Measure navigation" allows navigating into the geographic measure's hierarchy, changing granularity of the measure on the fly. For instance, since cities belong to departments (Figure 3b), "Measure navigation" operator permits to analyze polluted French departments (instead of cities) along time and pollutants dimensions. Moreover, to make the spatio-multidimensional paradigm more flexible and being closer to spatial analysis process, Bimonte et al. (2007b) propose a new kind of operators which change the structure of the spatial hypercube through the introduction of new spatial members into geographic dimension thanks to spatial analysis operators.

Figure 3. Spatio-multidimensional models a) Spatial measure, b) Geographic measure

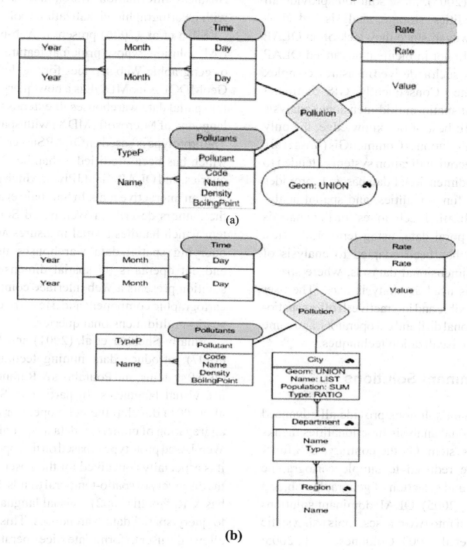

(a)

(b)

Spatial OLAP Tools: A Panorama

Bédard et al., (2005) identify three typologies of Spatial OLAP tools (OLAP dominant, GIS dominant and OLAP-GIS integrated), according to their OLAP and GIS functionalities. Some prototypes have been implemented. They allow an effective spatio-multidimensional analysis of spatial data warehouses thanks to advanced OLAP and GIS functionalities. However, an overall set of mandatory functionalities has not been defined,

yet. Indeed, the following SOLAP research tools' panorama reveals that spatial data mining tools, spatial analysis methods and geovisualization techniques should enrich spatio-multidimensional operators.

GIS Dominant Solutions

GIS dominant solutions simulate OLAP server thanks to a relational database modelled using the star or the snow-flake schema. As shown in

Bédard et al. (2005), these solutions provide all GIS functionalities: storage, analysis and visualization. However, since they lack of an OLAP Server, they do not implement advanced OLAP functionalities, such as derived measures, complex hierarchies, etc.. Consequently, GIS dominant solutions limit spatio-multidimensional analysis capabilities. To best of our knowledge, the only GIS dominant solution is CommonGis (Voss et al., 2004). It is a geovisualization system extended to support multidimensional databases. It provides multi-criteria functionalities, and spatial analysis and visualization techniques for the analysis of spatio-temporal data, using temporal series. CommonGIS has been adapted to analysis of spatio-multidimensional datasets, where spatial information is used as analysis axes. The user interface is flexible and interactive. It offers spatio-multidimensional drill and cut operators, and some advanced geovisualization techniques.

OLAP Dominant Solutions

OLAP dominant solutions provide all advanced multidimensional analysis functionalities thanks to an OLAP system. On the contrary, GIS functionalities are reduced to simple cartographic visualization and selection of geographic objects (Bédard et al., 2005). OLAP dominant solutions can be grouped into two classes: tools using static maps (Stolte et al., 2003; Colonnese et al., 2005; Mohraz, 2000) and tools using interactive maps (Silva et al., 2006; Sampaio et al., 2006; Shekhar et al., 2001; Han et al., 1997; Pourabbas & Rafanelli, 2002).

Polaris system (Stolte et al., 2003) allows the visualization of alphanumeric measures, using non-interactive maps incorporated into the cells of the pivot table. PostGeOLAP (Colonnese et al., 2005) is an open source SOLAP tool supporting numerical measures and spatial dimensions. It provides a set of methods to create spatio-multidimensional databases and materialize spatial views. In Mohraz (2000) the OLAP system SAP's

Business Information Warehouse is integrated with a cartographic visualization tool.

Silva et al. (2006) present a Web-based SOLAP solution, whose principal feature is the use of geographic Web services for the definition of GeoMDQL. GeoMDQL is a new query language for spatial data warehouses. It extends the OLAP language of Microsoft (MDX) with spatial types. The prototype is based on OLAP Server Mondrian, which has been modified to handle GeoMDQL queries, and OLAP client JPivot, which is coupled with an interactive map. In Sampaio et al. (2006), the authors describe a Web-based SOLAP system which handles spatial measures and allows querying spatial data warehouses using drill and cut operators on spatial dimensions. This solution presents a Web interface composed of a cartographic component and a text zone to define spatio-multidimensional queries.

Finally Shekhar et al. (2001) and Han et al. (1997) introduce data mining techniques into OLAP systems, and Pourabbas & Rafanelli (2002) use visual languages. In particular, Shekhar et al., (2001) develop the cube operator extending aggregation of numerical data to spatial data. The Web-based prototype is based on this operator, and it is especially conceived for the observation and the discovery of spatio-temporal trends. In Pourabbas & Rafanelli (2002) a visual language is used to query spatial data warehouses. This approach allows the user to formulate slice operations using an iconic language.

OLAP-GIS Integrated Solutions

OLAP-GIS integrated solutions combine GIS and OLAP functionalities. GIS analysis and visualization functionalities enrich and complete OLAP navigation and visualization functionalities, allowing a real and effective analysis of spatial data warehouses. Some OLAP-GIS integrated solutions have been developed (Rivest et al., 2005; Scotch & Parmanto, 2006; Matias & Moura-Pires, 2005; Escribano et al., 2007).

These solutions store spatial multidimensional data using a Spatial DBMS. Spatial data warehouses allow modelling complex spatial hierarchies, topological intersection relationships, and spatial/geographic measures. Star and snowflake schemas are modified to handle spatial data (Stefanovic et al., 2000; Malinowsky & Zimányi, 2007).

(S)OLAP Servers implement spatio-multidimensional operators explicitly taking into account spatial members' geometry to define cutting spatial predicates and to perform drill operators. They allow defining spatial members, hierarchies, measures and derived measures.

SOLAP clients improve OLAP clients thanks to cartographic visualization and interaction functionalities. They combine and synchronize tabular and graphic visualization components with interactive maps (Rivest et al., 2005). SOLAP operators are available through the simple interaction with maps. Each spatial level corresponds to a cartographic layer. Performing (S)OLAP operators on the pivot table and/or on the map will result in the calculation and displaying of a new clickable map (interactive map), merging different layers according to the different granularities selected for the spatial members, and displaying aggregated and/or detailed measures with visual variables and/or graphic displays (i.e. bars, pies, etc.) (Rivest et al., 2005).

For instance, considering the application of figure 2, one should be able to show and to interact with a map displaying average and minimum values for selected months and pollutants at the granularity of cities for one department, and at department level for the rest of the map.

In order to take advantage from human visual perception capabilities, interactive maps should be coupled with advanced geovisualization techniques such as MultiMaps, Space-Time Cubes, etc. (MacEachren et al., 2004). Finally, GIS operators are available through the cartographic component. Indeed, decision makers should be able to customize their maps, add layers, query the spatial data warehouse, use spatial analysis tools, etc.

Rivest et al. (2005) present a SOLAP tool which permits to enrich the elements of the spatial data warehouse with multimedia documents such as photos, videos, etc.. SOVAT (Scotch & Parmanto, 2006) extends SOLAP functionalities with (spatial) data mining tools (i.e. clustering, etc.). It provides also statistic and spatial analysis methods. The SOLAP tool described in Matias & Moura-Pires (2005) allows overlapping two hypercubes using their spatial dimensions. PIET (Escribano et al., 2007) is a Web-based SOLAP solution providing a new query processing method. Spatial members are first organized into open convex polygons, and then the overlay of these polygons is used to answer to multidimensional queries using user-defined window queries.

In the following paragraph we describe our OLAP-GIS integrated solution.

GeWOlap: Spatio-Multidimensional Analysis Tool

GeWOlap is a Web-based system for exploration and analysis of spatio-multidimensional databases (Bimonte et al., 2006; Bimonte et al., 2007a, Bimonte et al., 2007b). It provides advanced (S)OLAP and GIS functionalities through a flexible interactive and user-friendly interface. GeWOlap is based on three tier architecture.

The spatial data warehouse tier is implemented using Oracle for its native support for spatial data and its object-relational capabilities.

OLAP server Mondrian provides an easily customizable, full featured (i.e. aggregate tables, user-defined functions, complex hierarchies, MDX support, etc.) OLAP server. It is important to notice that no spatial extension has been integrated into Mondrian. Spatial data is represented using simple textual labels. In order to overcome this limitation, GeWOlap handles spatial data in the spatial data warehouse and client tiers, and it provides a mapping mechanism between spatial data and their textual representation in the OLAP Server.

The client tier is implemented using the OLAP client JPivot to provide JSP pages, and a Java

Figure 4. GeWOlap's user interface

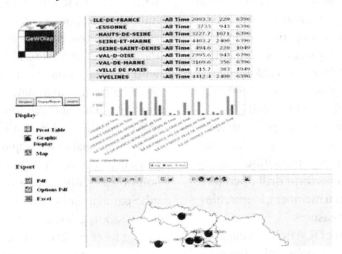

applet developed using MapXtreme Java (MapXtreme) to support map visualization/interaction and GIS functionalities. The client tier allows a visual representation of spatio-multidimensional structures [(geographic) dimensions and measures] through pivot table, graphic displays and interactive map.

Figure 4 displays the visual interface of GeWOlap for the application of figure 2. The pivot table represents pollution values for Ile de France region and for its departments (Essone, Hautes de Seine, etc.). The cartographic component shows a thematic map representing departments' pollution values using pie charts.

Spatio-multidimensional and GIS operators are accessible through the simple interaction with the pivot table and the interactive map of the client using only few mouse clicks.

In particular, GeWOlap provides a set of drill operators which are available through the interaction with the pivot table and the map: "roll-up drill-down replace", "drill-down position", "expand-all", "drill-through" (Bimonte et al., 2007a).

For instance, let us suppose that the user wishes to "see" the measures for departments of the Ile de France region. By pointing the mouse on that region she/he can apply the drill-down position operator (figure 5a). As a result, the pivot table displays average pollution values for the Ile de France region, and for other departments (Figure 5b). Several synchronization problems rise from the topological inclusion relationships between spatial members of different levels, and the number of measure values that must be displayed. For example, unlike the pivot table, the map cannot display at the same time a region and its departments, and visualize the pollution values for each pollutant granting a good cartographic readability.

The user can cut the hypercube by using the "Cube Navigator" tool provided by JPivot. The Cube Navigator provides a tree representation of dimension members which can be used to customize pivot table axes and select a sub-set of members. Moreover, GeWOlap extends OLAP cut operators by introducing two new cut operators: "Slice Predicate" and "Slice Position" (Bimonte et al., 2007b). Thanks to "Slice Predicate", the user can select spatial members by directly clicking on the interactive map. "Slice Predicate" allows cutting the hypercube through Spatial SQL queries.

Let us suppose the user is interested in pollution values for departments crossed by from the

Figure 5. Spatial Drill-down position, a) Input: Ile de France region, b) Output: Departments of Ile de France

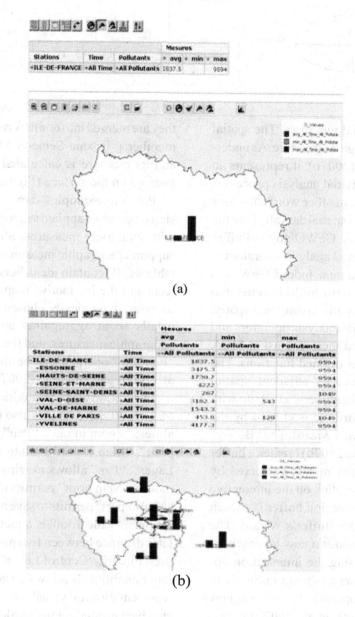

(a)

(b)

Seine river. Then, thanks to the Slice Predicate's wizard she/he defines its spatial query:

```
select * from MEASURES_VIEW, RIVERS
where (MEASURES_VIEW.NAME = 'Es-
sone') OR... OR (MEASURES_VIEW.
NAME = 'Yvelines') AND SDO_GEOM.
RELATE(MEASURES_VIEW.GEOM,
```

```
'ANYINTERACT', RIVERS.GEOM, 0.5)=
'TRUE' AND RIVERS.NAME = 'Seine'
```

As a result, the pivot table and the map show only the departments satisfying the spatial predicate.

Cut and drill operators allow to explore the spatial hypercube using, directly or not, the spa-

Figure 6. Overlay operator

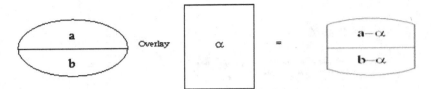

tial attribute of the spatial members. The spatial hypercube does not change its structure. As underlined in Bimonte, et al. (2007b), it represents an important limit, as the spatial analysis process is iterative and flexible, or, in other words, the user can change and transform spatial data all along the spatial decisional process. GeWOlap fits buffer, overlay and dissolve spatial analysis operators to the multidimensional paradigm. Indeed, GeWOlap provides three new spatio-multidimensional operators which dynamically create new spatial members thanks to spatial analysis operators and calculate their associated measures using MDX formula and/or Java user-defined functions. The "Dissolve" operator merges adjacent spatial members having an alphanumeric attribute with the same value. This attribute is chosen by the user through the Dissolve's wizard. The "Buffer" operator (Bimonte, et al., 2007b) creates a buffer region around one spatial member selected by the user through a mouse click on the interactive map. The distance of the region buffer is chosen by the user thanks to the Buffer's wizard. The GIS overlay operator creates a new layer whose features are obtained using the intersection operator on two input layers as shown in Figure 6. GeWOlap adapts this operator to create n new spatial members (Bimonte, et al., 2007b).

We present here an example of the "Dissolve" operator as it is representative of this class of operators. An example is shown in figure 7. Starting from the query represented in figure 7a, which shows pollution average values for Ile de France's departments, the analyst chooses the department type attribute. Since "Essone" and "Seine-et-Marne" are adjacent and their type is "Commercial", then

they are merged into one new region. A new spatial member ("Essone-Seine-et-Marne") is created, and its measure is calculated using a weighted average on the surface (Figure 7b).

Previous examples show spatio-multidimensional operators applied to geographic dimensions with numerical measures. Similarly, GeWOlap supports geographic measures. In this case, pivot table's cells contain identifiers of geographic objects and the interactive map shows geographic measure dynamically chosen by the user. More details about aggregation and visualization of geographic measures, and the implementation of "Permute" operator can be found in Bimonte et al. (2006) and Bimonte (2007).

In addition to spatio-multidimensional operators, GeWOlap provides also pure GIS functionalities: "Zoom in/out", "Pan", "Retrieve", "Map print", "Map export", "Rule tool" and "Control Layer". "Pan" allows moving the map using the mouse, "Map print" permits to print the map and "Map export" permits to save map in JPG and PDF formats. "Rule Tool" is a metric tool that calculates distance between two points selected by the user. Finally, "Control Layer" provides different functionalities. It allows customizing the visual representation of visual variables: colour, size, etc., backgrounding the spatio-multidimensional application by adding raster and/or vector layers, and querying the spatial data warehouse using Spatial SQL.

In conclusion, GeWOlap is a full-featured OLAP-GIS integrated solution, which supports geographic dimension and numerical measures, and implements drill and cut multidimensional operators. Moreover, GeWOlap enriches existing SOLAP

Figure 7. Dissolve operator, a) Input: Ile de France's departments, b) Output: Departments of Ile de France and the new spatial member Essone-Seine-et-Marne

(a)

(b)

tools functionalities supporting measures defined as geographic objects (geographic measures) and implementing three new spatio-multidimensional operators which change the structure of the spatial hypercube thanks to spatial analysis operators. However, some limits remain to overcome: the integration of ad-hoc indexing techniques (Papadias, et al., 2002) to improve the performance of our system, and the implementation of mechanisms for automatically detecting and computing spatial materialized views (Colonese et al., 2005).

FUTURE RESEARCH DIRECTIONS

Spatial OLAP technologies have reached maturity. They allow an effective multidimensional analysis of spatial data warehouses. However, the introduction of complex spatial data raises several problems.

Map generalization is mandatory for SOLAP systems (Bimonte, 2008). On the other hand, map generalization implies the reformulation of classical spatial hierarchies by introducing multi-association relationships and taking into account imprecise measures. (Un)Fortunately, visualization of multidimensional imprecise (spatial) data is an open issue (Pang, 2008).

Spatial OLAP models and tools are based on the vector representation of spatial data. Field data, which represent spatial data as a regular grid whose cells are associated with alphanumeric attributes, could be used for spatio-multidimensional analysis. Indeed, Ahmed & Miquel (2005) provide a continuous representation of spatial dimensions, but the introduction of field data as analysis subject remains unexplored. Aggregation of field data could be supported by Map Algebra operators. Map Algebra defines a set of operations on field data (local, focal and zone operators) (Tomlin, 1990). Adaptation of Map Algebra to multidimensional data structures, definition of pre-aggregation and visualization/interaction techniques for continuous measures are challenges to overcome for an effective SOLAP tool supporting field data.

The integration of trajectories data into data warehouses raises several problems because classical multidimensional models are based on discrete facts and dimensions and they do not take into account spatial predicates. This problem has been investigated by some works (Wan et al., 2007; Orlando et al., 2007) in the last years. However, the definition of a SOLAP client to visually query and analyze trajectory data warehouses is an unexplored important challenge.

Bertolotto et al. (2007) affirm that visual analysis of spatial data mining results is improved by exploiting the third dimension of spatial data through an interactive 3D geovisualization system. The integration of advanced geovisualization techniques within OLAP clients in order to support multidimensional 3D spatial data is an interesting research direction.

Finally, several semiology problems have to be solved for the correct and relevant visualization of measures. Measures can be displayed with labels but it is sometimes worthwhile to use more expressive, significant visual components. The

way measures will be displayed on the map must depend on several criteria: nature of the measure (quantitative or qualitative measure), number of measures to be displayed, and current representation of the spatial dimension (point, line or polygon). Moreover, GIS users are usually specific knowledge domain decision makers. GIS takes into account their profiles and preferences in order to provide well-suited cartographic visualization (Vangenot, 2001). Thus, the ambition is to define a method to automatically find out the most appropriate cartographic representation of SOLAP queries results. The visual variables (size, colours, etc.) and the graphic representation (i.e. bar, pie, etc.) used to represent measures on maps can be automatically deduced thanks to SOLAP query patterns taking into account number, type and current representation of dimensions, measures types, aggregation functions involved in the query and user profile and/or preferences (Bellatreche, et al., 2005).

CONCLUSION

Spatial OLAP refers to the introduction of spatial data into data warehouse and OLAP systems. SOLAP enhances decision analysis capabilities of OLAP systems allowing exploiting the complex nature of geographic information. SOLAP redefines main OLAP concepts. It defines spatial/geographic dimensions as dimensions with spatial attributes, spatial measures as a collection of spatial objects or the result of spatial operators, and geographic measures as geographic objects belonging to hierarchy schemas. SOLAP extends multidimensional navigation operators defining spatial drill and cutting operators which allow navigating into spatial/geographic dimensions and cutting the hypercube thanks to spatial and non-spatial predicates. Other spatio-multidimensional operators permit to change the structure of the spatial hypercube thanks to spatial analysis operators, to permute dimensions and geographic measures, and to navigate in the hierarchy of the geographic measure. SOLAP tools are based on the integration of OLAP and GIS functionalities. In this work, we have provided an analytical overview of SOLAP tools grouping them according to their architecture approach. We described our Web-based prototype (GeWOlap) for the multidimensional analysis of huge spatial datasets. GeWOlap combines SOLAP and GIS operators into a unique interactive and user-friendly framework. GeWOlap supports geographic dimensions and geographic measures, and it introduces some new spatio-multidimensional operators which allow to change the structure of the hypercube thanks to dissolve, buffer and overlay GIS operators.

REFERENCES

Ahmed, T., & Miquel, M. (2005). Multidimensional structures dedicated to continuous spatiotemporal phenomena. In M. Jackson, D. Nelson, & S. Stirk (Eds.), *Proceedings of the 22nd British National Conference on Databases* (Vol. 3567, pp. 29-40). Berlin, Germany: Springer.

Bédard, Y. (1997). Spatial OLAP. In *Proceedings of the 2nd Forum annuel sur la R-D, Géomatique VI: Un monde accessible*, Montréal, Canada.

Bédard, Y., Merrett, T., & Han, J. (2001). Fundaments of spatial data warehousing for geographic knowledge discovery. In H. Miller & J. Han (Eds.), *Geographic data mining and knowledge discovery* (pp. 53-73). London: Taylor & Francis.

Bédard, Y., Proulx, M., & Rivest, S. (2005). Enrichissement du OLAP pour l'analyse géographique: Exemples de réalisation et différentes possibilités technologiques. In *Revue des Nouvelles Technologies de l'Information, Entrepôts de données et l'Analyse en ligne* (pp. 1-20).

Bellatreche, L., Giacometti, A., Laurent, D., & Mouloudi, H. (2005). A personalization framework for OLAP queries. In I. Y. Song & Y. Trujillo (Eds.), *Proceedings of the ACM 8th International Workshop on Data Warehousing and OLAP* (pp. 9-18). New York: AMC Press.

Bertin, J., & Bonin, S. (1992). *La graphique et le traitement graphique de l'information*. Paris: Flammarion.

Bertolotto, M., Di Martino, S., Ferrucci, F., & Kechadi, T. (2007). Towards a framework for mining and analyzing spatio-temporal datasets. *International Journal of Geographical Information Science, 21*(8), 1–12. doi:10.1080/13658810701349052

Bimonte, S. (2007). *Vers l'intégration de l'information géographique dans les entrepôts de données et l'analyse en ligne: De la modélisation à la visualization*. Unpublished doctoral dissertation, INSA Lyon, France.

Bimonte, S. (2008). Des entrepôts de données, l'analyse en ligne et l'information géographique. *Journal of Decision Systems*.

Bimonte, S., Tchounikine, A., & Miquel, M. (2007). Spatial OLAP: Open issues and a Web based prototype. In M. Wachowicz & L. Bodum (Eds.), *Proceedings of the 10th AGILE International Conference on Geographic Information Science*.

Bimonte, S., Tchounikine, A., Miquel, M., & Laurini, R. (2007). Vers l'intégration de l'analyse spatiale et multidimensionnelle. In M. Batton-Hubert, T. Joliveau, & S. Lardon (Eds.), *Proceedings of the Colloque International de GEOmatique et d'Analyse Spatiale*.

Bimonte, S., Wehrle, P., Tchounikine, A., & Miquel, M. (2006). GeWOlap: A Web based spatial OLAP proposal. In R. Meersman, Z. Tari, & P. Herrero (Eds.), *Proceedings of the Workshop on Semantic-Based Geographical Information Systems* (Vol. 4278, pp. 1596-1605). Berlin, Germany: Springer.

Colonese, G., Manhaes, R., Montenegro, S., Carvalho, R., & Tanaka, A. (2005). PostGeoOlap: an open-source tool for decision support. In *Proceedings of the 2nd Simpósio Brasileiro de Sistemas de Informação*.

Escribano, A., Gomez, L., Kuijpers, B., & Vaisman, A. (2007). Piet: A GIS-OLAP implementation. In I. Y. Song & T. B. Pedersen (Eds.), *Proceedings of the ACM 10th International Workshop on Data Warehousing and OLAP* (pp. 73-80). New York: ACM Press.

Franklin, C. (1992). An introduction to geographic information systems: Linking maps to databases. *Database, 15*(2), 13–21.

Han, J., Kopersky, K., & Stefanovic, N. (1997). GeoMiner: A system prototype for spatial data mining. In J. Peckham (Ed.), *Proceedings of the ACM SIGMOD International Conference on Management of Data* (pp. 553-556). New York: ACM Press.

Inmon, W. H. (1996). *Building the data warehouse* (2nd ed.). New York: John Wiley & Sons.

Kouba, Z., Matousek, K., & Miksovsky, P. (2000). On data warehouse and GIS integration. In M. Ibrahim, J. Kung, & N. Revell (Eds.), *Proceedings of the 11th International Conference on Database and Expert Systems Applications* (Vol. 1873, pp. 604-613). London: Springer.

Longley, P., Goodchild, M., Maguire, D., & Rhind, D. (2001). *Geographic information systems and science*. New York: John Wiley & Sons.

MacEachren, A., Gahegan, M., Pike, W., Brewer, I., Cai, G., Lengerich, E., & Hardisty, F. (2004). Geovisualization for knowledge construction and decision support. *IEEE Computer graphics and application, 24*(1) 13-17.

MacEachren, A., & Kraak, M. (1997). Exploratory cartographic visualization: Advancing the agenda. *Computers & Geosciences, 23*(4), 335–343. doi:10.1016/S0098-3004(97)00018-6

Malinowsky, E., & Zimányi, E. (2004). Representing spatiality in a conceptual multidimensional model. In D. Pfoser, I. Cruz, & M. Ronthaler (Eds.), *Proceedings of the 12th ACM International Workshop on Geographic Information Systems* (pp. 12-22). New York: ACM Press.

Malinowsky, E., & Zimányi, E. (2005). Spatial hierarchies and topological relationships in SpatialMultiDimER model. In M. Jackson, D. Nelson, & S. Stirk (Eds.), *Proceedings of the 22nd British National Conference on Databases* (Vol. 3567, pp. 17-28). Berlin, Germany: Springer.

Malinowsky, E., & Zimányi, E. (2007). Logical representation of a conceptual model for spatial data warehouses. *Geoinformatica.*

Marchand, P., Brisebois, A., Bédad, Y., & Edwards, G. (2003). Implementation and evaluation of a hypercube-based method for spatio-temporal exploration and analysis. *Journal of the International Society of Photogrammetry and Remote Sensing, 59*(1), 6–20. doi:10.1016/j.isprsjprs.2003.12.002

Matias, R., & Moura-Pires, J. (2005). Spatial on-line analytical processing: A tool to analyze the emission of pollutants in industrial installations. In C. Bento, A. Cardoso, & G. Dias (Eds.), *Proceedings of the 5th International Workshop on Extraction of Knowledge from Databases and Warehouses.*

Mohraz, K. (2000). Geographical analysis in SAP business information warehouse. In K. Li, K. Makki, N. Pissinou, & S. Ravada (Eds.), *Proceedings of the 8th ACM Symposium on Advances in Geographic Information Systems* (pp. 191-193). Washington: ACM Press.

Orlando, S., Orsini, R., Raffaetà, A., Roncato, A., & Silvestri, C. (2007). Spatio-temporal aggregations in trajectory data warehouses. In I. Y. Song, J. Eder, & T. M. Nguyen (Eds.), *Proceedings of the 9th International Conference Data Warehousing and Knowledge Discovery* (Vol. 4654, pp. 66-77). Berlin, Germany: Springer.

Pang, A. (2008). Visualizing uncertainty in natural hazards. In A. Bostrom, S. French, & S. Gottlieb (Eds.), *Risk assessment, modeling and decision support: Strategic directions series: Risk, governance and society* (pp. 261-294). Berlin, Germany: Springer.

Papadias, D., Tao, Y., Kalnis, P., & Zhang, J. (2002). Indexing spatio-temporal data warehouses. In *Proceedings of the 18th International Conference on Data Engineering* (pp. 166-175). Los Alamitos, CA, USA: IEEE Computer Society.

Pourabbas, E., & Rafanelli, M. (2002). A pictorial query language for querying geographic databases using positional and OLAP operators. *SIGMOD Record, 31*(2), 22–27. doi:10.1145/565117.565121

Rivest, S., Bédard, Y., & Marcand, P. (2001). Towards better support for spatial decision-making: Defining the characteristics of spatial on-line analytical processing. *Journal of the Canadian Institute of Geomatics, 55*(4), 539–555.

Rivest, S., Bédard, Y., Proulx, M., Nadeaum, M., Hubert, F., & Pastor, J. (2005). SOLAP: Merging business intelligence with geospatial technology for interactive spatio-temporal exploration and analysis of data. *Journal of International Society for Photogrammetry and Remote Sensing, 60*(1), 17–33. doi:10.1016/j.isprsjprs.2005.10.002

Sampaio, M., Sousa, A., & Baptista, C. (2006). Towards a logical multidimensional model for spatial data warehousing and OLAP. In Y. Song & P. Vassiliadis (Eds.), *Proceedings of the 9th ACM International Workshop on Data Warehousing and OLAP* (pp. 83-90). New York: ACM Press.

Scotch, M., & Parmanto, B. (2006). Development of SOVAT: A numerical-spatial decision support system for community health assessment research. *International Journal of Medical Informatics, 75*(10-11), 771–784. doi:10.1016/j.ijmedinf.2005.10.008

Shekar, S., Lu, C., Tan, X., Chawla, S., & Vatsavai, R. (2001). Map cube: A visualization tool for spatial data warehouses. In H. Miller & J. Han (Eds.), *Geographic data mining and knowledge discovery* (pp. 74-109). London: Taylor & Francis.

Silva, J., Times, V., & Salgado, A. (2006). An open source and Web based framework for geographic and multidimensional processing. In H. Haddad (Ed.), *Proceedings of the ACM Symposium on Applied Computing* (pp. 63-67). New York: ACM Press.

Stefanovic, N., Han, J., & Kopersky, K. (2000). Object-based selective materialization for efficient implementation of spatial data cubes. *IEEE Transactions on Knowledge and Data Engineering, 12*(6), 938–958. doi:10.1109/69.895803

Stolte, C., Tang, D., & Hanrahan, P. (2003). Multiscale visualization using data cubes. *IEEE Transactions on Visualization and Computer Graphics, 9*(2), 176–187. doi:10.1109/TVCG.2003.1196005

Tomlin, D. (1990). *Geographic information systems and cartographic modeling*. Upper Saddle River, NJ: Prentice Hall.

Vangenot, C. (2001). Supporting decision-making with alternative data representations. *Journal of Geographic Information and Decision Analysis, 5*(2), 66–82.

Voss, A., Hernandez, V., Voss, H., & Scheider, S. (2004). Interactive Visual exploration of multidimensional data: Requirements for CommonGIS with OLAP. In *Proceedings of the 15th International Workshop on Database and Expert Systems Applications* (pp. 883-887). Los Alamitos, CA: IEEE Computer Society.

Wan, T., Zeitouni, K., & Meng, X. (2007). An OLAP system for network-constrained moving objects. In Y. Cho, R. Wainwright, H. Haddad, S. Shin, & Y. Koo (Eds.), *Proceedings of the ACM symposium on Applied computing* (pp. 13-18). New York: ACM Press.

Weibel, R., & Dutton, G. (2001). Generalizing spatial data and dealing with multiple representations. In P. Longley, M. Goodchild, D. Maguire, & D. Rhind (Eds.), *Geographic Information systems and science* (pp. 125-155). New York: John Wiley & Sons.

KEY TERMS AND DEFINITIONS

Spatial OLAP: Visual platform built especially to support rapid and easy spatio-temporal analysis and exploration of data following a multidimensional approach comprised of aggregation levels available in cartographic displays as well as in tabular and diagram displays.

Spatial Data Warehouse: Subject-oriented, non volatile, time variant and integrated repository of spatial data that is designed to facilitate reporting and spatial analysis.

Multidimensional Model: Conceptual model for the multidimensional analysis of huge datasets, based on the concepts of dimensions, facts and measures.

Geographic Information System: Information system for capturing, storing, analyzing, managing and presenting data that are spatially referenced.

Spatial Decision Support System: Interactive, computer-based system designed to support a user or group of users in achieving a higher effectiveness of decision making while solving a semi-structured spatial problem.

Section 2
Physical Design and
Self Turning

Chapter 7
View Selection and Materialization

Zohra Bellahsene
LIRMM-CNRS/Université Montpellier 2, France

ABSTRACT

There are many motivations for investigating the view selection problem. At first, materialized views are increasingly being supported by commercial database systems and are used to speed up query response time. Therefore, the problem of choosing an appropriate set of views to materialize in the database is crucial in order to improve query processing cost. Another application of the view selection issue is selecting views to materialize in data warehousing systems to answer decision support queries. The problem addressed in this paper is similar to that of deciding which views to materialize in data warehousing. However, most existing view selection methods are static. Moreover, none of these methods have considered the problem of de-materializing the already materialized views. Yet it is a very important issue since the size of storage space is usually restricted. This chapter deals with the problem of dynamic view selection and with the pending issue of removing materialized views in order to replace less beneficial views with more beneficial ones. We propose a view selection method for deciding which views to materialize according to statistic metadata. More precisely, we have designed and implemented our view selection method, including a polynomial algorithm, to decide which views to materialize.

INTRODUCTION

Nowadays, materialized views are increasingly being supported by a variety of commercial DBMS to speed up query response time. This technique is also very useful in data warehousing for optimizing OLAP queries. In such systems, data are extracted

in advance and stored in a repository. Then, user queries are addressed directly to the data warehouse system and processed without needing to access the data sources. At an abstract level, a data warehouse can be seen as a set of materialized views. Furthermore, new applications of the problem of view selection arise namely in data placement in

DOI: 10.4018/978-1-60566-756-0.ch007

distributed databases and in peer to peer data sharing systems.

The problem addressed in this paper is similar to that of deciding which views to materialize in data warehousing. However, most existing view selection methods are static. Moreover, none of these methods have considered the problem of dematerializing the already materialized views. Yet it is a very important issue since the size of storage space is usually restricted.

Many database systems support creation and use of materialized views. The presence of appropriate materialized views can significantly improve performance and speed up the processing of queries by several orders of magnitude. For this reason the problem of view selection has received significant attention in recent literature. The majority of these works (Yang, 1997; Kotidis, 1999; Theodoratos, 2001; Baril, 2003) presents the solution for data warehousing environments that are used for On-Line Analytical Processing (OLAP) and Decision Support System applications. The problem in this context is the following: given a database scheme R, a storage space B, and a workload of queries Q, choose a set of views V over R to materialize, whose combined size is at most B. The goal of view selection process is to find a set of views that minimizes the expected cost of evaluating the queries in Q. Traditionally, view selection has been carried out statically. With static view selection, a system administrator decides what kinds of queries might be carried out in the system. Several models and tools have been designed to take the expected query workload and choose set of views to materialize; e.g., (Yang, 1997; Gupta, 1999; Baril, 2003). Obviously, static selection of views has several weaknesses: (i) the query workload is often not predictable; (ii) even if the workload can be predicted, the workload is likely to change, and the workload might change so quickly that the system administrator cannot adjust the view selection quickly enough so the static view selection might very quickly become outdated. This means that the administrator should monitor the query pattern and periodically "recalibrate" the materialized views by rerunning these algorithms. This task for a large warehouse where many users with different profiles submit their queries is rather complicated and time consuming

Once the views are selected and are materialized, another problem arises. Each time a base table is changed, the materialized views and indexes built on it have to be updated (or at least have to be checked whether some changes have to be propagated or not). The problem of updating the views is known as the view maintenance problem. In most cases it is wasteful to maintain a view by re-computing it from scratch. Often, it is cheaper to use the heuristic of inertia (only a part of the view changes in response to changes in the base relations) and thus compute only the changes in the view to update its materialization (Gupta, 1995). This technique is called incremental view maintenance. However, not always the incremental maintenance is a right choice. For example, if an entire base relation is deleted, it may be cheaper to re-compute a view that depends on the deleted relation (if the new view will quickly evaluate to an empty relation) than to compute the changes to the view. The view maintenance cost constraint is very important for the view selection problem and cannot be ignored. Another kind of view maintenance, called *view adaptation* is the one occurring after schema evolution or after direct view query changes. The problem is that of propagating the schema change arising at the data sources or on the view schema to the materialized views (Bellahsene, 2004).

This chapter deals with the problem of dynamic view selection and with the pending issue of removing materialized views in order to replace less beneficial views with more beneficial ones. We propose a view selection method for deciding which views to materialize according to statistic metadata.

Contribution

We have designed a view selection method based on statistic information. This method provides the following features:

- It is dynamic: it treats a query as it arrives
- It is based on statistic measures for estimating the query processing
- It is using a replacement policy to materialize the most beneficial views
- The algorithm for finding the best views to materialize is polynomial

Outline

The rest of this chapter is organized as follows. In Section 2, we present the problem of view selection and a framework for representing the queries in order to detect common sub expressions. Section 3 presents our dynamic approach to view selection. The materialization and replacement policy and its related algorithms are described in Section 4. In Section 5, we present a tool based on our view materialization method for tuning the performance of the DBMS. We also show that is scalable and provides good performance. Finally, Section 6 presents related work and Section 7 contains concluding remarks and future work.

PRELIMINARIES

A view is a derived relation defined by a query in terms of source relations and/or other views. It is said to be materialized when its extent is computed and persistently stored. Otherwise, it is said to be virtual. We consider Selection-Projection-Join (SPJ) views that may involve aggregation and a group by clause as well.

Motivating Example

Let's start with a simple example showing how materialized views can improve query performance time in distributed context. Let us consider three sites S_1, S_2, S_3 which are connected by a slow wide-area network. S_1, S_2 and S_2, S_3 are connected by an edge with the speed 100 KB/sec, while the connection speed between S_2 and S_3 is 3 MB/sec. Let us consider three relations A, B, C stored at S_1, S_2, S_3 respectively and two queries q_1 and q_2 defined as follows. q_1=A equijoin C is posed frequently at S_2, and q_2 = A equijoin B is posed frequently at S_3. Suppose now that the query optimizer decides to execute all the queries at S_1 and the results size of q_1, q_2 are 1 MB, 2 MB respectively. So, the cost to answer q_1 each time at S_2 is 10 sec and to answer q_2 at S_3 is 20 sec, in addition to the cost to compute both queries at S_1. This cost has to be paid every time these queries are posed. While, if the result of q_1, q_2 are materialized at S_2, S_3 respectively, in this case only both queries has to be computed once at S1 and the results are shipped to S_2, S_3 to be materialized with the transfer cost of 10, 20 sec respectively. Then, subsequent queries could be performed with zero cost. Obviously, materialized views have significantly reduced the query response time. However, two problems can arise: First, sometimes the result of the queries is too large to fit in the available space at a specific site, so we can't materialize the entire workload and we have to select only the most beneficial queries to be materialized. Second, when the base relation is updated, then the view should be maintained and the cost of the view maintenance can cause overhead to the system. Assume in our example that the relation C is frequently updated, in this case materializing q_2 can be less attractive because the cost that we save for answering q_2 is now involved for maintaining the materialized view. Therefore, the view is considered as beneficial if and only if its materialization reduces significantly the query processing cost and without increasing significantly the view maintenance.

Another point should be taken into account. Assume in the previous example that q_1 is frequently used at both S_2, S_3 in this case materializing q_1 only at one site, e.g., S_1 can be benefit enough for the both sites as the communication cost between these sites are not high. And in this way the available storage at S_2 is saved for another benefit materialized view. Finally, this example demonstrates that the question of selecting appropriate views for materialization is not an obvious issue and should deal with different parameters like storage space constraint, view maintenance cost and communication cost.

VIEW SELECTION PROBLEM

The general problem of view selection is to select a set of views to materialize that optimizes both the view maintenance and query processing time given some constraints like storage space. To find the optimal solution satisfying all constraints is a NP-complete problem, therefore it is necessary to develop heuristics. In this chapter, we present a dynamic view selection method which includes a replacement policy of already materialized views.

More formally, given a set of source relations $R=\{R_1,R_2,...,R_n\}$ a set of conjunctive queries of workload $Q = \{Q_1,Q_2,...,Q_k\}$, the problem is to find a set of views to materialize $M=\{V_1,V_2,...,V\}$ under a storage space constraint. However, in this paper, the view selection algorithm is applied as a query arrives. Therefore, the workload is built incrementally.

Framework for Detecting Common Views

In this subsection, we present a framework for representing views to materialize in order to exhibit common sub-expressions between different queries. The Multi View Materialization Graph (MVMG) is similar to the AND-OR DAG representation of queries in multi query optimization. The MVMG is a bipartite Directed Acyclic Graph (DAG) composed of two types of nodes: AND-nodes and OR nodes. Each AND-node represents an algebraic expression (Select-Project-Join) with possible aggregate function. An OR node represents a set of logical expression that are equivalent (i.e., that yield the same result). The AND-nodes have only OR-nodes as children and OR-nodes have only AND-nodes as children. The MVMG represents AND-OR DAGs of several queries in a single DAG. The leaf nodes of the MVMG are equivalence nodes representing the base relations. In general, for each base relation, there is one leaf node except in case of a self join. Equivalence nodes in MVMG correspond to the views that are candidate to the materialization.

The queries used in this chapter are defined over the TPC-H schema described in Figure 1 . The *Part* table contains information about each product. The *Supplier* table describes the supplier of the products. Because a supplier is able to supply more than one product and a product may be supplied by several suppliers: there is a table *PartSupp* containing information about who supplies what products, in which quantity and so on. The Customer table describes the information concerning the clients like the name, address and the nation. The sales are represented by two relations: *Orders* and *Lineitem*. The table *Orders* contains information about the customer, the price of ordered items and so on. Finally, the *Lineitem* table contains for each ordered item, the ordered quantity and the corresponding supplier.

Let us consider the query Q_1, which finds the number of orders of Airbus planes ordered by different nations. Q_1: Select N.name, P.brand, O.orderdate, Sum(L.quantity)From Part P, Customer C, Orders O, Nation N, Lineitem LWhere P.type = 'airplane'and AND P.brand = 'Airbus' AND P.partkey = L.partkey AND L.orderkey =

Figure 1. Tables of TPC-H benchmark

```
Part(partkey, name, brand, type, size, retailprice)
Supplier(suppkey, name, address, nationkey, phone, acctbal)
PartSupp(partkey, suppkey, availqty, supplycost)
Customer(custkey, name, address, nationkey, phone, acctbal)
Orders(orderkey, custkey, orderstatus, totalprice, orderdate)
Lineitem(orderkey, partkey, suppkey, linenumber, quantity)
Nation(nationkey, name, regionkey, regionkey, comment)
Region(regionkey, name, comment)
```

O.orderkey AND O.custkey = C.custkey AND C.nationkey = N.nationkeyGroup by N.name P.brand, O.orderdate;

The AND-OR DAG representation of the query graph of query Q_1 is shown in Figure 2 (b). Circles represent AND nodes, i.e., operations and boxes represent OR nodes, i.e. equivalence nodes. In the transition from Figure 2 (a) to Figure 2 (b), new nodes are created to represent the equivalence nodes (e.g., node labeled $A1_{12}$ represents the result of the aggregation operation).

In this work, The MVMG is built incrementally because the view selection algorithm is applied as a query arrives. Indeed, the query tree is integrated into the MVMG. We borrow the rule provided in (Roy, 2002) for identifying common subexpressions. For example, equivalent nodes, obtained after applying join associativity property, are replaced by a single equivalence node.

We consider metadata like frequency at each node of the graph (i.e., at the operation and view nodes).

Figure 2. Query graph of Q (a) A possible query graph of Q_1 (b) AND-OR DAG of Q_1

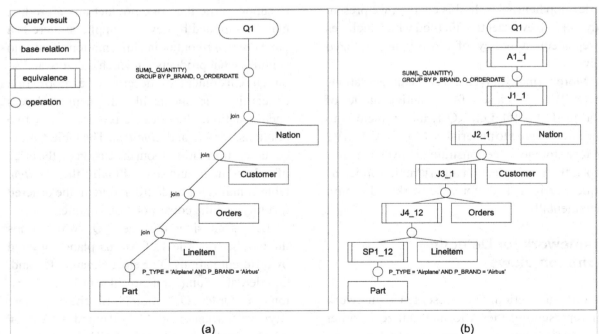

More precisely, at each node in the MVMG, are stored its frequency, size and meantime (execution time). While in related work, the frequency is considered at the user queries level. The first advantage of our approach is to exhibit frequent views even if the related query is not frequent. This means the view is used by many different queries. Therefore, the aim is to improve the efficiency of the view selection algorithm.

The second convenient feature appears at the operation level since we may take the parallelism into account. The MVMG framework also allows to clean the MVMG by eliminating the non-frequent views rather than entire queries. Building the MVMG is the main task for setting up the search space by identifying common subexpressions. This task is of importance similar to multi-query optimization. However, it is orthogonal to the view selection process itself. This paper focuses on the view selection process.

VIEW SELECTION STRATEGY

In this section, we present our method for dynamically selecting a set of views for a given query and a predefined storage space constraint. The constraint of view maintenance is relaxed since our method is dynamic: we are not considering a workload of a set of queries but a given query. However, our method takes the reuse parameter into account in order to reduce the view maintenance cost and the storage space. At first, as it was described in the previous section, the MVMG allows to detect common views. Secondly, the reuse is also handled by the frequency of a view.

Selection and Dynamic Materialization

The process of view selection/replacement is automatically triggered by the arrival of a user query or when an expert-user decides to materialize a query. Besides of the dynamic feature of the method, the other important argument of our solution is reducing the complexity of the view selection algorithm. The second argument for considering the views to materialize query by query relies in preserving the data independence whenever adding a query to the view configuration or removing one from it. Indeed, the side effect on existing queries is reduced since the view selection is applied query per query. In the related work since the view selection strategy consists in considering all equivalence nodes of the multi view query graph, the impact of adding or removing a query may lead to an important reorganization.

Criteria of Selection

To each view v is assigned a value, called *goodness(v)*, which represents the benefit of materializing v. This value is computed by the following formula: $goodness(v) = freq(v) \times cost(v)$ Where freq(v) is the access frequency of view v and cost(v) is its processing cost. Unlike related work, our approach is based on statistic metadata. The cost, for instance, is computed according to the average query processing time for a given view $v: cost(v) = meantime(v)$

Pre-Selection of Views per Query

At this stage, we try to avoid candidates which do not provide additional benefit to the set of already materialized views. A given query q is decomposed into a set of views. The method pre-selects a subset of views called candidate views V_c, from the set of views from q. $Goodness(V_c) = \sum goodness(v, V_c)$ be maximal $v \in V_c |V_c|$ be minimal Where: $goodness(v, V_c) = goodness(v)$ if no view in V_c is subsumed by v 0 else

The previous formula is designed in order to avoid the case where the view v is subsumed by another materialized view v' because materializing v provides no additional benefit for processing q. Unlike other approaches, ours tends to materialize

Figure 3. Example of view subsumption

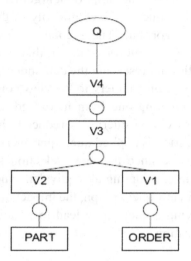

costly views in order to save work of frequently asked queries.

Furthermore, views may be selected for materialization even if it is the first time the query is executed. This is because some of its views could be shared with other queries, which have already been processed.

Let us illustrate this heuristic by considering the query Q depicted in Figure 3, which includes four views. Let us assume that V_3 is already materialized. Then, materializing V_1 or V_2 will not reduce the query processing time of Q.

OVERVIEW OF THE VIEW SELECTION ALGORITHMS

We present in the first part of this section the view selection algorithm, which allows selecting the best views for materialization. In the second part, we will discuss the replacement policy of already materialized views.

Pre-Selection Algorithm

The BestViews(q) algorithm, which is described below, provides for a given query q a set of can-

didate views for materialization. The decision for materializing them definitely is done according to the available storage space and regarding also the benefit of already materialized views. This is the task of the replacement algorithm, discussed in the second part. The algorithm requires a set of source relations V_R to answer q. The algorithm starts at the top of the query graph of q, but recursively builds from the bottom up a set of child nodes CV_C containing the best sub queries (nodes) for query q. At each iteration, the goodness of query q, is compared to the goodness of its candidate views CV_C. The result of the comparison is assigned to V_C.

For simplification we use the following notations:

- q represents the query as well as the view defined by this query.
- children(q) is the set of direct children of query q.

Complexity of the BestViews Algorithm

The algorithm performs a simple depth-first traversal of the query tree. Therefore, its complexity is O(n) where n is the number of nodes. Compared to our previous work, LevelSelection (Baril, 2003), the complexity of the BestViews(q) algorithm is similar to LevelSelection algorithm. Both the methods guarantee that no selected view can be subsumed by another one. However, BestViews(q) provides a better solution than LevelSelection in sense of goodness criteria (i.e., TotalCost in LevelSelection) since this algorithm was able to find only views to materialize at the same level of the query tree. Algorithm 1 *BestViews(q)*

```
Require: q, V_R ≠ φ
1:      if q ∈ V_R then
2:          V_c ← {q}
3:      else
4:          CV_c ← ∅
5:          for all q' ∈ children(q) do
6:              CV_c ←∪ BestViews(q')
```

```
7:      end for
8:          if goodness(q) ≥
goodness(CV_c) then
9:              V_c ← q
10:             else
11:             V_c ← CV_c
12:         end if
13:         return V_c
```

Materialization Decision

As it was said in the previous section, the final decision to materialize the candidate views is performed according to the storage space and the existing materialized views. Our general strategy is divided in two phases. Phase 1: While there is enough storage space, all the candidate views will be materialized. Phase 2: If the storage limit is reached, a candidate view will be materialized only if it proofs to be more beneficial than those which are already materialized. If so, these views should be removed to free the necessary storage space for materializing the new candidate.

Replacement Policy

The final decision is based on the notion of benefit to materialize view v. benefit(v) = goodness(v) - goodness(V⁻)

V⁻ is the set of already materialized views to be removed in order to free the necessary storage space.

The Benefit(v_{new}) algorithm evaluates the benefit of materializing v versus the loss of removing the views belonging to V⁻.

Replacement Algorithm

The Benefit algorithm is called once for every view v_{new} from the set of views V selected by the BestViews algorithm from any query. At the first stage (lines 4-10), the algorithm selects all materialized views v with a lower goodness value than v_{new} and adds these views to a set of candidate (for removal) views $V⁻_c$. In general the

size of $V⁻_c$ is much larger than the size of v_{new}. This means that not all views in $V⁻_c$ have to be dematerialized; just enough to materialize v_{new}. In the second stage of the algorithm (lines 11-14), we use knapsack algorithm to choose a subset V⁻ of views from $V⁻_c$ which have to be dematerialized in order to free the necessary space for v_{new}. The views left in $V⁻_c$ remain materialized. Algorithm 2: Benefit (v_{new})

```
Require: v_new, s, V_M
1:      V⁻ ← φ
2:      s_max ← totalspace(s) -
size(v_new)
3:      for all v ∈ V_M do
4:          if goodness(v) <
goodness(v_new) then
5:              V⁻_c ← V⁻_c ∪ {v}
6:          else
7:              s_max ← s_max -
size(v)
8:          end if
9:      end for
10:     if V⁻ = φ then
11:         b ← -∞
12:     else
13:         V⁻ ← V⁻_c - knapsack(V⁻
_c, s_max)
14:         b ← goodness(v_new) -
goodness(V⁻) - MaterCost(v)
15:     end if
16:     return b
```

The following notations are used:

- V_M is the set of materialized views, which are currently stored in space s.
- totalspace(s) returns the total capacity of s, and freespace(s) indicates the available space.
- $V⁻_c$ is the subset of materialized views, $V⁻_c ⊂ V_M$, candidate for deletion.
- V⁻ is a subset of materialized views, $V⁻ ⊂ V⁻_c$, to be deleted for storing v_{new} in its place.

Replacement Policy

If the available storage space is less than the size of v_{new} a certain number of materialized views need to be remove in order to free up enough storage space for materializing v_{new}. Therefore, the issue is to find the set of materialized views to be removed, say V^- so that:

- The free space should be sufficient: $size(V^-)$ + freespace $\geq size(v_{new})$.
- The loss is minimal: $goodness(V^-) \leq goodness(v_{new})$.

Finding the set of views to be removed is formed by solving an instance of the KNAPSACK problem: find the view with highest goodness to remain materialized and the rest V^- will be removed from P in order to free enough space to materialize v_{new}

Optimization. A candidate view will be materialized only if its benefit is strictly positive. Therefore, it is not necessary to consider the deletion of all the views having $goodness(v) > goodness(v_{new})$.

Complexity. The complexity of the algorithm is similar to the complexity of the knapsack problem,

$O(n \times m)$ where n is the number of candidate views for deletion, and m is equal to s_{max}. It is possible to choose a tradeoff between the quality of the solution provided by the knapsack algorithm and its execution time. The complexity depends on the number of views and the maximum size of storage space. We cannot reduce the number of views. However, it is possible to express the storage space and the size of views in terms of pages (the page size is to be appropriately chosen). Then, the storage space and the size of views should be expressed in number of pages. This will allow to reduce the execution time. In the counterpart, some solutions may be not found.

IMPLEMENTATION

MATUN: A Materialization-Based Tuning Tool

In this section, we will discuss a tool which we build from the ground up to facilitate different view materialization strategies using the algorithms presented in this paper. This tool, called MATUN, was created using the Java programming language and is therefore able to tune the performance of any JDBC compliant data source on several different platforms (cf. Figure 4).

Dynamic View Materialization Strategy

One of the important issues facing dynamic view materialization is how to implement the dynamic nature of view materialization. In order for the view materialization process to be dynamic, the set of best views have to be updated to reflect the (continuously) changing MVMG.

The most dynamic option would be to update, or choose, the set of best views whenever the MVMG changes, i.e., whenever a query is submitted to the data source. Unfortunately, this is also the most expensive option in terms of system resources. It follows that the system will be occupied with the view selection process. Another option would be to schedule the view selection processes periodically. This particular strategy omits the view selection process for a certain period of time and focuses on building the MVMG. Obviously, this strategy is less dynamic, but also less expensive. Both strategies are supported by the MATUN tool. In addition we have added support for 'refreshing' the MVMG to the second strategy. Refreshing the MVMG means eliminating infrequent views, as well as views which, haven't been accessed over a certain period of time. The process of refreshing the MVMG starts before the view selection and materialization process.

Figure 4. MATUN architectual overview

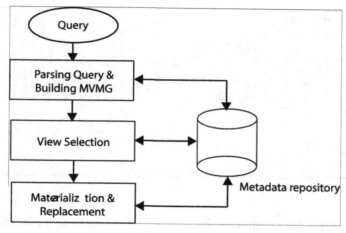

Overview of our Tool

MATUN provides the expert-user with a graphical user interface to manually add and remove queries to and from the MVMG. Using the materialize / dematerialize functions, the expert-user can decide whether or not the query should be considered for materialization / dematerialization. The materialize function starts the materialization process after integrating the new query into the MVMG. Once the expert-user decides to materialize the query, the view selection method will decide which views to materialize for improving the overall response time according to their frequency, goodness and the available storage space.

MATUN has several functions to manipulate the MVMG manually. However, it has three primary functions which we will outline. All these functions are available to the expert-user through the user interface shown in Figure 6. Queries in the MVMM can be selected to manually manipulate their frequency, meantime and size or to simply edit the query itself. These query statistics are used to calculate the cost and goodness of each query. The decision to materialize a query (or a fragment of it) is entirely based upon these values.

MATUN provides the option to generate query statistics automatically from a given data source based on the time it takes to answer a query and the algorithm used to estimate the number of disk pages needed to store the result set. However, these statistics are often misleading because of caching mechanisms used by the data source and optimistic space estimations.

MATUN tool represents the MVMG as a matrix, shown in Figure 5. A column represents a single view, and a row represents a single query. A zero simply means the view for that column is not being used by the query; one means otherwise. The matrix allows the expert user to evaluate frequently used views easily. And it helps decide which views to materialize /dematerialize manually.

Materialize Query. The materialize query function allows the expert-user to manually add queries to the MVMG either from a file or by using the build-in editor. Before a query is added to the MVMG it is parsed into its own AND-OR DAG. Once the query is added to the MVMG, the BestViews algorithm decides whether or not to materialize to query.

Dematerialize Query. This function allows the expert-user to clean the MVMG by deleting a set of selected queries and all its derived views which are not shared by other queries.

Refresh MVMG. Using the refresh MVMG function the expert-user can manually update

Figure 5. The multi view materialization matrix

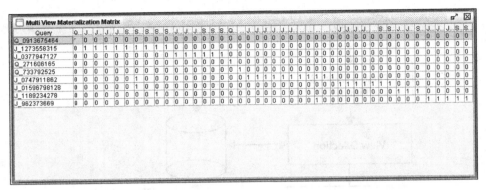

the set of materialized views. Re-computing the entire MVMG for each query submitted to the data warehouse can become extremely expensive and time consuming, therefore we've created the option to periodically re-compute all views in the MVMG and remove infrequent views.

In addition, the refresh function is also used to update the set of materialized views in the data warehouse to reflect the changes made to the original data sources.

MATUN provides the option to generate query statistics automatically from a given data source based on the time it takes to answer a query and the algorithm used to estimate the number of disk pages needed to store the result set. However, these statistics are often misleading because of caching mechanisms used by the data source and optimistic estimations.

RELATED WORK

A great deal of studies has been performed in the area of view selection problem in data ware-

Figure 6. MATUN user interface

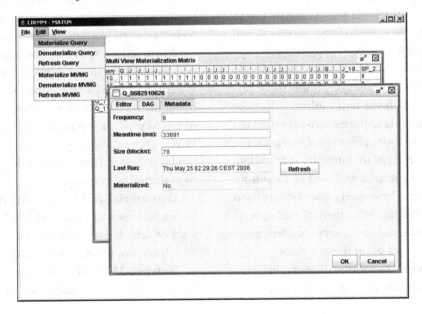

Figure 7. Edit query metadata

housing environment. The static approach as in (Gupta, 1999; Yang, 1997, Baril, 2003), provide framework for selecting views to materialize so as to achieve the best combination of good query performance and low view maintenance. As they are static approach, they assume fix workload.

Work reported in (Gupta, 1999) solves the view selection problem from another point of view. The principle of the solution is the view maintenance constraint.

The framework used to represent the queries is AND-OR View Graph derived from the AND-OR DAG representation as shown in figure 103, which is a directed acyclic graph with the base relations as sinks. However the authors study also a special case of an AND-OR DAG view graph, where exactly one view is used to compute another view. The authors consider the resource constraint is the maintenance cost, which is the time required for the incremental maintenance of views instead of the storage space and they refer to the problem as the maintenance-cost view-selection problem. This is more difficult than the view selection problem with a disk-space constraint because of the non-monotonic behaviour of the benefit function per unit of maintenance cost. That means that the maintenance cost of a view may decrease with selection of other views for materialization and this can prevent using the simple greedy algorithm for selecting the views. Therefore, they use the notion of inverted tree

set[1] to develop a greedy heuristic algorithm called *Inverted-tree Greedy Algorithm*, which delivers a near-optimal solution for a special case of OR view graphs. They prove that in OR view graph, an arbitrary set O can be partitioned into inverted tree sets such that the effective maintenance-cost of O with respect to an already materialized set M is greater than the sum of effective-costs of inverted tree sets with respect to M. So the algorithm will consider all the inverted tree set in the given view graph and selects the inverted tree set to materialize that has the most query-benefit per unit effective maintenance-cost. Finally, they present an optimal solution A* heuristic for the general case of AND-OR view graphs but it takes essentially more time than the previous one as it is exponential in the size of the input graph.

Work reported in (Yang, 1997) provides a static approach for selecting the appropriate set of views from the Multiple View Processing Plan (MVPP) which represents the query processing strategy of the entire workload. This approach was based on a cost model and has been implemented. However, this work focused on view maintenance problem without considering the query processing cost. Moreover, common sub-expressions have been exploited for improving view maintenance cost. However, the cost of maintenance used is the cost of reconstructing the view; they didn't take into account the incremental maintenance. The weak point of this approach is that there weren't any bounds in selecting the view. That's mean that they didn't take into account neither the storage space constraint. They suppose that there is no limit to materialize new view but this is not always possible in the real application.

Our Multi View Materialization Graph is close to the Multi View Processing Plan that has been described in (Yang, 1997). However, the evaluation cost of the query is not estimated according to the operation type. It seems that the estimated cost of a join is estimated as the same as the cost of a selection.

The Microsoft Research team presents another static approach reported in (Agrawal, 2000) by considering the storage space constraint. This approach deals with the issue of selecting both views and indexes to be materialized in order to optimize the physical design of the workload by taking into account the interaction between indexes and materialized views. Once a set of candidate indexes and candidate materialized views has been chosen, the system runs the configuration enumeration module to determine the ideal physical design, called a configuration. The configurations considered by the configuration enumeration module are compared for quality by taking into account the expected impact of the proposed configurations on the sum of the cost of queries in the workload. The configuration simulation and cost estimation module is responsible for providing this support. The goal of candidate materialized view selection is to eliminate materialized views that are syntactically relevant for one or more queries in the workload but are never used in answering any query, from entering the configuration enumeration phase in order to reduce the search space. However, one of the negative points for this approach is that it doesn't take the maintenance cost into account which can efficiently change the configuration.

In (Baril, 2003) the view selection is decided under space constraint. The framework chosen to represent the queries workload is The Multi View Materialization Graph (MVMG) which is similar

to the AND-OR DAG in multi query optimization (Roy, 2000). Each view of the query tree is associated to a level. The view selection problem here is solved in two phases, the first phase depends on local optimization by taking each query and preselect set of views which belong to the same level and which reduce the query processing cost if it is materialized without increasing significantly the view maintenance. While the second phase is the global optimisation where all the result collected from the first phase will be merged together and filtered according to its global benefit.

The authors present two polynomial algorithms to provide the solution based on the balance between query processing and maintenance cost. The first algorithm finds the level of each query in the workload which provide the minimal sum of query processing and view maintenance cost. The treatment is done in two main steps. The first one carries out a pre-selection of beneficial views. The second step computes the total cost (query plus maintenance) for each level of the query graph and selects the one which has the minimal sum of query processing and view maintenance cost.

In (Theodoratos, 2001) the dynamic data warehouse design is modeled as search space problem. Rules for pruning the search space have been proposed. The first rule relies on favoring the query rewriting that uses views already materialized. The second one modifies the previous rule to favor common sub expression. However, their view selection algorithm is still in exponential time. Besides, neither implementation and/or evaluation of their method have been performed.

The first dynamic approach dealing with the view materialization in data warehousing was DynaMat (Kotidis, 1999). This system aimed to unify the view selection and the view maintenance problems. The principle of this system is monitoring constantly the incoming queries and materializing their query results given the space constraint. During the update only the most beneficial subset of materialized views are refreshed within a given maintenance window. It provides a self-tuneable solution that relieves the warehouse administrator from having to monitor and calibrate the system constantly.

The view pool is the information repository used for storing materialized results as multidimensional data structures. For each query that arrives at the system, first the fragment locator determine if it can be answered from the already materialized view by linearly searching the pool in the aide of dictionary index. In the case of failure in finding any already materialized view, the query will be answered conventionally from the base tables. Either-way, after the result is computed and given to the user, it is tested by the Admission Control Entity which decides whether or not it is beneficial to store it in the Pool.

They provide a replacement policy based on the goodness of a view. Different kinds of goodness have been experimented: last date of access, use frequency, size and cost of re-computing a view. However, Dynamat's approach dealt with query per query and considers the materialization at the final result of a query. Hence, it did not use any framework to detect common views between queries for reuse purpose.

More recently, a formal study of the view selection problem focusing on its complexity has been done in (Chirkova, 2001). It shows notably that the cost model is a parameter of importance in the view selection setting.

In paper (Ghozzi, 2003) the authors studied the impact of the constraints on the manipulation of dimensional data. More precisely, it analyzed the repercussions of the constraint over the dimensional operators and the query optimization by exploiting the semantic constraints for the selection of materialized views. This approach uses a dimensional lattice which is based on the structure of the hierarchies and which also integrates the constraints. Thereafter, the views which do not satisfy the constraints are removed. The author did not propose an algorithm or view selection method, which could optimize the query processing indeed.

Another dynamic approach presented in (Schnaitter, 2006) provides the solution for materializing the indexes which can be seen as a special case of the materialized view. The authors introduce a novel self-tuning framework that continuously monitors the incoming queries and adjusts the system configuration in order to maximize query performance. They call it CoLT (Continuous On-Line Tuning). It supports the on-line selection of an effective set of indices for a relational query by the following steps:

1. CoLT builds a model of the current workload based on the incoming flow of queries.
2. It estimates the respective gains of different candidate indexes.
3. It selects those that would provide the best performance for the observed workload within the available space constraint.

Thus, the system performs continuous profiling and reorganization in order to match the most recent traits of the query workload.

Paper (Zhou, 2007) presents another idea to add the dynamicity to their approach. Unlike other dynamic approaches, the dynamicity is not applied for the selection of the view but instead they suppose that the materialized view is already selected. However, the dynamicity is applied at the view extent level. Therefore, the algorithm selectively materializes only the most frequently accessed tuples of the view, and these tuples can be dynamically changed.

When any query arrives to the system two step of testing are required in order to decide if it is possible to answer the query from the materialized part of the view. The first test could be accomplished at the optimization time as for regular view that tests the containment of the query in the view. However, the other can be done only at execution time which called guard condition. This condition checks whether one or a few covering values exist in the control table. The construction of the guard condition is done in the optimization time but its evaluation is delayed until the execution time. Thus, the query is guaranteed to be contained in the view if the guard condition evaluates to true. The query plan must also contain an alternative subplan, called a fallback plan that computes the query expression from other input sources in case the guard condition evaluates to false.

For the view maintenance, as only a small number of row are actually materialized so the view can be maintained more efficiently. However the existence of an exist clause in the dynamic view syntax prevent to apply the incremental view maintenance algorithms. The authors discuss how to update the view incrementally by replacing this clause. This can be achieved by either converting the subquery to a join clause or converting the view into an aggregation view and this depends on the control table if it contains duplicated tuples or not. However, this cache policy, which admits the new value on the second access, can cause an overhead and reduce the global performance of the system. For example if the workload is noisy, the system requires strong evidence on the pay-off of switching between the materialized rows due to short-lived transitions in the workload. While CoLT prevents the Self Organizer from "thrashing" when the workload is noisy by to selecting an index for materialization based on its long-term potential.

In conclusion, unlike most of previous work, our approach is dynamic and provides a replacement policy.

FUTURE TRENDS

Recently, businesses are beginning to rely on distributed rather than centralized database for many reasons:

(1) PC processors are cheaper and significantly more powerful than one big mainframe computer.

(2) New PCs can be added easily at any time in order to meet the company's new requirements.

(3) A centralized data server can become a bottleneck as a large user community contends for data server access.

(4) Data is unavailable when a failure occurs on the network. In these contexts, users are spread over the network, and each location may have different types of query characteristics and/or performance requirements.

The view selection problem and its generalizations will play an even greater role in these contents where data need to be placed intelligently over a wide area network. As the scale of distributed systems and applications keep growing, the peer to peer communication paradigm is now recognized as the key to scalability. In a peer to peer system, each peer may act both as a client and server so that the number of servers increases linearly with the size of the system thus ensures the scalability. Our focus is on peer-to-peer distributed database system (PDBS). Peers in a peer group have their own local databases but can also retrieve data at different rate from various points on the network. Information in these local databases can be shared among peers through user queries. PDBS can obtain tremendous performance and availability benefit by employing materialized views. A key factor to ensure good performance in such context is intelligent placement and replication of data at different nodes on the network. However, the membership and the query workload at any peer are dynamic and unpredictable therefore the proposed solution should be dynamic and treats the queries as it arises at any peer. We argue that the materialization technique can be applied in a P2P DBMS context for (i) saving work on frequently asked queries and (ii) increasing availability in cases of failure.

CONCLUSION AND FUTURE WORK

In this paper we have presented a new approach for the view selection problem. We designed a new method including a polynomial algorithm that we have implemented on Oracle DBMS. The main features of our method are:

- It decides dynamically for a given query which views are worthy to be materialized regarding the query processing cost, the available storage capacity and also the already materialized views.
- It favors the more costly queries.
- Its view selection algorithm is based on the meantime.
- It includes a replacement policy for removing already materialized views in order to replace the less beneficial views with more beneficial once.

Since our view selection algorithm is dynamic, it was very difficult to take the view maintenance cost into account. However, our method includes a repository of metadata about the sharing feature that will allow reducing the view maintenance cost. Our future work will address the problem of view selection and the placement of materialized views in a super-peer based PDMS.

REFERENCES

Agrawal, S., Chaudhuri, S., & Narasayya, V. (2000). *Automated selection of materialized views and indexes for SQL database.* Paper presented at the International Conference on Very Large Databases (VLDB00), Cairo, Egypt.

Baril, X., & Bellahsene, Z. (2003). *Selection of materialized views: A cost-based approach.* Paper presented at the International Conference on Advanced Information Systems Engineering.

Bellahsene, Z. (2004). View adaptation in the fragment-based approach. *IEEE Transactions on Knowledge and Data Engineering, 16*(11), 1441–1455. doi:10.1109/TKDE.2004.79

Chirkova, R., Halevy, A., & Suciu, D. (2001). *A formal perspective on the view selection problem.* Paper presented at the International Conference on Very Large Databases, Rome, Italy.

Ghozzi, F., Ravat, F., Teste, O., & Zurfluh, G. (2003). *Constraints and multidimensional databases.* In *Proceedings of the International Conference Enterprise CEIS* (pp. 104-111).

Gupta, A., & Mumick, I. (1995). Maintenance of materialized views: Problems, techniques, and applications. *Data Engineering Bulletin, 18*(2), 3–18.

Gupta, H., & Mumick, I. S. (1999). *Selection of views to materialize under a maintenance cost constraint.* Paper presented at the 7th International Conference on Database Theory.

Halevy, A. (2001). Answering queries using views: A survey. *The VLDB Journal, 10*(4), 270–294. doi:10.1007/s007780100054

Kotidis, Y., & Roussopoulos, N. (1999). DynaMat: *A dynamic view management system for data warehouses.* Paper presented at the ACM SIGMOD International Conference on Management of Data, Philadelphia, United States.

Roy, P. Seshadri, S., Sudarshan, S., & Bhobe, S. (2000). *Efficient and extensible algorithms for multiquery optimization.* Paper presented at the International Conference on Management of Data SIGMOD, San Diego, USA.

Schnaitter, K., Abiteboul, S., Milo, T., & Polyzotis, N. N. (2006). *COLT – Continuous Online Database Tuning.* Paper presented at the ACM SIGMOD Conference on Data Management, SIGMOD'06

TCP(2005). TCP Benchmark H Standard Specification Revision 2.3.0.

Theodoratos, D., Ligoudistianos, S., & Sellis, T. (2001). View selection for designing the global data warehouse. *Data and Knowledge Engineering Journal*, *39*, 219–240. doi:10.1016/S0169-023X(01)00041-6

Yang, J., Karlapalem, K., & Li, Q. (1997). Algorithm for materialized view design in data warehousing environment. *23rd International Conf. on Very Large Data Bases, VLDB'97, Athens, Greece* (pp. 136-145).

Zhou, J., Larson, P., Goldstein, J., & Ding, L. (2007). *Dynamic materialized views*. Paper presented at the International Conference of Data Engineering (ICDE'07).

KEY TERMS AND DEFINITIONS

View: A derived relation defined by a query in terms of source relations and/or other views.

Materialized View: A view whose its extent is computed and persistently stored. Otherwise, it is said to be virtual. *View maintenance* consists of maintaining the materialized views in response to data modifications to the source relations.

View Selection: is the process of choosing an appropriate set of views to be materialized that can improve the performance of the system and given a set of constraints like storage space, view maintenance, etc.

ENDNOTE

[1]   (Inverted Tree Set) A set of nodes R is defined to be an inverted tree set in a directed graph G if there is a subgraph (not necessarily induced) TR in the transitive closure of G such that the set of vertices of TR is R, and the inverse graph of TR is a tree.

Chapter 8
ChunkSim
A Tool and Analysis of Performance and Availability Balancing

Pedro Furtado
University of Coimbra, Portugal

ABSTRACT

Self-tuning physical database organization involves tools that determine automatically the best solution concerning partitioning, placement, creation and tuning of auxiliary structures (e.g. indexes), based on the workload. To the best of our knowledge, no tool has focused on a relevant issue in parallel databases and in particular data warehouses running on common off-the-shelf hardware in a shared-nothing configuration: determining the adequate tradeoff for balancing load and availability with costs (storage and loading costs). In previous work, we argued that effective load and availability balancing over partitioned datasets can be obtained through chunk-wise placement and replication, together with on-demand processing. In this work, we propose ChunkSim, a simulator for system size planning, performance analysis against replication degree and availability analysis. We apply the tool to illustrate the kind of results that can be obtained by it. The whole discussion in the chapter provides very important insight into data allocation and query processing over shared-nothing data warehouses and how a good simulation analysis tool can be built to predict and analyze actual systems and intended deployments.

INTRODUCTION

Data warehouses may range from few megabytes to huge giga- or terabyte repositories, so they must have efficient physical database design and processing solutions to allow for efficient operation. Physical database design concerns the layout of data and auxiliary structures on the database server and, together with the execution engine and optimizer, has a large influence on the efficiency of the system. This is especially relevant in parallel architectures that are setup to handle huge data sets efficiently. The data sets are partitioned into nodes and processed in a parallel fashion in order to decrease the processing burden and, above all, to allow the system to return fast results for near-to-interactive data exploration.

DOI: 10.4018/978-1-60566-756-0.ch008

For this reason, there has been a lot of emphasis on automatic workload-based determination of partitioning indexes, materialized views and cube configurations in the past.

We concentrate on a different issue of providing desired load and availability levels with minimum degree of replication in parallel partitioned architectures and on system planning, both in the presence of heterogeneity. Consider a shared-nothing environment created in an ad-hoc fashion, by putting together a number of PCs. A data warehouse can be setup at a low cost in such a context, but then not only partitioning but also heterogeneity and availability become relevant issues. These issues are dealt-with efficiently using load- and availability- balancing, where data is partitioned into pieces and replicated into processing nodes; there is a controller node orchestrating balanced execution, and processing nodes ask the controller node for the next piece of the data to process whenever they are idle (on-demand processing). Under this scheme, the best possible performance and availability balancing is guaranteed if all nodes have all the data (fully mirrored data), but smaller degrees of replication (partial replication) also achieve satisfactory levels of performance and load balancing without the loading and storage burdens of full mirroring. The issue then is how to predict and take decisions concerning the degree of partial replication that is necessary and how to size a system, which are objectives of the ChunkSim simulator that we present in this work. There is a tradeoff between the costs of maintaining large amounts of replicas (loading and storage costs) and the efficiency of the system in dealing with both heterogeneity/non-dedication of nodes and availability limitations, and there is a need to size a system while taking heterogeneity and replication alternatives into consideration. ChunkSim is a what-if analysis tool for determining the benefit of performance-wise placement and replication degree for heterogeneity and availability balancing in partitioned, partially replicated on-demand processing. Our contribution is to propose the

tool and the model underlying it and to use it for system planning and the analysis of placement and replication alternatives.

The chapter is organized as follows: in the Background section we review partitioning, replication and load-balancing. Our review of replication will include works on both low-level replication (Patterson et al. 1998), relation-wise replication (e.g. chained declustering by Hsiao et al. 1990) and OLAP-wise replication (e.g. the works by Akal et al. 2002, Furtado 2004 and Furtado 2005). Then we review basic query processing in our shared-nothing environment, in section 3. In section 4 we describe the ChunkSim Model and parameters, including also a discussion on Placement and Processing approaches. The ChunkSim tool and underlying model is discussed next, and finally we use the tool to analyze the merits of different placement and replication configurations.

BACKGROUND

Shared-nothing parallel systems (SN) are systems where a possibly large number of computers (nodes) are interconnected such that, other than the network, no other resources are shared. These architectures are scalable, in the sense that it is possible to add a large number of computing nodes to handle larger data sets efficiently. The idea is that, if each node is able to process its part independently of the remaining nodes, the system will have good scalability properties. On the other hand, interconnections between processing units may become a bottleneck if large amounts of data need to be exchanged between nodes. For this reason, physical database design and query processing optimizations are most relevant in SN systems. In this context, self-tuning database systems most often rely on what-if analysis to determine the relevant physical parameters and organization. For instance, the AutoAdmin project (Chaudhuri et al. 2007) supported the creation

Figure 1. Sample DW Star schema

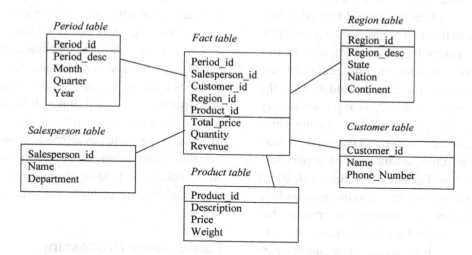

of an API for creating hypothetical indexes in a DBMS, and the physical database design tool in (Rao et al. 2002) tests hypothetical partitioning alternatives to determine the most appropriate configuration. In section 2.1 we review basic partitioning and data allocation principles that are useful in the SN context.

Given a data partitioning and allocation solution, query processing is also a most relevant issue, which we review in section 2.2. In section 2.3 we discuss replication and on-demand load-balancing, which are used to enable optimized performance and availability balancing.

Partitioning and Data Allocation

Automatic workload-based determination of partitioning and indexing configurations was explored in several works that include (Bellatreche et al. 2005, Furtado 2007, Rao et al. 2002, Sthor et al. 2000). Multi-Dimensional Hierarchical Fragmentation (Sthor et al. 2000) uses workload-based attribute-wise derived partitioning of facts and in-memory retention of dimensions for efficient processing, and introduces the use of join-bitmap indexes together with attribute-wise derived partitioning and hierarchy-aware processing for

very efficient partition-wise processing over star schemas; The Node Partitioned Data Warehouse (Furtado 2004, Furtado 2005, Furtado 2007) uses heuristics for efficient workload-based hash-partitioning in a shared-nothing environment; IBM shared-nothing approaches also use workload-based hash-partitioning together with what-if analysis, in order to determine the best physical design solution (Rao et al. 2002); The approach in (Bellatreche et al. 2005) proposes a genetic algorithm for schema partitioning selection, whereby the fact table is fragmented based on the partitioning schemas of dimension tables.

In this paper we assume a simple OLAP schema context similar to the one assumed in (Sthor et al. 2000), and describe next a typical partitioning and allocation scenario to help illustrate how it works: In relational databases, data warehouses are frequently organized as star schemas (Chaudhuri and Dayal 1997), with a huge fact table that is related to several dimension tables, as represented in Figure 1. In such schema, the fact tables (Sales fact in the Figure) store data to be analyzed and pointers to dimensions, while dimension information is stored in dimension tables (the remaining relations).

It is frequent for dimension tables to be orders of magnitude smaller than fact tables. When considering a parallel environment, this means that it is worth to partition the central fact table into multiple pieces that can be processed in parallel, while the dimension tables are left complete. In a shared-nothing environment, this means copying dimension relations into all nodes and dividing the fact throughout the nodes. This approach is very useful in what concerns parallel processing, since most operations can proceed in parallel (Furtado 2005), including processing of joins in parallel.

Works such as (Furtado 2007, Rao et al. 2002) deal with more complex schemas that may include bigger dimensions and multiple interconnected big relations that, for best performance, need to be partitioned. In those cases, simultaneous partitioning of multiple relations may pose problems to the parallel join operator. As a simple rule, if at most two of the relations participating in a join are partitioned, they can be partitioned by their common join key (equi-partition), and parallel join processing can proceed independently in all nodes; If, on the other hand, more than two relations need to be partitioned, then substantial exchanges of data may be necessary to process broadcast and redirected joins, as described in (Rao et al. 2002). When redirection is necessary, workload-based partitioning solutions as the ones referenced in (Furtado 2007, Rao et al. 2002) can be adopted, which try to co-locate the relations that result in highest query processing gains.

The IBM DB2 server (IBM 2008) allows the definition of any number of partitions (up to some limit) for dividing tables into a set of nodes. In that system parallel joins are processed in different manners, depending on the co-location status of joining relations: In co-located joins, the data is already partitioned according to the join hash values, so the join can occur in parallel with no data exchange requirements between nodes; In redirected joins the data is not co-located, but it is enough to re-locate the rows from one of the source data sets in order to proceed with a co-located join; In repartitioned join both source data sets need to be re-located in order to become co-located; In broadcast join one of the source data is broadcasted into all nodes to enable parallel joining with the other partitioned data set.

In this work we assume schemas and workloads that do not require redirection, that is, simple schemas such as the one in Figure 1, where there is a large fact and small dimensions, or schemas with at most two equi-partitioned relations (partitioned by the same key attribute), assuming that the remaining relations are replicated. Future work includes extending the current rationale of the ChunkSim simulator to deal with any generic schema.

Basic Query Processing

Given a data allocation in a shared-nothing environment, the next important issue is how queries are to be processed. Query plans are determined by a cost-based parallel query optimizer, which evaluates alternative query processing paths and chooses the most efficient, according to a cost model. The result of the optimization must then be re-written as a set of queries and data transfer operations. In this section we illustrate how queries can be decomposed into a number of smaller subqueries that will act on fragments independently in a SN architecture, with significant speedup. This subject has been discussed in several works (Akinde et al. 2003, Furtado 2005, Stohr 2000), our illustration being based on the parallel query processing approach followed by the Data Warehouse Parallel Architecture (DWPA) (Furtado 2005, Furtado 2007).

Figure 2 illustrates the basic architecture of the shared-nothing, node partitioned data warehouse. It includes three major entities: Query Submitter, Executor and the Controller. Submitters are simple services that may reside in any computer, do not require an underlying database server and submit queries to the system. Once submitted, the query is parsed and transformed into high-level actions by a query planner. These actions are then transformed into Command Lists for each Executor. Executors

Figure 2. The DWPA architecture

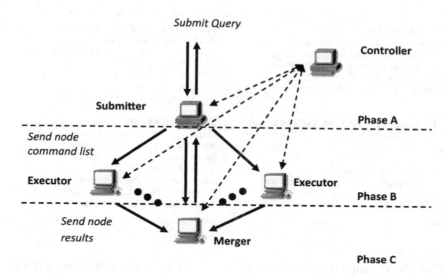

are services that maintain local database sessions and control the execution of commands locally and the data exchange with other nodes. Finally, the controller is a node which controls the whole system (it can be replicated for fault tolerance reasons), maintaining registries with necessary information. When nodes enter the system, they contact the controller to register themselves and to obtain all the necessary information. In DWPA, any computer can assume any role as long as it runs the corresponding service.

We will now describe basic query processing functionality. For simplicity, we start with the simplest possible example. Consider a single very large relation R partitioned into n nodes and a sum query over some attribute x of the relation. Formula (1) states that the sum of attribute x over all nodes is simply the sum of the sums of x in each node:

$$\sum x = \sum_{\text{all nodes}} \sum_{\text{over node}i}(x) \qquad (1)$$

The implementation of this very basic operation in DWPA involves the submitter parsing the initial query sum(x) from R and producing command lists for every node with the following operations:

1) a local query: sum(x) as sumx from Rlocal
2) data transfer commands for every executor node: send sumx to merger node
3) a merge query for the merger node: sum(sumx) from partial_results
4) a signal to the submitter to pull the results

The Merger node is an Executor that is chosen for merging the partial results if necessary. The query processing steps depend heavily on the placement layout of the data on the nodes. For instance, if relation R is replicated into all nodes or placed in a single node, the commands will be (executed in a single node):

1) a local query: sum(x) as sumx from R
2) signal the submitter to pull the results

More complex queries can be processed in a similar way, with some modifications. For instance, the following SQL query is from the TPC-H performance benchmark in (TPCC 2008) and computes the sales of each brand per month:SELECT p_brand, year_month, sum(l_quantity), count(*) FROM JOIN lineitem LI, part P, time T, supplier SWHERE year_month>= '1997' AND supplier =

Figure 3. Basic aggregation query steps

```
S1. Query submission:           S2. Query rewriting and
Select sum(a), count(a),        distribution to each node:
average(a), max(a), min(a),     Select sum(a), count(a), sum(a x
stddev(a), group_attributes     a), max(a), min(a),
From data set                   group_attributes
Group by group_attributes;      From data set
                                Group by group_attributes;


S3. Results sending/collecting: S4. Results merging:
Create cached table             Select sum(suma), sum(counta),
PRqueryX(node, suma, counta,    sum(suma)/ sum(counta),
ssuma, maxa, mina,              max(maxa), min(mina)
group_attributes)               (sum(ssuma) -
as <insert received results>;   sum(suma)²)/sum(counta), ga
                                From UNION_ALL(PRqueryX)
                                Group by group_attributes;
```

'X' GROUP BY to_char(l_shipdate,'yyyy-mm'), p_brand, year_month;

This typical query contains group-by attributes that allow the aggregation to be determined for each group. This aggregation can be handled using the following scheme: each node needs to apply an only slightly modified query on its partial data, and the results are merged by applying the same query again at the merging node with the partial results coming from the processing nodes.

Simple additive aggregation primitives are computed in each node, from which the final aggregation function is derived. The most common primitives are: (LS, SS, N, MAX, MIN: linear sum LS = sum(x); sum of squares SS = sum(x2); number of elements N, extremes MAX and MIN). Examples of final aggregation functions are:

$$COUNT = N = \sum\nolimits_{all\_nodes} N_{nodei} \tag{2}$$

$$SUM = LS = \sum\nolimits_{all\_nodes} LS_{nodei} \tag{3}$$

$$AVERAGE = \sum\nolimits_{all\_nodes} LS_{nodei} / \sum\nolimits_{all\_nodes} N_{nodei} \tag{4}$$

$$STDDEV = \sqrt{\frac{\left(\sum SS_{node_i} - \sum LS_{node_i}^{2} / N\right)}{N}} \tag{5}$$

This means that a query transformation step needs to replace each AVERAGE and STDDEV (or variance) expression in the SQL query by a SUM and a COUNT in the first case and by a SUM, a COUNT and a SUM_OF_SQUARES in the second case to determine the local query for each node. Figure 3 shows an example of aggregation query processing steps created by DWPA:

Given a basic query processing strategy described in this section, we proceed in the next section with background on replication and load-balancing.

Replication, Chunks and Load-Balancing

The use of replication for availability and load-balancing has been a subject of research for quite a while now. There are multiple levels at which to consider the replication issues. Mirrored disk drives (Tandem, 1987) and RAID disks (Patterson et al. 1998) are examples of storage organization level proposals; Multiple RAID alternatives were proposed, some emphasizing only reliability advantages, others with performance and reliability on their sight. At the networked data level, the concept of distributed RAID (ds-RAID) (Stonebraker et al. 1990) glues together distributed storage by software or middleware in a network-based cluster. The Petal project (Lee et al. 1996) built a prototype of ds-RAID and the work in (Hwang et al. 2002) further evolved the concept with an orthogonal striping and mirroring approach. These approaches are low-level data-block ones similar to RAID approaches, but at the networked multiple-nodes level. Their basic concepts are useful for parallel data warehousing, but they must be applied at a higher partition and processing units-level, since disk block-wise solutions would not spare very expensive data transfers from the disks to the processing nodes in order to retrieve whole partitions if we were to use low-level approaches for parallel inter-node processing in our setup.

At the OLAP query-processing level, in (Akal et al. 2002) the authors propose efficient data processing in a database cluster by means of full mirroring and creating multiple node-bound sub-queries for a query by adding predicates. This way, each node receives a sub-query and is forced to execute over a subset of the data, called a virtual partition. Virtual partitions are more flexible than physical ones, since only the ranges need to be changed, but do not prevent full table scans when the range is not small. The authors of (Lima et al. 2004) further propose multiple small sub-queries by node instead of just one (Lima et al. 2004b), and an adaptive partition size tuning approach. The rationale in all these works still suffer from data access-performance related limitations: full table scanning as in (Akal et al. 2002) by every or most nodes is more expensive than having each node access only a part of the data; the alternative in (Lima et al. 2004, Lima et al. 2004b) of reducing the query predicate sizes to avoid full table scans also has another limitation in that it assumes some form of index-based access instead of full scans. Unless the data is clustered index-key-wise (which should not be assumed), this can be slow for queries that need to go through large fractions of data sets (frequent in OLAP). These limitations are absent in physically partitioned data sets, as long as the query processor is able to restrict which partitions to access. For this reason,

we consider chunks, which are fixed size partitions that, besides partitioning, can also be used for replication and efficient load-balancing.

Basic partitioning into chunks can be implemented in any relational database management system (RDBMS), by either creating separate tables for each chunk or using the partitioning interface offered by the RDBMS.

The first issue concerning chunks is to define and enforce a convenient size, since chunks are the individual units that can be placed and processed in a highly flexible fashion, regardless of the partitioning approach. Since the focus of this work is on replication degree, load and availability balancing, and the solutions proposed are to be used generically with different partitioning approaches, we assume chunk target size and target size enforcement to be guaranteed by the partitioning approach itself and refer to these issues only briefly.

We assume a target chunk size value (e.g. in our experiments with TPC-H our target was approximately 250MB for base Lineitem table, noting that there is a fairly wide range of acceptable chunk size values which yield good performance, given a simple guiding principle: if there are too many very small chunks, there will be a large extra overhead related to switching disk scans among chunks, collecting partial results from each and merging all the results; If, on the other hand, the chunk is too large, we will not take full advantage of load-balancing opportunities.

Chunk target size enforcement is dependent on the partitioning approach. A chunk target size is a simple and always available way to influence the number and size of pieces that are an input to the allocation approach, which in turn is useful for the dynamic chunk-wise load and availability-balance. In contrast with what would be more sophisticated alternatives for optimization of chunk configuration, such as a benchmark or workload-based analysis, the simple specification of a chunk target size does not require further knowledge and adds only a simple target-related soft constraint to a partitioning approach. The target size objective can then be applied with any partitioning criteria – whether hash-based, round-robin, random, range-based or derived (dimension-attribute wise). For instance, given a dataset with size S and a target chunk size of C, the number of hash-buckets n in hash-based partitioning should be n=S/C, therefore chunk size enforcement is based on defining and reorganizing hash-range sizes (and chunks) accordingly when the actual chunk sizes rise above an upper limit beyond the chunk target size; In Round-robin or Random partitioning, the number of chunks is n=S/C and the rows are divided in round-robin or random fashion over those chunks; In dimension-attribute wise partitioning criteria, the target is used as an additional element in the determination of the attributes to use in the partitioning decision, as these are influenced by both workload-based determination of a suitable set of attributes and the desired number or size of chunks, as in (Sthor et al. 2000). Since there may be skew in the resulting chunks, skew-resistant partitioning approaches for hash, range and attribute-wise partitioning is a relevant related research issue for future work.

In what concerns load-balancing, there is a very large body of related work and we refer the reader to the review in (Lerner et al. 1998) and the thesis (Lerner et al. 1998b), where the author compares a wide range of approaches and concludes for on-demand, task stealing load-balancing. On-demand load-balancing, where consumers ask for further tasks as soon as they end the last one given to them, allows the system to adapt automatically and dynamically to different and varying skew, heterogeneity and non-dedication conditions.

CHUNK-WISE ON-DEMAND QUERY PROCESSING

Performance and availability balancing are tightly coupled to chunk-wise processing and chunk replication approaches. On-demand based load-balancing is a well-known pull-based approach which we review in this section: since executor nodes ask the controller for pieces of work as soon as they end processing the last piece they compromised with, the approach naturally balances node performance, availability and data processing skews. For this reason both our SN query processing architecture and the ChunkSim simulator implement chunk-wise on-demand processing, which we describe in this section.

In the previous section we described the logic behind data allocation, query processing and replication in SN systems. For dynamic load and availability balancing, the basic query processing is the same as before, but modified to deal with pieces of the data set – which we denote as chunks. A node will typically have several chunks and a chunk can reside in more than one node (replication) for balancing objectives. The query processing steps are the same as before, but apply to individual chunks, and an on-demand chunk processing strategy is implemented to deliver load- and availability- balancing. The load balancing algorithm is a simple on-demand one (Furtado 2008), based on a controller node shown in Figure 4. Although chunks can reside in any node, for algorithmic processing we consider that there is a primary node and replica nodes for a specific chunk. In lines 1 to 3, the controller notifies nodes to start demanding which chunks to process; From then on, each node enters a cycle asking for a chunk to process, getting the chunk identifier from the controller (lines 6 to 8) and processing that chunk. If there are no more primary chunks for the node to process, but there are still replica chunks (lines 9 to 11), it receives a replica chunk identifier and processes that chunk. The controller algorithm chooses a chunk from the node which still has the most original chunks to process, that is, with less chunk id deliveries to executing nodes so far.

Each node proceeds with this simple cycle until the controller has no more chunks to send to it, in which case it notifies the node that it ended. Upon

Figure 4. Load-balanced chunk processing algorithm

Algorithm 1 (On-demand Chunk Processing):
1. FOR (each node Ni holding chunks)
2.   Send the query to N_i to start demanding chunk queries
3.   Node[Ni]=STARTED

4. WHILE (there is at least one node with Node[N_i]=STARTED)
5.   Wait for demand received from any node N_d
6.   IF(at least 1 chunk left in N_d primary chunks)
7.   Send that chunk id to N_d for it to process
8.   Remove the chunk id from both chunk metadata copies
8.   ELSE
9.   IF(at least 1 chunk left in N_d replica chunks)
10.   Choose chunk of node with more chunks yet to process
11.   Send that chunk id to N_d for it to process
12.   Remove the chunk id from both chunk metadata copies
13.   ELSE // there was no chunk available for the node N_d to process
14.   Node[N_i]=ENDED

---

ending, the node proceeds to process a merge query and then to send the results to a merger node. The controller keeps track of how many nodes ended and ends the processing of the chunks as soon as all nodes ended. As soon as all results are in the merger node, the controller commands it to process the merge. In Figure 4 we focus only the chunk-processing part.

This on-demand load-balanced algorithm together with a replica placement approach is very flexible, in the sense that if any node gets delayed or is unavailable, other nodes holding its replicas are ready to help it as long as they finished their own work. This way, the algorithm handles every kind of heterogeneity and non-dedication delays gracefully. It also handles availability exceptions: If a node or a network segment becomes unavailable, the communication layer raises an exception and, after trying to reconnect, the controller flags it as unavailable. If the node was processing a query, the chunks processed by it are re-habilitated and the nodes can immediately start processing the corresponding chunks for which they may have a replica. Nodes that had already ended their

work for the query are also waken-up if they have replica chunks of the failing node.

The controller node can be chosen manually, and it may either be processing queries as well or only controlling. In a configuration with a few nodes, the bulk of the work is expected to be the processing and merging of queries/chunks, so that the coordinator functionality is expected to be light in comparison to that. Still, if there are many nodes, the controller may have a heavy burden receiving requests and answering them. We plan to explore this scalability issue in future work.

CHUNKSIM PERFORMANCE AVAILABILITY ANALYSIS

In this section we describe the ChunkSim model and tool. Section 4.1 describes parameters used by ChunkSim and section 4.2 describes data allocation and replication alternatives considered by the model for the SN system. Section 4.3 describes the experiments that ChunkSim implements to estimate performance and availability for system

Figure 5. ChunkSim workload properties, placement and replication layout parameters

> WP: $\{(Q_i, f_i)\}$ $t(C_lQ_iN_j)$ $tt(Q_i)$ $tm(Q_i)$ or $\{(Q_i, f_i)\}$ $t(CQ_iN_j)$ $tt(Q_i,N_j)$ $tm(Q_i,N_j)$;
> CL: $C_l(C_{key}, C_{sz})$ $\{(C_l, N_j)\}$
> RL: $\{C_l, \{N_j\}\}$

planning and analysis.

ChunkSim Model Parameters

ChunkSim builds a model of a system configuration that includes the set of parameters: Chunk Placement Layout (CPL), Workload Properties (WP) and Replication Layout (RL). With these parameters ChunkSim runs experiments and delivers a summary analysis of perofrmance and availability characteristics. The system configuration parameters may be collected from a running environment or be a what-if analysis for system deployment or reorganization.

Workload Properties (WP): a workload is typically characterized by a set of pairs of queries and their relative frequency of occurrence in the workload: $W=\{(Q_i, f_i)\}$. For ChunkSim WP purposes, we also collect the following parameters for each query Q_i ran on each node N_j:

Processing time statistic (average) of chunk C_l for query Q_i ran on node N_j: $t(C_lQ_iN_j)$;

Per node results Transfer and Merge query time statistic (average) for query Q_i: $tt(Q_iN_j)$, $tm(Q_iN_j)$;

The processing time statistics of individual chunks $t(C_lQ_iN_j)$ may be replaced by a further summarized version, the average chunk processing time (i.e. over all chunks) statistic for query Q_i ran on node N_j: $t(CQ_iN_j)$;

Chunk Placement Layout (CPL): the CPL refers to information on how chunks are placed into nodes. Chunk $C_l(C_{key}, C_{sz})$ is characterized by the chunk key (C_{key}) and a size in bytes (C_{sz}).

The chunk key is the partitioning criteria value that determined the chunk (ChunkSim needs only a unique chunk identifier), and chunk size is its resulting size in bytes. CPL is a set of pairs $\{(C_l, N_j)\}$.

Replication Layout (RL): RL information maintains a list of which nodes contain replicas of each chunk. For chunk C_l, the list is a set of nodes $\{N_j\}$.

The ChunkSim parameters discussed above are summarized in Figure 5.

The WP information is obtained by collecting runtime statistics, from either a production system or benchmark setup. A benchmark setup is one with at least a set of samples of the chunks in each node, together with replicated dimensions and a set of expected workload queries. This allows the simulator to collect expected chunk processing times for WP.

The CL and RL information are obtained as a result of the data allocation and replication actions described in the next subsection.

Data Allocation and Replication Alternatives

Consider a data set D that is partitioned into Cc chunks and placed into Nn nodes. For load and availability balancing, Cc>> Nn.

Data allocation refers to how chunks are placed in the system (the terms data allocation and placement are used interchangeably). Either manual or automatic specification of data allocation is possible. Custom Placement (Pl-C) refers to a system administrator specifying manually the chunk layout or, more likely, how many chunks there should be at each individual node, in which case chunks are placed automatically, according to those numbers. Regardless of whether automatic or manual data allocation was used initially, it is always possible for the system administrator to specify custom placements or modification of current allocation using the (Pl-C) functionality.

Automatic placement refers to approaches that determine chunk layouts automatically using some simple heuristic. Homogeneous Placement (Pl-H) refers to placing the same number of chunks in every node. It is the simplest placement alternative and has the merit that nothing is assumed concerning the performance of different nodes. A variation of homogeneous placement is Homogeneous Size Placement (Pl-Hsz), where placement targets similar total size of chunks among nodes, as opposed to similar number of chunks in Pl-H.

If WP statistics information is available, a Performance-Wise Placement (Pl-W) solution can be computed based on chunk processing times and query frequencies: Average Composed Time of Node j: $ACT(N_j) =$

$$\sum_{i=1}^{nQueries} \sum_{l=1}^{nChunks} f_i \times t(C_l Q_i N_j)$$

Performance Index of Node j: $PI_j = ACT(N_j) / \max_j \{ACT(N_j)\}$

Performance-wise placement places chunks in nodes according to the performance indexes, that is, nodes with higher performance indexes will have more chunks. Given

$$cumPI(i) = \sum_{j=0}^{i} PI_j,$$

Figure 7. Determination of PI_f

$$PI_f = \begin{cases} PI \times f & \text{iff} \quad PI \neq 1 \\ PI & \text{otherwise} \end{cases}$$

the following algorithm from (Furatdo 2008) achieves the objective shown in Figure 6.

If the performance indexes PI are all 1, the result of Pl-W defaults to homogeneous placement (Pl-H), and between (Pl-H) and (Pl-W) there is a wide range of possibilities. In order to allow the system administrator to choose these possibilities, we add Performance Factor-wise placement (Pl-Wf). This alternative uses a numeric factor f between 0 and 1 to smooth the weight of performance indexes in the data allocation decisions, therefore considering lower heterogeneity values among nodes. Figure 7 summarizes how the new performance factors are computed.

Given these modified performance factors, the same algorithm 2 of Figure 6 is then applied as for Pl-W.

Replica placement concerns how many copies there will be for chunks and where those copies will be placed. Custom replication (Rl-C) refers to the system administrator specifying replicas for individual chunks. Alternatively, it is possible to specify automated replica placement, whereby the system administrator specifies a replication degree and policy.

Definition - Replication degree: given a data set D that is partitioned into Cc chunks and placed into Nn nodes, the replication degree r is a real number between 0 and N_{n-1} determining how

Figure 6. Algorithm for performance-wise placement

> **Algorithm 2 (Performance-wise Placement):**
> for i in 1 to Nc (number of chunks)
>   place chunk(i) at node N(j) such that
>   cumPI(j-1) < i MOD cumPI(Nn-1) <= cumPI(j)

many replicas there will be for dataset D. Given a replication degree r, there will be $Cc + \lceil r \times Cc \rceil$ chunks in the system.

A replication degree of 0 means that the data set will have no replicas, no chunk will be replicated into any other node; A replication degree of 0.5 means that half the data set chunks will be replicated into additional nodes; A replication degree of 2 means that all chunks of a data set will have two replicas located in two other nodes. A replication degree of 15 in a 16-node system corresponds to full mirroring. In terms of size, a 100 GB data set will occupy a total of 1.6TB with full replication, 300 GB with $r=2$ and 150GB with $r=0.5$. The smallest the replication factor, the lower the loading and storage requirements.

Replication alternatives follow the same logic of placement alternatives, meaning that to Pl-C, Pl-H, Pl-W and Pl-Wf correspond Rl-C, Rl-H and Rl-W. These are denoted as replication policies.

This set of placement and replication alternatives is the basic set already implemented in ChunkSim and in the actual DWPA parallel data warehouse architecture prototype (Furtado 2007). Other semi-automated approaches can be added that may for instance take into account groups of nodes for availability or performance reasons.

ChunkSim Estimation of Performance and Availability

The ChunkSim simulator implements the data allocation alternatives (placement and replication) and collects the system configuration information (WP, CL and RL) that it needs to model the system. We further define a run and an experiment as the actions the simulator uses to output some analysis report:

Run: a run is a simple event-based simulation of the on-demand, chunk-wise processing algorithm of Figure 4, simulating on-demand assignment of chunks to nodes

for processing, local query runtimes, and results transfer and merge times (according to the WP information). The output of the simulation is the average expected runtime value (secs).

Experiment: an experiment is a set of runs with some parameter that varies in order to analyze the effect of that parameter on performance or availability properties of the system. Additionally, for statistics relevance, ChunkSim always runs a pre-defined number of times (100 by default) for each parameter value.

ChunkSim offers the following experiments:

Performance Analysis of Replication Degrees (PARD) – this experiment answers the question of how different replication degrees influence system performance;
Additional inputs: replication Degrees array;
Outputs: a set of tuples (Replication Degree, Time PL-H (LP), Time FM (LP), Time (LP), Time Query). The "Time (LP)" and "Time Query" fields are the average expected runtime of the Local Processing (LP) part of a query and of the whole Query, respectively (the LP part of a query is the fraction that is processed locally at each node, before transfer and merge times). The Time "PL-H (LP)" and "Time FM (LP)" fields are for comparison purposes, since they represent "Slow" Homogeneous Placement with no replicas (PL-H) and "Fast" Full Mirroring (FM) runtimes, respectively.

For illustration purposes, Table 1 shows an example of the output report of PARD (corresponding to the experimental setup that will be shown later on in section 5). In that table the Replication Degree (RD) quantifies how much replication there are for the chunks in the SN system. For instance, RD=10% means that only 10% of the fact chunks have one copy, while 100% means

Table 1. Extract of analysis report for replication degree

Replication Degree	Time PL-H (LP)	Time FM (LP)	Time (LP)	Time Query
10%	240	153.552276	239.607907	247.232275
25%	240	153.552276	238.044278	247.362589
50%	240	153.552276	232.592335	247.362589
75%	240	153.552276	219.842612	247.232275
100%	240	153.552276	207.945652	244.492903
150%	240	153.552276	198.712255	233.492903
200%	240	153.552276	185.513946	223.753531
300%	240	153.552276	179.151584	212.753531
400%	240	153.552276	175.329786	207.623217
500%	240	153.552276	173.505943	207.623217

that every chunk has a copy in the system. These results allow the user to see what performance benefit there may be from adding redundancy and also where the choice lies in the interval between the worst and best PL-H and FM times.

System Size Planning (SSZP) – this experiment answers the question of how the performance varies with different system sizes under specific placement and replication scenario, which can be used to determine the number of nodes for a dataset.

Additional inputs: Number of Nodes array;
Outputs: a set of tuples (Number of Nodes, Time (LP), Time Query). The "Time (LP)" and "Time Query" fields are the average expected runtime of the Local Processing part and of the whole Query, respectively. The Number of Nodes array specifies which alternatives should be tested.

Availability Analysis (AA) – this experiment answers the question of whether and how fast the system is able to provide answers for varying replication degrees when different sets of nodes are offline or fail.

Additional inputs: replication Degrees array (optionally, also an array listing the set of nodes that is offline, in case AA is used to characterize the behavior in a particular scenario in terms of which nodes are offline or fail);

Outputs: a set of tuples (Number Of Nodes Offline, Replication Degree, FailureRate, Time (LP), Time Query). The "Time (LP)" and "Time Query" fields are the average expected runtime of the Local Processing part and of the whole Query, respectively. The "Number Of Nodes Offline" and "Replication Degree" are self-explanatory. The "FailureRate" parameter is a number between 0 and 1 and represents the fraction of runs that could not end because a chunk was not present in any of the active nodes (the set of nodes remaining after taking nodes offline). Given that nodes are heterogeneous, may have heterogeneous data loads, and different nodes may fail, it is possible for a run to succeed (find all necessary chunks) while another one may fail (not being able to run for lack of at least one necessary chunk).

Table 2. Database setup for TPC-H SF 25

Relation		Placement	
	Size	N Chunks	Chunk Size
Lineitem	29GB	118	250MB
Orders	7.1GB	118	62MB
Customer	780 MB	copied	-
Supplier	50.4 MB	copied	-
Nation	Very small	copied	-
Region	Very small	copied	-

USING CHUNKSIM TO ANALYZE PERFORMANCE AND AVAILABILITY

In this section we show results from using ChunkSim to analyze an SN system running a typical data warehouse. We consider the dataset from the decision support benchmark TPC-H, with a scale factor of 25. Given that the TPC-H data set is not a pure star schema, we have chosen a subset of it that can be configured as a star. We used relations Lineitem, Orders, Region, Nation, Customer, Supplier, with relations Lineitem and Orders equi-partitioned on their join key. We also defined a target chunk size for relation Lineitem of 250 MB (we rounded this value to get 118 chunks). This determined chunk hash ranges on the orderkey attribute, which also determined the chunks for the Orders relation, so that Lineitem and Orders became equi-partitioned on their equi-join attribute. This allowed us to process the schema similarly to a star schema, where the fact is represented by a join between Lineitem and Orders and the dimensions are the remaining relations. Table 2 shows the sizes and number of chunks in the experimental setup.

The data sets were installed in 16 PCs from our lab. The PCs all ran Windows XP, with 2GB RAM, 200 GB disks and Ultra-ATA storage controller, but half the nodes were Pentium IV at 3GHz, while the other half were Pentium D at 3.40 GHz. The database engines are Postgres with shared_bufferes=32MB, tmp_buffers=100MB and work_mem=100MB. The system was optimized by installing indexes and analyzing the schema to allow the system to compute useful statistics. For runs on the nodes we used a DWPA (Furtado 2007) parallel database middleware prototype developed in our research lab and targeted at share-nothing environments. The prototype takes as input actions, which may be local SQL queries (queries to be executed in nodes), or data transfer operations among any nodes. When the load-balanced query action is requested, a controller node processes the query as discussed in previous sections.

The computed performance indexes were then obtained by running a TPC-H workload round-robin for 10 hours. The resulting performance indexes are shown next:

{1,1.037,1.21,1.047,1.123,1.0023,1.051,1.102,1.867,1.85,1.93,1.85,1.79,2.1,2.02,1.86}

ChunkSim also collected Workload Properties (WP) statistics from this test run. With that information and different Placement Layout (PL) and Replication Layout (RL) configuration alternatives, we then issued a set of experiments to illustrate the results given by ChunkSim. Given the ChunkSim results reports, we have built charts that allow us to better compare the alternatives tested by the simulator. In the next subsections we present the results of experiments with System Size Planning (SSZP), Performance Analysis of

Figure 8. System size planning analysis results

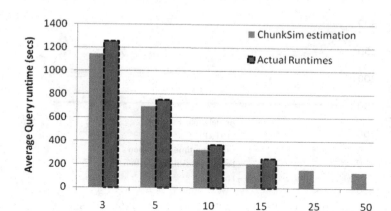

Replication Degrees (PARD) and Availability Analysis (AA).

System Size Planning (SSZP)

Our first experiment ran a System Size Planning analysis with ChunkSim, also repeating the same experiment in our lab setup to compare the estimation with actual runtimes. For these experiments the placement was homogeneous and the replication degree was 1 (one copy of each chunk). The results are shown in Figure 8. Since there were only 16 PCs in the physical setup and we wanted to include average runtime estimates for larger system configurations as well (25 and 50 nodes in the Figure), we assumed performance indexes for additional nodes beyond 16 using the same set of those 16 nodes in a round-robin fashion.

The results from Figure 8 show that the error in the ChunkSim average runtime estimation was within a 10% error from the actual runtimes for those combinations that were tested against both the simulator and the system (those with less than 16 nodes). It also allows the user to see what the average query runtime will be depending on the number of nodes. For instance, with 5 nodes the average runtime will be 695 secs, while with 25 nodes it will be 134 secs. We can also see that the

average runtime advantage of 50 nodes is very small when compared to 25 nodes, due to the increase in transfer and merge overheads among so many nodes.

Performance Analysis of Replication Degrees (PARD)

The PARD experiment allows us to analyze how different replication degrees affect runtime. For this experiment we considered homogeneous placement and varied the replication degree on 16 nodes. Figure 9 shows the results. The replication degree is depicted in the x-axis and represented as a fraction of the number of original chunks. There are two runtime interval boundings – the homogeneous (PL-H) and Full Mirroring (FM) curves (these concern only Local Processing) – and three more runtimes: the Local Processing estimation and the Query Runtime estimation are outputs of ChunkSim, while the Actual Query Runtime is the actual time taken in the lab experimental setup.

From Figure 9 we can see that ChunkSim does a good job estimating the runtime, and we can also see how the runtime evolves as the replication degree increases. One replica improves average query runtime by about 13%, and 2 replicas improve by about 23%, both when compared with

Figure 9. Performance analysis for replication degrees results

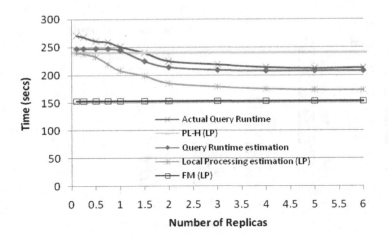

0.1 replicas. Beyond 2 replicas the improvement is small, at a significant increase in overall dataset size and therefore of loading and storage costs. This seems to indicate that 2 replicas would be an interesting option for this particular layout.

Availability Analysis (AA)

The next experiment predicts what happens when nodes go offline in our 16 node experimental setup using ChunkSim. Figure 10 shows the results. The point where each curve starts in Figure 10 indicates the minimum replication degree that is necessary in order to tolerate a certain number of node failures (we considered tolerance whenever the Failure Rate of experiment runs was below 10%).

Figure 10 indicates that while it is necessary to have at least 1 and 2 replicas to tolerate 1 and 2 node failures respectively, for this configuration 3, 4 and 5 node failures can be tolerated with 2, 3 and 3 replicas respectively. These experiment results also show a steep curve when 1 or 2 nodes fail with a replica degree less than 3. A similar behavior can be observed when 3 nodes fail with less than 4 replicas, when 4 nodes fail with less than 5 replicas and when 5 nodes fail with less than 6 replicas.

The observations from the previous experiments apply for the setting that was tested, concerning both dataset and chunk configurations, workload properties and performance indexes of the 16 nodes. With other settings, ChunkSim would allow us to reach conclusions and plan for the corresponding configurations as well. As a result, ChunkSim is an adequate tool to help plan, analyze and decide on the number of nodes, placement and replication layouts and replication degrees, depending on requirements concerning performance (average response times) and availability (tolerance to nodes failing or being offline) objectives.

CONCLUSIONS AND FUTURE WORK

In this paper we have proposed ChunkSim, an event-based simulator for analysis of load and availability balancing in chunk-wise parallel data warehouses. We discussed first how a shared-nothing system can store and process a data warehouse chunk-wise, and use an efficient on-demand processing approach. Then we discussed ChunkSim model parameters, the set of parameters that the simulator must collect to be able to simulate execution. We also discussed

Figure 10. Availability analysis results

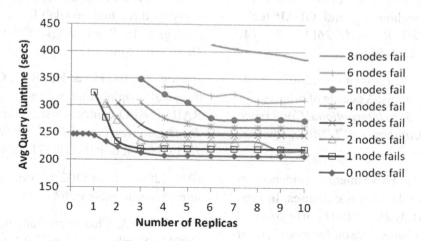

data allocation and replication alternatives that ChunkSim implements and the analysis that ChunkSim is currently able to run on performance and availability features. We have used Chunksim to analyze system size planning, peroformance analysis of replication degree and availability analysis, also comparing with results obtained in an actual deployment on 16 nodes. These results have shown that ChunkSim experiments can be used to characterize the behavior of the system with different placement and replication choices and in the presence of node failures. The results are also reasonably in aggreement with actual runs on the prototype system.

There are several related issues that deserve future work: in this work we assumed a star-schema, with multiple small dimensions which are copied into all nodes, and either a large fact (partitioned) or a set of equi-partitioned relations (also denoted as co-located). In the future ChunkSim should be extended to handle query processing with non co-located partitioned relations, in which case the model should include repartitioning costs (the costs from data exchange between nodes during the processing of joins); The current ChunkSim model assumes that every node sends its results to a single merge node, which will merge the incoming results from all nodes; We did not consider failures in the merge and controller nodes. In a future version of ChunkSim we expect to consider redundant merge and controler nodes and to study the impact of the additional overheads incurred in these cases; In order to optimize processing over a large number of nodes, it may be interesting to explore hierarchical aggregation (Furtado 2005) as well, whereby groups of nodes merge parts of the partial results in parallel and send the results to a next level in a hierarchical tree until a single final node merges the partial results to form the final result; In this setting, we also plan to consider node failures within the merge hierarchy.

REFERENCES

Akal, F., Böhm, K., & Schek, H.-J. (2002). OLAP Query Evaluation in a Database Cluster: A performance study on intra-query parallelism. East-European Conf. on Advances in Databases and Information Systems (ADBIS), Bratislava, Slovakia.

Bellatreche, L., & Boukhalfa, K. (2005). An evolutionary approach to schema partitioning selection in a data warehouse. *International Conference on Data Warehousing and Knowledge Discovery*.

Chaudhuri, S., & Dayal, U. (1997). An overview of data warehousing and OLAP technology. *SIGMOD Record, 26*(1), 65–74. doi:10.1145/248603.248616

Chaudhuri, S., & Narasayya, V. (2007). Self-tuning database systems: A decade of progress. In *Proceedings of the 33rd International Conference on Very Large Databases (VLDB07),* Vienna, Austria.

Furtado, P. (2004). Experimental evidence on partitioning in parallel data warehouses. In *Proceedings of the ACM DOLAP 04 - Workshop of the International Conference on Information and Knowledge Management,* Washington USA.

Furtado, P. (2004). Workload-based placement and join processing in node-partitioned data warehouses. In *Proceedings of the International Conference on Data Warehousing and Knowledge Discovery* (pp. 38-47), Zaragoza, Spain.

Furtado, P. (2005). Efficiently processing query-intensive databases over a non-dedicated local network. In *Proceedings of the 19th International Parallel and Distributed Processing Symposium.*

Furtado, P. (2005). Replication in node-partitioned data warehouses. *DDIDR2005 Workshop of VLDB 2005.*

Furtado, P. (2007). Efficient and robust node-partitioned data warehouses. In R. Wrembel and C. Koncilia (Eds.), *Data warehouses and OLAP: Concepts, architectures and solutions* (pp. 203-229). Hershey, PA: IGI Global.

Hsiao, H., & DeWitt, D. (1990). Chained declustering: A new availability strategy for multiprocessor database machines. *Intl. Conf. on Data Engineering.*

Hsiao, H., & DeWitt, D. (1990b). Replicated data management in the gamma database machine. *Workshop on the Management of Replicated Data.*

Hsiao, H., & DeWitt, D. J. (1991). A performance study of three high availability data replication strategies. In *Proceedings of the Parallel and Distributed Systems.*

Hwang, K., Jin, H., & Ho, R. S. C. (2002). Orthogonal striping and mirroring in distributed RAID for I/O-centric cluster computing. *IEEE Transactions on Parallel and Distributed Systems, 13*(1), 26–44. doi:10.1109/71.980025

IBM. (2008). IBM DB2 Server. Retrieved from http://www.ibm.com/db2.

Lee, E. K., & Chandramohan, A. Thekkath, P. (1996). Distributed virtual disks. In *Proceedings of the Seventh International Conference on Architectural Support for Programming Languages and Operating Systems.*

Lerner, A. (1998). *An architecture for the load-balanced parallel join operation in shared-nothing environments* (in Portuguese). M.Sc. Dissertation, Computer Science Department, Pontificia Univ. Catolica do Rio de Janeiro.

Lerner, A., & Lifschitz, S. (1998). A study of workload balancing techniques on parallel join algorithms. In *Proceedings of the International Conference on Parallel and Distributed Processing Techniques and Applications (PDPTA)* (pp. 966-973).

Lima, A. A., Mattoso, M., & Valduriez, P. (2004). *Adaptive virtual partitioning for OLAP query processing in a database cluster.* Paper presented at the 19th Brasilian Simposium on Databases SBBD, Brasília, Brasil.

Lima, A. A. B., Mattoso, M., & Valduriez, P. (2004). OLAP query processing in a database cluster. In *Proc. 10th Euro-Par Conf.*

Patterson, D. A., Gibson, G., & Katz, R. H. (1998). A case for redundant arrays of inexpensive disks (raid). In *Proceedings of the International Conference on Management of Data* (pp. 109-116).

Rao, J., Zhang, C., Megiddo, N., & Lohman, G. (2002). Automating physical database design in a parallel database. Proceedings of the ACM International Conference on Management of Data, 558-569, Madison, Wisconsin, USA, June 2002.

Stöhr, T., & Märtens, H. Rahm, E. (2000). Multi-dimensional database allocation for parallel data warehouses, In *Proc. 26th Intl. Conf. on Very Large Databases (VLDB)*.

Stonebraker, M., & Schloss, G. A. (1990). Distributed RAID - A new multiple copy algorithm. *International Conference on Data Engineering* (pp. 430-437).

Tandem (1987). *NonStop SQL, A distributed, high-performance, high-reliability implementation of SQL*. Paper presented at the Workshop on High Performance Transactional Systems.

Chapter 9
QoS–Oriented Grid–Enabled Data Warehouses

Rogério Luís de Carvalho Costa
University of Coimbra, Portugal

Pedro Furtado
University of Coimbra, Portugal

ABSTRACT

Globally accessible data warehouses are useful in many commercial and scientific organizations. For instance, research centers can be put together through a grid infrastructure in order to form a large virtual organization with a huge virtual data warehouse, which should be transparently and efficiently queried by grid participants. As it is frequent in the grid environment, in the Grid-based Data Warehouse one can both have resource constraints and establish Service Level Objectives (SLOs), providing some Quality of Service (QoS) differentiation for each group of users, participant organizations or requested operations. In this work, we discuss query scheduling and data placement in the grid-based data warehouse, proposing the use of QoS-aware strategies. There are some works on parallel and distributed data warehouses, but most do not concern the grid environment and those which do so, use best-effort oriented strategies. Our experimental results show the importance and effectiveness of proposed strategies.

INTRODUCTION

In the last few years, Grid technology became a key component in many widely distributed applications from distinct domains, which include both research-oriented and business-related projects. The Grid is used as an underlying infrastructure that provides transparent access to shared and distributed resources, like supercomputers, workstation clusters, storage systems and networks (Foster, 2001). In *Data Grids*, the infrastructure is used to coordinate the storage of huge volumes of data or the distributed execution of jobs which consume or generate large volumes of data (Krauter et al, 2002; Venugopal et al, 2006). Most of the works on data grids considers the use or management of large files, but grid-enabled Database Management Systems (DBMS) may be highly useful in several applica-

DOI: 10.4018/978-1-60566-756-0.ch009

tions from distinct domains (Nieto-Santisteban et al, 2005; Watson, 2001).

On the other hand, data warehouses are mostly read-only databases which store historical data that is commonly used for decision support and knowledge discovery (Chaudhuri & Dayal, 1997). Grid-based data warehouses are useful in many real and virtual global organizations which are generating huge volumes of distributed data. In such context, the data warehouse is a highly distributed database whose data may be loaded from distinct sites and that should be transparently queried by users from distinct domains.

But constructing effective grid-based applications is not simple. Grids are usually very heterogeneous environments composed by resources that may belong to distinct organization domains. Each domain administrator may have a certain degree of autonomy and impose local resource usage constraints for remote users (Foster, 2001).

Such site autonomy is reflected in terms of scheduling algorithms and scheduler architectures. The hierarchical architecture is one of the most commonly used scheduling architecture in Grids (Krauter et al, 2002). In such architecture, a *Community Scheduler* (or Resource Broker) is responsible to transform submitted jobs into tasks and to assign them to sites for execution. At each site, a *Local Scheduler* is used to manage local queues and implement local domain scheduling policies. Such architecture enables a certain degree of site autonomy.

Besides that, in Grids, tasks are usually specified together with Service Level Objectives (SLO) or Quality-of-Service (QoS) requirements. In fact, in many Grid systems, scheduling is QoS-oriented instead of performance-oriented (Roy & Sander, 2004). In such situations, the main objective is to increase user's satisfaction instead of achieving high performance. Hence, the user-specified SLOs may be used by the Community Scheduler to negotiate with Local Schedulers the establishment of Service Level Agreements (SLA). But SLOs can also be used to provide some kind of differentiation among users or jobs. Execution deadline and execution cost's limit are some example of commonly used SLOs.

We consider here the use of deadline-marked queries in grid-based Data Warehouses. In such context, execution time objectives can provide some differentiation between interactive queries and report queries. For example, one can establish that interactive queries should be executed by a 20 seconds deadline and that report queries should be executed in 5 minutes. In fact, different deadlines may be specified considering several alternatives, like the creation of privileged groups of users that should obtain responses in lower times or like providing smaller deadlines for queries submitted by users affiliated to institutions that had offered more resources to the considered grid-based data warehouse.

Data placement is a key issue in grid-based applications. Due to the grid's heterogeneity and to the high cost of moving data across different sites, data replication is commonly used to improve performance and availability (Ranganathan & Foster, 2004). But most of the works on replica selection and creation in data grids consider generic file replication [e.g. (Lin et al, 2006; Siva Sathya et al, 2006; Haddad & Slimani, 2007)]. Therefore, the use of specialized data placement strategies for the deployment of data warehouses in grids still remains an open issue.

In this chapter, we discuss the implementation of QoS-oriented Grid-enabled Data Warehouses. The grid-enabled DW is composed by a set of grid-enabled database management systems, a set of tools provided by an underlying grid resource management (GRM) system and hierarchical schedulers. We combine data partitioning and replication, constructing a highly distributed database that is stored across grid's sites, and use a QoS-oriented scheduling and a specialized replica selection and placement strategy to achieve high QoS levels.

This chapter is organized as follows: in the next Section we present some background on data grids and grid-enabled databases. Then, we discuss QoS-oriented scheduling and placement strategies for the Grid-based warehouse. In the following, we present some experimental results. Next, we draw conclusions. At the end of the chapter, we present some key terms definitions.

DATA GRIDS AND GRID-ENABLED DATABASES

The Grid is an infra-structure that provides transparent access to distributed heterogeneous shared resources, which belong to distinct sites (that may belong to distinct real organizations). Each site has some degree of autonomy and may impose resource usage restrictions for remote users (Foster, 2001).

In the last decade, some Grid Resource Management (GRM) Systems [for example, Legion (Grimshaw et al, 1997) and Globus Toolkit (Foster & Kesselman, 1997)] were developed in order to provide some basic functionality that is commonly necessary to run grid-based applications. Authorization and remote job execution management are among the most common features in GRM systems. Some of them also provide data management-related mechanisms, like efficient data movement [e.g. GridFTP (Allcock et al, 2005)] and data replica location [e.g. Globus Replica Location Service – RLS (Chervenak et al, 2004)].

In terms of grid job scheduling, there are three basic architectures (Krauter et al (2002): *centralized*, *hierarchical* and *decentralized*. In the first one, a single *Central Scheduler* is used to schedule the execution of all the incoming jobs, assigning them directly to the existent resources. Such architecture may lead to good scheduling decisions, as the scheduler may consider the characteristics and loads of all available resources, but suffers from a scalability problem: if a wide variety of distributed heterogeneous resources is available, considering all the resources' individual char-

acteristics when scheduling job execution may become very time consuming. In the hierarchical architecture, a *Community Scheduler* (or *Resource Broker*) is responsible to assign job execution to sites. Each site has its own job scheduler (*Local Scheduler*) which is responsible to locally schedule the job execution. The Community Scheduler and Local Schedulers may negotiate job execution and each Local Scheduler may implement local resource utilization policies. Besides that, as the Community Scheduler does not have to exactly know the workload and characteristics of each available node, this model leads to greater scalability than the centralized scheduling model. In the *Decentralized* model, there is no Central Scheduler. Each site has its own scheduler, which is responsible to schedule local job execution. Schedulers must interact to each other in order to negotiate remote job execution. Several messages may be necessary during the negotiation in order to do good job scheduling, which may impact the system's performance.

Some of the GRM systems have built-in scheduling policies, but almost all enable the user to implement its own scheduling policy or to use application-level schedulers. In this context, some *general purpose* application level schedulers were designed [e.g. Condor-G (Frey et al, 2001) and Nimrod-G (Buyya et al, 2000)]. These general purpose generally consider some kind of user-specified requirement or QoS-parameter (e.g. job's deadline), but may fail to efficiently schedule data-bound jobs.

Query scheduling strategies for data-bound jobs were evaluated by Ranganathan & Foster (2004). *Data Present* (DP), *Least Loaded Scheduling* (LLS) and *Random Scheduling* (RS) were compared. In RS, job execution is randomly scheduled to available nodes. In LLS, each job is scheduled to be executed by the node that has the lowest number of waiting jobs. Both in RS and LLS, a data-centric job may be scheduled to be executed by a job that does not store the required data to execute such job. In this case, remote data is fetched during job execution. In the DP strategy, each job is assigned to a node that stores the job's required input data. Ranganathan & Foster claim that, in most situations, DP has better performance than LLS and RS (as doing data movement across grid's nodes may be very time consuming).

There are several parameters that should be considered when scheduling data-centric jobs. These include the size of the job's input and output data, and the network bandwidth among grid's nodes. Park & Kim (2003) present a cost model that use such parameters to estimate job's execution time at each node (both considering that a job can be executed at the submission site or not, and that it may use local or remote data as input). Job execution is scheduled to the node with the lowest predicted execution time.

Although very promising, the grid-enabled database management systems were not largely adopted for a long time (Nieto-Santisteban et al, 2005; Watson, 2001). Watson (2001) proposed the construction of a federated system with the use of ODBC/JDBC as interface for heterogeneous database systems. In more recent work, web services are used as interface to database management systems. Alpdemir et al (2003) present an Open Grid Services Architecture [OGSA – (Foster et al, 2002)]-compatible implementation of a distributed query processor (Polar*). A distributed query execution plan is constructed by basic operations that are executed at several nodes.

Costa & Furtado (2008c) compares the use of centralized and hierarchical query scheduling strategies in grid-enabled databases. The authors present that hierarchical schedulers can be used without significant lose in the system's performance and can also lead to good levels of achievement of Service Level Objectives (SLOs). In Costa & Furtado (2008b) the authors propose the use of reputation systems to schedule deadline-marked queries among grid-enabled databases when several replicas of the same data are present at distinct sites.

In Grids, data replicas are commonly used to improve job (or query) execution performance and data availability. *Best Client* and *Cascading Replication* are among the dynamic file replication strategies evaluated by Ranganathan & Foster (2001) to be used in the Grid. In both models, a new file replica is created whenever the number of access to an existent data file is greater than a threshold value. The difference among the methods resides on where such new file is placed. The 'best client' of a certain data file is defined as the node that has requested for each more times in a certain time period. In the Best Client placement strategy, the new replica is placed at the *best client* node. In the Cascading Replication method, the new file is placed at the first node in the path between the node that stores the file that is being replicated and the *best client* node.

The Best Client strategy is used as an inspiration for the *Best Replica Site* strategy [(Siva Sathya et al, 2006)]. The main different among the this strategy and the original Best Client is that in *Best Replica Site* the site in which the replica is created is chosen considering not only the number of access from clients to the dataset, but also the replica's expected utility for each site and the distance between sites. Sathya et al (2006) also propose two other strategies: *Cost Effective Replication* and *Topology Based Replication*. In the first one, a cost function is used to choose in which site a replica should be created (the cost function evaluates the cost of accessing a replica at each site). In the latter, database replicas are created at the node that has the greatest number of direct connections to other ones.

Topology related aspects are also considered by Lin et al (2006) in order to choose replica location. The authors consider a hierarchical (tree-like) grid in which database is placed at the tree root. Whenever a job is submitted, the scheduler looks for the accessed data at the node in which the job was submitted. If the necessary data is not at such node, then the schedulers asks for it at the node's parent node. If the parent node does not have a

Figure 1. Sample Star Schema

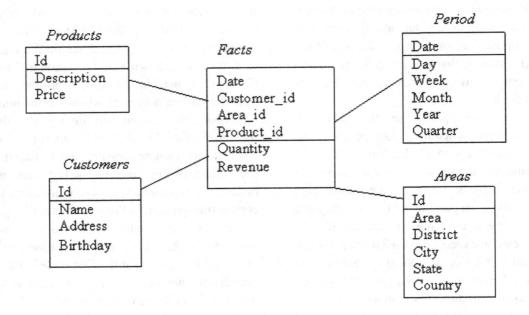

THE DISTRIBUTED QOS-ORIENTED WAREHOUSE

replica of the searched data, then the scheduler looks for it at the grandparent node, and so on. Whenever the number of searched nodes is greater than a defined value, a new data replica is created. Such newly created replica is placed at the node that maximizes the number of queries that can be answered without creating new replicas.

Maximizing the economic value of locally stored data is the objective of the strategy proposed by Haddad & Slimani (2007). In such strategy, there is a price to access each data fragment. Each node tries to foresee the future price of the fragments and stores the ones that are forecasted as the most valuable.

Most of the abovementioned strategies are oriented for file-based grids. Others are related to best-effort oriented scheduling in grid-enabled databases. But all of them are somehow related to the aspects we deal with in the next Sections. In the next Section, we discuss the architecture and scheduling for the QoS-oriented grid-based distributed data warehouse.

Data warehouses are huge repositories of historical data. They are subject-oriented: a certain subject (revenue, for example) is analyzed considering several distinct measures (e.g. time period). Each analyses measure domain is called a *dimension*. Therefore, the DW is a multidimensional space. Such space is commonly represented in relational databases as *star schemas* (Chaudhuri & Dayal, 1997), with several distinct *dimension tables* and a huge *facts table*. The dimensions tables store information about the analyze measures domains. The facts table stores data that represents the events of the real world and pointers to dimensions tables. Figure 1 presents an example of a star schema (in the remaining of this chapter, tables are considered to be conceptually organized in a star schema).

The Grid-based data warehouse is accessed by users of geographically distributed sites which may or may not belong to the same real organization, but that are put together within a grid infrastructure. Each site may share one or more resources to the grid. Examples of possible shared resources are storage systems, computer clusters and supercomputers.

Data warehouses are usually deployed at a single site. But that may not be the most effective layout in a grid-based DW implementation. In fact, in such environment, placing the entire database at a single site would be more expensive and time consuming than creating a distributed DW that uses the available distributed resources to store the database and to execute users' queries. It is important to consider that not only users are distributed across distinct grid sites but also that the warehouse's data may be loaded from several sites.

Hence, in the distributed Grid-based DW, data is partitioned and/or replicated at nodes from distinct sites and may be queried by any grid participant.

Best-Effort Approaches for Grid-Enabled Warehouses

There are some previous works on implementing and using grid-enabled data warehouses, but most use best-effort oriented approaches, which may not be the most adequate approach in grid based systems (as presented in the previous Section, grid scheduling is usually satisfaction-oriented).

High availability and high performance are the main concerns by Costa & Furtado (2006). Each participating site stores a partitioned copy of the entire warehouse. Intra-site parallelism is obtained by the use of the Node Partitioned Data Warehouse (NPDW) strategy (Furtado, 2004). Hierarchical scheduler architecture is used together with an on-demand scheduling policy (idle nodes asks the Central Scheduler for new queries to execute). Such model leads to good performance and high availability, but also consumes too much storage space, as the whole warehouse is present at each participating site.

The Olap-enabled grid (Lawrence & Rau-Chaplin, 2006; Dehne et al, 2007) is a two tier grid-enabled warehouse. The users' local domain is considered the first tier and stores cached data. Database servers at remote sites compose the second tier. The scheduling algorithm tries to use the locally stored data to answer submitted queries. If it is not possible, then remote servers are accessed.

The Globus Toolkit is used by Wehrle et al (2007) as an underlying infrastructure to implement a grid-enabled warehouse. Facts table data is partitioned across nodes participating nodes and dimension data is replicated. Some specialized services are used at each node: (i) an *index service* provides information about locally stored data; and (ii) a *communication service* is used to access remote data. Locally stored data is used to answer incoming queries. If the searched data is not stored at the local node, then remote access is done by the use of the communication service. This strategy and the abovementioned Olap-enabled strategy do not provide any autonomy for local domains.

Distributed Data Placement in QoS-Oriented DW

In data warehouses, users' queries usually follow some kind of access pattern, like geographically related ones in which users from a location may have more interest in data related to such location than in data about other locations (Deshpande et al, 1998). That may also be applicable for the grid. For instance, consider a global organization that uses a grid-based DW about sales which is accessed by users from several countries. The users in New York City, USA, may start querying data about sales revenue in Manhattan, and then do continuous drill-up operations in order to obtain information about sales in New York City, in New York State and, finally, in the USA. Only rarely New York users would query data about sales in France. In the same way, users from Paris may start querying the database about sales in France, and then start doing drill-down operations in order to obtain data about sales in Paris and, then, individually on each of its *arrondissements*.

In order to reduce data movement across sites (improving the system's performance) the grid-based DW tables are physically distributed across different sites. Such distribution is represented at a Global Physical Schema (GPS). Ideally, the physically used data distribution strategy is transparent to users, which should submit queries considering a unified Logical Model (LM).

Grids are highly heterogeneous environments. At each site, different types of resources may be available (like shared-nothing and shared-disk parallel machines, for example). It is somewhat difficult to find an intra-site allocation strategy that is optimal in the several possible situations. Therefore, each site may use its own local physical allocation strategy (e.g. Multi-Dimensional Hierarchical Fragmentation – MDHF (Stöhr et al, 2000) or Node-Partitioned Data Warehouse strategy - NPDW (Furtado, 2004). Each site's existent relations are represented in a Local Site Physical Schema (LSPS). This assumption fits well with the idea of domain autonomy, which is one of the grid's characteristics.

In the generic grid-based DW, nodes from any site can load data to the database. But the same data cannot be loaded from distinct sites. This leads to the idea that each piece of data has a single site (to which we call Data Source Site) that is its primary source. In order to reduce data movement across grid's sites (considering the abovementioned geographically related access patters), each site should maintain a copy of the facts data it has loaded into the DW (in this chapter, we consider that tables in the LM are organized in a star schema). This generates a globally physically partitioned facts table which uses the values of a site source attribute as partitioning criteria.

Depending on the implementation, the site source attribute values may be combined with values of other existent dimensions. In fact, the repartitioning of each facts table site source-based fragment into several smaller fragments can

benefit the system in several ways. For instance, in such situation, each smaller fragment can be replicated to distinct sites, what would increase the system's degree of parallelism. Besides that, depending on the selection predicate, some queries may access only a set of the smaller fragments, which would be faster than accessing the whole original site source-based fragment. These two situations are represented in Figure 2. Therefore, even at the global level, other partitioning criteria should be used together with the site source attribute. The use of the most frequently used equi-join attributes as part of the partitioning criteria for the facts table can improve performance, by reducing data movement across sites when executing queries [as it does in shared-nothing parallel machines (Furtado, 2004b)].

Besides facts table's partitions, each site should also store dimension tables' data. Full replication of dimension tables across all sites may be done to reduce inter-site data movement during query execution and to improve data availability. Such strategy is feasible when dimension tables are small (this also facilitates system management). But when large dimension tables are present, they can be fragmented both at intra-site and inter-sites levels in order to improve performance and QoS-levels. Intra-site dimension table fragmentation strategy depends on the locally chosen physical allocation strategy (which is dependent on the type of locally available resources, as discussed earlier). Inter-sites large dimension tables' fragmentation should be done using a strategy similar to the one of facts table fragmentation: initially, dimension data should remain at its *Data Source Site*. Inter-site replication is done when necessary. Derived partitioning of the facts table can also be done, improving the system's performance as join operations can be broken into subjoins that are executed in parallel at distinct sites. Although the use of facts table derived partitioning depends on the semantics of stored data, such kind of partitioning should be used together use the aforementioned partitioning based on the site source attribute.

Figure 2. Examples of benefits on the use of smaller facts table fragments at the global level

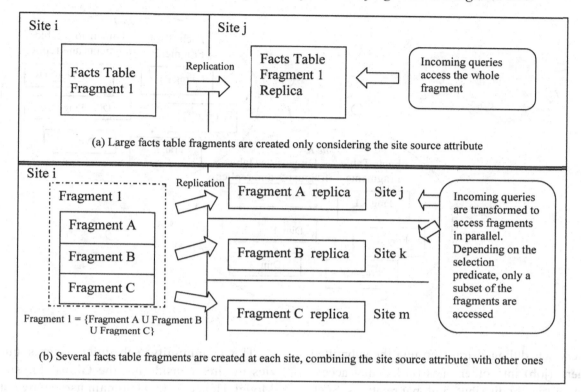

(a) Large facts table fragments are created only considering the site source attribute

Fragment 1 = {Fragment A U Fragment B U Fragment C}

(b) Several facts table fragments are created at each site, combining the site source attribute with other ones

In the case of large dimension tables' fragmentation, some data replication may also occur. For instance, let's consider a grid-DW of a nation-wide retail store. There are several sites participating in such grid-DW, each one at a distinct state. In such warehouse, a (large) dimension table stores information about customers. Such table may be fragmented according with the location in which the customer buys. Initially, each customer's information would be at a single site. But when a certain customer travels (or moves) to another state and buys at stores from such state, his/her information may also appear in the state's database. When there is dimension table (fragment) replication at distinct sites, a replica consistency strategy may be necessary. There are several works in the literature about algorithms to efficiently maintain replica consistency in distributed and grid-based databases [e.g., (Akal et al, 2005; Breitbart et al, 1999; Chen et al, 2005)].

Hence, in the GPS, the facts table is partitioned by the combination of the site source attribute with the other most frequently used equi-join attributes. Derived facts table partitioning may be used. Each site stores the partitions from which the site is the Data Source Site. Large dimension tables are fragmented and small dimension tables replicated at all sites. A fragmented *site source* dimension table (each site storing only its own information) should be used. Such data distribution strategy is represented in Figure 3. Facts table's fragments are replicated across grid's sites in order to improve performance and availability.

The QoS-Oriented Query Scheduling

Users submit queries to the grid-based DW considering the Logical Model. Ideally, the physically used data distribution strategy should be transparent to users. Hence, the first phase in

Figure 3. Global physical allocation example

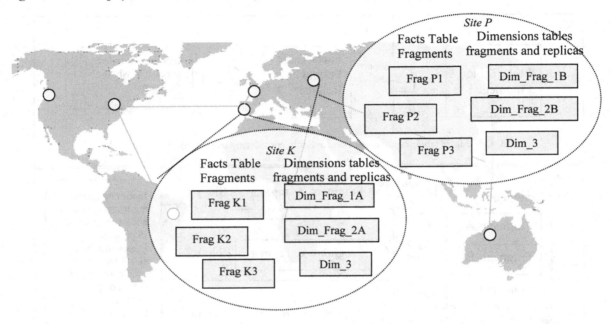

query scheduling is transforming the submitted query (job) into other ones (tasks) that access the physically distributed global relations. Such transformation is similar to the ones presented at (Furtado, 2004b).

The generated tasks are assigned to sites by a Community Scheduler. At each site, a Local Scheduler is responsible to manage task execution. If domain specific physical layout is used, the Local Scheduler must also do the conversion of the globally specified task into other queries that access the physically existent relations. The Community Scheduler specifies the necessary requirements (execution deadlines) of each task (rewritten query) in order to execute the user's query by the desired QoS level. Then, there is a task execution negotiation phase among the Community Scheduler and Local Schedulers, in order to verify if each of the rewritten queries (tasks) can be executed by its deadline. If any task cannot be executed by the specified deadline, then user is notified that the required SLO cannot be achieved and a new one must be specified, or the query execution would be canceled.

The Community Scheduler assigns queries to sites considering the Global Physical Model. Hence, if local domain uses some data partitioning policy different from the one used at the global level (e.g. large dimension table partitioning, as in the abovementioned NPDW strategy), then the Local Scheduler should transform the globally specified query into the ones that should be locally executed. Besides that, results merging should also be done at local site level in order to send back a single result, which is correspondent to the query (task) the site has received.

EVALUATING IF A SLO CAN BE ACHIEVED

Let's consider a user-submitted query Q with a deadline interval d. The system must estimate the query's total execution time (*tet*) and compare it with d in order to verify if the query can or cannot be executed by its deadline. When the system estimates that the execution can be done according to the specified SLO ($d \geq tet$), it starts query execution. Otherwise, query execution is not started and user is informed that the established SLO cannot be achieved.

In order to predict the *tet* value, the system estimates the execution time of each of the query's tasks (task finish time – *tft*), considering three key time components for each query (task):

(i) The query execution time at a local site (local execution time - *let*);

(ii) The necessary time to transfer required data to the site (data transfer time – *dtt*);

(iii) The necessary time to transfer the query's results back from the chosen site (results transfer time – *rtt*).

The *tft* value of a single task at a certain site is computed by Equation 1. An upper bound estimated value for the users' query execution (*tet*) is obtained by Equation 2.

$$tft = let + dtt + rtt \qquad (1)$$

$$tet = Max(tft) \qquad (2)$$

To estimate the value of *tft*, the Community Scheduler must have some estimative of its components. First of all, it predicts the values of *dtt* and *rtt*, with the support of a grid infrastructure network monitor tool [like the Network Weather Service – NWS - (Wolski, 1997)]. Such tool is used to predict network latency (L) and data transfer throughput (TT) between sites. The Community Scheduler uses such predicted values for network characteristics together with estimated dataset sizes (obtained by database statistics) to predict *dtt* and *rtt* (a predicted transfer time (*tbs*) of a dataset of size z between sites i and j can be obtained by Equation 3).

$$tbs_{i,j} = L + \left(\frac{z}{TT} \right) \qquad (3)$$

On the other hand, the Community Scheduler does not have control of intra-set data placement and query execution. Therefore, it is somewhat difficult to make such module estimate tasks' execution time. Such estimation is done by local schedulers. In fact, in QoS-oriented scheduling, the Community Scheduler does not have to know the exactly necessary time to execute a query: local schedulers must commit themselves to execution the assigned queries by a certain time interval. Such interval is the maximum value that *let* (mlet) can assume in order to finish the user's query execution by the specified SLO.

Hence, for each task, the Community Scheduler computes the *mlet* value (Equation 4) and uses such value as a task deadline when negotiating with local schedulers.

$$mlet \leq d - (dtt + rtt) \qquad (4)$$

Figure 4 presents a general view of the SLO-aware scheduling model.

LOCAL SCHEDULERS AND SERVICE LEVEL AGREEMENTS

When estimating if a user's query can be executed by the proposed deadline, the Community Scheduler must consider the necessary time to execute each rewritten query at local sites (*let*). But not only the Community Scheduler does not have total control of the execution environment, but also each site can have local domain policies that can constraint the use of local resources by remote users. Therefore, the necessary time to execute each task should be predicted by local schedulers.

But in QoS-oriented scheduling, each site may not inform the Community Scheduler the exact predicted query execution time. On the other hand, local schedulers should commit themselves to execute the negotiated query by

Figure 4. General view of the SLO-aware scheduling model

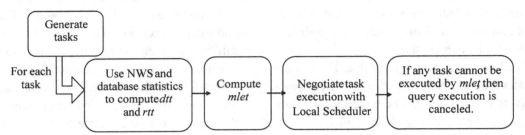

a certain deadline (*mlet*) that is specified by the Community Scheduler. When a local scheduler agrees to execute a query by a certain deadline, it makes a SLA (Service Level Agreement) with the Community Schedule.

When a SLA is signed, the local scheduler is committed to execute the query by the negotiated deadline. But it can, for instance, reorder local query execution (do not have to execute each of the incoming queries as fast as possible) or change the number of queries that are concurrently executed at the local DBMS (multi-programming degree).

The QoS-OES (Costa & Furtado, 2008) scheduler is an example of QoS-oriented query scheduler that can be used in such context. Such module is a generic external scheduler that is used as a middleware between the DBMS and its users. The QoS-OES is capable to estimate query execution time in a multi-query environment and to commit itself to execute a submitted query by a certain deadline, as soon as the specified deadline time is greater than the predicted query execution time.

Caching and Replication for QoS

Grids are highly heterogeneous environments in which the use of database replicas can lead to great performance improvement and to high QoS levels. But as the problem of choosing the optimal number of database replicas and doing the optimal placement of such replicas into the

nodes of a distributed environment is NP-hard (Loukopoulos & Ahmad, 2000), some heuristics should be used. The heuristics used in this Section are QoS-oriented, which means they intend to increase the system's SLO-achievement rate (SLO-AR).

The SLO-AR (Costa & Furtado, 2008b) is a performance metric that aims to indicate how well a system is performing on executing jobs by specified service level objectives. It is defined as the relation between the number of queries whose execution finishes by the required deadline (N) and the number of queries in the submitted workload (W).

Therefore, the SLO-Oriented replica selection and placement strategy aims at increasing the number of queries that the system executes by the specified SLOs. In order to do that, a benefit-based mechanism is implemented by a Replication Manager (RM), as it is described below.

INTER-SITE QOS-ORIENTED DYNAMIC REPLICATION

The RM monitors the number of times that a SLO-objective cannot be achieved due to the inexistence of a certain dataset (e.g. facts table fragment) at a certain site and computes the total benefit value (β) that the system would have if a replica of such dataset is created. When β is greater than a threshold value, the system considers the possibility of creating the data replica at the evaluated site (at this point we refer that replicas of input datasets are created. Latter in this chapter, we discuss how to determine if such datasets are fact's table fragments or computed chunks).

In order to implement such policy, when the Local Scheduler cannot execute the task (query) by the specified *mlet* time, it should evaluate if it would achieve the specified deadline if a replica of a given dataset is present at the site.

When the Local Scheduler predicts that it would achieve the required task's deadline if a certain replica is locally stored, it informs the Replication Manager what is such replica. In such situation, the value of β for the specified dataset is incremented by a certain δ value (benefit of the considered input data set replica to the system), as represented in Equation 5. However, the δ value of each task should vary over time, in order to differentiate the benefit for old queries from the ones for newer queries. Therefore, a time discount function may be used in order to compute δ, as presented in Equation 6.

$$\beta = \sum_i \delta_i \qquad (5)$$

$$\delta_i = e^{-\left(\frac{\Delta t}{\lambda}\right)} \qquad (6)$$

In Equation 6, Δt represents the time window between the task execution time (of the query that would be benefited by the input dataset replication) and current time and λ enables the use of different time intervals [as defined in (Huynh et al, 2006)].

Whenever β is greater than a threshold value for a certain dataset/site, the site is marked as a candidate to receive a replica of the considered dataset. Indeed, the replica is immediately created if there is enough disk space. Otherwise, the system would have to evaluate if some of the existent data replicas (of another datasets) should be replaced or not by the new replica candidate. In order to do that, RM also maintains the benefits score of existing dataset replicas. Such score is

computed in the same way that β and δ values of inexistent replicas are computed. If the β value of an existing replica is lower than the one of a replica candidate, then a replica replacement is done. Otherwise, the system maintains the already existing replicas.

LOCAL CACHING AND INTRA-SITE REPLICA CANDIDATES

Facts' table fragments are natural candidates for inter-site replication, as discussed previously in this Chapter. When a Local Scheduler evaluates that a certain deadline would be achieved if its site stores a local copy of a certain fragment, it informs the Replication Manager which considers such fragment as a dataset that is candidate for inter-site replication. Such fragment may be replicated or not depending on its benefit for the system.

As discussed before, each site is autonomous to implement its own data placement (and replication) strategy. Besides that, each site may also implement its own data caching mechanism. There are some caching mechanisms that are benefited by the multidimensional nature of warehouse data. Chunked-based caching (Deshpande et al, 1998; Deshpande & Naughton, 2000) is one of those specialized mechanisms for the DW.

In chunk-based caching, DW data to be stored in the cache is broken up into chunks that are cached and used to answer incoming queries. The list of necessary chunks to answer a query is broken into two: (i) chunks that may be obtained (or computed) from cached data; and (ii) chunks that have to be recovered from the data warehouse database. In such method, sometimes it is possible to compute a chunk from chunks from different levels of aggregation (each aggregation level corresponds to a group-by operation) (Deshpande & Naughton, 2000).

Such computed chunk based mechanism may be implemented by local schedulers to implement

Figure 5. Experimental setup description

Site Id	CPU Rating (MIPS) x 10^3	Storage Space (GB)	Number of Grid-DW Users at the Site	Number of Submitted Queries
1	49.0	2,750	24	135
2	62.0	1,800	32	141
3	20.0	1,000	8	47
4	21.0	500	16	77
5	14.0	1,350	24	114
6	70.0	2,500	48	252
7	7.0	350	8	42
8	3.0	100	4	26
9	6.0	250	8	41
10	1.0	80	4	25
11	80.0	5,000	24	100

local caching. But chunks of results or computed chunks can also be considered as candidates for replication by Replication Manager. In such context, when a local scheduler evaluates that a certain missing chunk would enable the site to execute a task by a certain deadline that would be achieved without such chunk, the local scheduler must send to the Replication Manager the identification of such chunk. Then, the RM would consider the chunk as a dataset candidate for replication in its benefit-based dynamic replica selection and placement mechanism.

EXPERIMENTAL EVALUATION

The QoS-oriented scheduling and dynamic replication mechanisms were experimentally evaluated in a simulation environment. The experimental setup is composed by 11 sites, which were inspired in the experimental testbed used in (Sulistio et al, 2007) and in the LHC Computing Grid Project sites (Bird et al, 2005). Figure 5 presents the main characteristics of the used sites.

A Star Schema-based DW is considered. Facts table is partitioned into 121 fragments. Fragments

sizes are generated considering Pareto's power-law distribution [which fits well for data grids files (Sulistio et al, 2007)], with a 1Gb mean fragment size. Initially, each site stores the same number of facts table fragments (11 fragments).

Two distinct network topologies are used in our tests (represented in Figure 6). The first one is a hierarchical topology, in which sites are organized in a binary tree according to their ids [hierarchical topologies are also considered in real projects, like the LHC Computing Grid Project - data storage and analysis project for CERN's Large Hadron Collider (Bird et al, 2005)]. The second network model is a nonhierarchical topology, dual ring topology. In such topology, there is no central root site (eliminating a possible bottleneck in the system) and each site is directly connected to two other sites. Data movement in the rings is done in opposite directions. In all the tests, we consider a data transfer rate of 50Mbps and a latency of 10 milliseconds.

The considered query workload is composed of 1,000 tasks (re-written queries). Tasks' sizes vary about 2,000 kMIPS ± 30%, which means that a typical task execution would take about 30 minutes in the least powerful site and 40 seconds

Figure 6. Experimentally tested network topologies

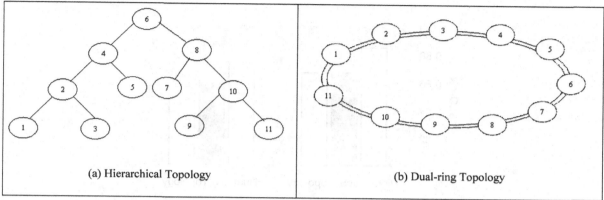

(a) Hierarchical Topology   (b) Dual-ring Topology

in the most powerful one. Figure 5 presents the number of queries submitted at each site. In order to model that, we consider that each query may be submitted by a user from any site, but the probability of a query being submitted by a specific site is proportional to the number of DW users at the site. Users' access patterns were modeled considering that half of the tasks access data stored at the same site that submitted the job.

In order to evaluate the effectiveness of the QoS-aware scheduling and dynamic replication strategies, we have made several tests using the QoS-oriented scheduling and three different data dynamic replication strategies: (i) the QoS-aware, (ii) Best Client (BC) and (iii) Data *Least Loaded* (DLL). Variations of the BC strategy are used by Ranganathan & Foster (2001) and Siva Sathya et al (2006). The DLL is used by Ranganathan & Foster (2004). Both in the BC and in DLL, each site monitors the number of data access at the data replicas it stores, computing the number of times the fragment was requested. When such number is greater than a threshold value, a fragment replica is created at another site. In BC, the fragment replica is created at the site that has more times demanded for the considered fragment. In DLL, fragment replica is created at the site that has the least remaining work to execute.

The obtained SLO-AR values are represented in Figure 7. All the evaluated dynamic replication

methods lead to good SLO-AR. Such success ensures the quality of the used QoS-oriented hierarchical scheduling model. But the obtained results also present the benefits of the proposed QoS-aware dynamic data replication and placement, as it was the method that leads to the highest value of SLO-AR.

In Figure 8 we present the measured throughput for the evaluated strategies. Once again, the proposed QoS-aware replication strategy leaded to the highest values in the two tested network configurations. This happens because such placement strategy has the same objective of the used query scheduling strategy. Therefore, not only it increases the number of queries that the Community Scheduler agrees to execute but also lead to a better resource utilization than the other replica selection and placement methods.

The number of created replicas per method was almost the same and no method created a huge number of replicas for the same data fragment (as show in Figure 9). In fact, the success of the QoS-aware scheduling method is mostly related to its replica placement strategy.

In Figure 10, we present the number of created replicas per site for the Hierarchical Topology. Let's analyze site 6: such site is almost the most powerful one and it is the site that have the highest number of submitted queries. This is also the site on which the BC method created the highest

Figure 7. SLO-achievement rate

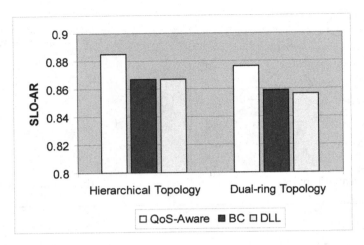

number of data replicas. But as the BC method places too much replicas at such site, the scheduler assigns too much queries for site 6 (what puts it into a too high load situation and decreases performance, leading to a lower SLO-achievement rate) or schedules queries to other sites that are near site 6 but that do not have the same data replicas (in such case, data movement is done during query execution, which also decreases the system performance).

On the other hand, the QoS-aware placed high number of replicas at sites 3-5 than the other methods. Such sites are of medium powerful ones and are relatively near of sites 1, 2 and 6 (the three sites with the highest number of submitted queries). This way, many of the queries submitted at sites 1, 2 and 6 can be executed at sites 3-5 with a good performance (no database copy is done during execution, only results - which are relatively small in size - are transferred through sites during query execution). In contrast, the DLL strategy placed many replicas on not so powerful sites (like 10 and 7). This happened as the DLL strategy evaluated that such sites had a small size

Figure 8. Measured throughput

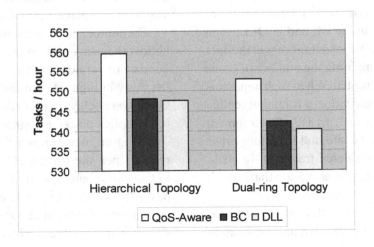

Figure 9. Number of replicas per facts table fragment - hierarchical topology

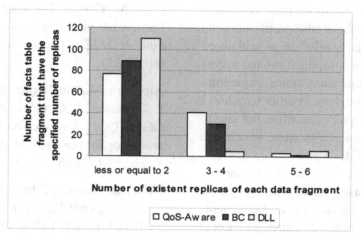

of pending work. But such sites take too much time to execute a query, and the Community Scheduler rarely assigns query execution for such sites. Therefore, the replicas created by DLL were somehow of less utility to the system.

CONCLUSION

Grid-based data warehouses are useful in many global organizations which generates huge volumes of distributed data that should be transpar- ently queried by the organizations participant's. In such environment, the Grid is used as basic infrastructure for the deployment of a large dis- tributed mostly read-only database. But due to the grid's special characteristics, like resource heterogeneity, geographical dispersion and site autonomy, the efficient deployment of huge data warehouses over grid-connected sites is a special challenge.

In this chapter, we present QoS-oriented scheduling and distributed data placement strat- egies for the grid-based warehouse. We discuss

Figure 10. Number of facts table fragments at each site in hierarchical topology

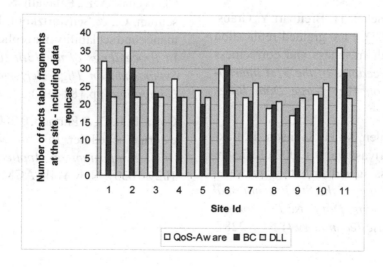

the use of a physically distributed database, in which tables are both partitioned and replicated across sites. The use of facts' table partitioning and replication is particularly relevant as grid users' queries may follow geographical related access patterns. Inter-site dimension tables fragmentation and replication are done in order to achieve good performance in query execution but also to reduce data movement across sites, which is a costly operation in grids.

Incoming queries are rewritten into another ones (tasks) that are assigned to sites by a Local Scheduler based on Service Level Agreements between the Community Scheduler and Local Schedulers The use of a hierarchical scheduling model leads to good SLO-achievement rates and also maintains site autonomy, as each site's Local Scheduler may implement its own scheduling strategy.

Dynamic data replication is very important in grid-based data bound jobs. In the grid-enabled warehouse, dynamic replication of facts table fragments or of computed chunks is important to improve the systems' performance. The QoS-oriented dynamic replica selection and placement is especially important to increase the SLO-achievement rate in grid-enabled warehouses.

REFERENCES

Akal, F., Türker, C., Schek, H., Breitbart, Y., Grabs, T., & Veen, L. (2005). Fine-grained replication and scheduling with freshness and correctness guarantees. In *Proceedings of the 31st international Conference on Very Large Data Bases* (pp. 565-576).

Akinde, M. O., Böhlen, M. H., Johnson, T., Lakshmanan, L. V., & Srivastava, D. (2002). Efficient OLAP query processing in distributed data warehouses. In *Proceedings of the 8th international Conference on Extending Database Technology: Advances in Database Technology.* (LNCS 2287, pp. 336-353.

Allcock, W., Bresnahan, J., Kettimuthu, R., & Link, M. (2005). The Globus striped GridFTP framework and server. In *Proceedings of the 2005 ACM/IEEE Conference on Supercomputing* (pp.54-65).

Alpdemir, M., Mukherjee, A., Paton, N., Watson, P., Fernandes, A., Gounaris, A., & Smith, J. (2003). OGSA-DQP: A service-based distributed query processor for the Grid. In *Proceedings of UK e-Science All Hands Meeting.*

Bird, I. & The LCG Editorial Board (2005). LHC Computing Grid Technical Design Report [LCG-TDR-001, CERN-LHCC-2005-024].

Breitbart, Y., Komondoor, R., Rastogi, R., Seshadri, S., & Silberschatz, A. (1999). Update propagation protocols for replicated databates. *SIGMOD Record, 28*(2), 97–108. doi:10.1145/304181.304191

Chaudhuri, S., & Dayal, U. (1997). An overview of data warehousing and OLAP technology. *SIGMOD Record, 26*(1), 65–74. doi:10.1145/248603.248616

Chen, G., Pan, Y., Guo, M., & Lu, J. (2005). An asynchronous replica consistency model in data grid. In *Proceedings of Parallel and Distributed Processing and Applications - 2005 Workshops* (LNCS 3759, pp. 475-484).

Chervenak, A. L., Palavalli, N., Bharathi, S., Kesselman, C., & Schwartzkopf, R. (2004). Performance and scalability of a replica location service. In *Proceedings of the 13th IEEE international Symposium on High Performance Distributed Computing* (pp.182-191).

Costa, R. L. C., & Furtado, P. 2008. A QoS-oriented external scheduler. In *Proceedings of the 2008 ACM Symposium on Applied Computing* (pp. 1029-1033). New York: ACM Press.

Costa, R. L. C., & Furtado, P. (2008). QoS-oriented reputation-aware query scheduling in data grids. In *Proceedings of the 14th European Conference on Parallel and Distributed Computing (Euro-Par)*.

Costa, R. L. C., & Furtado, P. (2008). Scheduling in Grid databases. In *Proceedings of the 22nd international Conference on Advanced information Networking and Applications – Workshops* (pp. 696-701).

Deshpande, P., & Naughton, J. F. (2000). Aggregate aware caching for multi-dimensional queries. In *Proceedings of the 7th international Conference on Extending Database Technology: Advances in Database Technology vol. 1777* (pp. 167-182).

Deshpande, P. M., Ramasamy, K., Shukla, A., & Naughton, J. F. (1998). Caching multidimensional queries using chunks. In A. Tiwary & M. Franklin (Eds.), *Proceedings of the 1998 ACM SIGMOD international Conference on Management of Data (Seattle, Washington, United States, June 01 - 04, 1998)* (pp. 259-270). New York: ACM Press.

Foster, I. Kesselman, C. Nick, J., & Tuecke, S. (2002). *The physiology of the grid: An open grid services architecture for distributed systems integration* (Globus Project Tech Report).

Foster, I., Kesselman, C., Tsudik, G., & Tuecke, S. (1998). A security architecture for computational grids. In *Proceedings of the 5th ACM Conference on Computer and Communications Security. CCS '98* (pp. 83-92).

Foster, I. T. (2001). The anatomy of the grid: Enabling scalable virtual organizations. In *Proceedings of the 7th international Euro-Par Conference on Parallel Processing* (LNCS 2150, pp. 1-4).

Furtado, P. (2004). Workload-based placement and join processing in node-partitioned data warehouses. In *Proceedings of the 6th International Conference on Data Warehousing and Knowledge Discovery* (LNCS 3181, pp. 38-47).

Furtado, P. (2004). Experimental evidence on partitioning in parallel data warehouses. In *Proceedings of the 7th ACM international Workshop on Data Warehousing and OLAP* (pp. 23-30).

Haddad, C., & Slimani, Y. (2007). Economic model for replicated database placement in Grid. In *Proceedings of the Seventh IEEE international Symposium on Cluster Computing and the Grid* (pp. 283-292). IEEE Computer Society.

Huynh, T. D., Jennings, N. R., & Shadbolt, N. R. (2006). An integrated trust and reputation model for open multi-agent systems. *Autonomous Agents and Multi-Agent Systems, 13*(2), 119–154. doi:10.1007/s10458-005-6825-4

Krauter, K., Buyya, R., & Maheswaran, M. (2002). A taxonomy and survey of grid resource management systems for distributed computing. *Software, Practice & Experience, 32*(2), 135–164. doi:10.1002/spe.432

Lawrence, M., & Rau-Chaplin, A. (2006). The OLAP-Enabled Grid: Model and query processing algorithms. In *Proc. of the 20th international Symposium on High-Performance Computing in An Advanced Collaborative Environment (HPCS)*.

Lima, A., Mattoso, M., & Valduriez, P. (2004). Adaptive virtual partitioning for OLAP query processing in a database cluster. In *Proceedings of the Brazilian Symposium on Databases (SBBD)* (pp. 92-105).

Lin, Y., Liu, P., & Wu, J. (2006). Optimal placement of replicas in data grid environments with locality assurance. In *Proceedings of the 12th international Conference on Parallel and Distributed Systems - Vol 1 (2006)* (pp. 465-474).

Loukopoulos, T., & Ahmad, I. (2000). Static and adaptive data replication algorithms for fast information access in large distributed systems. In *Proc. of the 20th Intern. Conference on Distributed Computing Systems (ICDCS)*.

Nieto-Santisteban, M. A., Gray, J., Szalay, A., Annis, J., Thakar, A. R., & O'Mullane, W. (2005). When database systems meet the grid. In *CIDR* (pp. 154-161).

Park, S., & Kim, J. (2003). Chameleon: A resource scheduler in a data grid environment. In *Proceedings of the 3st international Symposium on Cluster Computing and the Grid*. IEEE Computer Society.

Poess, M., & Othayoth, R. K. (2005). Large scale data warehouses on grid: Oracle database 10g and HP proliant servers. In *Proc. of the 31st international Conference on Very Large Data Bases* (pp. 1055-1066).

Ranganathan, K., & Foster, I. (2004). Computation scheduling and data replication algorithms for data Grids. In *Grid resource management: State of the art and future trends* (pp. 359-373). Norwell, MA: Kluwer Academic Publishers.

Roy, A., & Sander, V. (2004). GARA: A uniform quality of service architecture. In Grid resource management: State of the art and future trends (pp. 377-394). Norwell, MA: Kluwer Academic Publishers.

Siva Sathya, S., Kuppuswami, S., & Ragupathi, R. (2006). Replication strategies for data grids. *International Conference on Advanced Computing and Communications. ADCOM 2006 (*pp 123-128).

Stöhr et al, 2000 Stöhr, T., Märtens, H., & Rahm, E. 2000. Multi-Dimensional Database Allocation for Parallel Data Warehouses. In Proceedings of the 26th international Conference on Very Large Data Bases. 273-284.

Transaction processing council benchmarks (2008). Retrieved from http://www.tpc.org

Venugopal, S., Buyya, R., & Ramamohanarao, K. (2006). A taxonomy of Data Grids for distributed data sharing, management, and processing. *ACM Computing Surveys, 38*(1), 3. doi:10.1145/1132952.1132955

Watson, P. (2001). *Databases and the grid.* UK e-Science Technical Report Series.

Wehrle, P., Miquel, M., & Tchounikine, A. (2007). A grid services-oriented architecture for efficient operation of distributed data warehouses on Globus. In *Proceedings of the 21st international Conference on Advanced Networking and Applications (AINA)* (pp. 994-999).

Wolski, R. (1997). Forecasting network performance to support dynamicscheduling using the network weather service. In *Proceedings of the 6th IEEE international Symposium on High Performance Distributed Computing (August 05 - 08, 1997)* (pp. 316). IEEE.

KEY TERMS AND DEFINITIONS

Community Scheduler: It is a specialized middleware, responsible for matching users' jobs requirements with the available resources in a grid by the interaction with local schedulers. It assigns jobs to sites through a process that, besides requirement matchmaking, can also comprise some kind of negotiation with local schedulers. Sometimes it is also called Resource Broker or Meta-scheduler.

Data Grid: A Grid environment whose services are mainly used to deal with (including to store, process, replicate and move) huge volumes of distributed shared data or over which are executed grid-based applications that consume or generate huge volumes of data.

Grid: The term Grid is a basic infrastructure used to interconnect and provide access to widely distributed, and possibly heterogeneous, shared resourced that may belong to distinct organizations.

Grid Resource Management System: It is the resource management system that runs over the grid and is used to manage the available shared resources, providing a wide range of services (like efficient data movement, replica management and remote job submission and monitoring) to grid-based applications.

Grid-Enabled Databases: A set of Database Management Systems (DBMS) which are physically distributed and are queried by grid users through the use of a middleware together with a Grid Resource Management System.

Quality-of-Service (QoS): The term was first coined in the networking-related field in order to identify the ability of a certain technology to do resource reservation in order to provide different priority to distinct applications or users. More recently, it can also be used as a users' satisfaction degree or the ability to provide predictable performance levels that are according to users' expectations.

Service Level Agreement (SLA): An agreement that is firmed between a service provider and a service consumer, and which defines the service levels (possibly in terms of Service Level Objectives) that should be provided for several characteristics (like performance and availability) of the provided services. It may also define guarantees and penalties (for the case of non compliance with the SLA).

Service Level Objective (SLO): It is a target value used to measure the performance of a service provider in what concerns to a specific characteristic, like response time or throughput. Its definition may also contain information about how the SLO is measured and the measurement period.

Section 3
Evolution and Maintainance Management

Chapter 10
Data Warehouse Maintenance, Evolution and Versioning

Johann Eder
University of Klagenfurt, Austria

Karl Wiggisser
University of Klagenfurt, Austria

ABSTRACT

Data Warehouses typically are building blocks of decision support systems in companies and public administration. The data contained in a data warehouse is analyzed by means of OnLine Analytical Processing tools, which provide sophisticated features for aggregating and comparing data. Decision support applications depend on the reliability and accuracy of the contained data. Typically, a data warehouse does not only comprise the current snapshot data but also historical data to enable, for instance, analysis over several years. And, as we live in a changing world, one criterion for the reliability and accuracy of the results of such long period queries is their comparability. Whereas data warehouse systems are well prepared for changes in the transactional data, they are, surprisingly, not able to deal with changes in the master data. Nonetheless, such changes do frequently occur. The crucial point for supporting changes is, first of all, being aware of their existence. Second, once you know that a change took place, it is important to know which change (i.e., knowing about differences between versions and relations between the elements of different versions). For data warehouses this means that changes are identified and represented, validity of data and structures are recorded and this knowledge is used for computing correct results for OLAP queries. This chapter is intended to motivate the need for powerful maintenance mechanisms for data warehouse cubes. It presents some basic terms and definitions for the common understanding and introduces the different aspects of data warehouse maintenance. Furthermore, several approaches addressing the problem are presented and classified by their capabilities.

DOI: 10.4018/978-1-60566-756-0.ch010

INTRODUCTION

The standard architecture for data warehouse systems are *multidimensional databases*, where *transactional data* (*cell values*) are described in terms of master data (*dimensions* and *dimension members*). Whereas today's commercial systems are well prepared to deal with changes in the transactional data, they are, surprisingly, not able to deal with changing master data in a satisfactory way. Nonetheless, such changes frequently occur (restructuring in organizations, new laws, mergers and acquisitions, product portfolio restructuring, etc.). All these changes have to be represented in the information systems, and thus, must somehow be modeled also in the data warehouse. For data warehouses the adequate representation and treatment of such changes is even more crucial than in standard database applications, since data warehouses are intended to represent also historical data which – changes occurring – might be quite incompatible.

A simple example illustrating the problem of missing data is querying the number of inhabitants in the European Union for the last 25 years. This query seems rather straightforward and the numbers should not leave much space for interpretation. But, one has to be aware of some changes: First of all, the geopolitical entity "European Union" only exists since 1993, succeeding the "European Community", which itself was originally named "European Economic Community". Furthermore, in the considered period (1983 to 2008), the European Union grew from 12 to 27 members. Finally, with the reunification of East- and West-Germany in 1990 one of the member countries had a massive internal reorganization. So if querying the number of inhabitants from 1983 to 2008, how can the resulting numbers be compared? When querying this data from the Eurostat website, one has to choose the "geopolitical entity" (EU-27, EU-25, one or more counties, …) for which the data should be retrieved. If, for instance, EU-25 is chosen, the population for

these 25 countries is returned also for the years before their membership. But of course, the overall sum of returned inhabitants for the year 1987 does not match the real number of people living in the European Union at that time. Comparing the numbers of 1990 and 1991, where the organization itself did not change, may indicate a massive increase of inhabitants. In reality, the 1991 number also contains the 16.4 million people of former East-Germany. Eurostat, for instance, takes this into account, and presents numbers of the united Germany also for the years before 1991. Another example for an unclear inclusion are the Baltic countries or Slovenia. They did not even exist before 1991, but were parts of other countries, which, of course, never were parts of the European Union. An alternative to presenting such "adjusted data" is to display the "historical truth", i.e. include the numbers of different countries only after they joined the European Union. This may make sense in some situations, in others, such results may be useless.

An example demonstrating the effect of changing semantics could be to retrieve the Gross National Product of the countries in the European Union from 1983 to 2008. Besides the problems induced by the structural changes described above, i.e. whether and how to include numbers for a specific country, this query illustrates the changing semantics problem: As of 1999 and 2002, a common European currency, the Euro, was introduced as deposit currency and cash money respectively, in many – but not all – of the member countries. Thus, before 1999 the Gross National Product of different countries was expressed in the local currency, but as of 1999 it is given in Euro. Before 1999 for comparing the GNP of different countries, it is obvious that the numbers must be brought to a common base, i.e. the same currency, to be comparable. But what about statistics for a single country? For Austria, 1 Euro exchanges 13.7603 Austrian Schillings. So, someone comparing the Austrian Gross National Product from 1990–2006 without considering the

Euro would notice a giant retracement in the year 1999. But, of course, someone who knows about the Euro can divide each value given in ATS by 13.7603 and then compare the values.

Besides such simple "unit changes" there may be also more complex semantic changes for dimension members. Consider a query analyzing the unemployment rate in the European Union. Not only that it is calculated in different ways for various countries, the calculation mode has also been changed several times in the last few years, for instance whether people who are attending coursed offered by federal employment offices are counted as unemployed or not. Such calculation methods may be contained in the data warehouse definition as formulae for a certain member.

Generally, the three basic aspects of change management in data warehouses can be identified as follows:

1. **Being aware about changes happening:** First of all, to be able to manage changes, it is necessary to be *aware of their existence.* This awareness can easily be seen from two typical reasons for data warehouse structure changes. The first reason are *changes in the real world.* that is represented by the data warehouse, for instance creation of a new department, a merge of different departments, or new countries joining the European Union.. The second reason for modifications in the data warehouse are *changing requirements,* for instance analyzing not only the turnover in a company, but also the gain, or keeping track of unemployment rates, which were not recorded before.

2. **Identifying the changes in the system:** As today's typical data warehouse systems typically do not support changing structure data, they also may not be able to provide information about them, for instance some sort of a change log, even if the happened, e.g. by some automatic ETL process recreating the data warehouse from its sources.

The administrator is then, being aware that changes happened, in charge of finding the modifications and correctly dealing with them. Executing this task manually is very time consuming and also error prone, especially if the affected dimensions are large and the changes are rather small.

3. **Dealing with the influence of structure changes on the cell data:** Some structural changes may have heavy influence on the cell data. One of the main reasons for data warehouse maintenance is *comparability* of cell data. Now comparing cell data stemming from before and after a structural change may be very complex or even impossible, because of the influence of the structure changes on the cell data. In this context two major problems can be identified

   a. **Missing Data:** If elements are inserted or removed from the structure, cell data may not be available for the whole period of analysis (e.g. missing data for new countries in the European Union).

   b. **Incorrect Data:** If structure elements are changed, their semantics may change. This could have an influence on the calculation of cell values. Thus, if comparing cell values from before and after the change, equal values may have a different meaning and vice versa (e.g. different methods for calculating the unemployment rate).

These examples illustrate the problems induced by changing structures on a very simple level. Froeschl, Yamada and Kudrna (2002) call this the *problem of footnotes in statistics,* i.e. many values have to be tagged with their correct semantics. When being aware of such semantic and structural changes, interpreting "strange" results may be cumbersome but possible. But if someone does not even know that there were changes, analyzing query results may be impossible or, even worse, lead to wrong decisions. One possible solution to this problem is data transformation, i.e. viewing old data under new structures or vice versa. One may define the semantics of a query, and the system has – provided that the necessary information is available – the ability to include only the desired data, exclude undesired data and adjust the data to the desired structure and semantics.

BACKGROUND: THE DATA WAREHOUSE MAINTENANCE PROBLEM

The standard architecture and modeling approach for data warehouses is the multidimensional data cube. A multidimensional data cube consists of a set of *Dimensions,* each of them comprising a set of *Dimension Members* (also called simply *Members*). Dimensions are hierarchically organized into a set of *Categories* or *Dimension Levels,* each of them having assigned a set of members. The members themselves are also hierarchically structured, accordingly to the categories they are assigned to. Dimensions and categories define the *schema* of the cube, whereas the members are called the *instances.* Schema and instances together define the *cube structure.* Selecting one member from each dimension defines a *Data Cell,* containing either a *Cell Value* or a NIL value. Although there is no standardized terminology in data warehousing till today, these basic terms are widely accepted. The terms *Fact* and *Measure* are sometimes used with different semantics. In this chapter they are used as follows: A fact is a dimension member in the *Fact Dimension,* representing a certain subject of analysis (for instance Turnover). The term measure is used synonym to cell value.

Problems of Cube Structure Changes

It is obvious that the cube structure is modeling a certain part of the real world. For instance, departments and divisions of a company will somehow be represented in a cube used in that company. Thus, there may be a Company dimension comprising members for the departments and divisions. And, as the real world tends to change, such changes must also be represented in the cube structure.

Changes can happen on the schema level, i.e. dimensions or categories are changed, or on the instance level, i.e. the members are changed.

Figure 1 shows examples for schema and instance changes. It contains three different version of a cube structure in a car dealer's data warehouse. For sake of simplicity, only the Cars dimension is depicted. The dealer sells different car models of different brands. Each model has assigned a user defined attribute Engine Power. Traditionally, for German cars this is given in horsepower, whereas for English models it is given in kilowatt. In the second version there are various instance changes: the new model BMW1 is introduced and Silver Spirit is renamed to Silver Spirit II. In version 3 there is also a schema change. Due to the merge of BMW and Rolls Royce on the one hand and Mercedes and Chrysler on the other hand, a new dimension level is introduced. Of course for this new level also new members are created and the existing members are relocated accordingly. The brand Puch is discontinued, the model attached to it is now sold under the brand of Mercedes. The new brand Chrysler with one car model is introduced, whereas the Phantom V is removed from the product portfolio. The attribute for the engine power is unified to kilowatt. All these structure modifications are due to changes in the data warehouse's application domain. A modification resulting from a changed requirement can for instance be the introduction of a member profit in the facts dimension, depicting the car dealers wish to keep track of his profit.

Figure 1. Schema and instance changes in the example company

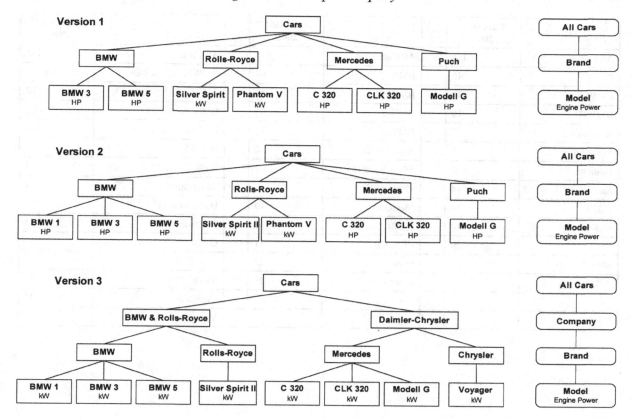

From the view of structural changes, these reorganizations do not cause any problems. But what about the data? Table 1 shows the cell data for the cube in the years 2005, 2006 and 2007, i.e. for the Versions 1, 2 and 3 respectively. A possible chart resulting from this data without considering changes may look like shown in Figure 2. Without knowing about the changes, interpretation of this chart is not possible.

Levels of the Maintenance Problem

As defined above, the cube's structure consists of schema and instances. A data warehouse maintenance system must be able to keep track of changes in both of them. Thus, on the schema level it must provide operations for *Insertion, Deletion* and *Change* of dimension and categories. Category changes are, for instance, addition or deletion of user defined attributes. Also the hierarchical relations between different categories may be subject to change. On the instance level, the system must provide operations for the *Insertion, Deletion* and *Change* of dimension members, as well as operations for changing the hierarchical relations between the dimension members.

Recording and managing structure changes is only one aspect of the maintenance problem. The cell data contained in the data warehouse depends on the structure. Thus, modifications of the structure may lead to inconsistencies in the cell data. So it may have to be adjusted to be consistent again. Such adjustments could range from simple reaggregation to complex data transformations, because, for instance, the unit of a fact has changed. For the example given above, a data adjustment may be the recalculation for the brand Mercedes, representing that Model G is now sold under this brand.

Table 1. Cell data for the example company

	Cars sold 2005			Cars sold 2006			Cars sold 2007
All Cars	111		All Cars	145		All Cars	181
BMW	40		BMW	67		BMW&Rolls-Royce	71
BMW 3	30		BMW 1	20		BMW	67
BMW 5	10		BMW 3	35		BMW 1	22
Rolls-Royce	7		BMW 5	12		BMW 3	34
Silver Spirit	3		Rolls-Royce	6		BMW 5	11
Phantom V	4		Silver Spirit II	3		Rolls-Royce	4
Mercedes	44		Phantom V	3		Silver Spirit II	4
C 320	34		Mercedes	49		Daimer-Chrysler	110
CLK 320	10		C 320	38		Mercedes	75
Puch	20		CLK 320	11		C 320	40
Modell G	20		Puch	23		CLK 320	11
			Modell G	23		Modell G	24
						Chrysler	35
						Voyager	35

Figure 2. Example charts for changed structure

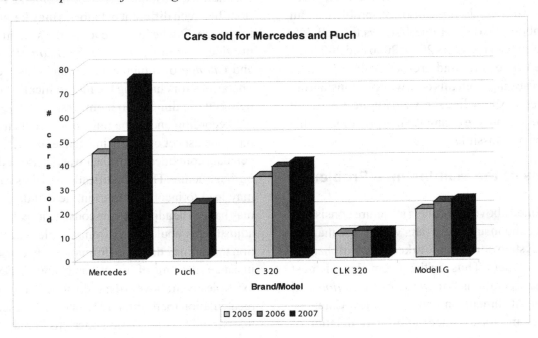

Impacts of Data Warehouse Changes on Cell Data

The different types of changes in data warehouse structures affect the assigned cell data in different ways. The following impacts on the cell data can be identified:

- **Additional Cell Data:** Additional data is most times expressed by new structure elements not depending on previously existing elements, either on the schema (dimension, categories) or on the instance (dimension members) level. The problem with additional cell data is that it is oftentimes not available for the past thus, leading to *missing data*. An example could be new countries joining the European Union.

- **Removed Cell Data:** When dimension members or categories are completely removed from the data warehouse structure, also the assigned cell data should no longer be part of the cube. For instance, data from countries leaving the European Union should not be contained in statistics any longer.

- **Restructuring of Cell Data:** Restructuring cell data can happen in various forms: aggregation hierarchies may change, new aggregation levels may be created, dimension members may be split or merged, the unit of a fact may change. All these restructurings have in common that the cell data for the new version can – to a certain extent – be calculated from the old structure. Not dealing with such changes may lead to *incorrect data*. Examples for this type of changes may be the split of a country in the European Union into two independent countries, or the changing the currency.

- **Change of Cell Data Calculation:** Cell data may also be calculated from various external data sources by some given formulae. Such calculation rule may change.

Not dealing with such changes may again lead to *incorrect data*. An example for this type may be changing the calculation rule for the unemployment rate.

- **Changing Cell Data:** Typically, cell data contained in a data warehouse is non-volatile, thus not changing any more (Inmon 2005, p. 29). Therefore changing cell data is typically not considered during of data warehouse maintenance.

Data Warehouse Evolution and Versioning

When it comes to changing systems, one question always arising is whether to keep previous versions available or not. This also applies to data warehouse maintenance. With *Data Warehouse Evolution* every modification (or every set of modifications applied in one transaction) of the structure leads to a new version of this structure and the previous version is lost. The contained cell data has to be transformed to be consistent with the new structure. Queries can only be executed based on the newest structure. With *Data Warehouse Versioning* also every modification (or every set of modifications applied in one transaction) of the structure leads to a new version of this structure, but the previous version is kept available and may be restored. Existing cell data does not need to be adapted, but can be stored following is origin structure version. This enables queries spanning multiple structure versions.

Comparing these two possibilities reveals advantages and disadvantages for both of them: When using the evolution approach, one does not need to keep track of old versions, which reduces data management effort and as all data is adapted to the current version, no adaptations have to be done during runtime, which means a better query performance, compared to the versioning approach. On the other hand, evolution lacks the possibility of multiversion queries and as the data has to be transformed, change operations may take quite a long time. The versioning approach allows multiversion queries, and data does not have to be transformed when applying modifications. On the other hand, when running a multiversion query, data may have to be adapted, which leads to worse performance, compared to the evolutionary approach. Furthermore, keeping track of past versions is a non-negligible data management effort.

Aspects of Time in the Data Warehouse

Time is a key issue in data warehousing, because when supporting the decision process, computing historical trends may be necessary (Rizzi and Golfarelli, 2006). In data warehouses one can distinguish three different kinds of time:

1. **Valid Time of Cell Data:** In a multidimensional cube usually the Time dimension is used to represent the history of changing transaction data. Cell data, which is related to a specific dimension member from the time dimension is valid at the time point or interval represented by that member.
2. **Transaction Time of Cell Data:** Based on the assumption of nonvolatility, for most application the transaction time of cell values, i.e. the time when data is current in the data warehouse, is not considered to be relevant. When this assumption is violated and transaction data which is already stored in the data warehouse is changed afterwards, transaction time bay become an important aspect, as it allows traceability for query results (Rizzi and Golfarelli, 2006).
3. **Valid Time of Structure Data:** Data warehouse structures need to be maintained. Structure elements may be inserted, deleted or changed. To be able to determine the data warehouse's structure at a given point in time, structures have to be assigned a valid time. Today's data warehouse systems typically

provide very little support for changing structures.

Data warehouse maintenance mostly deals with the third aspect, i.e. valid time of structure data.

Subsuming the above the following definition can be given for data warehouse maintenance, evolution and versioning: The process and methodology of performing changes on the schema and instance level to represent changes in the data warehouse's application domain or requirements is called *Data Warehouse Maintenance*. *Data Warehouse Evolution* is a form of data warehouse maintenance where only the newest data warehouse state is available. *Data Warehouse Versioning* is a form of data warehouse maintenance where all past versions of the data warehouse are kept available. Dealing with changes on the data level, mostly insertion of new data, is not part of data warehouse maintenance, but part of a data warehouse's normal operation. (Eder and Wiggisser, 2009, p. 1)

THE COMET TEMPORAL DATA WAREHOUSE

Eder and Koncilia (Eder & Koncilia, 2001; Eder, Koncilia, & Morzy, 2002) suggest the COMET Metamodel for temporal data warehouses. This model is based on the multidimensional data model. All elements (dimensions, categories, dimension members, ...) and relations between them get assigned a timestamp $[T_s; T_e]$ where T_s identifies the first point in time where the given element is valid, and T_e defines the last point in time of the validity of the element. An ending timestamp of *NOW* defines elements for which the end of validity is yet unknown. Operations for inserting, deleting, and updating structure elements are provided, as well as operations for changing hierarchical relations between these elements, for instance creating a new aggregation hierarchy. On the member level, also the complex operations *Split* – i.e. a single dimension member is separated into several members – and *Merge* – i.e. several dimension members are combined into a single one – are supported.

An advantage of this approach is its independence from the data warehouse system in use (Eder, Koncilia, & Wiggisser, 2006). The versioned structure data and the metadata is stored independently from the data warehouse system in a relational database, thus virtually any data warehouse system can be supported with temporality. As COMET works independently from any particular data warehouse system, the changes log between two versions may not always be readily available to be integrated in the COMET database. For that purpose, the framework provides a change detection mechanism based on directed acyclic graphs. COMET compares the graph representing the last known structure version in the database to the graph representing the current version in the data warehouse systems and suggests and edit script, which represents the differences between the two graphs. Such a change detection can only be semiautomatic, because to definitely confirm the calculated differences, external knowledge which can only be provided by a human user is necessary.

The COMET approach supports versioning and therefore all previous structure versions are recorded. If an element changed at time T_i, a new version of this element with valid time *[T_i; NOW]* is created in the relational database. The previous version is updated by assigning the ending timestamp T_{i-1}. For creating a new structure element at time T_i, the respective data is inserted into the relational database and given the timestamp *[T_i; NOW]*. Deleting a structure element at timepoint T_i is done by changing the ending timestamp from *NOW* to T_{i-1}. It is important to note that no data is physically deleted from the relational database.

All elements with the same end of validity build a so called structure version, which represents a version of the cube valid at a certain point of time. Structure versions are contiguous, thus there are no holes in the version history of a cube. A particular version of a structure element may be part of several structure versions, but within a single structure version, only one version of an element can be valid.

Between different versions of a dimension member so called *transformation functions* are defined, which allow to transform the assigned cell values between different structure versions with a certain weighting factor *w*. Such a transformation may for instance be the transformation from Austrian Schillings into Euro for all money related members in the fact dimensions, for which new versions have been created in the year 2002. In this case the factor *w* would have a value of 0.07267. Of course such transformations may be far more complex than just such "unit transformations". For instance in the case of a split, there may exist different weighting factors for each successor, defining the split ratios.

The set of all these transformation functions may be modeled as a matrix or as a directed acyclic graph (Eder & Wiggisser, 2008). The matrix approach allows simple and intuitive modeling of the transformation process. The cell data is represented as n-dimensional matrix, transformation data is modeled as two-dimensional matrix for each dimension. The transformation is done by standard matrix multiplication. As many data cubes are only sparsely populated and also the amount of changes is assumed to be rather small, this matrix multiplication is not the most efficient way for transformation. The graph approach is intended to give a more efficient representation. Cell data and transformation functions are represented by nodes and edges, respectively. Thus, only populated cells have to be included. As each edge stands for a multiplication and each node stands for a cell, it is desirable to have the transformation graph minimized, i.e. containing the least possible number of nodes and edges. For independent transformations – that are transformations which do not affect different versions of the same member – it is possible to change the order

Figure 3. Architecture of DWT (Adapted from Eder and Wiggisser (2006))

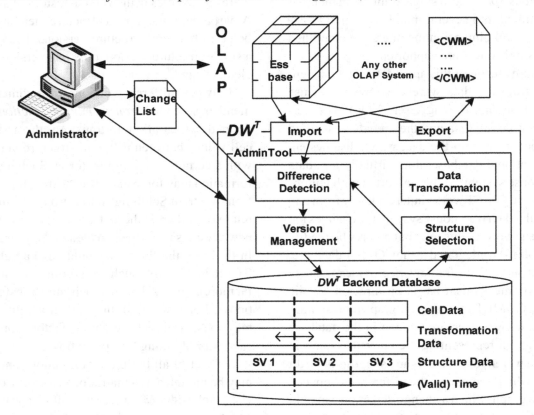

in which these transformations are executed, thus to minimize the graph.

The architecture of a prototypic implementation of the COMET Metamodel, called DW^T is shown in Figure 3[REMOVED REF FIELD]. The whole system is based on the backend database, which contains the versioned structure information, the transformation functions and the cell data. DW^T is independent from any specific data warehouse system. For each system to be supported, an import and export interface has to be implemented. These interfaces are responsible for reading/writing structure and cell data from/to the particular system. Structure data read from an external data warehouse system is compared to the last version stored in the backend database (if available) by the difference detection component. If there is some external knowledge about the changes available in computer readable form

it can be imported as well. With the differences generated the version management component creates a new structure version and stores it into the backend database. When reestablishing a particular structure version from the backend database, the structure selection component reads all necessary data from the backend database. Cell data and transformation data are handled by data transformation component. The export interface is responsible for writing the structure data the transformed cell data into the external data warehouse system.

OTHER APPROACHES ADDRESSING THE MAINTENANCE PROBLEM

There are several other approaches dealing with the data warehouse maintenance problem. Most of them are scientific ones, but two of them are included in commercial products. In this section some of these approaches are presented and compared by their capabilities.

Approach of Kimball: Slowly Changing Dimensions

Kimball (1996) was probably the first discovering the need for evolving structures in a data warehouse and introduces three methods for dealing with so called *slowly changing dimensions*. The first method simply suggests overwriting old instances with their new values, thus tracking a change history is not possible. The second method consists of creating a new instance for each change. This will create a version history, but means additional effort in data management. One has to introduce a surrogate key, because the natural primary keys may not be unique any longer. For relating various versions of an instance to each other, creating a time stamp for the validity of each version is proposed. The third method proposes creating a new attribute for the instance, so the original and the current attribute value can be saved. This can, of course, only handle two versions of an instance. All three methods are quite straightforward and only allow very basic modifications on the instance level. Impacts of structure changes on the cell data are not considered. Furthermore, they are only applicable for slowly changing dimensions and not for what Kimball calls a *rapidly changing monster dimension* (Kimball and Ross, 2002). For this type of changes, they suggest swapping out frequently changing attributes (e.g. age or income of a customer) into so called *minidimensions*. With their help the original member remains unchanged and if an attribute changes, just another member in the minidimension is used.

Approach of Yang and Widom

Yang and Widom (1998) present an approach that allows building a temporal data warehouse for tem-

poral and non-temporal data sources. This work is based on the assumption of a data warehouse being only a view over the sources. It contains temporal query language and a framework to create and incrementally update temporal views over the history of instances. As such a history may not always be available in the sources, auxiliary data is stored in the data warehouse to enable self-maintaining views.

Approach of Hurtado, Mendelzon and Vaisman

The approach of Hurtado, Mendelzon and Vaisman (Hurtado, Mendelzon & Vaisman, 1999; Vaisman & Mendelzon, 2001) proposes a temporal multidimensional model and a temporal query language. It allows modifications of schema and instances. The temporal dimension schema is defined as a directed acyclic graph. Each node represents a dimension level. The edges connecting the levels are labeled with a time interval denoting the time when the edge is valid. The same approach is used for dimension members, i.e. the nodes represent dimension members and the edges between them are labeled with their valid time. This model assumes that only the relations between the nodes, and not the nodes themselves, change. The temporal query language TOLAP can be used to execute queries over a set of temporal dimensions and fact tables.

Approach of Blaschka, Sapia and Höfling: Fiesta

The *Framework for Schema Evolution in Multidimensional Databases (FIESTA)* (Blaschka, Sapia and Höfling, 1999) supports a schema design technique and some evolution operations. The authors derive the need for an evolution methodology from the fact that the data warehouse design process is an iterative process. The proposed evolution algebra supports modifications on the schema level. Instance evolution is not supported directly, but the instances are adapted automatically according to the changes on schema level, either physically in the database or logically with views and filters.

Approach of Quix

Quix (1999) provides a framework for quality-oriented evolution of data warehouse views. The author proposes a data warehouse process model to capture dynamic aspects by representing the data warehouse evolution as a special process. The main focus is on the maintenance of evolving data warehouse views. Metadata is provided to keep track of the history of changes in the conceptual and logical schema. Consistency rules are defined guarantee consistency when quality factors have to be re-evaluated.

Approach of Sarda

Sarda (1999) presents a formal model for a temporal data warehouse that supports multiple hierarchies, a symmetric treatment of dimensions and measures and many-to-many relationships among dimension levels. The authors provide a mapping from their formal temporal ware house model to a relational model. History is recorded for dimension members as well as for relations between them.

Approach of Ravat and Teste

Ravat and Teste (2000) introduce an object-oriented approach to data warehouse modeling. They define a *Warehouse Class Extension* (the instances extracted from the sources) as current state, a set of historical states, and a set of archived states for the instances. Whereas historical states are available on detailed level, archived states can only be queried on an aggregated level. The main focus is laid on modeling of data warehouses.

Approach of Body, Miquel, Bedard and Tchounikine

Body, Miquel, Bedard and Tchounikine (2003) present their approach for handling evolution in multidimensional structures. As basis for their approach they define a temporal multidimensional model. Based upon this model a set of evolution operators is defined. The multidimensional model comprises the typical elements of a data warehouse structure, i. e. dimensions, levels, dimension members and hierarchical relations. All of the elements on the instance level are timestamped, schema elements are not evolvable. Furthermore, it contains a so called confidence factor, describing the reliability of data, for instance if it is source or mapped data, and a mapping relationship that describes the mapping between two versions of a dimension member. Operations are only defined on the member level. There are operations for creating new members, removing and reclassifying (i. e. moving) members, and create associations between versions of a member.

Approach of Kaas, Pedersen and Rasmussen

Kaas, Pedersen and Rasmussen (2004) present their approach for supporting schema evolution for star and snowflake schema. In contrast to other approaches, this methodology takes into account the special needs of an evolving star or snowflake schema using a relational database as data storage. They provide a rich set of changing operations, including operations for inserting and deleting dimensions, categories and dimension members. For each of the operations, the impact on existing queries and the complexity of applying the operation is evaluated. These evaluations are compared for the case of an underlying star and snowflake schema. From these comparisons the authors conclude that a star schema is more robust in case of structure evolution. Data transformation is not captured in this paper, but considered as future work.

Approach of Golfarelli, Lechtenbörger, Rizzi and Vossen

Golfarelli, Lechtenbörger, Rizzi and Vossen (2004; 2006) present their approach for schema versioning in data warehouses. Based on a graph model (called *schema graphs*) of the data warehouse schema they present their algebra for schema modifications. This approach supports versioning, therefore, past versions are not lost. Based on those schema versions the authors describe a mechanism to execute cross-version queries, with the help of so called augmented schemas. For creating such an augmented schema, an old schema version is enriched with structure elements from a subsequent version, so that the data belonging to the old schema version can be queried as if it followed the new version.

Approach of Malinowski and Zimanyi

Malinowski and Zimanyi (2006) present an approach for representing time-varying data in dimensions. Based on their MultiDimER (Malinowsky & Zimanyi, 2004) they present a set of temporal extensions that allow conceptual representation of time-varying levels, attributes and hierarchies. They describe the versioning of levels and hierarchies. When describing time varying levels, they actually refer to modeling changes in the members contained in this level. With respect to hierarchies, the authors distinguish between temporal levels and non-temporal relations between them, temporal levels and temporal relations between them, and non-temporal levels and temporal relations between them. Based on these scenarios the authors extend their MultiDimER metamodel to include the capability of expressing these changes. Additionally, means for transforming MultiDimER into a classical Entity Relationship model are proposed. As the approach is more concerned about conceptual modeling of changes, considerations about dealing with cell data are not included.

Approach of SAP AG

Besides these scientific approaches, there are also two commercial products including support for changing structures in data warehouses. SAP AG (2000) presents an approach capable of producing four different types of reports: a report using today's constellation, a report using an old constellation, a report showing the historical truth and a report showing comparable results. This approach is limited to basic operations on dimension members and does not allow to transform cell data between structure versions.

Approach of KALIDO

The KALIDO Dynamic Information Warehouse (2004) supports some aspects of data warehouse maintenance. Dealing with changes is realized by the so called Generic Data Modeling. The data warehouse model consists of three categories of data: the *transaction data*, describing the activities of the business and the facts associated with them, the *business context data*, which is the analog to the instances, and the *metadata*, which among others comprises parts of the schema. With evolving the business context data, instance evolution is supported.

Comparison of Approaches

After having presented the various approaches, Table 2 shows a classification of them with respect to the following features:

1. **Level of Maintenance:** Does the approach support schema maintenance, instance maintenance or both of them?
2. **Type of Historization:** Does the approach support versioning or evolution?

Of course, the desired feature combination would be an approach supporting versioning on schema and instance level, because this offers

Table 2. Classification of approaches

	Versioning	Evolution
Schema and Instance	Eder et al., Malinowski et al.	Hurtado et al., Kaas et al.
Schema only	Golfarelli et al.	Blaschka et al., Quix
Instance only	SAP AG, Ravat et al., Sarda, Body et al.	Kimball, Yang et al, Kalido

the biggest flexibility. On the other hand, it can be seen that the current commercial approaches both support maintenance only on instance level. But nevertheless, selection considering these two features only may not be sufficient. Table 3 compares some the approaches (two of them quite established and two rather new ones) with respect to a set of additional features. The selection of approaches for the comparison is based on their similarity, i.e. the selected approaches follow similar principles, which allows to define a set of features applicable to all of them. A plus in a cell expresses that the respective approach supports the feature. A minus means that the respective feature is not supported by that approach.

1. **Valid time for hierarchical relations:** Does the approach support valid time for the relations between dimension members?
2. **Valid time for dimension members:** Does the approach support valid time for dimension members?
3. **Data transformation or multiversion queries:** Does the approach support queries spanning several structure versions or transformation of cell data between structure versions?
4. **Complex Operations:** Does the approach support operations other then insert, delete, update (for instance split or merge)?
5. **Formal Temporal Model:** Is a formal model for the temporalization provided?
6. **Changes in Time/Fact dimension:** Does the approach allow changes in the Time and/or Fact dimension?
7. **Modeling Technique:** Is the approach based on a particulare technique for multidimensional modeling, possibly presented by the authors?

Related Problems

Besides the classical maintenance requirements of keeping managing structural changes in a data

Table 3. Features of different maintenance approaches

	Eder et al.	Hurtado et al.	Golfarelli et al.	Malinowski et al.
Valid time for hierarchical relations	+	+	+	+
Valid time for dimension members	+	-	-	+
Data transformation / multiversion queries	+	-	+	-
Complex operations	+	+	-	-
Formal Temporal Model	+	+	+	+
Changes in Time/Fact dimension	+	-	+	-
Modelling Technique	-	-	+	+

warehouse, maintenance methodologies can also be used to facilitate so called *what-if-analysis*. Bebel, Wrembel and others (2004, 2007) present an approach for the management of multiversion data warehouses. They differentiate between real versions and alternative versions. The former are used to historicize data warehouse modifications resulting from real world changes. Alternative versions facilitate to create several versions, each of them representing a possible future situation and then apply what-if-analysis on them. Additionally, alternative versions may be used to simulate data warehouse modification for optimization purposes.

Shahzad, Nasir and Pasha (2005) present a similar approach for enabling evolution and versioning in data warehouses that supports the simulation of business scenarios with alternative versions. Based on the formal model of a so called versioned multidimensional schema, they introduce a set of operations on the schema and instance level. All the operations are defined by a changing-algebra defined upon the multidimensional model. The versioning function supports both versioning and evolution. To support simulation of business scenarios so called real versions and alternative versions may be created. The problem of data transformation following the change operations is not dealt with.

Another instance of data warehouse maintenance is the so called *View Maintenance*. The classical data warehouse maintenance deals with structural changes, and often assumes the data warehouse structure to be rather independent from the underlying sources. View maintenance, on the other hand, interprets the data warehouse as a materialized view of the sources. Thus, changes in the sources directly affect the data warehouse. For instance, Zhuge, Garcia-Molina, Hammer and Widom (1995) present an approach to synchronize changes in the source data to the materialized view. The main problem here is to decide whether to update or to recalculate the view from scratch. But as this, and also similar, approaches only deal

with changes of transaction data they are out of scope for this chapter. Bellahsene (2002) presents an approach for structural view maintenance, i.e. updating the view definition with changes from the underlying data sources. The presented operations only cover addition and deletion of attributes of the source schema. Also here the main question is, whether an update of the view is possible and cheaper than recalculation.

FUTURE TRENDS

Current commercial systems assume that the data warehouse structure is defined at design time and does not change afterwards. Therefore the support of structure modifications is rather limited. On the other hand, real-world systems are used in evolving application domains. Thus, the demand for modifications is present, because the system has to be consistent with its application domain and requirements. Despite the fact that more effort is put into integrating maintenance capabilities into commercial data warehouse systems, current products are still not well prepared for this challenge.

Schema and instance maintenance are quite elaborated in current research approaches, but efficient cell data transformation between different structure versions is still subject to research. The two main problems with data transformation are first of all to define semantically correct transformation functions, which express the user's requirements and expectations. The second problem is the huge amount of data, which has to be dealt with. Related to data transformation are also multiversion queries. The problem with such queries is again their semantic definition, i.e. whether and how to include cell data related to elements which are not valid of the whole period of consideration.

CONCLUSION

Maintenance is an important aspect in the data warehouse domain. Typically, data warehouse systems are used in a changing environment thus the need for evolving systems is inevitable. This chapter provides some simple, but yet illustrating examples that motivate the need for data warehouse maintenance.

Founded on basic data warehouse concepts, the levels of data warehouse maintenance are introduced. Data warehouse structure may change on the schema (i.e. dimensions and categories) and instance (i.e. dimension members) level. Not only the structure elements themselves, but also the relations between them may change. When keeping track of structure changes, one has also to decide whether to use an evolutionary or versioning approach. Keeping available prior versions may for instance be necessary for legal reasons. Besides managing these structural changes, another important aspect of data warehouse maintenance is dealing with the impact of structure changes on the cell data. Modifications of structure data may corrupt the structural and/or semantic consistency of the associated cell data.

There are several approaches dealing with the data warehouse maintenance problem. One of them, namely the COMET metamodel for Temporal data warehouses, is presented in some details. Several other approaches addressing the data warehouse maintenance problem are shortly introduced. After their introduction, some of the presented approaches are compared with respect to several features. Approaches dealing with problems related to data warehouse maintenance are presented to mark the boundaries of this research area.

REFERENCES

Bellahsene, Z. (2002). Schema evolution in data warehouses. *Knowledge and Information Systems, 4*(3), 283–304. doi:10.1007/s101150200008

Blaschka, M., Sapia, C., & Höfling, G. (1999). On schema evolution in multidimensional databases. In M. Mohania & A. M. Tjoa (Eds.), *Proceedings of the 1st International Conference on Data Warehousing and Knowledge Discovery* (pp. 153-164). Heidelberg: Springer.

Body, M., Miquel, M., Bedard, Y., & Tchounikine, A. (2003) Handling evolutions in multidimensional structures. In U. Dayal, K. Ramamritham, & T.M. Vijayaraman (Eds.), *Proceedings of the 19th International Conference on Data Engineering* (pp. 581-591). New York: IEEE Computer Society.

Dynamic Information Warehouse, K. A. L. I. D. O. (2004). *A technical overview*. Retrieved May 8, 2007 from http://www.kalido.com

Eder, J., & Koncilia, C. (2001). Changes of dimension data in temporal data warehouses. In Y. Kambayashi, M. Mohania, & W. Wöß (Eds.), *Proceedings of the 3rd International Conference on Data Warehousing and Knowledge Discovery* (pp. 284-293). Heidelberg: Springer.

Eder, J., Koncilia, C., & Morzy, T. (2002). The COMET metamodel for temporal data warehouses. In A. Pidduck, et al. (Eds.), *Proceedings of the 14th International Conference on Advanced Information Systems Engineering* (pp. 83-99). Heidelberg: Springer

Eder, J., Koncilia, C., & Wiggisser, K. (2006). Maintaining temporal warehouse models. In L. Xu & A. M. Tjoa (Eds.), *Proceedings of the IFIP International Conference on Research and Practical Issues of Enterprise Information Systems* (pp. 21-30). Heidelberg: Springer

Eder, J., & Wiggisser, K. (2008). Modeling transformations between versions of a temporal data warehouse. In *Proceedings of ER 2008 Workshops.* Heidelberg: Springer

Eder, J., & Wiggisser, K. (2009). Data warehouse maintenance, evolution and versioning. In L. Liu & T. Özsu (Ed.), *Encyclopedia of Database Systems.* Heidelberg: Springer.

Froeschl, K., Yamada, T., & Kudrna, R. (2002). Industrial statistics revisited: From footnotes to meta-information management. *Österreichische Zeitschrift für Statistik, 31*(1), 9-34.

Golfarelli, M., Lechtenbörger, J., Rizzi, S., & Vossen, G. (2004). Schema versioning in data warehouses. In S. Wang et al. (Eds.), *Conceptual Modeling for Advanced Application Domains, ER 2004 Workshops* (pp. 415-428). Heidelberg: Springer.

Golfarelli, M., Lechtenbörger, J., Rizzi, S., & Vossen, G. (2006). Schema versioning in data warehouses: Enabling cross-version querying via schema augmentation. *Data & Knowledge Engineering, 59*(2), 435–459. doi:10.1016/j.datak.2005.09.004

Hurtado, C., Mendelzon, A., & Vaisman, A. (1999). Updating OLAP Dimensions. In *Proceedings of the ACM Second International Workshop on Data Warehousing and OLAP* (pp. 60-66), New York: ACM Press.

Inmon, W. (2005) *Building the data warehouse* (4th ed.) New York: John Wiley & Sons.

Kaas, C., Pedersen, T. B., & Rasmussen, B. (2004). Schema evolution for stars and snowflakes. In *Proceedings of the 6th International Conference on Enterprise Information Systems* (pp. 425-433).

Kimball, R. (1996). Slowly changing dimensions. *DBMS Magazine, 9*(4), 14.

Kimball, R., & Ross, M. (2002). *The data warehouse toolkit.* (2nd ed.) New York: John Wiley & Sons.

Malinowski, E., & Zimányi, E. (2004). OLAP hierarchies: A conceptual perspective. In J. Persson & J. Stirna (Eds.), *Proceedings of the 16th International Conference on Advanced Information Systems Engineering* (pp. 477-491). Heidelberg: Springer.

Malinowski, E., & Zimányi, E. (2006). A conceptual solution for representing time in data warehouse dimensions. In M. Stumptner, S. Hartmann, & Y. Kiyoki (Eds.), *Proceedings of the 3rd Asia-Pacific Conference on Conceptual Modelling* (pp 45-54). Newcastle: CRPIT

Quix, C. (1999). Repository support for data warehouse evolution. In S. Gatziu et al. (Eds.), *Proceedings of the 1st International Workshop on Design and Management of Data Warehouses* (p. 4). CEUS-WS.org

Ravat, F., & Teste, O. (2000). A temporal object-oriented data warehouse model. In M. Ibrahim, J. Küng, & N. Revell (Eds.), *Proceedings of the International conference on Database and Expert Systems Applications* (pp. 583-592). Heidelberg: Springer

Rizzi, S., & Golfarelli, M. (2006). What time is it in the data warehouse? In A. Tjoa & J. Trujillo (Eds.), *Proceedings of the 8th International Conference on Data Warehousing and Knwoledge Discovery, DaWaK 2006* (pp. 134-144). Heidelberg: Springer

SAP. (2000). *Multi-dimensional Modeling with BW: ASAP for BW Accelerator.* Retrieved May 8, 2007 from http://sap.com

Sarda, N. (1999). Temporal issues in data warehouse systems. In *Proceedings of the International Symposium on Database Applications in Non-traditional Environments* (pp. 27-34). New York: IEEE Computer Society

Shahzad, M. K., Nasir, J. A., & Pasha, M. A. (2005). CEV-DW: Creation and evolution of versions in data warehouse. *Asian Journal of Information Technology*, *4*(10), 910–917.

Vaisman, A., & Mendelzon, A. (2001). A temporal query language for OLAP: Implementation and case study. In G. Ghelli & G. Grahne (Eds.), *Proceedings of the 8th International Workshop on Database Programing Languages* (pp. 78-96). Heidelberg: Springer

Wrembel, R., & Bebel, B. (2007). Metadata management in a multiversion data warehouse. *Journal on Data Semantics*, *8*, 118–157.

Yang, J., & Widom, J. (1998). Maintaining temporal views over non-temporal information sources for data warehousing. In H-J. Schenk, F. Saltor, I. Ramos, & G. Alonso (Eds.), *Proceedings of the 1998 International Conference on Extending Database Technology* (pp. 389-403). Heidelberg: Springer

Zhuge, Y., Garcia-Molina, H., Hamer, J., & Widom, J. (1995). View maintenance in a warehousing environment. In M. Carey & D. Schreider (Eds.), *Proceedings of SIGMOD* (pp. 316-327). New York: ACM Press

Chapter 11
Construction and Maintenance of Heterogeneous Data Warehouses

M. Badri
Crip5 Université Paris Descartes, France & Lipn Université Paris Nord, France

F. Boufarès
Lipn Université Paris Nord, France

S. Hamdoun
Lipn Université Paris Nord, France

V. Heiwy
Crip5 Université Paris Descartes, France

K. Lellahi
Lipn Université Paris Nord, France

ABSTRACT

The data necessary to decisional ends are increasingly complex. They have heterogeneous formats and come from distributed sources. They can be classified in three categories: the structured data, the semi-structured data and unstructured data. In this work, we are interested in the field of data integration with the aim of construction and maintenance of warehouses whose sources are completely heterogeneous and belonging to the various categories. We propose a formal framework based on the definition of an integration environment. A set of "integration relationships" between the components of the sources is thus defined: an equivalence relation and a strict order relation. These relationships are independent of any data sources modelling. These last can be then heterogeneous and having different models and/ or categories. Two different physical architectures, to create and maintain the warehouses and the ma-terialized views, are given.

DOI: 10.4018/978-1-60566-756-0.ch011

INTRODUCTION

Nowadays, the current informational environment is characterized by strongly distributed heterogeneous data. Complex applications such as knowledge extraction, data mining, learning and web applications use heterogeneous and distributed data sources (Boussaïd, Darmont, Bentayeb & Loudcher-Rabaseda, 2008). Thus the need of integrating and manipulating of large amount of data is more and more increasing. In the absence, first, of tools for the heterogeneous data integration, and second, of formalisms for modelling the integration of these data, we propose in this chapter early attempts to formalise the integration of heterogeneous data and their maintenance. Indeed, the data can be classified in three categories: structured (relational and object data), semi-structured (HTML, XML, graphs) and unstructured (text, images, sounds) (see figure 1).

Our contribution is twofold: the first part of our work concerns the beginning of the Data Warehouse (DW) life cycle: the building of DW from heterogeneous sources and the second part is related to the maintenance phase.

In the literature (Da Silva, Filha, Laender & Embley, 2002; Saccol & Heuser, 2002; Kim & Park, 2003; Beneventano, Bergamaschi, Castano, Antonellis, Ferrara, Guerra, Mandreoli, Ornetti & Vincini, 2002), there is no consensus on the significance of heterogeneity. According to the domain and the type of considered application, the treatment and the interpretation of heterogeneity were made in several ways. Considering this ambiguous interpretation of heterogeneity, we adopt, in our integration work, the definitions below which will enable us to treat all categories together.

Data sources are known as heterogeneous if they check one of the two following properties:

1) They belong to the same category of data but they have different modellings;
2) They belong to different data categories.

Thus, the integration of a relational database (DB) and of an object-relational one is an example of handling heterogeneous data sources. It is the same case for a relational and an XML DBs.

A DW results from data sources integration. It is a subject-oriented, integrated, time-variant,

Figure 1. The heterogeneity of DW's sources

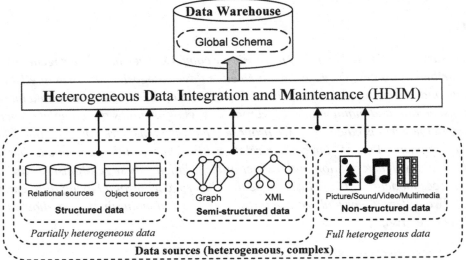

and non-volatile collection of data in support of management's decision making process (Inmon, 1995). A heterogeneous DW is a one whose sources are heterogeneous.

Our theoretical approach allows us the integration of various heterogeneous data sources (DS) (Hamdoun, 2006; Hamdoun, Boufarès & Badri, 2007; Badri, 2008). This approach takes as an input an integration environment (see figure 2) as a set of DS and a set of relationships between them and returns a DW. Because it deals with heterogeneous data, our approach proposes an unified formal theoretical representation of them. It is general and applicable for any kind of integration. We will be able for instance to duplicate databases or to create several versions of databases (Hamdoun, 2006; Hamdoun, Boufarès & Badri, 2007; Badri, 2008).

During several years, DW maintenance was considered as a real-time processing operation and many works (O'Gorman, Agrawal & El Abbadi,1999; Zhang & Rundensteiner, 2000; Laurent, Lechtenborger, Spyratos & Vossen, 2001) proposed algorithms and techniques to solve and manage concurrent DW updates. Since we

believe that the special need of using DW does not has a transactional nature. And these last years, some DW maintenance works (Rantzau, Constantinescu, Heinkel & Meinecke, 2002; Engstrom, Chakravarthy & Lings, 2003) focused on the heterogeneity of DS. They used mapping solutions (from XML to relational or vice versa). A state of the art can be found (Badri, Boufarès, Ducateau & Gargouri, 2005).

In this chapter, we are interested in the data integration with the aim of building and then of maintaining heterogeneous warehouses. It is structured as follows. Section 2 deals with the heterogeneous data integration. We introduce various data sources (relational, object-relational and XML) and propose a generic model to represent them (Hamdoun, 2006; Hamdoun, Boufarès & Badri, 2007; Badri, 2008).

We also present the integration environment as well as the different steps of the integration process. Two possible physical architectures for the heterogeneous DW (Badri, Boufarès & Heiwy, 2007) are presented in the third section. Section 4 presents our incremental maintenance method to integrate updates incoming from heterogeneous

Figure 2. Example of an integration environment

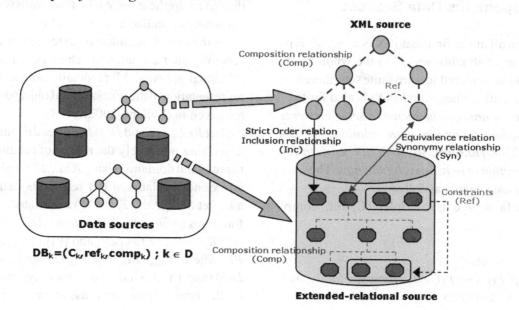

$DB_k=(C_k, ref_k, comp_k)$; $k \in D$

sources. We focus on aggregates maintenance with showing the limitations of the commercial WMS (Warehouse Management System) and propose some interesting solutions to overcome them (Badri, Boufarès, Ducateau & Nefoussi, 2006; Badri, Heiwy & Boufarès, 2008). Our work is tested exemplified on a real example which have been generated using Oracle 11g Data Base Management System (DBMS). Our results are compared to Oracle ones. Finally, our future work is given as a conclusion.

HETEROGENEOUS DATA INTEGRATION: A FORMAL APPROACH

In this section we present a theoretical approach that allows the integration of various heterogeneous data sources (DS) (Hamdoun, 2006; Hamdoun, Boufarès & Badri, 2007; Badri, 2008). This approach takes as an input an integration environment (a set of DS and a set of relationships between them) and returns a DW. It is generated by applying a set of algorithms we have developed.

A Formal Approach for Modelling Heterogeneous Data Sources

Let us recall at the first that if X is a set, $|X|$ represents its cardinality and $P(X)$ the whole of its parts. The considered sets are finite sets, therefore $|X|$ is a positive integer and $P(X)$ is also finite.

A data source can be seen as a set of elements accompanied by one or more relationships between them. However, we limit our work to the consideration of only two relationships. Thus, we model a data source as follows:

A data source is a triplet (C, ref, comp) where:

- C is a set;
- *ref: $P(C) \rightarrow P(C)$ is a binary relation such that: X ref $Y \Rightarrow |X| = |Y|$; and*

- *comp: $C \rightarrow P(C)$ is a function such that c $\notin$ comp(c) for any c $\in$ C.* An element of C is called a data source component. A component c is called simple if *comp(c)* = $\varnothing$.

Any data source comes with a type system in which data are interpreted. Each simple component is interpreted in the system by a basic type like integer, real, char, boolean. The type constructors must allow us the interpretation of all the components.

Let us now see how to represent relational, object-relational and XML data using our formal approach.

Relational and object-relational models revisited: The definition of a relational or object-relational database can be done in two steps: the first step allows us to describe the structure of the objects of the real world to be stored and the second step permits to define the objects to represent.

In terms of the data models, the description of the objects structures is called the database schema. The data (the objects themselves), constitute the database instance. Moreover, the specification of a set of constraints, called integrity constraints give the possibility to be restricted with the relevant data of an application. An instance satisfying the constraints is called a database state.

In the sequel, we mean by extended-relational schema either a relational schema or an object-relational schema. More details on the formal representation of the relational and object database are given in (Lellahi, 2002).

Let *REL*, *ATT* and *DOM* be three disjoined sets describing intuitively the names of relations, attributes and domains. Using *REL*, *ATT* and *DOM*, an extended-relational DB schema is defined as a triplet $S = (R_s, ATT_s, DOM_s)$ associated to three functions $(dom_s, att_s, [[\ ]]_s):dom_s: ATT_s \rightarrow DOM$; $att_s: R_s \rightarrow P_f(ATT) \setminus \{\varnothing\}$; and $[[\ ]]_s: DOM_s \rightarrow TYPES$ where $R_s \subseteq REL$, $ATT_s \subseteq ATT$ and $DOM_s \subseteq DOM$ and TYPES indicates various types defined by the type system, dom_s associates to each attribute name a domain, att_s associates for each relation the set of attributes which compose it and $[[\ ]]_s$ associates, for each domain, a type of data and $ATT_s = \cup_{R \in Rs}\ att_s(R)$.

An instance of S is a function $\delta_s: R_s \longrightarrow \cup_{R \in Rs}(Inst_s(R))$ *such that* $\delta_s(R) \in Inst_s(R)$ *for any* $R \in R_s$, where $Inst_s(R) = P_f(dom_s(R))$ and $dom_s(R) = \prod_{A \in atts(R)}([[dom_s(A)]]_s)$.

A (relational or object) database is a triplet (S, K_s, δ_s) *where S is a schema,* K_s *a set of constraints and* δ_s *an instance of S satisfying the constraints.*

The state δ_s *is called the current state.*

An Extended-Relational DB as a Data Source

Let $S = (R_s, ATT_s, DOM_s)$ be an extended-relational schema. In our formal approach, S can be seen as a data source in the following way:

- The set of components $\mathbf{C} = ATT_s \cup R_s$ a component c of C has one of the two following forms: c=DB.R.A or c=DB.R with $R \in R_s$ and $A \in ATT_s$.
- The ref function, makes it possible to identify the external references in the database, it is defined as follows:

$X\ ref\ Y \Leftrightarrow X \subset ATT_s, Y \subset ATT_s$ and X are an external reference to Y.

- The comp function describes both schema relations and composed attributes and is defined in the following way:

comp: $ATT_s \cup R_s \rightarrow P_f(ATT_s \cup R_s)$

comp(X)=Y $\Leftrightarrow$ X $\in R_s$, Y $\subset ATT_s$ and Y = $att_s(X)$ or X $\in ATT_s$, X is a composed attribute, and Y $\subset ATT_s$, Y is the set of the attributes composing X.

XML model revisited The definition of an XML database is also done in the following two steps: first to describe the structure of the objects of the real world that we want to store (hierarchical structure schema) and second to define the objects to represent (database instance). The description

of the database schema can be done using a DTD or an XML schema (Gardarin, 2002).

Let ELEM and DOM be two disjoined sets describing intuitively the sets of XML elements and domains.

An XML DB schema using (ELEM, DOM) is a pair $S = (E_s, DOM_s)$ associated to three functions: $dom_s: E_s^s \rightarrow DOM$; $att_s: E_s \rightarrow P_f(E_s)$; and $[[\ ]]_s: DOM_s \rightarrow TYPES$ where TYPES indicates the various types of the considered system type, *doms* associates to each name of simple XML element a domain, *att$_s$* associates to each XML element the set of elements it is composed of and $[[\ ]]_s$ associates for each domain a type of data.

An instance of S is a function $\delta_s: E_s^s \longrightarrow \cup_{R \in Rs}([[dom_s(E)]]_s)$ *such that* $\delta_s(E) \in [[dom_s(E)]]_s$ *for any* $E \in E_s^s$.

A (XML) database is a triplet (S, K_s, δ_s) *where S is a schema,* K_s *is a set of constraints and* δ_s *is an instance of S satisfying the constraints. The state* δ_s *is called current state.* An XML DB as a data source:

Let $S = (E_s, DOM_s)$ be an XML schema. In our formal definition of data sources, S can be seen as a data source as follows:

- The set of components $C = E_s$; Let us denote by E_s^s and E_s^c the set of the simple elements and composed elements, respectively.
- The *ref* relationship, makes it possible to identify the external references in the database, it is defined as follows: X ref Y $\Leftrightarrow$ X $\subset E_s^s$, Y $\subset E_s^s$ and X is an external reference to Y.
- The function comp is the function *att$_s$*.

Note: The originality of our approach is the ability to represent heterogeneous models in the same way. A data source can be seen then as a set of components (simple or composed) and a set of relationships.

2.2 The Integration Environment

Let us first point out the following two definitions:Equivalence relation: a binary relation R on a set X is an equivalence relation if:

a)   R is reflexive: x R x, for any x ∈ X;
b)   R is symmetric: x R y, y R x, for any x, y ∈ X;
c)   R is transitive: x R y and y R z ⇒ x R z, for any x, y, z ∈ X.

Strict partial order: A binary relation R, on a set X, is said to be a strict partial order relation on X if:

a)   R is irreflexive: x R y ⇒ x ≠y, for any x, y ∈ X;
b)   R is transitive: x R y et y R z ⇒ x R z, for any x, y, z ∈ X;
c)   *R is antisymmetric: x R y ⇒ ¬ (y R x), for any x, y ∈ X.*

Most of the time, an *integration environment* is made of a *set of data sources* and of a *set of "integration relationships"* between the various sources which are used during the extract process. Thus we define an integration environment as follows (see figure 2).

An integration environment is a triplet (E,S,I) where: $E = \{DB_k, k \in D\}$ is a set of data sources with $DB_k = (C_k, ref_k, comp_k)$ and D a finite set used for indexing. S is an equivalence relation on the set $C = \cup_{k \in D}(C_k)$ and I is a strict order relation on C.

Notes:

- This definition is independent of the model of each source. Consequently, data sources can be heterogeneous (modelled differently and/or belonging to different categories).
- Each DB_k indicates a different data source. We suppose that different DB_k does not

have common ingredients. In other words, there are no components having the same names in two different sources. In fact, $k \in D$ can be seen like a name for the source DB_k and consequently k simulates the prefix's attribution of components of DB_k by the name of the source.

Example 1: An example of integration environment can be the triplet (E,S,I) such that:

- $E = \{DB_1, DB_2\}$ with $DB_1 = (C_1, ref_1, comp_1)$ and $DB_2 = (C_2, ref_2, comp_2)$.
- $C_1 = \{x_1, x_2, x_3, x_4, x_5, x_6\}$, $ref_1 = \varnothing$ and

$comp_1(x_1) = \{x_2, x_3\}$, $comp_1(x_4) = \{x_5, x_6\}$, and $comp_1(x) = \varnothing$ for all $x \notin \{x_1, x_4\}$.

- $C_2 = \{y_1, y_2, y_3, y_4, y_5, y_6, y_7, y_8, y_9, y_{10}\}$, $\{y_3\}$ $ref_2\ \{y_1\}$ and $\{y_3\}\ ref_2\ \{y_8\}$

$comp_2(y_2) = \{y_4, y_3\}$, $comp_2(y_5) = \{y_1, y_6\}$, $comp_2(y_7) = \{y_8, y_9, y_{10}\}$, and $comp_2(y) = \varnothing$ for all $y \notin \{y_2, y_5, y_7\}$

- $x_2 S\ y_3$ et $y_3 S\ x_2$ and x S x for any $x \in C_1 \cup C_2$
- $x_3 I\ y_4$

2.3 The Integration Process

Our integration approach takes as an input an integration environment (containing a set of heterogeneous DB and a set of relationships between them) and returns a data warehouse DW. This DW is composed of a set of views on the data sources.

Let (E,S,I) be an integration environment where $E = \{DB_k, k \in D\}$ and each $DB_k = (C_k, ref_k, comp_k)$ is a data source. Our integration approach is made up of five main steps (Hamdoun, 2006).

In the first step (*The choice of the DW com-*

ponents), the set L of the components of the warehouse is selected. L constitutes the set of the components needed in the DW. We suppose that the set of the components of the warehouse is a subset of all the components of the various DBs. In other words we have: $L \subseteq \cup_{k \in D}(C_k)$. Consequently, $L = \cup_{k \in D}(L_k)$ where $L_k = L \cap (C_k)$.

We suppose that $L \neq \varnothing$ and some L_k can be empty with $C_k \cap C_{k'} = \varnothing$ and $L_k \cap L_{k'} = \varnothing$ for any $k \neq k'$. Thus, for all $x \in L$, a single $k \in D$ exists such that $x \in L_k$.

Example 2: Considering example 1, the set L of the components of the warehouse is $L = \{x_1, x_5, y_1, y_2, y_7\}$ with $L_1 = \{x_1, x_5\}$ and $L_2 = \{y_1, y_2, y_7\}$

The second step (*The decomposition of the whole components of the warehouse*) consists in replacing recursively all the composite element by their components. We defined as simple component, every component c such that $comp(c) = \varnothing$. It thus acts, in this step, to recursively replace every non simple component c of L ($comp(c) \neq \varnothing$) by all the elements of comp(c), until there is only simple components.

Let DB = (C, ref, comp) be a DS. Let us denote that C^S is the set of simple components. The decomposition of the composed components is made using the recursive function (Hamdoun, 2006) decomp: $C \rightarrow P(C^S)$. It is defined as follows: if $decomp(c) := \{c\}$ then $comp(c) = \varnothing$, else $decomp(c) := \cup_{c' \in comp(c)}(decomp\ (c'))$

In fact, decomp(c) makes simple the set of components which took part in the construction of c.

Example 3: By considering example 2, the result of the decomposition is the following set: L' = $\{x_2, x_3, x_5, y_1, y_4, y_3, y_8, y_9, y_{10}\}$.

The third step consists in filtering the components set. This one is refined using the two relations S and I of the selected environment. Indeed, two sub-steps of filtering are carried out on the set L according to these relations. The first filtering operation, using the partial order I, consists in leaving the components corresponding *to the maximum elements* with respect to the partial order I. Recall

that: X is a maximum element in a partial order if it does not exist *y* such that *y > x*.

Example 4: According to the example 3, L' becomes L'=$\{x_2, x_3, x_5, y_1, y_3, y_8, y_9, y_{10}\}$.

In this second filtering operation, for each equivalence class of the relation S, only one representative is left and others are deleted. The choice of this representative element is arbitrary and does not intervene in the integration process.

Example 5: By supplementing example 4, L' becomes the following set: L'=$\{x_2, x_3, x_5, y_1, y_8, y_9, y_{10}\}$. The set L', result of the filtering, is thus formed: L'⊆L. L' can be written as follows: L'=$\cup_{k \in D}(L'_k)$ avec $L'_k = L' \cap (L_k)$.

Note: In the realization of these two filtering operations the order of processing is crucial (filtering by using I then filtering by using S). The following example illustrates the two results obtained if the order is not respected.

Example 6: Let us suppose that L'=$\{x_2, y_3, y_5\}$ and assume $x_2 S\ y_3$ and $y_5 I\ x_2$. The result of filtering by using I is L'=$\{x_2, y_3\}$ then by applying S we obtain L'=$\{y_3\}$. The result of filtering by using S leads to L'=$\{y_3, y_5\}$; then by applying I we obtain L'=$\{y_3, y_5\}$.

The fourth step (*The generation of the total schema of the DW*) is made up applying the four following sub-steps:

a) Construction of the graphs associated with the sources: In each graph G_k corresponding to a data source DB_k, the nodes represent all the components $c \in C_k$ where not exists $c' \in C_k$ with $c \in comp_k(c')$. The edges rely each couple of nodes (n(c), n(c')) corresponding to a couple of components (c, c') such that $\exists X \subset comp_k(c), Y \subset comp_k(c.)$ with X ref_k Y.

Example 7: By supplementing example 5 we obtain the two graphs shown in Figure 3.

b) Detection of the connected sub-graphs: a graph is qualified as connected when it

Figure 3.

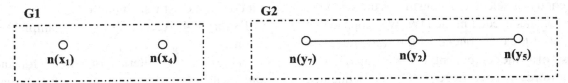

exists at least one path between each couple of nodes. In this step we detect the related connected sub-graphs of each graph G_k. The graph G_k is then the union of its connected sub-graphs. Let us note $\lceil_k$ the set of these sub-graphs: $\lceil_k = \{G_{ki} / i \in T_k\}$ where T_k is an indexing set for $\lceil_k$

Example 8: By supplementing example 7, G_1 is formed by two connected subgraphs G_{11} et G_{12} and G_2 contains only one connected subgrap $G_{21} = G_2$ (seeFigure 4). $\lceil_1 = \{G_{11}, G_{12}\}$ et $\lceil_2 = \{G_{21}\}$.

c) Unions of the related sub-graphs: it is realized by taking each time only one connected sub-graph from each graph G_k. Let's have $T = \prod_{k \in D} T_k$ et $d = |D|$. for each $u = (u_1, \ldots, u_d) \in T$ we consider the graph R_u *formed by the union of all the* G_{ui} (i=1,…,d). Since these graphs do not have neither common nodes nor common edges. The union of the considered graphs means their juxtaposition.

We denote by R the set of the obtained graphs: $R = \{R_u / u \in T\}$.

Example 9: By supplementing example 8, we obtain the following set $R:R = \{R_1, R_2\}$ with $R_1 = G_{11} \cup G_{21}$ and $R_2 = G_{12} \cup G_{21}$

d) Generation of a view schema for each sub-graph: We associate a view to each union of sub-graphs realized. The views components constitute the intersection of L' and all the sub-components of the components associated to the nodes of these sub-graphs.

Example 10: By supplementing example9, two view's schemas W_1 and W_2 are obtained. $W_1 = \{x_2, x_3, y_1, y_8, y_9, y_{10}\}$ and $W_2 = \{x_5, y_1, y_8, y_9, y_{10}\}$.

The fifth step of our approach (*Building the Data warehouse*) gives the possibility to build the views feeding the DW. For every view W to build, the algorithm ConstrView() allows the integration of various and heterogeneous data.

Let us note that:

•   A set of fictitious components (of CompNull names) is created in order to ensure Union-compatibility between the built queries if $SI_w = \varnothing$.

•   The procedure Create_View(Q) consists in carrying out a selection query of the various components appearing in Q. According to the warehouse model this query can be translated. Thus, the procedure depends on the adopted modelling for the source and the DBMS used. It also depends on

Figure 4.

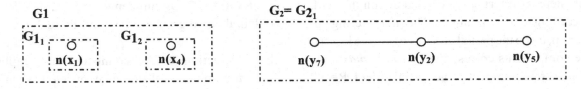

the chosen modelling for the warehouse. The latter is closely related to those of the sources as well as the applicability domain. For instance, when the sources are belonging to different categories and the applicability requires a frequent exchange of data between various systems, the XML representation can be chosen for the DW.

Algorithm ConstrView (W)

```
for each k ∈ D doQ := empty view /*
initialization of an empty view*/
W:= empty viewW 0 := (L'_k) ∩ W /*
W0 is the set of the components of
W belonging to DB_k*/
W' := W - W 0 /* W' is the set of
the components of W not belonging
to DB_k*/
y := |W 0| /* y is the cardinality
of W' */
for each w' ∈ W do
SI_w' := (S'(skl(w'), w',k) ∪
I'(skl(w'), w',k))
/* skl function to identify the
source */
/* SIw'contains the set of the syn-
onymous components of w' in DB_k and
the set of the components of DB_k in-
cluded in w'*/
end for
for each (a_1,...,a_y) ∈ ∏_{w'∈W'} (SI_w') do
Q :=W0 ∪ {a_1,...,a_y}
/*Q contains the set of the compo-
nents to extract from DB_k*/
Q := Q (union) Create_View(Q)/* Q
contains the partial result from
DB_k*/
end for
W := W (union) Q
end for
```

- The procedure Create_View(Q) gives the possibility to create a view. Types are associated to the various components of the view. These types associated to the DBMS are used.

Most of the time, types corresponding to a component and those which are bound to it by the relation S (an equivalence class β) are compatible. Let T_y be the set of these types. Thus, for each equivalence class β, there exists a type t' such that $\forall\ t_i \in Ty,\ t_i \rightarrow^* t'$.

In this case, the type associated with the selected representative is t'. In the same way, all types corresponding to an ordered set α of components (according to the ordered relation I) in L' are compatible. Let *Typ* be the set of these types. Thus, for each ordered set α of components in L', there exists a type t' such that $\forall\ t_i \in Typ, t_i t_i \rightarrow^* t'$. Note that t' is the type associated with the component corresponding to the maximum of α.Example 11:The following results are obtained by applying the algorithm using example 10:To built W_1 two queries are generatedSource DB_1: Q = {x_2, x_3,CompNull$_1$,CompNull$_2$,CompNull$_3$, CompNull$_4$} Source DB_2: Q' = {CompNull$_1$,CompNull$_2$, y_1, y_8, y_9, y_{10}}

To built W_2 two queries are generated:Source DB_1: Q = {x_5,CompNull$_1$,CompNull$_2$,CompNull$_3$, CompNull$_4$}Source DB_2: Q' = {CompNull$_1$, y_1, y_8, y_9, y_{10}}

Then the structure of the DW is described as:W_1={ x_2, x_3, y_1, y_8, y_9, y_{10}} and W_2={ x_5, y_1, y_8, y_9, y_{10}}

A META-SCHEMA FOR TWO POSSIBLE PHYSICAL ARCHITECTURES

Let us note that the DW obtained by our following integration process is independent of any architecture. Indeed, the returned views are logical and have no information about their physical structure. Thus, they can be implemented in any model such as relational, object-relational or XML. Moreover, we have the possibility to implement our warehouse under two different architectures: the classical star architecture (called Ws) and the *flat architecture* (called Wp). In the Wp architecture, the idea is to keep the views like they are returned from the integration process. This independence is seen as a further advantage of our proposed approach. Two physical architectures are then possible for every logical DW. Whatever the chosen architecture, the data warehouse is considered as a set of facts and dimensions. The warehouse creator clarifies the type of the chosen physical architecture and its request (the list L of the components requested) according to meta-model given below in Figure 5.

The presented meta-schema can handle multiple DW. Each of these data warehouses is considered as a set of views (DW_Views), cubes and lattices (Lattice). OLAP cubes and lattices are presented in (Badri, 2008). The views are those obtained by our integration process, where each view corresponds to one or more queries. A view is described by a fact and dimensions. We can

combine multiple hierarchies in one dimension. Each of these hierarchies has one or several levels of granularity. Each level is related to a component and a single sequence over a given hierarchy. The components of the DW are derived from attributes belonging to the DS.

The meta-base built from this meta-schema is used to ensure the transition from star to flat DW schema and vice versa. A transformation procedure is carried out using the ConstrView() algorithm which is launched for each dimension and for each fact. More details and choice criteria between these two architectures can be found in (Badri, Boufarès & Heiwy, 2007).

Example 12: Using the meta-schema, the data warehouse W, obtained in example 11, is composed of two facts: $F_1 = \{x_2, x_3\}$ and $F_2 = \{x_5\}$ and three dimensions: $D_1 = \{y_1, y_8\}$, $D_2 = \{y_9\}$ and $D_3 = \{y_{10}\}$.

Figure 5. The DW meta-schema

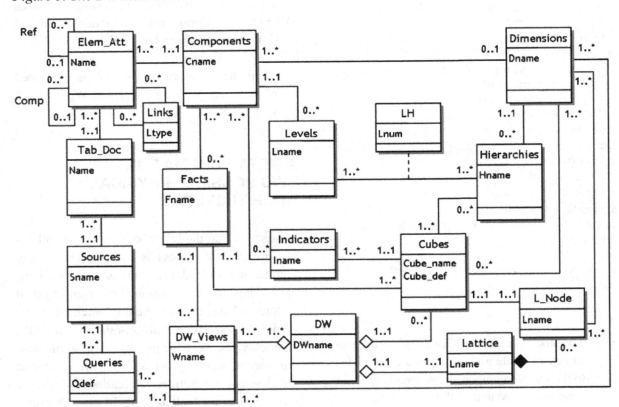

Figure 6. The two architectures of the DW of the example 12

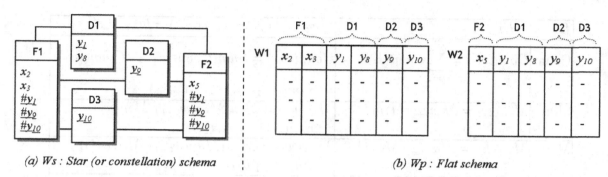

(a) Ws : Star (or constellation) schema   (b) Wp : Flat schema

W can be created according to two possible different architectures (see Figure 6).

INCREMENTAL MAINTENANCE OF DATA AND AGGREGATES

To help decision making, aggregates are computed over DW. These aggregates can be calculated in the same way using Ws architecture as well as Wp. They are stocked in materialized views (MV) called in some systems Automatic Summary Table (AST). We discuss in this section different ways to refresh these MV.

Updates realized on the source level are reflected in the warehouse according to our ConstrView() algorithm. This implies the update of the aggregates in the view MV of this warehouse. Our maintenance method consists in carrying out an incremental update of MV. In the case of a flat architecture (Wp), it is achieved by computing ΔWp resulting from the sources updates. It is the same case for star architecture Ws (compute delta update for every fact and/or dimension which is affected by the new update). To maintain MV we need to calculate MV' on ΔWp. The new values of MV are obtained by applying a full outer join operation between MV and MV'. But before explaining our incremental maintenance method, let us describe the aggregate functions and their differences. The aggregate functions belong to different categories and are not all refreshed in the same way. Indeed, given two sets A and B of integers: $average(A \cup B) \neq average(average(A), average(B))$ whereas $max(A \cup B) = max(max(A), max(B))$.

In Palpanas, Sidle, Cochrane & Pirahesh, 2002; Chou & Zhang, 2004, the aggregate functions have been classified into three categories:

- **distributive** aggregate functions: a function f is distributive if for a group G, $f(G)$ can be computed from $f(G_s)$ values where G_s are the G sub-groups. **COUNT ALL, MAX, MIN** and **SUM** are examples of distributive functions.

- **algebraic** aggregate functions: a function f is called algebraic if for a group G, $f(G)$ can be computed from a fixed number of intermediate aggregates computed on G_s sub-groups. This extra data is usually stored in auxiliary tables/views. **AVG, VARIANCE** and **STDDEV** are examples of algebraic functions.

- and **holistic** aggregate functions: the number of intermediate aggregates is unknown. There is no known method to compute incrementally this kind of aggregates. The only available solution remains in exploring all data sources. This third class of functions is not considered treated in this work. **COUNT DISTINCT** and **RANK** are examples of holistic functions.

Figure 7. Computing distributive functions

f	$f(E)$	$f(w_t) = h(f(w_{t-1}), f(w'_t)) = h(v_{t-1}, v'_t)$
Count	$Count(E) = \sum_{i=1}^{n} count(E_i)$	$Count(w_t) = Sum(Count(w_{t-1}), Count(w'_t))$ $= Sum(v_{t-1}.a_{count}, v'_t.a_{count})$
Min	$Min(E) = Min_{i=1}^{n}(Min(E_i))$	$Min(w_t) = Min(Min(w_{t-1}), Min(w'_t))$ $= Min(v_{t-1}.a_{Min}, v'_t.a_{Min})$
Max	$Max(E) = Max_{i=1}^{n}(Max(E_i))$	$Max(w_t) = Max(Max(w_{t-1}), Max(w'_t))$ $= Max(v_{t-1}.a_{Max}, v'_t.a_{Max})$
Sum	$Sum(E) = \sum_{i=1}^{n} Sum(E_i)$	$Sum(w_t) = Sum(Sum(w_{t-1}), Sum(w'_t))$ $= Sum(v_{t-1}.a_{Sum}, v'_t.a_{Sum})$

Our objective is to update aggregate values without computing them again from all data. Some classical computing technics (Palpanas, Sidle, Cochrane & Pirahesh, 2002; Chou & Zhang, 2004) are used below.

Let w be a DW obtained from one or more data sources (DB$_s$ with s $\in$ [1..b]) and let ΔT be a sequence of updates from one or several sources.

By applying the ConstrView() algorithm on ΔT, we obtain w' such that $w' = ConstrView(\Delta T)$. We note that w and w' have the same logical schema. Let w_t (respectively w'_t) be a version (respectively an update) of the DW at the instant t. Maintaining data of a DW consists in computing a new DW version: $w_t = w_{t-1} \cup w'_t$.

Let us consider now that a materialized view v, defined on the DW w, is the result of computing aggregate functions with $v = f(w)$. We can then calculate v', defined on w', with the same manner: $v' = f(w')$.

Let us consider that: $W = \{w_i, i \geq 1\}$ the set of DWs and $V = \{v_i, i \geq 1\}$ the set of all MV computed on W. $V^A \subset V$ the set of all special materialized views called auxiliary MV. f an aggregate function defined as follow: $f: W \to V$; $f(w_t) = v_t$ Since $w_t = w_{t-1} \cup w'_t$; we can then write $f(w_t) = f(w_{t-1} \cup w'_t) = v_t$

According to the definitions given above, one can find that:

- for a **distributive** function f, a function

$h: V \times V \to V$; $h(v_{t-1}, v') = v_t$ such that $f(w_{t-1} \cup w') = h(f(w_{t-1}), f(w'))$ We have then $f(w_t) = f(w_{t-1} \cup w'_t) = h(f(w_{t-1}), f(w'_t)) = h(v_{t-1}, v'_t) = v_t$

- for an **algebraic** function f, an aggregate function g and a function h^A such as:

$g: W \to V$; $g(w_t) = v_t^A$ $h^A: V^A \times V^A \to V$ with $h(v_{t-1}^A, v'_t^A) = v$ $f(w_{t-1} \cup w') = h^A(g(w_{t-1}), g(w'_t))$

We have then $f(w_t) = f(w_{t-1} \cup w'_t) = h^A(g(w_{t-1}), g(w'_t)) = h(v_{t-1}^A, v'_t^A) = v_t$

Let us apply the above results to the most frequently used functions into practice (such as count, sum, max, min, variance, stddev).

The next two figures (Figure 7 and Figure 8) summarize the used technique to maintain incrementally aggregate functions.

Let E_i be a set of discrete elements such that: $E_i = \{x_{i1}, x_{i2}, x_{i3}, ..., x_{ip}\}$ with $|E_i| = Count(E_i)$ and $Avg(E_i)$ the arithmetic average.

$E = \cup_{i=1}^{n}(E_i)$ is a set with $\cap_{i=1}^{n}(E_i) = \emptyset$ and $|E| = \sum_{i=1}^{n}(count(E_i))$

And $v_t.a_f$ the aggregate value of the function f computed on w_t and stored in the view v at the

Figure 8. Computing algebraic functions

f	$f(E)$	$f(w_t) = h^A(g(w_{t-1}), g(w_t')) = h(v_{t-1}^A, v_t'^A)$
Avg	$Avg(E) = \dfrac{\sum_{i=1}^{n} Sum(E_i)}{\sum_{i=1}^{n} count(E_i)}$	$Avg(w_t) = \dfrac{Sum(Sum(w_{t-1}), Sum(w_t'))}{Sum(Count(w_{t-1}), Count(w_t'))}$ $= \dfrac{Sum(v_{t-1}^A.a_{sum}, v_t'^A.a_{sum})}{Sum(v_{t-1}^A.a_{count}, v_t'^A.a_{count})}$
Var	$Var(E) = \dfrac{\sum_{i=1}^{n}\Big(Count(E_i) \times (Var(E_i) + Avg(E_i)^2)\Big)}{\sum_{i=1}^{n} Count(E_i)}$ $- \left(\dfrac{\sum_{i=1}^{n} Sum(E_i)}{\sum_{i=1}^{n} Count(E_i)}\right)^2$	$Var(w_t) = \dfrac{X_1}{X_2} - \left(\dfrac{X_3}{X_4}\right)^2$ where: $X_1 = Sum(Count(w_{t-1})(Var(w_{t-1}) + Avg(w_{t-1})^2),$ $Count(w_t')(Var((w_t')) + Avg(w_t')^2))$ $= Sum(v_{t-1}^A.a_{count}(v_{t-1}^A.a_{var} + v_{t-1}^A.a_{avg}^2),$ $v_t'^A.a_{count}(v_t'^A.a_{var} + v_t'^A.a_{avg}^2))$ $X_2 = Sum(Count(w_{t-1}), Count(w_t'))$ $= Sum(v_{t-1}^A.a_{count}, v_t'^A.a_{count})$ $X_3 = Sum(Sum(w_{t-1}), Sum(w_t'))$ $= Sum(v_{t-1}^A.a_{sum}, v_t'^A.a_{sum})$ $X_4 = Sum(Count(w_{t-1}), Count(w_t'))$ $= Sum(v_{t-1}^A.a_{count}, v_t'^A.a_{count})$

instant t.Example 13:Let v be the materialized view computed on the DW (Ws) resulting from example 12.

v is defined, using SQL statements, as follow:

```
CREATE MATERIALIZED VIEW V as
SELECT y10, MIN(x2) as M, AVG(x3)
as A, COUNT(x3) AS C, SUM(x3) as S
FROM F1
GROUP BY y10;
```

After receiving source updates, one compute F1_prim using the ConstrView() algorithm.

Then v_prim is computed, from F1 prim, as it is done for v.

According to Figures 7 and 8 the SQL query to be developed for incremental maintenance (of Min and Avg functions), instead of computing again v values, is:

```
SELECT DECODE(V.y10,NULL, V_PRIM.
y10, V.y10),
DECODE(V.M,NULL,V_prim.M,DECODE(V_
prim.M,NULL,V.M,
DECODE(abs(V_PRIM.M-V.M),V_PRIM.M-
V.M, V.M, V_PRIM.M))) as M,
DECODE(V_PRIM.M,NULL,V.A,DECODE(V.
```

```
A,NULL,V_PRIM.A, (V_PRIM.S + V.S)/
(V_PRIM.C + V.C))) as A
FROM V FULL OUTER JOIN V_prim ON
V.y10=V_prim.y10 ORDER BY 1;
```

CONCLUSION

In this work, we propose a formal framework which treats integration of heterogeneous data sources from various categories. This approach is based on the definition of an *integration environment*. This last is seen as a set of data sources associated with a set of *"integration relationships"* between the sources components.

The originality of our work, contrary to various works on integration, lies in the fact of covering the integration of all the categories of data considered at the same time and in the proposition of a theoretical approach of the data integration. Our approach is general and is applicable to any type of integration. For instance, it is possible to duplicate databases or to create several versions of one or many databases at the same time. We propose to implement a heterogeneous DW in two possible physical architectures. We give method to rewrite computing aggregates functions for incremental maintenance of MV.

An heterogeneous data integration tool (HDIM prototype) and procedures of incremental maintenance are under development. We plan now to compare our measure on different DBMS (Oracle, DB2 and SqlServer) (see Figure 9).

REFERENCES

Badri, M. (2008). *Maintenance des entrepôts de données issus de sources hétérogènes*. PhD thesis, University Paris Descartes.

Badri, M., Boufarès, F., Ducateau, C. F., & Gargouri, F. (2005). Etat de l'art de la maintenance des entrepôts de données issus des systèmes d'information hétérogènes. *Cinquièmes Journées Scientifiques GEI* (pp. 13-18).

Badri, M., Boufarès, F., Ducateau, C. F., & Nefoussi, R. (2006). Maintenance des vues matérialisées hétérogènes sous oracle. *In Workshop SID Systèmes d'Information Décisionnels . INFORSID, 2006*, 8–14.

Badri, M., Boufarès, F., & Heiwy, V. (2007). Des critères pour choisir l'architecture physique d'un entrepôt de données hétérogènes. *In Workshop ASD Atelier des systèmes décisionnels.*

Figure 9. Comparison performance between HDIM MV maintenance and Oracle MV refreshing

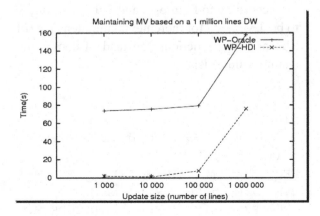
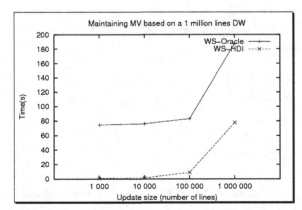

Badri, M., Heiwy, V., & Boufarès, F. (2008). Mise à jour incrémentale des agrégats: Cas des indicateurs ROLAP dans les entrepôts de données. *In CNRIUT'08*.

Beneventano, D., Bergamaschi, S., Castano, S., Antonellis, V. D., Ferrara, A., Guerra, F., et al. (2002). Semantic integration and query optimization of heterogenous data sources. In *Proceedings of the workshops on advances in Object-Oriented Information Systems (OOIS)* (LNCS 2426).

Boussaïd, O., Darmont, J., Bentayeb, F., & Loudcher-Rabaseda, S. (2008). Warehousing complex data from the Web. [invited paper]. *International Journal of Web Engineering and Technology, 4*(4), 408–433. doi:10.1504/IJWET.2008.019942

Chou, P. L., & Zhang, X. (2004). Computing complex iceberg cubes by multiway aggregation and bounding. In *DaWaK* (pp.108-117).

Da Silva, A. S., Filha, I. M. R. E., Laender, A. H. F., & Embley, D. W. (2002). Representing and querying semistructured Web data using nested tables with structural variants. In *Proceedings of the 21st International Conference on Conceptual Modeling* (LNCS 2503, pp. 135-151).

Engstrom, H., Chakravarthy, S., & Lings, B. (2003). Maintenance policy selection in heterogeneous data warehouse environments: A heuristics-based approach. In *DOLAP Proceedings* (pp. 71-78).

Gardarin, G. (2002). *Des bases de données aux services Web*. Edition Dunod - Paris.

Hamdoun, S. (2006). *Construction d'entrepôts de données par intégration de sources hétérogènes*. PhD thesis, University Paris Nord.

Hamdoun S., Boufarès F. & Badri M. (2007). Construction et maintenance des entrepôts de données hétérogènes. *Revue e-TI, (4)*.

Inmon, W. H. (1995). Multidimensional databases and data warehousing. *Data Management Review*.

Kim, H. H., & Park, S. S. (2003). Building a Web-enabled multimedia data warehouse. *In Proceedings of the Web Communication Technologies and Internet-Related Social Issues (HSI2003)* (LNCS 2713, pp. 594-600).

Laurent, D., Lechtenborger, J., Spyratos, N., & Vossen, G. (2001). Monotonic complements for independent data warehouses. *The VLDB Journal, 10*(4), 295–315. doi:10.1007/s007780100055

Lellahi, S. K. (2002). Modelling data and objects: An algebraic viewpoint. *Theoretical aspects of computer science, advanced lectures (First summer school on theoretical aspects of computer science) (. LNCS, 2292*, 113–147.

O'Gorman, K., Agrawal, D., & El Abbadi, A. (1999). Posse: A framework for optimizing incremental view maintenance at data warehouse. In *DaWaK '99, London, UK* (pp. 106-115). Springer-Verlag.

Palpanas, T., Sidle, R., Cochrane, R., & Pirahesh, H. (2002). Incremental maintenance for non-distributive aggregate functions. In *VLDB* (pp. 802-813).

Rantzau, R., Constantinescu, C., Heinkel, U., & Meinecke, H. (2002). Champagne: Data change propagation for heterogeneous information systems. In *VLDB '02, VLDB Endowment* (pp. 1099-1102).

Saccol, D. B., & Heuser, C. A. (2002). Integration of XML Data. In *Proceedings of VLDB workshop on Efficiency and Effectiveness of XML Tools and Techniques (EEXTT) and of the international Conference on Advanced Information System Engineering (CAISE) workshop on Databases in Telecommunications and Web (DTWeb2002) Revised papers* (LNCS 2590, pp. 68-80).

Zhang, X., & Rundensteiner, E. A. (2000). Dyda: Dynamic data warehouse maintenance in a fully concurrent environment. In *DaWaK 2000: Proceedings of the Second International Conference on Data Warehousing and Knowledge Discovery, London, UK* (pp. 94-103). Springer-Verlag.

Section 4
Exploitation of Data Warehouse

Chapter 12
On Querying Data and Metadata in Multiversion Data Warehouse *

Wojciech Leja
Poznań University of Technology, Poland

Robert Wrembel
Poznań University of Technology, Poland

Robert Ziembicki
Poznań University of Technology, Poland

ABSTRACT

Methods of designing a data warehouse (DW) usually assume that its structure is static. In practice, however, a DW structure changes among others as the result of the evolution of external data sources, the changes of the real world represented in a DW, and new user requirements. The most advanced research approaches to managing the evolution of DWs are based on temporal extensions and versioning techniques. An important feature of a DW system supporting evolution is its ability to query different DW states. Such querying is challenging since different DW states may differ with respect to their schemas. As a consequence, a system may not be able to execute a query for some DW states. Our approach to managing the evolution of DWs is based on the so-called Multiversion Data Warehouse (MVDW) that is composed of the sequence of DW versions. In this chapter, we contribute a query language called MVDWQL for querying the MVDW. The MVDWQL supports two types of queries, namely content queries and metadata queries. A content query is used for analyzing the content (i.e., data) of multiple DW versions. A metadata query is used for analyzing the history of evolution of the MVDW. The results of both types of queries are graphically visualized in a user interface.

INTRODUCTION

Contemporary manner of managing enterprises is based on knowledge. Typically, knowledge is gained from the advanced analysis of various types of data processed and collected during the lifetime of an enterprise. In practice, within the same enterprise data are stored in multiple heterogeneous

DOI: 10.4018/978-1-60566-756-0.ch012

and autonomous storage systems that often are geographically distributed. In order to provide means for the analysis of data coming from such systems, a data warehouse architecture has been developed (Jarke et al., 2003; Widom, 1995). The data warehouse architecture, firstly, offers techniques for the integration of multiple data sources in one central repository, called a data warehouse (DW). Secondly, it offers means for advanced, complex, and efficient analysis of integrated data.

Data in a DW are organized according to a specific conceptual model (Gyssens & Lakshmanan, 1997; Letz, Henn, & Vossen, 2002). In this model, an elementary information being the subject of analysis is called a *fact*. It contains numerical features, called *measures* (e.g., quantity, income, duration time) that quantify the fact and allow to compare different facts. Values of measures depend on a context set up by *dimensions*. A dimension is composed of *levels* that form a hierarchy. A lower level is connected to its direct parent level by a relation, further denoted as →. Every level l_i has associated a domain of values. The finite subset of domain values constitutes the set of *level instances*. The instances of levels in a given dimension are related to each other, so that they form a hierarchy, called a *dimension instance*. A typical example of a dimension, is *Location*. It may be composed, for example, of three hierarchically connected levels, i.e., *Shops→Cities→Regions*. An example instance of dimension *Location* may include: {*Macys→New Orleans→Lousiana*}, {*Timberland→Houston→Texas*}.

In practice, this conceptual model of a DW can be implemented either in multidimensional OLAP servers (MOLAP) or in relational OLAP servers (ROLAP). In a MOLAP implementation, data are stored in specialized multidmensional data structures whereas in a ROLAP implementation, data are stored in relational tables. Some of the tables represent levels and are called *level tables*, while others store values of measures, and are called *fact tables*. Level and fact tables are typi-

cally organized into a star schema or a snowflake schema (Chaudhuri & Dayal, 1997).

DW Evolution

For a long period of time, research concepts, prototypes, and commercial DW systems have assumed that the structure of a deployed DW is time invariant. This assumption turned out to be false. In practice, a DW structure may evolve (change) among others as the result of the evolution of external data sources, the changes of the real world represented by a DW, new user requirements, as well as the creation of simulation environments (Mendelzon & Vaisman, 2000; Rundensteiner, Koeller, & Zhang, 2000; Wrembel, 2009).

The most advanced research approaches to managing the evolution of DWs are based on temporal extensions (Bruckner & Tjoa, 2002; Chamoni & Stock, 1999; Eder & Koncilia, 2001; Eder, Koncilia, & Morzy, 2002; Letz et al., 2002; Malinowski & Zimányi, 2008; Schlesinger et al., 2001), and versioning extensions (Body et al., 2002; Golfarelli et al., 2004; Mendelzon & Vaisman, 2000; Ravat, Teste, & Zurfluh, 2006; Rizzi & Golfarelli, 2007; Vaisman & Mendelzon, 2001). Concepts from the first category use timestamps on modified data in order to create temporal versions. In versioning extensions, a DW evolution is managed partially by means of schema versions and partially by data versions. These concepts solve the DW evolution problem partially. Firstly, they do not offer a clear separation between different DW states. Secondly, they do not support modeling alternative, hypothetical DW states required for simulations and predictions within the so-called 'what-if' analysis.

In order to eliminate the limitations of the aforementioned approaches, we proposed the so-called *Multiversion Data Warehouse* (*MVDW*). The *MVDW* is composed of the sequence of DW versions, each of which represents either the real-world state within a certain period of time or a 'what-if' simulation scenario (Bębel et al., 2004).

The important functionality of a DW system that supports evolution is a query language capable of: (1) querying multiple DW states (versions) that differ with respect to their schemas and presenting query results to a user in a meaningful way and (2) querying metadata on the history of DW changes. Designing such a query language is challenging since DW versions may differ with respect to their schemas (e.g., one schema version may store attribute *amount*, whereas another may not or may store a corresponding attribute but with a different name).

Few languages for querying evolving data warehouses have been proposed so far in the research literature, e.g., (Mendelzon & Vaisman, 2000; Vaisman & Mendelzon, 2001), (Eder & Koncilia, 2001; Eder et al., 2002), and (Rizzi & Golfarelli, 2007). The languages, however, either are not capable of querying DW versions that differ with respect to their schemas or do not allow to query metadata.

A more detail analysis of related approaches to managing evolution in databases and data warehouses as well as approaches to querying evolving databases and data warehouses can be found in (Wrembel, 2009).

Chapter Contribution

This chapter contributes the so-called *Multiversion Data Warehouse Query Language* (*MVDWQL*) developed for querying the *MVDW*. The language proposed in this chapter is the extension of our previous works (Morzy & Wrembel, 2004; Wrembel & Bębel, 2007; Wrembel & Morzy, 2006) with respect to the functionality that allows to explicitly query metadata on the *MVDW*. To this end, two types of queries on metadata are supported, namely:

- Queries searching for DW versions that include an indicated DW object (a level table, fact table, attribute, dimension, dimension instance) or its equivalent existing in other DW versions;

- Queries retrieving the history of the evolution of an indicated DW object (a level table, fact table, attribute, dimension, dimension instance).

In this chapter we discuss the functionality of *MVDWQL* queries, their syntax, and how the queries are processed. We discuss how to handle queries that address DW versions that differ with respect to their schemas. We outline our prototype *MVDWQL* software. Finally, we summarize the chapter.

MULTIVERSION DATA WAREHOUSE

DW Versions

The Multiversion Data Warehouse is composed of the sequence of DW versions. A *DW version* is composed of a DW schema version and a DW instance version. The *DW schema version* describes the structure of a DW within a given time period, whereas the *DW instance version* represents the set of data described by its schema version.

We distinguish two types of DW versions, namely real and alternative ones (Bębel et al., 2004). Real versions are created in order to reflect changes in a real business environment. *Real versions* are linearly ordered by the time they are valid within. *Alternative versions* are created mainly for simulation purposes, as part of the 'what-if' analysis. Such versions represent virtual business scenarios.

Versions of the *MVDW* form a *DW version derivation tree*. Each node of this three represents a DW version (real or alternative), whereas edges represent *derived-from* relationships. The root of the DW version derivation tree is the first real version. Figure 1 schematically shows an example DW version derivation tree where R_i represents a real version and A_i represents an alternative version.

Figure 1. An example DW version derivation tree consisting of real and alternative DW versions

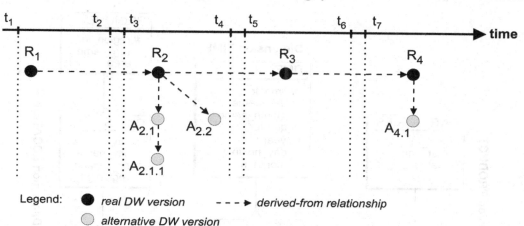

Every DW version is valid within a certain time period represented by two timestamps, i.e., *begin validity time* (BVT) and *end validity time* (EVT) (Bębel et al., 2004; Wrembel & Bębel, 2007), as shown in Figure 1. For example, real version R_1 is valid from time t_1 (BVT) until t_2 (EVT) whereas R_4 is valid from t_7 until present. Alternative versions are valid within the same time period as their parent version, e.g., $A_{2.1}$ is valid from t_3 until t_4.

Metadata Describing MVDW

In order to provide the support for schema and data versioning as well as for querying the *MVDW*, the set of well defined metadata is required. In our approach we developed the metaschema of the *MVDW* (Wrembel & Bębel, 2007) that allows to store data on: (1) the structure and content of every DW version, (2) changes applied to DW versions, (3) data conversion methods, which are required for querying, (4) transactions run in the system. The metaschema is general and it is applicable to a ROLAP and a MOLAP implementation. It is composed of *dictionary tables*.

DW Version Change Operations

After being explicitly derived, a DW version may be modified by means of 15 elementary operations on a schema, further called *schema change operations* and by means of 7 elementary operations on dimension instances, further called *instance change operations*. These operations allow to handle all typical changes that may be required in practice. Multiple schema change operations and instance change operations may be applied to the same DW version.

Schema change operations include: creating a new dimension, creating a new level, connecting a level into a dimension hierarchy, disconnecting a level from a dimension hierarchy, removing a level, removing a dimension, creating a new attribute for a level, removing an attribute from a level, changing the domain of a level or a fact attribute, creating a new fact, creating a new attribute for a fact, removing an attribute from a fact, creating an association between a fact and a level, removing an association between a fact and a level, removing a fact.

Instance change operations include: inserting a new level instance, associating a level instance with its parent level instance, associating a fact instance with a bottom level instance, deleting

Figure 2. The example schema of a data warehouse on sales of products

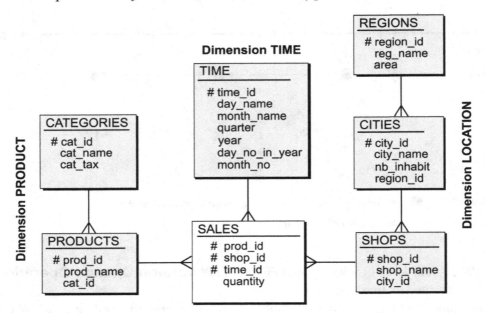

a level instance, reclassifying a level instance, merging *n* instances of a given level into a new instance of the same level, splitting an instance of a given level into *n* new instances of the same level.

In order to illustrate some of the version change operations let us consider a DW schema from Figure 2. In this schema, the central *Sales* fact table references via foreign keys three level tables, namely *Products* (in dimension *Product*), *Time* (in dimension *Time*), and *Shops* (in dimension *Location*).

Case 1: Reclassifying level instances. Let us assume that initially, in April 2004, in real version denoted as *R_April*, there existed 3 shops (instances of the *Shops* level table), namely *ShopA*, *ShopB*, and *ShopC*. These shops were selling *porotherm bricks* (the instance of the *Products* level table) with 7% of VAT (the instance of the *Categories* level table). Let us further assume that in May, *porotherm bricks* were reclassified to 22% VAT category. This reclassification was reflected in a new real DW version, denoted as *R_May*. The reclassification was also registered in a dedicated dictionary table storing mappings between new and old level instances.

Case 2: Merging or splitting level instances. Let us assume that in June, shops *ShopA* and *ShopC* were merged into one shop *ShopAC* in a new real DW version *R_June*. Similarly as in Case 1, mappings between shops in DW versions *R_May* and *R_June* are stored in a dedicated dictionary table. For more advanced splitting or merging operations it will be necessary to provide backward and forward conversion methods for converting fact records from an old to a new DW version. If such methods are explicitly implemented and provided by a DW user/administrator, then their names are registered in a dedicated dictionary table.

Splitting level instances is handled in a similar way as merging, by storing appropriate records in a dedicated dictionary table.

Case 3: Different table names. In this case, a table (either fact or level) in a parent DW version and its equivalent table in a child DW version differ only with respect to their names. The change of a fact table and a level table name is registered in a dedicated dictionary table.

Case 4: Different attribute names and domains. Differences in the names of attributes existing in a table in a parent and a child DW version are registered in a dedicated dictionary table. Corresponding attributes of two tables in two adjacent DW versions may differ also with respect to their domains. In order to compare the values of such attributes, their values have to be convertable to each other. In the *MVDW*, conversion methods are used for this purpose. As an example we may consider changing prices of products from Polish Zloty to Euro. Appropriately defined conversion methods from PLN to EUR and vice versa will allow to compare sales of products expressed in these two currencies.

QUERYING THE CONTENT OF MULTIVERSION DATA WAREHOUSE

In the *MVDW*, data of user interest are usually distributed among several DW versions and a user may not be aware of the location of the particular set of data. Moreover, DW versions being addressed in queries may differ with respect to their schemas and the structure of dimension instances. Such DW versions will further be called *heterogeneous*. Querying heterogeneous DW versions is challenging and requires intensive usage of metadata. In our approach, we developed the *MVDWQL* query language, capable of:

- Querying the content of multiple heterogeneous DW versions (Morzy & Wrembel, 2004; Wrembel & Bębel, 2007; Wrembel & Morzy, 2006), such queries will be further called *content queries*;
- Querying metadata describing DW versions, such queries will be further called *metadata queries*.

In this section we focus on content queries whereas in the next section we focus on metadata queries.

Querying Real and Alternative DW Versions

With the support of the *MVDWQL* a user can query either a single DW version or multiple DW versions, real and alternative ones. A query that addresses a single DW version will be further called a *singleversion query* (SVQ), whereas a query that addresses multiple DW versions will be further called a *multiversion query* (MVQ).

The set of real DW versions addressed in a MVQ is indicated by a user either by specifying a time interval, represented by version begin and version end validity times or by specifying the set of version identifiers $VID_1, ..., VID_n$. In the first case, the SELECT command uses the VERSION FROM start_date TO end_date clause. In the second case, the SELECT command uses VERSION IN ($VID_1, ..., VID_n$) clause. If the version selection criteria point to one DW version, then a MVQ becomes a SVQ. If clauses VERSION FROM and VERSION IN are omitted in a MVQ, then the query will address all real DW versions.

Processing Multiversion Queries

Parsing and executing a MVQ is performed in the five following steps (Wrembel & Bębel, 2007).

1. **Constructing the set of DW versions:** The set $S^V = \{V_1, V_2, ..., V_n\}$ of DW versions (either real or alternative ones) that is addressed in a MVQ is constructed taking into account version begin and end validity times or explicitly provided version identifiers.

2. **Decomposing MVQ:** Next, for every DW version V_i belonging to S^V, the system constructs an appropriate singleversion query SVQ_i. In this process, the differences in schema versions are taken into consideration. If some tables and attributes changed their names from one version to another, then their names are found in an appropriate dictionary table and are used for constructing SVQ_i.

3. **Executing SVQs:** Every SVQ_i constructed in step 2 is executed in its own DW version V_i.

4. **Returning SVQ results:** The results of singleversion queries obtained in step 3 are returned and presented to a user separately. Additionally, every result is annotated with: (1) an information about a DW version the result was obtained from, (2) metadata about schema (e.g., attribute/table renaming, attribute domain modification) and dimension instance changes (e.g., reclassifying, splitting, or merging level instances) between adjacent DW versions addressed by the MVQ.

5. **Integrating SVQ results:** Results of single-version queries obtained in step 3 may be in some cases integrated into one consistent set that is represented as if it was stored in a DW version specified by a user. It must be stressed that in many cases such an integration will not be possible since DW versions may differ with respect to their schemas and structures of dimension instances (Morzy & Wrembel, 2004). The integration of SVQ results will be possible if a MVQ addresses attributes that are present (or have equivalent attributes) in all queried DW versions and if there exist conversion methods between adjacent DW versions (if such conversions are needed). Integrating results obtained by SVQs is defined by including in a MVQ the MERGE INTO VID_i clause, where VID_i denotes the identifier of a DW version whose schema version will be used as a destination schema for all the obtained results of SVQs.

Querying Heterogeneous DW Versions

In this section we will illustrate how a MVQ is executed on heterogeneous DW versions. Five typical cases will be considered.

Case 1: Reclassifying Level Instance

Let us consider the MVQ given below that computes net and gross total sales of products in DW versions from April (R_April) until May (R_May). Notice that the DW versions are selected by means of using their validity times. Recall that in May *porotherm bricks* were reclassified to 22% VAT category and the information about this reclassification is stored in a dedicated dictionary table.

```
SELECT sum(sa.amount *
  pr.item_price * vc.vat_value),
  sum(sa.amount * pr.item_price),
  pr.name product
FROM sales sa, products pr,
        vat_categories vc
WHERE sa.prod_id=pr.prod_id
AND pr.cat_id=vc.cat_id
GROUP BY pr.name
VERSION FROM '01-04-2004'
  to '30-05-2004'
```

During a parsing phase, the query is decomposed into two SVQs: one for version R_April and one for R_May. Next, the two SVQs are executed in their proper DW versions. After executing the SVQs, the result of SVQ addressing version R_May is augmented and returned to a user with metadata describing changes in the structure of the *Product* dimension instance made in R_May, as shown below. This way, a sales analyst will know that a gross sales increase from April to May was at least partially caused by VAT increase.

```
Reclassified key [br1(porotherm) ->
vc7(VAT 7%)] to
[br1(porotherm)) -> vc22(VAT 22%)]
in table PRODUCTS
```

Case 2: Merging or Splitting Level Instances

Let us consider a MVQ computing monthly gross sales of products in shops in the period from 01-05-2004 until 30-06-2004, i.e., addressing two DW versions *R_May* and *R_June*. Recall that in June *ShopA* and *ShopC* were merged into *Shop_AC* and the information about this merging is stored in a dedicated dictionary table. Similarly as in the above case, the MVQ is decomposed into two SVQs, one addressing DW version *R_May* and one addressing DW version *R_June*. The result of the SVQ addressing *R_June* will be annotated with the following metadata informing about merging shops:

```
Merged key [sh1(ShopA), sh3(ShopC)]
to [sh4(ShopAC)] in table SHOPS
```

Case 3: Different Table Names

Recall that metadata on the changes of table names are stored in a dedicated dictionary table. The contents of the table is used while parsing a MVQ in order to find the right name of a table in every DW version of interest. Appropriate table names are then used in SVQs. Next, query results are annotated with metadata informing about table names changes. Let us assume that in our example fact table *Sales* was renamed to *Poland_Sales* in a DW version *R_July*. If we execute the query from Case 1 addressing DW versions from March to July, then the result of the SVQ query addressing *R_July* will be annotated with:

```
Table SALES renamed to POLAND_SALES
```

Case 4: Different Attribute Names and Domains

In order to find out whether attributes changed their names or domains in DW versions and in order to find the right attribute name in every DW version being addressed in a MVQ, while parsing the MVQ, the system searches the content of dedicated dictionary tables. Appropriate attribute names are then used in SVQs. Next, the results of SVQs are annotated with metadata informing about changing attribute names.

If for example, attribute *quantity* in table *Sales* is renamed to *nb_sold* in a DW version from August, then the result of a SVQ addressing a DW version from August will be annotated with:

```
Attribute 'QUANTITY' in table SALES
renamed to 'NB_SOLD'
```

Case 5: Missing Attributes

Table attributes may exist in some DW versions but they may be dropped in other DW versions. An attribute that does not exist in some DW versions will be called a *missing attribute* in these versions. Missing attributes can appear in the SELECT, WHERE, GROUP BY, HAVING, and ORDER BY clauses. Missing attributes may in some cases prevent from executing SVQs. For example, let us assume that in DW versions from January, February, and March the *Sales* fact table includes attribute *quantity*. Attribute *total_price* was added to *Sales* in DW version from April. The attribute also exists in DW versions from May and June. A MVQ computing not only sum(quantity) but also sum(total_price) of products sold by shops in the period from 1st January, 2004 until 30th June, 2004 can be answered only in the last three DW versions. In this case, the system removes sum(total_price) from SVQs addressing versions from January, February, and March. Such modified SVQs are executed in these three DW versions and their results are returned to a user. Moreover, the result of the SVQ addressing DW version from April is augmented with the following metadata informing about the added attribute:

```
Attribute 'TOTAL_PRICE' in table
SALES added
```

If attribute a_i used in the WHERE, GROUP BY, and HAVING clauses is missing in DW versions V_i and V_j, then SVQs are not executed in these versions. In these cases, a user is notified about missing attributes by means of metadata that are returned instead of query results. The reason for such a behavior is to not return to a user data that he/she is not requesting since excluding missing attributes from these clauses changes the meaning of a query. SVQs are executed only in these DW versions where a_i exists or has its equivalent attribute.

If attribute a_i used in the ORDER BY clause is missing in DW versions V_i and V_j, then the attribute is excluded from SVQs addressing V_i and V_j and the SVQs are executed in their DW versions. The returned results are not sorted by a_i and they are augmented with metadata notifying a user about missing attribute a_i.

If attribute a_i used in the SELECT clause is missing in DW versions V_i and V_j, then the attribute is excluded from SVQs addressing V_i and V_j and such modified SVQs are executed in their DW versions.

Attributes dropped from tables in some DW versions are handled in a similar way as added attributes.

Integrating Results of SVQs

In order to provide a global view on analyzed data, SVQs may be integrated into one consistent result. The integration is done as follows. Firstly, the system finds out a common set of attributes/expressions used in the SELECT clause of SVQs. Tables that changed their names and attributes that changed their names and/or domains from version to version are also included in the set. Secondly, a temporary table is being created for holding partial results. Next, partial queries are executed and all obtained partial results are stored in the temporary table. While loading a partial result, data are transformed by conversion methods, if needed, in order to form a consistent result. Finally, the integrated result is returned to a user by a query on the temporary table.

Notice that missing attributes used in the SELECT, WHERE, GROUP BY, and HAVING clauses prevent from the full integration of partial results.

Missing Attributes in SELECT, WHERE, GROUP BY, and HAVING

Let us assume that attribute a_m and a_n in fact table F are missing in DW versions V_i and V_j. Let us further consider a MVQ that selects F.a_m, F.a_n, F.a_o, F.a_p, ..., from versions V_i, V_j, V_k, and V_m. The query will be decomposed into four SVQs. SVQs addressing V_i and V_j will have attributes a_m and a_n removed from their SELECT clauses. Such partial queries will not be integrated in the second step as the structures of their results differ from the structures of the results obtained by SVQs addressing V_k and V_m.

Missing attributes a_m and a_n in DW versions V_i and V_j specified in WHERE, GROUP BY, and HAVING cause that SVQs can be executed only in these DW versions that contain a_m and a_n, i.e., V_k and V_m. As a consequence, only the results of SVQs from V_k and V_m will be integrated.

QUERYING METADATA IN MULTIVERSION DATA WAREHOUSE

With the support of the *MVDWQL* a user can explicitly query metadata for the purpose of analyzing the change history of either the whole *MVDW* or some DW versions. The functionality of the language allows to execute two types of queries, namely: (1) a query searching for DW versions that include an indicated schema object or a dimension instance, and (2) a query retrieving the evolution history of an indicated schema object or a dimension instance. A query of the first type will be called a *version query* and a query of the second type will be called an *object evolution query.*

Version Query

In particular, a version query allows to search for DW versions that include:

1. an attribute of a given name and a type or an equivalent attribute (in the case of changing attribute names in DW versions) in a fact or a level table;
2. a table (either fact or level) of a given name or an equivalent table (in the case of changing table names in DW versions);
3. a table (either fact or level) that has a given exact or partial structure;
4. a dimension that has a given exact or partial structure;
5. a dimension instance that has a given exact or partial structure.

The result of a version query is a DW version derivation tree that allows to track the existence of a specified DW object in the DW versions of interest. A version query is expressed by means of the SHOW VERSIONS HAVING clause, followed by keywords specifying the type of an object being searched. The set of keywords includes: ATTRIBUTE, LEVEL TABLE, FACT TABLE, DIMENSION, DIMENSION ... INSTANCE. In each of these five types of a version query a user specifies the definition of the searched object. This object definition is valid for an indicated DW version. The DW version where the specified object exists will be called a *base version*. A base version is selected by means of the IN VERSION version_name clause.

A version query can address either all or some DW versions. The set of DW versions being queried is constrained by means of the VERSION FROM start_date [TO end_date] clause, similarly as in content queries. Notice that the TO end_date

clause is optional. If it is not specified in a query, then the query addresses all DW versions whose BVT is greater or equal to start_date. If the whole VERSION FROM clause is omitted, then all existing DW versions are queried.

Below we describe the syntax of each of the aforementioned five types of a version query and illustrate them with examples.

VQ1. DW versions containing an attribute of a given name and type

The general syntax of the query is shown below. attr_name is the name of an attribute being searched. The optional OF TYPE type_name clause allows to specify attribute type. The FROM {LEVEL|FACT} TABLE table_name clause allows to specify whether the attribute of interest belongs to a level or fact table whose name is specified as table_name.

```
SHOW VERSIONS HAVING ATTRIBUTE
attr_name [OF TYPE type_name]
FROM {LEVEL|FACT} TABLE table_name
IN VERSION version_name
[VERSION FROM start_date
  [TO end_date]]
```

The below example query searches for DW versions containing attribute *reg_name* of type *varchar2* and the length equal 20 characters, belonging to fact table called *Regions*. This attribute and the table originally exist in DW version *R_March*, which is the base version as specified in the IN VERSION 'R_March' clause. The set of searched DW versions is constrained to versions whose validity times are within the range from *01-02-2004* to *28-02-2004*. Notice that attribute *reg_name* could change its name and/or its type in some DW versions. All attributes equivalent to *reg_name* will also be taken into consideration.

```
SHOW VERSIONS HAVING ATTRIBUTE
reg_name OF TYPE varchar2(20)
```

```
FROM FACT TABLE Regions
IN VERSION 'R_March'
VERSION FROM '01-02-2004'
  TO '28-02-2004'
```

VQ2. DW versions containing a fact or a dimension level table of a given name

The general syntax of the query is shown below. The mutually exclusive keywords LEVEL and FACT are used for specifying a level or a fact table, respectively, similarly as in the query of type *VQ1*. The meaning of other clauses is the same as discussed for the query of type *VQ1*.

```
SHOW VERSIONS HAVING
{LEVEL|FACT} TABLE table_name
IN VERSION version_name
[VERSION FROM start_date
  [TO end_date]]
```

The below example query searches for DW versions containing fact table called *sales* in base version *R_March*. Notice that this table could change its name in some DW versions. In this case, all tables equivalent to *Sales* will also be taken into consideration. Since the VERSION FROM clause was omitted, the query addresses all existing DW versions.

```
SHOW VERSIONS HAVING FACT TABLE
Sales
IN VERSION 'R_March'
```

VQ3. DW versions containing a fact or a dimension level table of a given name and structure

The general syntax of the query is shown below. The mutually exclusive keywords LEVEL and FACT are used for specifying a level table or a fact table, respectively. Additionally, the structure (schema) of a table have to be specified. To this end, the OF [EXACT] STRUCTURE clause is

used. The structure that a table of interest should have is specified by means of the set of attributes and, optionally, their types. The optional EXACT keyword allows to express that the table of interest should have exactly the same structure as specified in the query, i.e., the table should be composed of only the specified attributes. Omitting the EXACT keyword results in searching for a table whose schema contains at least the specified attributes.

```
SHOW VERSIONS HAVING
(LEVEL|FACT) TABLE table_name
OF [EXACT] STRUCTURE (
  attr_name
    [OF TYPE type_name],
  attr_name
    [OF TYPE type_name], ... )
IN VERSION version_name
[VERSION FROM start_date
  [TO end_date]]
```

The below example query searches for DW versions containing a level table, named *Products* in base version *R_March*. Additionally, the table is composed in *R_March* of exactly three attributes, namely *prod_id*, *prod_name*, and *cat_id*. Notice that the types of attributes are out of user interest (the OF TYPE clause was omitted). Notice also that the table name and attribute names could change in some DW versions. In this case, their equivalents in other DW versions will also be taken into consideration. The VERSION FROM clause restricts the set of searched DW versions to these whose BVT is equal to or greater than *01-01-2004*.

```
SHOW VERSIONS HAVING
LEVEL TABLE Products
OF EXACT STRUCTURE
  ( prod_id, prod_name, cat_id )
in version 'R_March'
VERSION FROM '01-01-2004'
```

VQ4. DW versions containing a dimension that has a given structure

The general syntax of the query is shown below. The structure of the dimension of interest is specified by means of clause OF [EXACT [UP|DOWN]] STRUCTURE. The structure of a dimension is expressed by means of level's hierarchy. The optional EXACT keyword allows to express that the structure of a dimension has to be exactly as specified in the query. The optional EXACT UP keywords allow to express that the structure of a dimension has to match the specified structure from a top level towards lower levels. The optional EXACT DOWN keywords allow to express that the structure of a dimension has to match the specified structure from a bottom level towards upper levels.

```
SHOW VERSIONS HAVING
DIMENSION dimension_name
OF [EXACT [UP|DOWN]] STRUCTURE
   (level_name -> level_name ... ->
   level_name)
IN VERSION version_name
[VERSION FROM start_date
   [TO end_date]]
```

For example, in the below query the search criteria are defined for base version *R_April* (as specified in IN VERSION 'R_April'). In this version, dimension *Product* is composed of hierarchically connected two levels, such that *Products→VAT_Categories*, as specified in the OF STRUCTURE clause. Notice that dimension name and level names could change in some DW versions. In this case, all dimensions equivalent to *Product* and all levels equivalent to *Products* and *VAT_Categories* will also be taken into consideration. Notice also that the EXACT keyword was omitted in the query. As a consequence, all *Product* dimensions (and their equivalents) are taken into consideration whose hierarchies include level *Products* as a lower level and *VAT_Categories* as

its direct upper level, regardless other levels that may exist as lower levels of *Products* and upper levels of *VAT_Categories*.

```
SHOW VERSIONS HAVING
DIMENSION Product
OF STRUCTURE (Products ->
   VAT_Categories)
IN VERSION 'R_April'
VERSION FROM '01-04-2004'
   TO '30-05-2004'
```

If we modify the above example query so that the OF EXACT DOWN STRUCTURE (Products→VAT_Categories) clause is included in the query, then the query will search for dimensions *Product* (and their equivalents) whose structure matches the specified hierarchy from the bottom. In this case, all dimensions of structure *Products→VAT_Categories→...→...* would be taken into consideration. The usage of the OF EXACT UP STRUCTURE (Products→VAT_Categories) clause will result in searching for dimensions *Product* (and their equivalents in other DW versions) whose structure matches the specified hierarchy from the top. In this case, all dimensions of structure *...→...→Products→VAT_Categories* will be taken into consideration.

VQ5. DW versions containing a dimension instance that has a given structure

The general syntax of the query is shown below. The structure of the dimension instance of interest is specified by means of the OF [EXACT [UP|DOWN]] STRUCTURE clause, similarly as in the query of type *VQ4*. A dimension instance is specified by means of attribute values belonging to levels.

```
SHOW VERSIONS HAVING
DIMENSION dimension_name
INSTANCE OF [EXACT [UP|DOWN]]
```

```
STRUCTURE
(table_name.attr_name(value) ->
 table_name.attr_name(value) -> ...
 table_name.attr_name(value))
IN VERSION version_name
[VERSION FROM start_date
  [TO end_date]]
```

For example, the below query searches for DW versions in which in base version *R_June*: (1) dimension *Location* is composed of three hierarchically connected levels *Shops→Cities→Regions*, as specified in the INSTANCE OF EXACT STRUCTURE clause, (2) the instance of dimension *Location* is defined on attributes *Shops. shop_name*, *Cities.city_name*, and *Regions. reg_name*, and (3) the dimension instance has the following structure *Auchan→Warsaw→Central*. Keyword EXACT causes that only dimension instances whose structure is exactly as specified in the query are considered. Since the VERSION FROM clause was omitted, the query will address all existing DW versions. Notice that the dimension, the level tables and their attributes could change their names in other DW versions. In this case their equivalents in other DW versions will also be considered by the query.

```
SHOW VERSIONS HAVING
DIMENSION Location
INSTANCE OF EXACT STRUCTURE
(Shops.shop_name('Auchan') ->
 Cities.city_name('Warsaw') ->
 Regions.reg_name('Central'))
IN VERSION 'R_June'
```

Object Evolution Query

An object evolution query allows to retrieve the evolution of:

1. an indicated attribute of a fact or a level table;
2. an indicated fact or level table;

3. an indicated dimension;
4. an indicated dimension instance.

The result of an object evolution query is the history of the evolution of a specified object. This history includes a DW version derivation tree and metadata describing the structure of the object in each of the retrieved DW versions.

An object evolution query is expressed by means of the SHOW EVOLUTION OF clause, followed by keywords specifying the type of an object whose evolution is to be retrieved. Similarly as for a version query, the set of keywords includes: ATTRIBUTE, LEVEL TABLE, FACT TABLE, DIMENSION, DIMENSION ... INSTANCE. An object evolution query can address either all existing DW versions or some versions. The set of DW versions being queried can be constrained by means of the VERSION FROM start_date [TO end_date] clause. Its meaning is exactly the same as for a version query.

Below we describe the syntax of each of the aforementioned four types of an object evolution query and illustrate the queries with examples.

OEQ1. Evolution of an attribute

The general syntax of the query is shown below. The name of an attribute whose evolution is to be retrieved follows the ATTRIBUTE keyword. The attribute belongs either to a level or a fact table. The name of this table is specified in clause FROM {LEVEL|FACT} TABLE table_name.

```
SHOW EVOLUTION OF
ATTRIBUTE attribute_name
FROM {LEVEL|FACT} TABLE table_name
IN VERSION version_name
[VERSION FROM start_date
  [TO end_date]]
```

For example, the below query retrieves the evolution history of attribute called *amount* in table *Sales*, in base version *R_February*. Notice that a table name and an attribute name could change in some DW versions. In this case, equivalent tables and attributes are taken into consideration. Since the VERSION FROM clause was omitted, the query will address all existing DW versions.

```
SHOW EVOLUTION OF
ATTRIBUTE amount
FROM FACT TABLE Sales
IN VERSION 'R_February'
```

OEQ2. Evolution of a fact or dimension level table

The general syntax of the query is shown below. The name of a fact or a level table whose evolution is to be retrieved follows the FACT TABLE and LEVEL TABLE keywords, respectively.

```
SHOW EVOLUTION OF
{LEVEL|FACT} TABLE table_name
IN VERSION version_name
[VERSION FROM start_date
  [TO end_date]]
```

For example, the below query retrieves the evolution of a level table whose name is *Shops* in base version *R_April*. The history of evolution is retrieved from DW versions whose validity times are within the specified range in the VERSION FROM ... TO ... clause. Similarly as in the above queries, level tables (in other DW versions) equivalent to *Shops* are also considered by the query.

```
SHOW EVOLUTION OF
LEVEL TABLE Shops
IN VERSION 'R_April'
VERSION FROM '01-01-2004'
  TO '30-05-2004'
```

OEQ3. Evolution of a dimension

The general syntax of the query is shown below. For a specified dimension that follows keyword DIMENSION, the evolution of a specified hierarchy is retrieved. The name of hierarchy whose evolution history is to be retrieved follows keyword HIERARCHY.

```
SHOW EVOLUTION OF
DIMENSION dimension_name
HIERARCHY hierarchy_name
IN VERSION version_name
[VERSION FROM start_date
  [TO end_date]]
```

For example, the below query retrieves the evolution of hierarchy *H_product* belonging to dimension *Product* in base version *R_March*. The evolution history is retrieved in all DW versions since the VERSION FROM clause was not specified. Dimensions and hierarchies that changed their names in some DW versions and that are equivalent to *H_product* and *Product* are also considered by the query.

```
SHOW EVOLUTION OF
DIMENSION Product
HIERARCHY H_product
IN VERSION 'R_March'
```

OEQ4. Evolution of a dimension instance

The general syntax of the query is shown below. Similarly as in the query of type *VQ5*, a dimension instance is specified by means of attribute values belonging to levels. A dimension name follows keyword DIMENSION. A dimension instance is specified in clause INSTANCE OF STRUCTURE.

```
SHOW EVOLUTION OF
DIMENSION dimension_name
INSTANCE OF STRUCTURE
(table_name.attribute_name(value)
->
  table_name.attribute_name(value)
-> ...
 table_name.attribute_name(value))
IN VERSION version_name
[VERSION FROM start_date
  [TO end_date]]
```

For example, the below query retrieves the evolution of the instance of dimension *Product* existing in base version *R_March*. In this version, dimension *Product* is composed of two hierarchically connected levels, i.e., *Products* and *Categories*, such that *Products→Categories*, as specified in clause INSTANCE OF STRUCTURE. The dimension instance is defined on attributes *Products.prod_name* and *Categories.cat_name*. The instance has the following structure *porotherm brick→vat 7%*. Since the VERSION FROM clause was omitted, the query will address all existing DW versions. Notice that the dimension, the level tables and their attributes could change their names in other DW versions. In this case their equivalents in other DW versions will also be considered by the query.

```
SHOW EVOLUTION OF
DIMENSION Product
INSTANCE OF STRUCTURE
(Products.prod_name
   ('porotherm brick') ->
 Categories.cat_name('vat 7%'))
IN VERSION 'R_March'
```

PROTOTYPE IMPLEMENTATION OF *MVDWQL*

The feasibility of the proposed *MVDWQL* was verified in the prototype *MVDW* system. In this section we present the technical architecture of the *MVDW* system, an application for executing content queries and an application for executing metadata queries.

Technical Architecture

The *MVDW* system is composed of the *MVDW storage* and six software modules (cf. Figure 3), namely: (1) *MVDW manager*, (2) *MVDW management interface*, (3) *content query manager*, (4) *content query interface*, (5) *metadata query manager*, and (6) *metadata query interface*. The modules are implemented in Java and they connect to the *MVDW storage* by means of JDBC.

The *MVDW storage* manages and stores metadata describing the *MVDW*, DW schema versions, and DW instance versions. The *MVDW manager* is responsible for managing DW schema and DW instance versions. In particular, it is responsible for: (1) deriving new DW versions, (2) executing schema change operations, instance change operations, and fact instance modifications, (3) creating new schema objects from scratch, (4) loading data into DW instance versions, and (5) transactional management of the *MVDW*. The *MVDW* is managed by means of the *MVDW management interface*. The *content query manager* is responsible for parsing and executing multiversion queries and for returning their results (possibly integrated) to the *content query interface*. The *content query interface* is responsible for entering MVQs for execution and presenting their results to a user. It visualizes the results of MVQs as texts and charts. Similarly, the *metadata query manager* is responsible for parsing and executing metadata queries and for returning the results for visualization. Metadata queries are entered for execution and their results are presented to a user by means of the *metadata query interface*. The parser of metadata queries is build based on the *SableCC* library. The visualization software is based on *JGraph* and *JGraphpad pro*.

Figure 3. The software architecture of the MVDW prototype

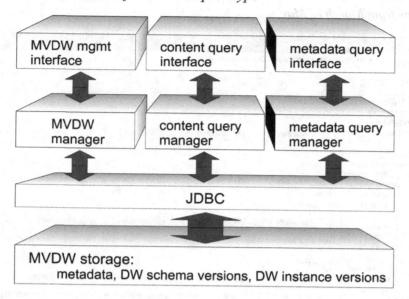

Content Query Interface

The results of multiversion queries are presented in the *content query interface* as: (1) separate results of singleversion queries and (2) an integrated result, if an integration is possible. Additionally, every result of a SVQ is annotated with version information and metadata describing changes applied to a DW schema and the structure of dimension instances in adjacent DW versions.

The example screen shot of the *content query interface* is shown in Figure 4. It is composed of two panels. The left-hand side panel - an *object navigator* allows to browse through DW schema versions and DW instance versions. The right-hand side panel - *query visualizer* is used for visualizing the results of MVQs.

The screen shot shown in Figure 4 displays the results of a MVQ that addresses DW versions from March (denoted as *RV3*) to May (denoted as *RV5*). As we can observe in Figure 4, each of the addressed DW versions contains its own partial result, denoted as *Version RV3*, *Version RV4*, and *Version RV5*. Every partial result, can be displayed either in a text form (available under the *View data* button) or as a chart (available under the *View chart*

button). Moreover, one can view a SVQ passed for execution in a given DW version (available under the *View query* button). For every partial result, one can show or hide metadata describing schema and dimension instance changes between adjacent DW versions that are queried (available under the *View changes/Hide changes* button). For example, in Figure 4 metadata describing changes made to *RV4* as compared to *RV3* inform a user that table called *Sale* in *RV3* was renamed to *Poland_Sale* in *RV4*. In *RV5* two products were reclassified to another VAT category. *Common result* contains an integrated result from the three addressed DW versions.

Metadata Query Interface

The results of metadata queries, both version queries and object evolution queries, are visualized in the *metadata query interface*.

Version Query Visualization

As mentioned before, the result of a version query is a DW version derivation tree. In the tree, we use different colors for representing different DW

221

Figure 4. The example screen shot of the content query interface presenting the result of a MVQ that addresses versions from March to May

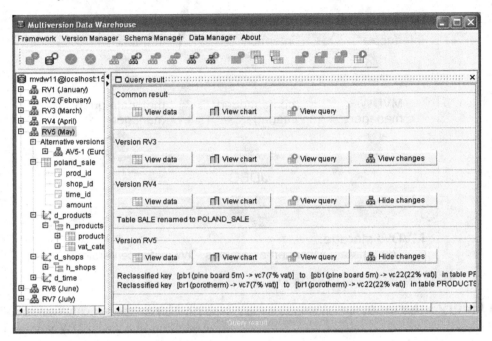

versions. The root of a DW version derivation tree is yellow-colored. Real DW versions are blue-colored, whereas alternative DW versions are red-colored. Regardless a version type, if a version does not contain the searched object, then it is gray-colored, otherwise it is colored as mentioned above.

The example screen shot of the *metadata query interface* is shown in Figure 5. Similarly as in the *content query interface*, it is composed of the *object navigator* and the *query visualizer*. Figure 5 displays the results of a version query searching for DW versions that contain hierarchy *H_Product* in dimension *Product* in base version from February. Ellipses represent DW versions and arrows represent derived-from relationships. *RV1*, *RV2*, and *RV3* represent real DW versions, whereas *AV31*, *AV32*, and *AV321* represent alternative DW versions.

Detail metadata are displayed after clicking on the node of the version derivation tree. The metadata are visualized in a window shown in Figure 6. It displays four types of metadata, namely: (1)

query information - providing an information on the executed query (query type, i.e., a version query or an object evolution query, its base version, and the query version range), (2) *current version* - providing an information on the DW version that is represented by the selected node (the information is retrieved from the *VERSIONS* dictionary table), (3) *image query object* - which is the graphical visualization of an object specified in the version query, and (4) *query object* - which provides an information on an object specified in the version query.

Object Evolution Query Visualization

As mentioned before, the result of an object evolution query is the evolution history of a specified object. This history is visualized by a DW version derivation tree (similarly as a version query) but the derivation tree is augmented by the graphical representation of the structure of the searched object.

Figure 5. The example screen shot of the metadata query interface showing the result of a version query

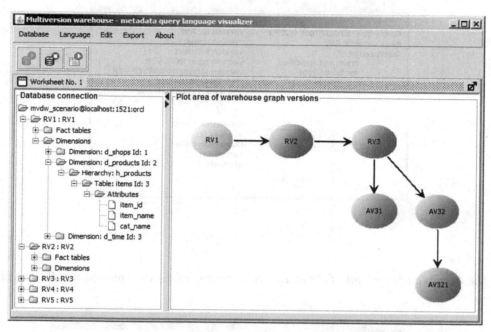

An example screen shot that displays the results of an object evolution query is shown in Figure 7. The query retrieves the evolution of hierarchy *H_Product* in dimension *Product* that originally exists in base version from March. As we can observe in Figure 7, the hierarchy in dimension *Product* is graphically displayed next to the DW version that includes the hierarchy. For example, in DW version *RV1*, hierarchy *H_Product* includes only one level *Items*. In *RV2*, the hierarchy is composed of two hierarchically connected levels, namely *Products→Categories*.

Similarly as for a version query, a detail information on the searched object in a selected DW version is available after clicking on the node of a version derivation tree.

SUMMARY

In this chapter we presented the *MVDWQL* query language, for the Multiversion Data Warehouse.

The *MVDWQL* allows to: (1) query multiple DW versions that differ with respect to their schemas, (2) augment query results with metadata describing changes made to the queried DW versions, and (3) explicitly query metadata on the history of DW changes and visualize their results. Two types of queries on metadata are supported, namely: (1) queries searching for DW versions that include an indicated DW object and (2) queries retrieving the history of the evolution of an indicated DW object. The *MVDW* and *MVDWQL* have been successfully implemented in a prototype system.

Since a few years data warehouses are applied to the integration and analysis of complex data, e.g., XML, spatio-temporal, and multimedia. Moreover, semantic Web, knowledge bases, ontology based systems, and various reasoning technologies are becoming components of decision support systems. It is likely that these various systems will also suffer from structural and content changes in data sources and will face the same problems as traditional data warehouses.

Figure 6. The example screen shot of a window visualizing detail metadata

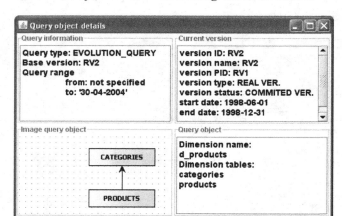

Figure 7. The example screen shot of the metadata query interface showing the result of an object evolution query

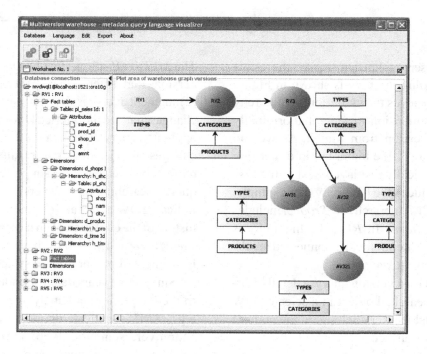

We believe that the concept of the *MVDW* and its *MVDWQL* query language will be useful for these new areas of DW and OLAP applications.

REFERENCES

Bębel, B., Eder, J., Koncilia, C., Morzy, T., & Wrembel, R. (2004). Creation and management of versions in multiversion data warehouse. In

Proc. of ACM Symposium on Applied Computing (SAC) (pp. 717-723).

Body, M., Miquel, M., Bédard, Y., & Tchounikine, A. (2002). A multidimensional and multiversion structure for OLAP applications. In *Proc. of ACM Int. Workshop on Data Warehousing and OLAP (DOLAP)* (pp. 1-6).

Bruckner, R., & Tjoa, A. M. (2002). Capturing delays and valid times in data warehouses - towards timely consistent analyses. [JIIS]. *Journal of Intelligent Information Systems, 19*(2), 169–190. doi:10.1023/A:1016555410197

Chamoni, P., & Stock, S. (1999). Temporal structures in data warehousing. In Proc. of *Int. Conference on Data Warehousing and Knowledge Discovery (DaWaK)* (LNCS 1676, pp. 353-358).

Chaudhuri, S., & Dayal, U. (1997). An overview of data warehousing and OLAP technology. *SIGMOD Record, 26*(1), 65–74. doi:10.1145/248603.248616

Eder, J., & Koncilia, C. (2001). Changes of dimension data in temporal data warehouses. In *Proc. of Int. Conference on Data Warehousing and Knowledge Discovery (DaWaK)* (LNCS 2114, pp. 284-293).

Eder, J., Koncilia, C., & Morzy, T. (2002). The COMET metamodel for temporal data warehouses. In *Proc. of Conference on Advanced Information Systems Engineering (CAiSE)* (LNCS 2348, pp. 83-99).

Golfarelli, M., Lechtenbörger, J., Rizzi, S., & Vossen, G. (2004). Schema versioning in data warehouses. In *Proc. of ER Workshops* (LNCS 3289, pp. 415-428).

Gyssens, M., & Lakshmanan, L. V. S. (1997). A foundation for multidimensional databases. In Proc. of *Int. Conference on Very Large Data Bases (VLDB)* (pp. 106-115).

Jarke, M., Lenzerini, M., Vassiliou, Y., & Vassiliadis, P. (2003). *Fundamentals of data warehouses.* Springer-Verlag.

Letz, C., Henn, E. T., & Vossen, G. (2002). Consistency in data warehouse dimensions. In *Proc. of Int. Database Engineering and Application Symposium (IDEAS)* (pp. 224-232).

Malinowski, E., & Zimányi, E. (2008). *Advanced data warehouse design: from conventional to spatial and temporal applications.* Springer.

Mendelzon, A. O., & Vaisman, A. A. (2000). Temporal queries in OLAP. In *Proc. of Int. Conference on Very Large Data Bases (VLDB)* (pp. 242-253).

Morzy, T., & Wrembel, R. (2004). On querying versions of multiversion data warehouse. In *Proc. of ACM Int. Workshop on Data Warehousing and OLAP (DOLAP)* (pp. 92-101).

Ravat, F., Teste, O., & Zurfluh, G. (2006). A multiversion-based multidimensional model. In *Proc. of Int. Conference on Data Warehousing and Knowledge Discovery (DaWaK)* (LNCS 4081, pp. 65-74).

Rizzi, S., & Golfarelli, M. (2007). X-time: Schema versioning and cross-version querying in data warehouses. In *Proc. of Int. Conference on Data Engineering (ICDE)* (pp. 1471-1472).

Rundensteiner, E., Koeller, A., & Zhang, X. (2000). Maintaining data warehouses over changing information sources. *Communications of the ACM, 43*(6), 57–62. doi:10.1145/336460.336475

Schlesinger, L., Bauer, A., Lehner, W., Ediberidze, G., & Gutzman, M. (2001). Efficiently synchronizing multidimensional schema data. In *Proc. of ACM Int. Workshop on Data Warehousing and OLAP (DOLAP)* (pp. 69-76).

Vaisman, A., & Mendelzon, A. (2001). A temporal query language for OLAP: Implementation and case study. In *Proc. of Int. Workshop on Database Programming Languages (DBPL)* (LNCS 2397, pp. 78-96).

Widom, J. (1995). Research problems in data warehousing. In *Proc. of ACM Conference on Information and Knowledge Management (CIKM)* (pp. 25-30).

Wrembel, R. (2009). A survey on managing the evolution of data warehouses. [IGI Global.]. *International Journal of Data Warehousing and Mining, 5*(2), 24–56.

Wrembel, R., & Bębel, B. (2007). Metadata management in a multiversion data warehouse. *Journal on Data Semantics (JODS)*, **8**, 118-157. LNCS 4380.

Wrembel, R., & Morzy, T. (2006). Managing and querying versions of multiversion data warehouse. In *Proc. of Int. Conference on Extending Database Technology (EDBT)* (LNCS 3896, pp. 1121-1124).

ENDNOTE

* This work was supported from the Polish Ministry of Science and Higher Education grant No. N N516 365834

Chapter 13
Ontology Query Languages for Ontology-Based Databases
A Survey

Stéphane Jean
LISI/ENSMA and University of Poitiers, France

Yamine Aït Ameur
LISI/ENSMA and University of Poitiers, France

Guy Pierra
LISI/ENSMA and University of Poitiers, France

ABSTRACT

Current databases and their associated languages allow a user to exploit data according to their logical model. Usually, there is a gap between this logical model and the actual concepts represented. As a consequence, exploiting, exchanging and integrating data stored in databases are difficult. To overcome these problems, several approaches have proposed to extend current databases with ontologies. We called Ontology-Based Databases (OBDB) such databases. However, current database languages such as SQL have not been designed to exploit ontologies. Thus, a new generation of languages we called ontology query languages has emerged. The goal of this chapter is to provide an up to date survey on ontology query languages. We survey languages coming from the Semantic Web community as well as those coming from the database community.

INTRODUCTION

Data warehouses are designed to aggregate data and allow decision makers to obtain accurate, complete and up to date information. In current data warehouses, queries are issued to the logical model of data, making direct use of the table and column information that describes the persistence structure. Usually, there is a gap between this logical model and the actual business concepts used by decision makers. As a consequence, users of data warehouses have to use existing documentation (e.g, data dictionaries) - if any and if not out of date – to discover the meaning of tables and columns. This makes using and querying a data warehouse problematic for all users that have not designed it.

DOI: 10.4018/978-1-60566-756-0.ch013

Defined by Gruber as "an explicit specification of a conceptualization", ontologies have been proposed to explicit the semantics of data. They allow to describe, in a consensual way, the relevant concepts of a given application domain. Thus, the idea to describe a data warehouse with ontologies in order to make explicit the semantics of data stored has emerged (Xuan et al., 2006). This idea is concretized by introducing an ontological layer in a data warehouse. This layer can be used by decision makers to express queries using business concepts they are used to manipulate. However, existing query languages such as SQL or OQL have not been designed to exploit ontologies. For this purpose, a new generation of query languages, called *ontology query languages*, has emerged.

The goal of this chapter is to provide an up to date survey on the capabilities of existing ontology query languages to manage databases extended with ontologies we call *ontology-based databases (OBDBs)*. Previous surveys on ontology query languages (Bailey et al. 2005; Haase et al. 2004) have focused on the capabilities of Semantic Web query languages to manage RDF-Schema ontologies and data whatever be the used storage system. In this chapter, we propose to complete these previous surveys by taking a database-oriented point of view. Thus, this chapter discusses two representatives of Semantic Web query languages, namely SPARQL (Prud'hommeaux and Seaborne, 2008) and RQL (Karvounarakis et al., 2004) as well as two representatives of database-oriented ontology query languages namely, Oracle extension to SQL (Chong et al., 2005; Wu et al., 2008) and OntoQL (Jean, 2007; Jean et al., 2006) .

This chapter is organized as follows. In section 2, we present our point of view on domain ontologies and their classification. We conclude this section by describing our proposed extension of the traditional ANSI/SPARC database architecture with ontologies. Requirements for an exploitation language of this proposed architecture are then defined in section 3. These requirements are used to compare some existing Semantic Web

Query Languages and database-oriented ontology query languages in section 4 and 5. Finally, section 6 concludes this comparison and introduces future work.

DOMAIN ONTOLOGIES AND THEIR APPLICATION TO DATABASE

In this section, we present the database-oriented point of view on ontologies we take (Jean et al., 2007b; Fankam et al., 2008) to compare existing ontology query languages.

Definition and Classification of Domain Ontologies

Several definitions have been proposed for an ontology (Gruber, 1993; Guarino, 1998). In our work a domain ontology is "a formal and consensual dictionary of categories and properties of entities of a domain and the relationships that hold among them". This definition emphasizes three criteria that distinguish ontologies from other models used in Computer Science. An ontology is:

1. *formal*: it is based on a logical axioms and may be processed by computers; so checking consistency and performing automatic reasoning are made possible;
2. *consensual* in a community, i.e. several members have agreed upon the concepts represented in the ontology;
3. has the *capability to be referenced*. A universally unique identifier can be used to define the semantic of a piece of data, whatever are the modeling schema of the ontology and the data model.

All ontologies are not similar. We distinguish the three following categories:

*   *Conceptual Canonical Ontologies (CCOs)* provide concepts definitions

Figure 1. The onion model of domain Ontology

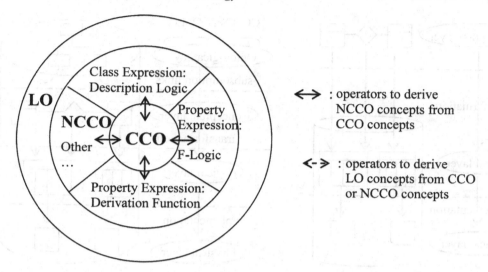

without redundancy. In CCOs (for example, (IEC61360-4, 1999)), information is represented in terms of classes and properties that have unique identifiers.

- *Non Conceptual Canonical Ontologies (NCCOs)* contain not only primitives concepts (canonical) but also defined concepts, i.e. those concepts for which the ontology provides a complete axiomatic definition by means of necessary and sufficient conditions expressed in terms of other - primitive or defined - concepts.

- *Linguistic Ontologies (LOs)* define terms appearing in the universe of discourse of a given domain. Relationships between terms are captured in a semi-formal way by linguistic relationships (e.g, synonymy or hyponymy). An example of LO is Wordnet.

These three categories of ontologies can be combined into a layered model, called the Onion Model, shown in Figure 1. At the heart of this model is a CCO. It provides with a formal basis to model and to exchange efficiently the knowledge of a domain. From primitive concepts of the CCO, a NCCO can be designed. This NCCO provides

constructors to relate different conceptualizations made on this domain. Finally, a LO may provide a natural language representation of NCCO or CCO concepts, possibly in the various natural languages where these concepts are meaningful.

When they are designed according to the onion model, ontologies have always a canonical layer, they may have a non canonical layer and they always have a minimum of linguistic aspects and in particular, terms that denote the represented concept. In this chapter, we focus on the exploitation of such ontologies in databases.

Extension of the ANSI/SPARC Architecture with Ontologies

The major objectives of a database are to ensure an efficient management of data and to provide access to data independently of their physical representation. The ANSI/SPARC architecture has been proposed to fulfil these objectives. It distinguishes two main access levels:

- the *physical level* which defines how data are stored and managed using a file management system;
- the *logical level* which defines how data are

Figure 2. Proposed extension of ANSI/SPARC architecture

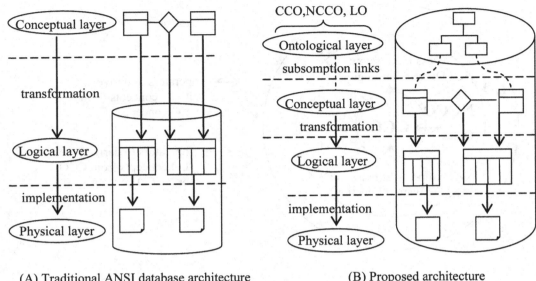

(A) Traditional ANSI database architecture   (B) Proposed architecture

structured using the database data model (e.g., the relational or object model).

When designing a database according to this architecture, a large amount of data semantics may be lost during the transformation from the conceptual model (CM) to a logical model. Moreover, the meaning of the CM is not formally documented, and thus it cannot be stored in the database. To solve these difficulties, references to an ontology appear as a relevant solution. Thus, we propose to extend this architecture with the ontological level. This level defines explicitly data semantics. Moreover, the CM will be modelled by referring to the ontology concept to which they correspond. This extended architecture is shown in Figure 2.

Figure 2(A) presents the traditional database architecture. A conceptual model is represented in a modeling language like Entity-Relationship. Then, it is often used to generate automatically the logical model of data. This logical model is represented at the physical level by a set of files. In Figure 2(B) we propose to extend this architecture with the following elements.

- *Ontological level.* It is composed of one (or several if the scope of the system encompasses the domain of several existing ontologies) ontology defining the concepts of the universe of discourse in terms of well-defined classes and properties.
- *Subsumption links.* They link the ontological and conceptual levels, thus defining the set of ontology concepts used to fulfil applications requirements. The meaning of these links, represented in the CM by the absolute identifier of an ontology concept, is that the CM concept is equal or is a special case of the referenced ontology concept (i.e., subsumption).

The goal of this chapter is to study capabilities of existing ontology query languages to exploit the OBDB architecture proposed in this section. This language should (1) be *homogeneous*, i.e. it should provide an access to the different levels of this architecture meaningful for the end-user and (2) it should exploit the specificities of these different levels. We detail these requirements in the next section.

Figure 3. Running example

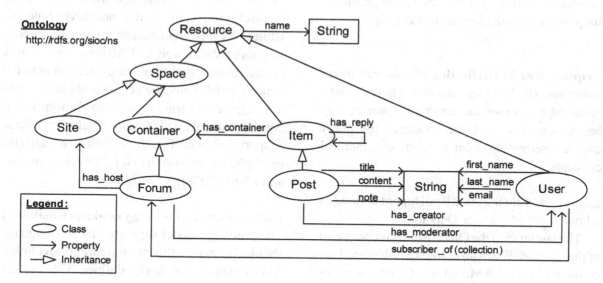

REQUIREMENTS FOR AN EXPLOITATION LANGUAGE OF OBDB

To illustrate our proposed requirements for an exploitation language of the OBDB architecture presented in the previous section, we use the ontology presented as a graph on Figure 3. This example is an extract of the SIOC ontology (*http://sioc-project.org/*). This ontology describes the domain of on-line communities. A forum (Forum) is hosted by a site (Site) administered by a moderator (has_moderator). Users (User) can subscribe to forums (subscriber_of) and create messages (Post) on these forums (has_container). Several answers may be provided for a given message (has_reply).

Requirements Resulting from the Onion Model

One of the most important characteristics of the ANSI/SPARC architecture is to separate the physical and logical representation of data. Defining, manipulating and querying data at the logical level independently of their physical representa-

tion are possible. Our architecture adds one more independency, representing both the conceptual and the ontological description of the represented data. Thus, exploitation of data independently of their logical schema is possible.

Requirement 1: (Queries at the ontological level) The language should allow to express queries at the ontological level independently of the logical representation (schema) of data.

Example. Retrieve all (direct and/or indirect) instances of the class Item.

Another fundamental characteristic of the ANSI/SPARC architecture is to define an external level. This level defines external schemas (views) that reflect users perception of the application domain (e.g., woman in place of person whose gender is female). These views can be used to define queries. The query engine rewrites them according to the logical model of data. In our architecture, the NCCO layer of an ontology provide views at the onlogical level. It allows each user to represent its own perception of the application domain by defining non canonical concepts expressed in terms of other - canonical or non canonical - concepts. Thus, the language should support the exploitation of such concepts.

Requirement 2: (Definition of non canonical concepts) The language should support the definition of non canonical concepts. Queries may be expressed using these concepts, the query engine interpreting them in terms of canonical concepts.

Example. Create the class PostDupont defined as all messages of the user Dupont.

The last layer of the Onion Model is composed of the LO part. When an ontology is designed according to the Onion Model, its LO part associates to each concept, one or several terms and textual definitions. These linguistic definitions allow human users to understand the ontology and to reference ontology concepts using their names. These linguistic definitions are often given in different natural languages. To make it easy for members of different countries to use the same ontologies, the language may support the definition and exploitation of multilingual LO.

Requirement 3: (Linguistic exploitation) The language should support the definition and exploitation of linguistic definitions of concepts that may be defined in different natural languages.

Example. Return the first name and last name of users with a query written using English names of concepts and one using French names.

The Onion Model is based on the complementarity of ontology models. Indeed, many ontology models have been proposed such as RDF-Schema (Brickley and Guha, 2004), OWL (Dean and Schreiber, 2004) or PLIB (Pierra, 2008). All these ontology models have constructors to define a CCO composed of classes, properties, datatypes, and instances. In addition to these core constructors, each ontology model provides specific constructors to define an ontology. For

example, PLIB provide constructors to define precisely and contextually primitive concepts while OWL provides conceptual equivalence constructors to define a NCCO. All these constructors are useful to define an ontology according to the Onion Model. Thus, the language should be able to integrate constructors coming from different ontology models. This feature would also help to support evolution of existing ontology models (for example, the support of OWL2 (Patel-Schneider and Motik, 2008)).

Requirement 4: (Ontology model extensibility) The ontology model supported by the language should be extendable to support its evolution and to manage ontologies defined with another ontology model.

Example. Add the OWL constructor AllValues-From (a class composed of all instances whose values of a given property are all instances of a given class) to the ontology model supported by the language.

Requirements Resulting from Preserving Compatibility with the ANSI/SPARC Architecture

Our proposed architecture extends the ANSI/ SPARC architecture, and thus, it also includes the usual logical level. Since many applications have been built using the SQL language to manipulate data at this level, the language should support manipulation of data not only at the ontological level (see previous section) but also at the logical level. Thus, the language will keep upward compatibility for existing applications and will permit to manipulate data at the different levels of our proposed architecture.

Requirement 5: (SQL compatibility) The language should permit the manipulation of data at the logical level preserving SQL compatibility.

Example. Assuming that instances of the class User are stored in the table T_User (uri, first_name, last_name, email), retrieve all users using a SQL query.

Designing a layered architecture has the drawback to increase the complexity of data processing in upper levels. The introduced complexity has in general consequences on efficiency of query processing. In such architecture, one way to optimize processing at a given level is to use the lower level (e.g., create an index to optimize logical queries). In the proposed architecture, the ontological level has been added on top of the conceptual level. Thus, to optimize query processing at this level, the DBMS shall provide an access to the lower level, i.e. the conceptual level.

Requirement 6: (Access to the conceptual model of data) The language should allow to define, manipulate and query the conceptual model of data from the ontological level.

Example. Create the conceptual model of data corresponding to the class User knowing that only the properties first_name, last_name and email will be used in the target application.

Requirements on the Expressive Power of the Language

In traditional databases, the data definition language (DDL) is used to create tables and the data manipulation language (DML) to insert rows with their properties values. The DML has the advantage to be a powerful declarative language being combined with the query language. In the proposed architecture both ontologies and data are stored. A data definition and manipulation languages is required to define and manipulate them.

Requirement 7: (Ontology & data definition and manipulation) The language should offer a definition and manipulation language for ontologies and data.

Example. Create the class User of our example and add some instances.

Ontologies are a conceptualization of a domain aiming at covering a wide and diverse range of technical and business requirements. As a consequence, ontologies usually define a lot of concepts. For example, the IEC ontology (IEC61360-4, 1999) on the domain of electronic components contains approximately 100 classes and more than 1000 properties. Moreover, users of an ontology are rarely its designer. Thus, users should have a mean to discover ontologies with the language.

In addition, since an ontology defines generally a lot of concepts, a hierarchy of classes may have many levels. When a query is expressed on a class at a given level, the result may contain instances of this class and of its subclasses. Thus, these instances can be associated to different ontological description that the user may want to retrieve. This example shows the need to be able to query both ontologies and data. Notice that this capability would also be useful to extract a part of an ontology with its instances. In traditional languages, this operation requires the composition of two queries. Thus, this capability would be useful in distributed architecture where the network trips have to be minimized.

Requirement 8: (Queries on ontologies and on ontologies and data) The language should offer querying capabilities on ontologies and both on ontologies and data.

Example. Return all instances of Resource. For each instance, retrieve also the classes it belongs to.

In this section, we have defined a requirement specification for an exploitation language of the OBDB architecture defined in section 3. A language fulfilling these requirements would allow to fully exploit this architecture. Using these requirements, we are now able to compare existing ontology query languages.

ANALYSIS OF SEMANTIC WEB ONTOLOGY QUERY LANGUAGES

A lot of ontology query languages have been proposed in the context of the Semantic Web. In a recent survey (Bailey et al., 2005), these languages are classified in seven categories (SPARQL family, RQL family, languages inspired from XPath, XSLT or XQuery, languages in controlled English, languages with reactives rules, deductive languages and other languages). In this section, we present a representative language of the two first categories that fit the most with the requirements we have defined.

SPARQL

The first category of language is named "SPARQL familiy". It is composed of the languages SPARQL (Prud'hommeaux and Seaborne, 2008), RDQL (Seaborne, 2004), SquishQL (Miller et al., 2002) and TriQL (Caroll et al., 2005). These languages consider all information (both ontologies and instances data) as a set of RDF triples (subject, predicate, object). As a representative we have chosen SPARQL which is a W3C Recommendation.

SPARQL is a graph-matching query language. A query consists of a pattern (a set of triples with variables and filters) defined in the WHERE clause. This pattern is matched against a data source, and the values obtained from this matching are processed in the SELECT clause to give the answer. We describe more precisely this language by discussing its capability w.r.t. the defined requirements.

Requirement 1 (Queries at the ontological level)

Example. The following SPARQL query[1] can be used to rretrieve the instances of the class Item.

```
SELECT ?i
WHERE {?i rdf:type sioc:Item}
```

Explanation. The triple in the FROM clause introduces the variable ?i (a variable is prefixed by ?) to iterate over instances of the class Item. This variable is specified in the SELECT clause to return its values.

However, the result of the previous query depends on the triples represented in the OBDB. On the one hand, if for a class C, a triple (i, rdf:type, C) is represented for each direct or indirect instance of C, then the previous query returns also all the instances of the class Post subclass of Item. On the other hand, if a triple (i, rdf:type, C) is represented only for each direct instance of C, then the query returns only direct instances of C unless the query interpreter computes the transitive closure of the subsumption relationship. Thus, the SPARQL fulfill partially this requirement. Ontological queries can be expressed but their results depend on the represented triples or of their interpretation.

Requirement 2 (Definition of non canonical concepts)

SPARQL does not provide a data definition language. Thus, it can not be used to define non canonical concepts. However, if these concepts have been defined in the data source, SPARQL provides a CONSTRUCT query form that can be used to compute automatically their instances. *Example.* Compute instances of the class PostDupont

```
CONSTRUCT ?p rdf:type
sioc:PostDupont
WHERE {?p rdf:type sioc:Post . ?p
sioc:has_creator "Dupont"}
```

Explanation. The WHERE clause retrieves instances (?p) of the class Post created by the user Dupont. The CONSTRUCT clause replaces the traditional SELECT clause. It is constructed as a WHERE clause (a set of triples with variables and

Table 1.

SELECT ?fn ?ln WHERE {?u rdf:type ?c . ?c rdfs:label "User"@en . ?u sioc:first_name ?fn . ?u sioc:last_name ?ln}	SELECT ?fn ?ln WHERE {?u rdf:type ?c . ?c rdfs:label "Utilisateur"@fr . ?u sioc:first_name ?fn . ?u sioc:last_name ?ln}

filters). The result is a new RDF graph constructed by replacing variables in the CONSTRUCT clause by values satisfying the WHERE clause. Thus, each post created by Dupont is associated to the class PostDupont in the resulting graph.

Thus, SPARQL fulfill partially requirement 2. It can not be used to define non canonical concepts but permits to compute their instances (*extension*). Notice that the CONSTRUCT query form produces a new RDF graph. As a consequence and contrary to views of databases, extensions of non canonical concepts have to be recomputed whenever extensions of corresponding canonical concepts are modified (in our example, each time a message is added or deleted by Dupont).

Requirement 3 (Linguistic exploitation)

SPARQL is equipped with operators to manipulate string defined in different natural languages. *Example.* Return the first name and last name of users with a query written using English names of concepts and one using French names (Table 1).

Explanation. The query written using English (resp. French) names is on the left (resp. right) part. The WHERE clause of this query retrieves instances (?u) of a class (?c) whose name in English (suffix @en) is User. The query written in French is equivalent to this one. The suffix @ fr allow to use the French name of the class User ("Utilisateur").

Thus, SPARQL fulfil requirement 3. It provides also other functions to manipulate multilingual ontologies. For example, the lang function return the natural language of a given string.

Requirement 4 (Ontology Model Extensibility)

SPARQL does not provide a definition language for ontology and thus we can not define the OWL AllValuesFrom constructor (sample example). However, since SPARQL has been designed for RDF, it considers an OWL ontology as a set of triples that use the OWL constructors defined in the OWL namespace. Thus, it can be used to query OWL ontologies but the semantics of OWL constructors has to be coded in the query interpreter.

Requirements 5 and 6 (Compatibility with the Traditional Database Architecture)

Even if a SPARQL query has a form similar to an SQL query (clauses SELECT-FROM-WHERE), it is adapted to RDF (triples) querying and thus it is different from SQL (requirement 5). In addition, data schema is considered fixed (subject, predicate, object) and thus SPARQL does not provide any operator to modify it (requirement 6).

Requirement 7 (Ontology & Data Definition and Manipulation)

Currently, SPARQL provides only a query language; it is not equipped with a definition and manipulation language (requirement 7). Thus, definition and manipulation of data are considered external functionalities provided by the data source. The need of a standard mechanism to update data sources has been addressed in

(Seaborne and Manjunath, 2008) with the proposition of SPARQL/Update. But, this language is not yet integrated in the recommendation of the W3C.

Requirement 8 (Queries on Ontologies and on Ontologies and Data)

Since, SPARQL considers all information as RDF data, it can be easily used to combined ontology and data querying.*Example*. Return all instances of Resource with the classes it belongs to.

```
SELECT ?i ?c
WHERE {?i rdf:type sioc:Resource .
?i rdf:type ?c}
```

Explanation. The first triple of the WHERE clause retrieves instances (?i) of the class Resource. The second triples retrieves classes (?c) these instances belong to.

Notice that in this example, like in all SPARQL queries, results depend on the triples represented in the data source and/or the interpretation of these triples by the query interpreter.

RQL

The second category of Semantic Web languages is called "RQL family". It is mainly composed of the languages RQL (Karvounarakis et al., 2004), SeRQL (Broeskstra and Kampman, 2003) and eRQL (Tolle and Wleklinski, 2004). We have chosen to discuss the RQL language which is the most complete.

RQL has been designed following a functional approach similar to the object-oriented language OQL (Cattell, 1993). Thus, simple queries consist of function calls (e.g, SubClassOf(Resource) to retrieve all subclasses of Resource). More elaborate queries can be defined using a traditional SELECT-FROM-WHERE syntax. The FROM clause introduces path expressions (with vari-

ables) built from a set of predefined basic path expressions and operators (e.g., C{X} is a basic path expression that introduces a variable X on all instances of the class C). The WHERE clause is used to define conditions on variables introduced in the FROM clause. Finally, the SELECT clause defines the variable projected in the result (like in SPARQL).

RQL is also composed of a manipulation language named RUL (Magiridou et al., 2005) and a view language named RVL (Magkanaraki et al., 2004). We present these different languages by discussing capabilities of RQL to fulfil the proposed requirements.

Requirement 1 (Queries at the Ontological Level)

The data model of RQL is based on RDF-Schema. To distinguish clearly the data, ontology and ontology model levels, the data model of RQL has some restrictions compared to RDF-Schema (e.g., a class can not be subsumed by an ontology model constructor). Yet, this model contains the main constructors of RDF-Schema (class, property and subsumption) and thus, queries at the ontological level are possible.*Example*. Retrieve all instances of the class Item

```
SELECT I
FROM sioc:Item{I}
```

Explanation. The FROM clause introduces the variable I on all (direct and indirect) instances of the class Item. The SELECT clause projects URI of these instances. To retrieve only direct instances, the class Item must be prefixed with ^ (i.e., tem)

Requirement 2 (Definition of Non Canonical Concepts)

The view language associated to RQL (RVL) can be used to represent non canonical concepts such as OWL restrictions.*Example.* Create the class PostDupont defined as all messages of the user Dupont.

```
CREATE NAMESPACE myview=&http://
www.lisi.ensma.fr/ex-view.rdf#
  VIEW rdfs:Class("PostDupont")
       Property(P, PostDupont,
range(P))
       FROM Property{P}
       WHERE domain(P) >= sioc:Post
  VIEW PostDupont(P), title(P, T),
has_creator(P, C)
FROM sioc:Post{P}.sioc:title{T},
{P}sioc:has_creator{C}
  WHERE C = "Dupont"
```

Explanation. In RVL, views (non canonical concepts) are separated from classes (canonical concepts). Thus, a new namespace is created for views (http://www.lisi.ensma.fr/ex-view.rdf). The first VIEW clause is used to create the view PostDupont with all properties defined on the class Post. This is done using a RQL query that searches all properties defined on Post or on a superclass of Post (domain(P)>= sioc:Post). The second VIEW clause is used to compute instances of the view PostDupont by searching all messages (P) with their title (T) that have been created by Dupont (C). Notice that, for conciseness, we have only retrieved values of the title property. To define the complete view, other properties values must be searched.

Thus, RQL fulfil requirement 2. However, notice that the distinction between canonical and non canonical concepts forbids the definition of subsumption relationships between these two kind of concepts. Thus, it is necessary to reproduces manually this behaviour (by importing properties and their values in the NCCO).

Requirement 3 (Linguistic Exploitation)

RDF-Schema allows to associate names defined in different natural languages to classes and properties. It permits also to define string values in different natural languages. RQL does not exploit these features.

Requirement 4 (Ontology Model Extensibility)

The ontology model supported by RQL is composed of the constructors Class and Property. This ontology model can be extended by specialization of these two constructors. But, a constructor can not be added if it does not inherit from Class or Property. For example, this limitation prevents to add the Document constructor of PLIB (to describe a concept by a document) or the Ontology constructor of OWL (to regroup all concepts defined in an ontology). Moreover, if these capabilities are defined on the data model of RQL, the language does not provide any operator to use them. Thus, we can not use RQL to define the OWL AllValuesFrom constructor.

Requirements 5 and 6 (Compatibility with the Traditional Database Architecture)

The syntax of RQL is close to the one of object-oriented languages. However, it keeps no compatibility with SQL (requirement 5). In addition, RQL considers all instances as a URI independently of the classes it belongs to and of its properties values. Thus, it can not be used to manipulate the data schema (requirement 6).

Requirement 7 (Ontology & Data Definition and Manipulation)

As we have seen in requirement 4, RQL does not provide a syntax to define the ontology model used. But RVL provides constructors to create new classes and properties and RUL can be used to insert new instances. *Example*. Create the class User of our example and add some instances.

```
VIEW Class("User")<Resource>
    Property("first_name", User,
xsd:string)
    Property("susbscriber_of",
User, Forum)
INSERT User(&http://www.lisi.ensma.
fr/Dupont)
INSERT first_name (&http://www.
lisi.ensma.fr/Dupont, "patrick")
```

Explanation. The constructor Class takes only one parameter: the URI of the class to define (for readability we use only the name User). This class is defined as a subclass of Resource (operator <>). Its properties are defined with the Property constructor. It takes three parameters: URI, domain and range of the property to define. The language RUL is then used to insert one instance of the class User. The operation INSERT is first used to define the URI of the instance and then to define its properties values (we define only value of the property first_name).

As this example shows, the RVL language is not a complete data definition language. It can only be used to create classes with a URI and properties with a URI, their domain and range. Other characteristics of classes and properties (e.g., names in different natural languages) can not be specified. On the other hand, RUL provides a complete set of operations (INSERT-MODIFY-DELETE) to manipulate data.

Requirement 8 (Queries on Ontologies and on Ontologies and Data)

RQL is equipped with powerful path expressions that make it possible to query both ontologies and data. *Example*. Return all instances of Resource with the classes it belongs to.

```
SELECT U $C
  FROM $C{U}
  WHERE C <= sioc:Resource
```

Explanation. The basic path expression $C{U} of the FROM clause introduces a variable U that denotes direct instances of a class $C (variables for classes are prefixed by $ in RQL). The WHERE clause adds a condition to retrieve only direct instances of Resource or of a subclass of Resource. Finally, the SELECT clause projects the URI of instances and classes.

In this section, we have discussed capabilities of Semantic Web query languages w.r.t. the defined requirements. In next section, we study other languages that have been designed to keep some degree of compatibility with traditional databases.

ANALYSIS OF DATABASE-ORIENTED ONTOLOGY QUERY LANGUAGES

Several languages have been defined specifically for exploiting ontologies stored in databases such as Oracle extension to SQL (Chong et al., 2005; Wu et al., 2008), OntoQL (Jean et al., 2006), SOQA-QL (Ziegler et al., 2005) or CQL (Mizoguchi-Shimogori et al., 2002). In this section we discuss the most recent and active approaches i.e., Oracle extension to SQL and the OntoQL exploitation language.

Oracle Extension to SQL

The main objective of Oracle (Chong et al., 2005; Wu et al., 2008) was to provide efficient RDF data querying capabilities that integrate smoothly with SQL queries. The proposed solution is a SQL table function to query RDF data.

The table function named RDF_MATCH takes four parameters. The first parameter is a graph pattern to be matched. This graph pattern is defined with a syntax similar to the clause WHERE of SPARQL (basically a set of triples with variables). The second parameter specifies the RDF graph to be queried. The third parameter specifies the rulebase (if any) that must be used to infer new RDF data. A rulebase is composed of a set of rules. Each rule consists of a left hand side graph pattern for the antecedents, filter conditions, and a right hand side graph pattern for the consequents. Notice that RDF-Schema inference rules (e.g, transitive closure of the subsumption relationship) is created by the system (named rdfs) and available to users. Finally, the last parameter specifies user-defined namespaces aliases. The RDF_MATCH function returns a table having a column for each variable used in the graph pattern. Thus, this function can be seamlessly combined with SQL queries.

A strong effort has been made to optimize the RDF_MATCH function. Indeed, this function is rewritten has a SQL query so that it can be optimized with the rest of the query. Moreover, indexes and materialized views are used to execute efficiently queries. Scalability of the proposed approach has been demonstrated on 80 million RDF triples.

Requirement 1 (Queries at the Ontological Level)

The RDF_MATCH function can be used to express ontological queries decomposed in a triples pattern. *Example*. Retrieve instances of the class Item.

```
SELECT t.i
FROM TABLE(RDF_MATCH('(?i rdf:type
Item)', NULL, NULL, NULL))
```

Explanation. The table function RDF_MATCH is used in the clause FROM of the query. It only takes a simple graph pattern as parameter to

search instances of the class Item (?i). This function returns a table with a column named i for the variable ?i. This variable can be projected in the SELECT clause.

Like SPARQL, result of the previous query depends on the triple represented in the RDF data source. For the RDF_MATCH function, it depends also of the rulebase specified. Indeed, if we specify the rdfs rulebase in the previous example, all (direct and indirect) instances of Item will be returned (the transitive closure of the subsumption relationship is computed by a rule).

Requirement 2 (Definition of Non Canonical Concepts)

The data manipulation language of SQL can be used to define the non canonical class PostDupont A rule can be used to compute automatically its extension (set of instances).*Example[2]*. Create the class PostDupont defined as all messages of the user Dupont.

```
INSERT INTO rdf_example
        VALUES ('PostDupont',
rdf:type, rdfs:Class)
SELECT i FROM TABLE(
    RDF_MATCH('(?i rdf:type PostDu-
pont)', NULL, rb_example, NULL)
```

The rulebase rb_example contains the following rule:

```
('(?p rdf:type Post)(?p has_creator
?c)',
'?c = Dupont',
'(?p rdf:type PostDupont)')
```

Explanation. In this example, we suppose that a table named rdf_example has been created to store RDF data. An Insert statement is used to insert the class PostDupont. Instances of PostDupont can be retrieved through a SQL query that uses the RDF_MATCH function. This function infers all instances of PostDupont thanks to a rule. The meaning of this rule is the following. If a message ?p has been created by ?c (antecedent defined in the first parameter) which is Dupont (filter defined in the second parameter), then ?p is inferred to be an instance of PostDupont (consequent defined in the third parameter).

Requirement 3 (Linguistic Exploitation)

Like SPARQL, the graph pattern of the RDF_ MATCH function can use string values suffixed by a language code (e.g., @fr for a French string). Thus, our sample queries can be written like in SPARQL (see section 4).

Requirement 4 (Ontology Model Extensibility)

Like SPARQL, the RDF_MATCH function has been designed for RDF data and thus, it considers OWL ontology as a set of triples that use the OWL constructors defined in the OWL namespace. However, contrary to SPARQL, predefined rule-bases are provided to take into account semantics of OWL constructors.

Requirements 5 and 6 (Compatibility with the Traditional Database Architecture)

The RDF_MATCH function is directly integrated in SQL (requirement 5). To use this function, a table has to be created to store triples. Materialized views are automatically created to optimize queries on this table. However the representation of triples in this table can not be customized (requirement 6).

Requirement 7 (Ontology & Data Definition and Manipulation)

The data manipulation language of SQL can be used to create classes and instances. *Example.*

Create the class User of our example and add some instances.

```
INSERT INTO rdf_example VALUES
('User', rdf:type, rdfs:Class)
INSERT INTO rdf_example
VALUES ('User', rdfs:subClassOf,
'Resource')
INSERT INTO rdf_example
VALUES ('first_name', rdf:type,
rdf:Property) ...
INSERT INTO rdf_example VALUES
('User1', rdf:type, User)
INSERT INTO rdf_example VALUES
('User1', first_name, 'Patrick') …
```

Explanation. All information has to be inserted as RDF triples. Thus, many INSERT statements are necessary to insert the class User with its properties and its instances.

As this example shows, usage of the DML of SQL can be tedious to create ontologies and their instances.

Requirement 8 (Queries on Ontologies and on Ontologies and Data)

Since, the RDF_MATCH function provides similar graph pattern matching capabilities as SPARQL, it can be used to combined ontology and data querying.

Thus, the RDF_MATCH is a powerful extension of SQL to query RDF data. In the next section we discuss the OntoQL exploitation language that extends SQL following a different approach.

OntoQL

OntoQL (Jean, 2007; Jean et al., 2006) has been defined specifically for OBDBs. To exploit data, OntoQL has been defined in different layers:

- data access at the logical level by compatibility with SQL;
- data access at the ontological level, CCO layer. Primitive concepts being mainly

defined with object-oriented constructors, OntoQL adapts and extends SQL99 providing powerful relational-object operators;

- data access at the ontological level, NCCO layer. OntoQL provides a View Definition Language for defining and querying defined concepts;

- data access at the ontological level, LO layer. Each class and each property can be referenced by a name (in a given natural language) in an OntoQL query.

Ontologies being recorded in OBDBs, OntoQL provides an Ontology Definition, Manipulation and Query Language (ODL, OML and OQL) to exploit them. To keep a uniform syntax, these languages have been designed to keep a syntax near SQL99. They are based on a core ontology model that contains the main constructors of existing ontology models. This core ontology model is an object-oriented model composed of classes and properties named entities and attributes to distinguish them from ontology classes and properties. This core ontology model can be extended with new entities and new attributes using the ODL. Since this model can be extended, names of entities and attributes are not encoded as keywords in the OntoQL grammar but they are prefixed by the character #.

Requirement 1 (Queries at the Ontological Level)

Ontological queries can be expressed following a SQL-like syntax.*Example*. Retrieve instances of the class Item.

```
SELECT uri
  FROM Item
 USING NAMESPACE 'http://rdfs.org/
sioc/ns'
```

Explanation. The USING clause is used to define a default namespace for the query. When

the SIOC namespace is set, each element without prefix (e.g., Item) is searched in this ontology. This query retrieves all instances of Item. To retrieve only direct instances, one can use the ONLY operator like in SQL99 (i.e., ONLY(Item)).

Requirement 2 (Definition of Non Canonical Concepts)

OntoQL provides a View Definition Language to define non canonical concepts.*Example*. Create the class PostDupont defined as all messages of the user Dupont.

```
CREATE #Class PostDupont AS VIEW
UNDER Post
CREATE VIEW OF PostDupont AS
  SELECT * FROM Post AS p
WHERE p.has_creator.last_name =
'Dupont'
```

Explanation. The first statement creates the class PostDupond as a non canonical concept (keyword VIEW), subclass of Post. The second statement defines the extension of this class by providing an OntoQL query that computes its instances.

When non canonical classes are defined using OWL constructors (e.g., restrictions), an inference engine can automatically compute subsumption relationships between canonical and non canonical concepts. OntoQL (like RQL) has not this capability: canonical and non canonical classes must be placed manually in the hierarchy.

Requirement 3 (Linguistic Exploitation)

In OntoQL, each class and each property can be referenced by a name in a given natural language. It makes it possible to write the same query in many natural languages.*Example*. Return the first name and last name of users with a query written using English names of concepts and one using French names (Table 2).

Explanation. The USING clause of OntoQL can be used to specify the natural language in which a query is expressed. The left query used English names. For names with a space (e.g., first name) double quotes are used. The right query is equivalent but written with French names.

Requirement 4 (Ontology Model Extensibility)

The ontology model supported by OntoQL can be extended using its ODL. *Example.* Add the OWL constructor AllValuesFrom

```
CREATE ENTITY #AllValuesFrom UNDER
#Class(
    #onProperty REF(#Property),
    #allValuesFrom REF(#Class)
)
```

Explanation. An OWL restriction being a class, the ALLValuesFrom constructor is added as a subentity of #Class. This entity has an attribute #allValuesFrom to specify the class in which its instances take their values for the property defined by the attribute #onProperty.

When an extension is made by specialization, like in the previous example, new entities inherit the behaviour of their super entities. This behaviour is defined in the operational semantics of the core ontology model. Thus, every specialization of the entity #Class defines a new category of classes which supports by inheritance the usual behaviour of a class. As a consequence, each OWL restriction may be associated to a container to store its instances. These instances may be computed using a view (all instances having all values of a property in a given class). However, OntoQL does not provide yet the capability to express this semantics.

Table 2.

SELECT "first name", "last name" FROM User USING LANGUAGE EN	SELECT prénom, nom FROM Utilisateur USING LANGUAGE FR

Requirement 5 (SQL Compatibility)

If a default namespace is not specified, each element of an OntoQL query without a namespace alias prefix is considered as an element of the logical model (a table or a column). Thus, an OntoQL query without namespace specification is considered as a SQL query (requirement 5). Moreover, the semantics of OntoQL (an algebra) has been defined so that each operator returns a relation (Jean et al., 2007a). Thus, queries at the logical level and ontological level can be combined (like Oracle).

Requirement 6 (Access to the Conceptual Model of Data)

OntoQL provides basic functionalities to define and access the conceptual model of data. *Example.* Create the conceptual model corresponding to the class User knowing that only the properties first_name, last_name and email will be used in the target application.

```
CREATE EXTENT OF User ("first
name", "last name", email)
TABLE T_User (first_name, last_
name, email)
```

Explanation. The CREATE EXTENT statement defines the conceptual model corresponding to a class specifying the set of properties used to describe instances of this class. The TABLE clause is used to choose the logical implementation of this conceptual model (i.e., tables and columns necessary).

Currently, in OntoQL, the conceptual model of data can only be defined through a subset of the ontology.

Requirement 7 (Ontology & Data Definition and Manipulation)

The data manipulation language of SQL can be used to create classes and instances.*Example.* Create the class User of our example and add some instances.

```
CREATE EXTENT OF User ("first
name", "last name", email)
TABLE T_User (first_name, last_
name, email)
CREATE #Class User UNDER Resource (
DESCRIPTOR (#name[fr] = 'Utilisa-
teur)
  #property ("first name" String,
"last name" String, …)
)
INSERT INTO User VALUES('User1',
'Patrick', 'Dupond')
```

Explanation. The first statement creates the class User. This class is defined as a class (#Class), subclass of Resource. The name in French of this class is specified in the DESCRIPTOR clause. The #property clause is used to create properties having User as domain. The second statement supposes that we have created an extent for the class User (see previous requirement). It uses a SQL-like INSERT statement to insert an instance.

One limitation of the data manipulation language of OntoQL is that it does not support multi-instanciation, i.e., that an instance may belong to many classes not linked by subsumption relationships. This limitation allows to define an efficient storage structure when instances have many properties values (Dehainsala et al., 2007).

Requirement 8 (Queries on Ontologies and on Ontologies and Data)

OntoQL is equipped of operators to combine ontologies and data querying. In particular, it provides the TYPEOF operator to return the class an instance belongs to.*Example.* Return all instances of Resource with the classes it belongs to.

```
SELECT r.uri, TYPEOF(r).#name[en]
FROM Resource AS r
```

Explanation. The FROM clauses introduces the alias r on instances of the class Resource. For each instance, its URI is projected as well as the name in English of the class it belongs to (retrieved with the TYPEOF operator).

This brief presentation of OntoQL ends our analysis of capabilities of ontology query languages to exploit OBDBs. We draw main conclusions in the next section.

CONCLUSION

In this chapter, we have presented capabilities of the main ontology query languages to exploit databases extended with ontologies. To compare these languages, we have first defined a set of requirements for an architecture that extends the traditional ANSI/SPARC architecture with conceptual and ontological levels. Then, we have discussed the capabilities of two Semantic Web query languages (SPARQL and RQL), and two database-oriented ontology query languages (Oracle extension to SQL and OntoQL) to fulfill these requirements. The result of this study is summarized in Table 3. In this table, the symbol · is used when the requirement is fulfilled, o when it is partially fulfilled, and when it is not fulfilled.

Table 3. Analysis of the main ontology query languages w.r.t. to the defined requirements

	SPARQL	RQL	Oracle	OntoQL
Queries at the ontological level	o	•	o	•
Definition of non canonical concepts	o	o	•	o
Linguistic exploitation	•	-	•	•
Ontology model extensibility	o	o	•	o
SQL compatibility	-	-	•	•
Access to the conceptual model of data	-	-	-	o
Ontology & data definition and manipulation	-	o	o	o
Queries on ontologies and on ontologies and data	•	•	•	•

Results presented in Table 3 lead us to draw the following conclusions. The main drawback of SPARQL and Oracle approaches to query OBDBs is that they consider all information as RDF data. As a consequence, when querying at the ontological level, the semantics of the ontology models has to be coded either in the query interpreter of SPARQL or by a set of deductive rules in the Oracle approach. Moreover, they don't provide operators to exploit this semantics (e.g., an operator to retrieve direct instances of a class). Another consequence is that the syntax of these two languages is adapted to query triple data. As a consequence, an ontological query has to be decomposed in triples (e.g, (?i rdf:type User) (?i sioc:name ?n) for retrieving names of users) which can be tedious for users.

On the contrary, the semantics of RQL and OntoQL are based on the core constructors of ontology models. They provide a syntax near the one of object-oriented query languages. We think that this syntax is more adapted for ontologies than a triple syntax because ontologies share many constructors with the object-oriented data model.

However, RQL and OntoQL may benefit from efforts made by Oracle to provide semantics technologies. Indeed, Oracle provides customizable and optimized triple storage with capability to load quickly a huge amount of RDF data. Thus, Oracle provides the built-in functions to serve as a scalable storage structure for RQL or OntoQL. Moreover, Oracle is now equipped with an inference engine for RDFS/OWL constructs which will be particularly useful for RQL and OntoQL to take into account the semantics of OWL. As a future work we plan to put this observation in application by implementing OntoQL on top of Oracle.

REFERENCES

Bailey, J., Bry, F., Furche, T., & Schaffert, S. (2005). Web and Semantic Web query languages: A survey. In *Reasoning Web, First International Summer School* (LNCS, pp. 35-133).

Brickley, D., & Guha, R. V. (2004). *RDF Vocabulary Description Language 1.0: RDF Schema*. World Wide Web Consortium. Retrieved from http://www.w3.org/TR/rdf-schema

Broekstra, J., & Kampman, A. (2003). SeRQL: A second generation RDF query language. In *SWADEurope Workshop on Semantic Web Storage and Retrieval*.

Carroll, J. J., Bizer, C., Hayes, P., & Stickler, P. (2005). Named graphs, provenance and trust. In *Proceedings of the 14th international conference on World Wide Web (WWW'05)* (pp. 613-622). New York: ACM Press.

Cattell, R. G. G. (1993). *The object database standard: ODMG-93*. Morgan Kaufmann.

Chong, E. I., Das, S., Eadon, G., & Srinivasan, J. (2005). An efficient SQL based RDF querying scheme. In *Proceedings of the 31st International Conference on Very Large Data Bases (VLDB'05)* (pp. 1216-1227).

Dean, M., & Schreiber, G. (2004). *OWL Web ontology language reference*. World Wide Web Consortium. Retrieved from http://www.w3.org/TR/owl-ref

Dehainsala, H., Pierra, G., & Bellatreche, L. (2007). OntoDB: An ontology-based database for data intensive applications. In *Proceedings of the 12th International Conference on Database Systems for Advanced Applications (DASFAA'07)* (LNCS 4443, pp. 497-508).

Fankam, C., Jean, S., Bellatreche, L., & Ameur, Y. A. (2008). Extending the ANSI/SPARC architecture database with explicit data semantics: An ontology-based approach. In R. Morrison, D. Balasubramaniam, & K. E. Falkner (Eds.), *Proceedings of the 2nd European Conference on Software Architecture (ECSA'08)* (LNCS 5292, pp.318-321).

Gruber, T. R. (1993). A translation approach to portable ontology specifications. *Knowledge Acquisition*, 5(2), 199–220. doi:10.1006/knac.1993.1008

Guarino, N. (1998). Formal ontology and information systems. In N. Guarino (Ed.), *Proceedings of the 1st International Conference on Formal Ontologies in Information Systems (FOIS'98)* (pp. 315). IOS Press.

Haase, P., Broekstra, J., Eberhart, A., & Volz, R. (2004). A comparison of RDF Query languages. In *Proceedings of the 3nd International Semantic Web Conference (ISWC'04)* (pp. 502-517).

IEC61360-4 (1999). *Standard data element types with associated classification scheme for electric components - Part 4: IEC reference collection of standard data element types, component classes and terms* (Tech. Rep., International Standards Organization).

Jean, S. (2007). *OntoQL, un langage d'exploitation des bases de donnes base ontologique*. PhD thesis, LISI/ENSMA and University of Poitiers.

Jean, S., Aït-Ameur, Y., & Pierra, G. (2006). Querying ontology based database using OntoQL (an Ontology Query Language). In *Proceedings of On the Move to Meaningful Internet Systems 2006: CoopIS, DOA, GADA, and ODBASE, OTM Confederated International Conferences (ODBASE'06)* (LNCS 4275, pp. 704-721).

Jean, S., Aït-Ameur, Y., & Pierra, G. (2007a). An object-oriented based algebra for ontologies and their instances. In *Proceedings of the 11th East European Conference in Advances in Databases and Information Systems (ADBIS'07)* (LNCS 4690, pp. 141-156).

Jean, S., Pierra, G., & Aït-Ameur, Y. (2007b). Domain ontologies: A database-oriented analysis, *Lecture Notes in Business Information Processing: Volume 1* (pp. 238-254). Berlin: Springer.

Karvounarakis, G., Magkanaraki, A., Alexaki, S., Christophides, V., Plexousakis, D., Scholl, M., & Tolle, K. (2004). RQL: A functional query language for RDF. In P. M. D. Gray, L. Kerschberg, P. J. H.King, & A. Poulovassilis (Eds.), *The functional approach to data management: Modelling, analyzing and integrating heterogeneous data.* (LNCS, pp. 435-465).

Magiridou, M., Sahtouris, S., Christophides, V., & Koubarakis, M. (2005). RUL: A declarative update language for RDF. In *Proceedings of the 4th International Semantic Web Conference (ISWC'05)* (pp. 506-521).

Magkanaraki, A., Tannen, V., Christophides, V., & Plexousakis, D. (2004). Viewing the Semantic Web through RVL lenses. *Journal of Web Semantics*, *1*(4), 359–375. doi:10.1016/j.websem.2004.06.004

Miller, L., Seaborne, A., & Reggiori, A. (2002). Three implementations of SquishQL, a simple RDF query language. In *Proceedings of the 1st International Semantic Web Conference (ISWC '02)* (pp. 423-435).

Mizoguchi-Shimogori, Y., Murayama, H., & Minamino, N. (2002). Class query language and its application to ISO13584 parts library standard. In *Proceedings of the 9th European Concurrent Engineering Conference (ECEC '02)* (pp. 128-135).

Patel-Schneider, P. F., & Motik, B. (2008). OWL2 Web ontology language: Mapping to RDF graphs. *W3C Working Draft 08 October 2008*. Retrieved from http://www.w3.org/TR/owl-ref

Pierra, G. (2008). Context representation in domain ontologies and its use for Semantic integration of data. [JODS]. *Journal of Data Semantics*, *X*, 173–210.

Prud'hommeaux, E., & Seaborne, A. (2008). SPARQL query language for RDF. W3C *Candidate Recommendation 15 January 2008*. Retrieved from http://www.w3.org/TR/rdf-sparql-query

Seaborne, A. (2004). RDQL– A query language for RDF. *W3C Member Submission 9 January 2004*. Retrieved from http://www.w3.org/Submission/2004/SUBM-RDQL-20040109

Seaborne, A., & Manjunath, G. (2008). SPARQL/Update: A language for updating RDF graphs. Retrieved from http://jena.hpl.hp.com/~afs/SPARQL-Update.html

Tolle, K., & Wleklinski, F. (2004). *Easy RDF query language (eRQL)*. Retrieved from http://www.dbis.informatik.uni-frankfurt.de/~tolle/RDF/eRQL

Wu, Z., Eadon, G., Das, S., Chong, E. I., Kolovski, V., Annamalai, M., & Srinivasan, J. (2008). Implementing an inference engine for RDFS/OWL constructs and user-defined rules in Oracle. In *Proceedings of the 24th International Conference on Data Engineering (ICDE '08)* (pp. 1239-1248).

Xuan, D. N., Bellatreche, L., & Pierra, G. (2006). A versioning management model for ontology-based data warehouses. In *Proceedings of the 8th International Conference on Data Warehousing and Knowledge Discovery (DaWak '06)* (pp. 195-206).

Ziegler, P., Sturm, C., & Dittrich, K. R. (2005). Unified querying of ontology languages with the SIRUP Ontology Query API. In *Datenbanksysteme in Business, Technologie und Web (BTW '05)* (pp. 325-344).

KEY TERMS AND DEFINITIONS

Ontology: a formal and consensual dictionary of categories and properties of entities of a domain and the relationships that hold among them.

Ontology-Based Database (OBDB): a data source which contains i) a (local) ontology, ii) possibly some references from this ontology to external (shared) ontologies, iii) a set of data, iv) and finally a relationship between each data and the ontological notion which explicit its meaning. An OBDB has two main characteristics: i) both ontologies and data are represented in a unique database and the same processing can be applied on them (Insert, Update, Querying, Versioning, etc.); ii) any data is associated to an ontological element which defines it meaning and vice versa (Dehainsala et al., 2007).

Ontology Query Language: a language that has been designed to exploit ontologies and their instances.

ENDNOTES

[1] For readability and conciseness, we omit specifications of namespaces and use names instead of URI.

[2] For conciseness, we use a simplified syntax. For more details, the interested reader can consult the Oracle documentation (http://www.oracle.com/technology/tech/semantic_technologies/index.html)

Chapter 14
Ontology–Based Database Approach for Handling Preferences

Dilek Tapucu
IYTE, Izmir, Turkey

Gayo Diallo
LISI/ENSMA, Poitiers, France

Yamine Ait Ameur
LISI/ENSMA, Poitiers, France

Murat Osman Ünalir
Ege University, Izmir, Turkey

ABSTRACT

Information systems now manage huge amount of data. Users are overwhelmed by the numerous results provided in response to their requests. These results must often be sorted and filtered in order to be usable. Moreover, the "one size fits all" approach has shown its limitation for information searching in many applications, particularly in the e-commerce domain. The capture and exploitation of user preferences have been proposed as a solution to overcome this problem. However, the existing approaches usually define preferences for a particular application. Thus, it is difficult to share and reuse the handled preferences in other contexts. In this chapter, we propose a sharable, formal and generic model to represent user's preferences. The model gathers several preferences models proposed in the Database and Semantic Web communities. The novelty of our approach is that the defined preferences are attached to the ontologies which describe the semantic of the data manipulated by the applications. Moreover, the proposed model offers a persistence mechanism and a dedicated language; it is implemented using Ontology-Based Databases (OBDB) system extended in order to take into account preferences. OBDB manage both ontologies and the data instances. The preference model is formally defined using the EXPRESS data modelling language which ensures us a free ambiguity definition and the approach is illustrated through a case study in the tourism domain.

DOI: 10.4018/978-1-60566-756-0.ch014

INTRODUCTION

The rapid growth and the wide adoption of internet technology make available a huge amount of data managed by various information systems. When searching over these disseminated data, users are often submerged by the numerous returned results in response to their requests. These results must often be sorted and filtered in order to identify the relevant information. Despite the fact that the "one size fits all" approach has shown its limitation in many applications particularly in the e-commerce domain, our targeted application domain, most information systems do not take into account the variety of users' need and preferences.

Capturing and exploiting user's preferences have been proposed as a solution to this problem in many domains including database systems (Kießling and Kostler, 2000; Kießling, 2002; Chomicki, 2003; Agrawal and Wimmers, 2000; Koutrika and Ioannidis, 2004; Viappiani et al., 2006; Das et al., 2006), Data Warehouse (Bellatreche et al., 2005), the Semantic Web (Siberski et al., 2006; Gurský et al., 2008; Toninelli et al., 2008), Information Retrieval (Daoud et al., 2007) and Human Computer Interaction (Cherniack et al., 2003). Although preferences are defined using an ontology in some approaches, most of the previously cited work, and particularly in the Database domain, the preferences and their model are defined according to the logical model underlying the targeted system. The use of the preferences requires having knowledge of this logical model.

Preferences express the sense of wishes and preference based search is a popular approach for helping consumers to find relevant items. Users would like to find the best matches between their wishes and the reality. Modelling preferences is difficult because human preferences are complex, multiple, heterogeneous, changing, and even contradictory. Moreover, they are complex to evaluate and according to the user's goals and his/her current task, they should be evaluated in the context they have been expressed.

Within most existing information systems, even if the notion of preference has been integrated in various application domains, it is not explicitly modelled. They are often hard encoded and disseminated throughout the applications that exploit these information systems. Therefore, they can not be shared and must be defined and updated for each application. This is a burden for users and yields to another layer of heterogeneous modelling.

To overcome these drawbacks, we propose an ontology based approach of preference model which relies on an ontology based database system (OBDB), namely OntoDB (Dehainsala et al., 2007; Pierra et al., 2005). The proposed model is formally described using the EXPRESS modelling language and the approach takes benefits from the OntoDB system which offers a flexible mechanism for storing together an ontology, its model and its instances. Nowadays, ontologies are well accepted as formal knowledge organisation systems which describe the explicit semantics of entities manipulated in a given domain (Gruber, 2003). Domain ontologies are used to provide definitions and specifications of these manipulated entities. These entities are defined following the ontology model.

Our contribution in this article is twofold. Firstly, we propose a shared and generic model to represent user preferences. Then, we describe how preferences model can be attached to an ontology and manipulated on the meta-model level. The sharable preferences model has been formally defined using the EXPRESS modelling language in order to make its definition ambiguity free. Indeed, EXPRESS is equipped with a powerful constraints language allowing defining precisely the semantics of the defined model.

The rest of the chapter is subdivided as follows. The next section gives an overview of the preferences handling in the database, Semantic Web and Data Warehouse areas. In addition, to make the chapter self-explanatory, we give an overview of the different ODBD existing approaches and we explain why we have chosen OntoDB. Moreover, we describe briefly the EXPRESS data modelling language which is used to formally define our model. The different models that are manipulated in our approach are described in this language. We detail afterward our approach of preferences model and formally describe its three components using EXPRESS. The integration of the preference model into the OntoDB system is presented in this section as well. Before concluding and outlining some future directions of this research work, we illustrate the approach of preferences model by an implementation within the tourism domain.

BACKGROUND

This section addresses the state of the art in two directions followed by this article. On the one hand, we overview the preference modelling approaches in the areas of databases and of Semantic Web, and on the second hand the database system that embed ontologies and their instances. Our goal is to study the existing approaches in order to propose a preference model as generic as possible.

Related Work on Preferences Models

Handling preferences has been addressed in various information systems research areas. The related work described in this section is mainly concentrated on two major subareas: Databases, Semantic Web and data warehouse domains.

Preferences in Databases

Handling preferences in the database domain has been addressed in many research work (Kießling and Kostler, 2000; Kießling, 2002; Chomicki, 2003; Agrawal and Wimmers, 2000; Koutrika and Ioannidis, 2004; Viappiani et al., 2006; Das et al., 2006). Preferences in this context are defined on the logical model level of the database, specifically on the column values of the tables. According

to the type of used metric, two different ways of expressing preferences have been proposed: *qualitative* and *quantitative* approaches.

Qualitative approaches (Chomicki, 2003; Kießling, 2002) allow users to define (relative) preferences between tuples. The preferences are defined on the content and define a binary relation between tuples (Chomicki, 2003). For example, if we consider two tuples t_1 and t_2, the expression $t_1 > t_2$ means that the user prefers the tuple t_1 rather than t_2. Kießling and Kostler follow a qualitative approach as well, named *constructor* approach. The preferences are expressed by a strict partial order and are formally described by first order logical formulas (Kießling, 2002). The defined constructors are integrated within the Preference SQL relational language (Kießling, and Kostler 2000). For instance, the constructor *Highest*(*c*) is used to express that for 2 tuples t_1 and t_2, we prefer the tuple having the higher value for the column *c*. This approach is referred as the BMO (*Best Match Only*) query model and is identical to the *winnow* operator defined by Chomicki (Chomicki, 2003).

Quantitative approaches in the other hand allow users to define scoring functions to compute a numeric score or an absolute preference for each tuple (Agrawal and Wimmers, 2000; Koutrika and Ioannidis, 2004; Das et al., 2006). The results are sorted according to this score. In this context, Agrawal and Wimmers define preferences by introducing a preferred value for each column in the database's tables (Agrawal and Wimmers, 2000). For instance, let us consider the table Hotel defined as *Hotel*(*name*, *priceMin*, *priceMax*). The preference < *,40,80 > indicates that preferred hotels are those having room price between 40 and 80. This preference is then used to compute a score between 0 and 1 for each hotel. Koutrika and Ioannidis introduce the notion of *atomic preferences* by specifying a set of pair < *condition*, *score* > where *condition* is a condition on the values of columns and *score* is the degree of interest between 0 and 1 of this condition (Koutrika and Ioannidis, 2004). Atomic preferences can be combined and used to derive *implicit preferences*. For example, considering the same table Hotel, the expression < *Hotel.name* =0 *Sophitel*, 0.8 > indicates that the interest degree of *Sophitel Hotels* is 0.8.

Following the quantitative approach as well, Das et al. (Das et al., 2006) propose a presentation based preferences of user profiling. These preferences define an order relation between the tuples returned by a given query. In this case two tuples are compared after accessing data sources. The comparison is based on a set of selected attributes. The presentation is expressed by the selection of a set of relevant attributes and by displaying the corresponding tuples in the tables and ranked according to their importance.

These approaches are strongly linked to the logical model of the database. Therefore, a good knowledge of this logical model is required for an efficient exploitation of these models. They implement various operators including *winnow* (Chomicki, 2003), Top(k) (Theobald et al., 2004), Skyline (Brzsnyi et al., 2001), Pareto (Viappiani et al., 2006) and Preferring preference operator (Kießling, 2002) which are applied on the database table's columns.

Preferences in Semantic Web

The notion of preference is a crucial issue in the Semantic Web area. The Semantic Web is a vision where data on the Web can be defined and linked in such a way that they can be understandable and be processed by machines and not only by humans (Berners-Lee et al., 2001). The Internet enables user to access a vast amount of available information, but this often results in the inability to find the relevant and needed information. Thus, in order to provide more accurate information, the various Internet portals, and more generally the Semantic Web must support profile based search and preferences based browsing.

Different models of preferences have been proposed in the literature (Siberski et al., 2006; Gurský et al, 2008; Toninelli et al., 2008; Sieg et al., 2007).

The *Local Preference Model* is proposed by Gurský et al. in order to model complex user preferences (Gurský et al, 2008). They consider that complex preferences reflect more accurately real life preferences. They use a fuzzy based approach for preferences description. Firstly, nominal and ordinal attributes are used to define local preferences. Then, their combination with user's local preferences produces global preferences. For example, the global preference *good hotel(x)* can be defined by the combination of the two local preferences expression *good price(x)* and *good starRating(x)*.

Toninelli et al. introduce the *Ontology Based Preference Model* approach by defining a meta model (Toninelli et al., 2008). In this approach, value and priority preferences are specified. For example, to find high standard hotels, the quality of the service must be a priority.

Siberski et al. propose an extension of the SPARQL query language (SPARQL, 2008) by introducing the *Preferring* modifier (Siberski et al. 2006). This modifier allows users to define Boolean and scoring preferences. For instance, the expression < *rating = excellent* > specifies an excellent hotel.

Sieg et al. present an ontology based approach for personalising Web information access (Sieg et al., 2007). The user interests are captured implicitly by a context defined through the notion of ontological user profiles. This context model for a user is represented as an instance of reference domain ontology. The concepts of the ontology are annotated by *interest scores* derived and updated implicitly according to the user's behavior.

Preferences in Data Warehouses

There is a few works on preferences in the data warehouse context compare to database and Se-

Table 1. Preference definition approaches in Databases, Semantic Web and and Data Warehouses domains

Author	Domain (DB/SW/DW)	Approach	Preferences Model Level	Query Operator	Storage of Preferences Model
Kießling (2002-2003)	DB	Qualitative	Logical	Preference SQL	NO
Chomicki (2003)	DB	Qualitative	Logical	Winnow	NO
Agrawal & Wimmers (2000)	DB	Quantitative	Logical	NO	NO
Koutrika & Ioannidis (2006)	DB	Quantitative	Logical	NO	NO
Das et al. (2006)	DB	Quantitative	Logical	NO	NO
Siberski et al. (2006)	SW	Boolean/ Scoring preferences	Semantic	SPARQL Clause Preferring	NO
Sieg et al. (2007)	SW	Ontological User Profiles	Semantic	NO	NO
Gurský et al. (2008)	SW	Fuzzy based/ Ontology	Semantic	NO	NO
Toninelli et al. (2008)	SW	Middleware-level/ Meta Model	Semantic	NO	NO
Bellatreche et al. 2005 Mouloudi et al. 2006	DW	Qualitative	Logical	NO	NO

mantic Web, except the works done by (Bellatreche et al., 2005; Mouloudi et al. 2006). They present a personalization framework for OLAP queries. They give end user the possibility to specify her/his preferences (e.g., the presence of a given dimension of a data warehouse in the final result) and her/his visualisation constraint to display the result of an OLAP query. The visualisation constraint represents the size of device (PDA, mobile phone, etc.) used to display the result of a query. The authors present some issues on the impact of preferences on physical design of a data warehouse (data partitioning, index and materialized view selection). This work did not present query operator handling preferences.

The presented approaches are summarized in Table 1. We classified them according to 5 criterions. The first criterion indicates whether the considered approach is presented in the context of Databases (DB), Semantic Web (SW) or Data Warehouse (DW). The second criterion indicates the followed approach (qualitative, quantitative, etc.). The third criterion indicates at what level (physical, logical, semantic) preferences are defined. The fourth criterion indicates whether there is a specific operator for querying with preferences. Finally, the last criterion indicates whether the considered approach offers the possibility to store physically the preferences model.

By analysing the above table, we note that the notion of preferences as considered in the databases domain is introduced mainly at the logical level. Preferences are defined on top of the manipulated models themselves and consequently, they depend on the model they extend. In the Semantic Web domain, even if an ontology is used to define preferences, the approaches are static and not enough flexible and generic to handle different preference models and are hardly adaptable in other contexts. This is because these approaches handle mostly preferences at ontology's instances level. For the storage issue, any of the approaches provide a real storage possibility of preferences model. Some of them hard code the models in the application (e.g. (Siberski et al, 2006)). None of the previously mentioned approaches offer simultaneously the possibility to define preferences at the semantic level, allow their persistence and provide a dedicated language for querying with preferences facilities.

To overcome these drawbacks, we propose an approach of preferences management by introducing a data model which is abstracted from the concerned database logical model. Indeed, our approach is based on an Ontology Based Database (OBDB) system which offers a persistence mechanism allowing the storage of both preferences and the actual data in the same infrastructure. The OBDB approach offers also the possibility to manage the ontology which describes the content of the database. Our approach acts at the semantic level by dynamically linking the preference model to the ontology describing the meaning of the semantic data.

Ontology Based Database (OBDB)

Over the last years, many OBDB architectures have been proposed in the literature. They can be classified in 3 categories according to the schemas they handle.

Single triple-based table approach. In this category, information is represented in a single schema composed of a unique triple table (subject, predicate, object) (Harris and Gibbins, 2003; Chong et al., 2005; Petrini and Risch, 2007; Alexaki et al., 2001; Broekstra et al., 2002; Ma et al., 2004; Dehainsala et al., 2007; Pierra et al., 2005). This table, called vertical table (Agrawal et al., 2001) can be used both for the ontology and the instances descriptions. However, this approach raises serious performance issues when queries require many self-joins over this table.

Double schema approach. In this approach, ontology descriptions and instance data are stored separately in two different schemas (Alexaki et al., 2001; Broekstra et al., 2002; Ma et al., 2004). The schema for ontology descriptions depends on the ontology used model (e.g., RDFS (Lassila, 1999), OWL (McGuinness et al., 2004), PLIB (IS010303.02, 1994). It is composed of a set of tables used to store each ontology modelling primitive like classes, properties and subsumption relationships. For the instances data, different schemas have been proposed; i) a vertical table to store instance data as triples (Ma et al., 2004; Broekstra et al., 2002); ii) a binary representation where each class is represented by an unary table and each property by a binary table (Alexaki et al., 2001; Broekstra et al., 2002; Pan and Heflin, 2003; Abadi et al., 2007); iii) finally, a table per class representations (also known as class-based representations) has been proposed where a table having a column for each property associated with value for at least one instance of a class is associated to each class (Dehainsala et al., 2007; Park et al., 2007). These three basic approaches have also some small variants. For more detail, the user may refer to (Theoharis et al., 2005). Separating representation of ontology descriptions and instance data leads to better performance and query response time. However, this approach assumes a fixed ontology model.

The OntoDB approach. OntoDB (Dehainsala et al., 2007; Pierra et al., 2005) proposes to add another schema to the previous approach. This schema, called meta-schema, records the ontology model into a reflexive meta-model. For the ontology schema, the meta-schema plays the same role as the one played by the system catalog in traditional databases. Indeed, the meta schema supports: (1) a generic access to the ontology, (2) the evolution of the used ontology model, and (3) the storage of different ontology models

Figure 1. The OntoDB Four Parts architecture

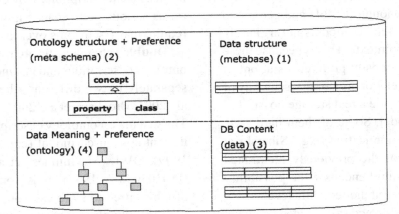

including OWL, DAML+OIL (McGuinness et al., 2002) and PLIB.

The Different Components of OntoDB

OntoDB ensures the persistence of both models and their instances. A dedicated language, OntoQL, has been implemented in order to manipulate and query the different components of the OntoDB system. The OntoDB architecture is composed of four parts described in Figure 1. These components are briefly summarised as follows.

- **The *meta-base* part (1)**. The meta-base, also often called *catalog system*, is a traditional part of any database. It contains system tables used to manage all the data contained in the database. In OntoDB, it contains specifically the description of all the tables and columns defined in the three other parts of the architecture.
- **The *data* part (3)**. It represents the objects of domain described by the entities (classes and properties) provided by an ontology. These objects are represented following the table per class approach.
- **The *ontology* part (4)**. It contains all the ontologies that define the semantics of the various domains covered by the database.

OntoDB initially supports the PLIB ontology model.

- **The *meta-schema* part (2)**. The meta-schema part records the model of the ontology used into a reflexive meta-model. For the ontology part, the meta schema part plays the same role as the one played by the meta-base in traditional databases systems.

The OntoQL Language for OntoDB

The OntoQL language has been designed to exploit the power offered by the OntoDB architecture (Jean et al., 2005; Jean et al., 2006). Indeed, OntoQL is able to access and manipulate the model, its instances and the meta-model.

OntoQL can deal both with the entities of an ontology and their instances. Moreover, the language supports the manipulation of the model that describes the ontology (e.g.#class, #property, #datatype). It is equipped with a data definition language DDL (CREATE and ALTER clauses), a data manipulation language (INSERT, UPDATE and DELETE clauses) and a query facility language (SELECT clause). Syntactical details of the language are given in the Table2.

Let us for instance consider the tourism domain. An ontology for this domain manipulates entities

Table 2. Syntax of the OntoQL language

Data Definition Language (DDL)
- The create class statement:
<class definition>::= "CREATE" <entity id> <class id> [<view clause>] [<under clause>]
[<descriptor clause>] [<properties clause list>]
-The alter class statement:
<alter class statement>::= "ALTER" <class id> [<descriptor clause>] [<alter class action>]
Manipulation Language (DML)
- The insert statement:
<insert statement>::= "INSERT" "INTO" <category id> <insert description and source>
- The update statement:
<update statement>::= "UPDATE" <category id polymorph> "SET" <set clause list> ["WHERE" <search condition>]
- The delete statement:
<delete statement>::= "DELETE" "FROM" <category id polymorph> ["WHERE" <search condition>]

including Hotels, Prices, Rate. Some examples of instances in this domain include *Ibis Poitiers* (Hotels), *Paris* (Cities). OntoQL can deal both with the mentioned entities and their instances (Table 3).

Handling Non Functional Properties in OBDB

In the OntoDB architecture previously presented, the different models store both the ontology and its instances. They also store the meta model of the ontology. This approach is based on an extensive use of meta modelling techniques. However, all the described OBDB approaches lack to offer primitives that are able to represent non functional aspects related to the ontology models such as quality of service, preferences or security. Indeed, most of the well known ontology models including OWL and PLIB do not provide built-in constructors to represent these notions.

To overcome the problem of handling non functional characteristics, specific attributes (e.g., note, remark) are introduced or particular proper-

ties are defined. Rather than extending a specific ontology model and being linked to the specific extended ontology model, our proposal consists in introducing a side model describing the non functional entities together with the model of the ontology model inside the same OBDB. The advantage of this approach is the possibility to adapt non functional descriptions to any ontology model keeping its definition unchanged and preserving upward compatibility. Technically, this extension is possible only if the meta-model that describe the model of the ontology can be manipulated. Indeed, such an extension requires being able to attach any element of the model of the ontology to the model of the non functional elements. The OntoDB approach offers this manipulation facility thanks to the availability of the meta-schema previously outlined.

Before we give the details of our approach, we end our state of the art by giving an overview of the EXPRESS language used to model the side models associated to an ontology model expressed in the meta-schema part.

Table 3. Hotel class creation with an OntoQL statement

CREATE #CLASS Hotel (id int, name String, starRate int, price int, airCond boolean, tv boolean, wifi boolean, pool boolean, jakuzi boolean, tennisCourt boolean, casino boolean);	INSERT INTO Hotel (id, name, starRating, price, airCond, tv, wifi, pool, jakuzi, tennisCourt, casino) VALUES (52, 'HotelIBIS', 4, 75, true, true, true, false, false, false, false);

Table 4. Entity Definition and Instantiation in EXPRESS

Entity Definition	
ENTITY A;	**ENTITY** B;
att_A(?):INTEGER;	att_1:REAL;
INVERSE;	att_2: LIST [0:?] OF STRING;
att_1:B **FOR** att_3;	att_3:A;
END ENTITY;	**END** ENTITY;
Entity Instance	
#1=A(3);	
#2=B(4.0,('HELLO','BYE'), #1);	

The Express Data Modelling Language

EXPRESS is a data modelling language that combines ideas from the entity-attribute-relationship family of modelling languages with object modelling ideas of the late 1980s. It became an international standard (ISO 10303-11) in 1994.

The major advantage of this language is its capability to describe structural, descriptive and procedural concepts in a common data model and semantics. This integration avoids the use of several models and languages that require bridging over the gap between all the defined models (like in UML). A data model in EXPRESS is represented by a set of schemas that may refer to each other. Each schema contains two parts. The first part is a set of entities that are structured in an object-oriented approach (supporting multiple inheritances). The second part contains procedures, functions and global rules used to express constraints.

Entity definition. Entities are named and defined by a set of attributes (which may be an empty set) assigned to each entity. Each attribute has a domain (where it takes its values) defining a data type. It can be either a simple (e.g., integer, string) or a structured (e.g., lists, sets, bags) domain or an entity type meaning that an attribute is a type of another entity.

Table 4 shows the entity B with three attributes: a real, a list of strings and a relationship with another entity A which has only one integer attribute. att_1 is an inverse attribute of entity A, corresponding to the inverse link defined by attribute att_3 in entity B. Entities may have instances. Each entity has an identifier. The attribute values are either literal values of the EXPRESS simple or structured built-in types or they are references to other entity instances.

An example of the model extension associated to the previous entity definitions is shown in the same table. The #2 instance of the entity B, where att_1 evaluates to 4.0, att_2 is the list ('hello', 'bye') and att_3 points the particular instance #1 of the entity A where its att_A attribute evaluates to 3.

Multiple inheritance. Inheritance (single and multiple) is introduced by the SUPERTYPE and SUBTYPE EXPRESS keywords. The SUBTYPE clause occurring in an entity E is followed by the enumeration of the set of entity names representing the superclasses of E.

Constraining entities. It is possible to limit the allowed set of instances of the data models to those instances that satisfy some stated constraints. EXPRESS uses first order logic which is completely decidable since the set of instances is finite. Constraints are introduced thanks to the WHERE clause that provides for instance invariant, and to the global RULE clause that provides for model invariant. Derivations and constraints are the only places where functions may occur. They are inherited. Set inclusion defines the semantics of the EXPRESS inheritance mechanism.

Graphical representation. To help the user to understand the EXPRESS data models, the EXPRESS-G graphical representation has been defined. It represents the structural and descriptive constructs of the EXPRESS language (classes and attributes) but the procedural constructs (derivation and rules) are not represented. The example of Figure 2 illustrates an EXPRESS-G representation of a simple data model related to geometrical entities.

In this example, a geometric entity can be

Figure 2. EXPRESS-G representation of geometric entities

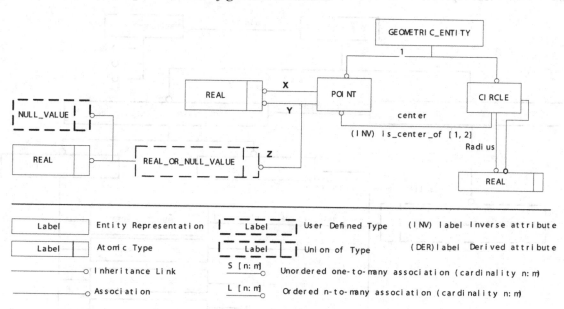

either a circle or a point. A circle has a center and a radius, and a derived attribute perimeter. A point has coordinates X, Y, Z but Z may have either a real value or a null value introduced by the SELECT (sum of types) type real or null value. Finally in this model, a point can be the centre of two circles at the maximum. This is specified by the inverse attribute *is center_of*. For more information on the EXPRESS language, the reader may refer to (IS010303.02, 1994; Schenck and Wilson, 1994).

In this example, a geometric entity can be either a circle or a point. A circle has a centre and a radius, and a derived attribute perimeter. A point has coordinates X, Y, Z but Z may have either a real value or a null value introduced by the SELECT (sum of types) type real or null value. Finally in this model, a point can be the center of two circles at the maximum. This is specified by the inverse attribute *is_ centre_of*. For more information on the EXPRESS language, the reader may refer to (IS010303.02, 1994; Schenck and Wilson, 1994).

In this section, we have reviewed the main

work related to preference handling in the database and the Semantic Web areas. A brief description of the main ontology based database approaches has been given and the OntoDB system presented. The EXPRESS data modelling language, used to describe formally our preferences model, has been presented as well. In the following section, the details of our approach for preferences handling are presented. We also describe how it is articulated with the model of the ontology.

ONTOLOGY-BASED DATABASE WITH PREFERENCES

In order to represent user's preferences, we propose a modular, sharable and generic model of preferences. Below, this model is formally defined using the EXPRESS data modelling language in order to make it sharable. Thanks to its formal definition, the resulting preference model is ambiguities-free. Indeed, EXPRESS is equipped with a powerful constraints language allowing to defining precisely the semantics of the model being described. The

Figure 3. Graphical representation of the preference model

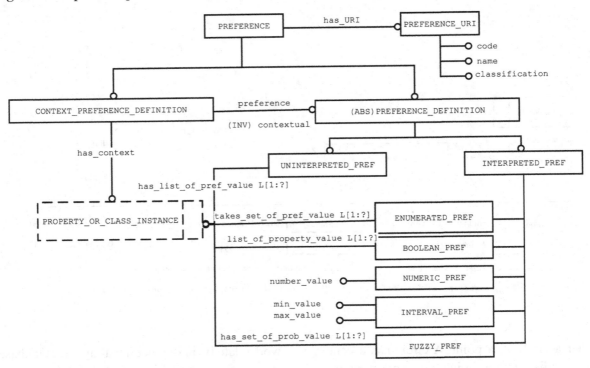

following section details the preference model and shows how it can be integrated to the OntoDB system in order to express preferences on any set of data semantically described by an ontology.

Three distinct elements, detailed below, compose the model: i) the ontology model resource; ii) the preference model; iii) and finally the link between these 2 resources. The model is presented on Figure 3.

The definition of the preference model compiles the different models found in the literature. We have separated preferences that are generic from those depending on the context where they are defined. Preferences may be either interpretable or non interpretable. By interpreted preferences, we mean those preferences that are enumerated by a given user or a system designer without any associated interpretation procedure.

Each preference is associated with a set of attributes that give a characterisation for this preference. Attributes code, name and classifi-

cation represent respectively an identifier URI, a name and the classification associated to this preference (e.g., cost, star rating, or distance). Its specification in EXPRESS (PREFERENCE_URI) is shown in Table 6. As an example, we define the preferences 'cheap' or 'expensive', 'far' or 'near'. The corresponding characteristics are given by #2, #3, #60, #61 instances of Table 6. Notice that the PREFERENCE_URI entity is separately defined and could be interpreted from a more general knowledge model. An ontology for example can be used to give a more precise description of the semantic annotation of a preference.

Table 5. Representation of ontology model resource

PROPERTY_OR_CLASS_INSTANCE
TYPE PROPERTY_OR_CLASS_INSTANCE SELECT (PROPERTY_VALUE, CLASS_VALUE); END TYPE;

Table 6. Definition and instantiation of PREFERENCE_URI

PREFERENCE_URI Definition
ENTITY PREFERENCE_URI code: INTEGER; name: STRING; classification: STRING; END ENTITY;

Figure 4. Graphical representation of ontology resource definition

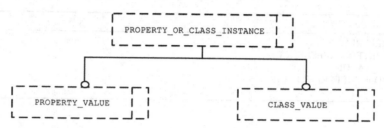

Ontology Model Resource Definition: Property_ or_Class_Instance

Our approach consists in associating any preference model to any ontology resource model that allows to manipulating the model of the ontology through its meta-model. Indeed, according to Figure 4, the preference resource concept of the preference model is associated to the Property_ Or_Class_Instance entity of the ontology model. The ontology's instances are taken into account in the preference model by referring to their corresponding ontology's entities. Preferences can be expressed on property or class instances.

The PROPERTY_OR_CLASS_INSTANCE resource is defined in EXPRESS according to the expression in Table 5. It represents a property instance or a class instance. Indeed, as it is shown in Figure 2, this resource is a select type (union of types) between the CLASS_VALUE type and PROPERTY_VALUE type available in any existing ontology model.

The preference model introduces specific resources allowing to defining preferences. Two categories of preferences are introduced: interpreted and uninterpreted preferences.

Interpreted Preferences

Interpreted preferences are those preferences that can be given an interpretation through of an evaluation. The nature of their definition depends on the attached interpretation function. They can be associated to an evaluation or interpretation procedure. For example, we can interpret the preference *cheap(x)* as being *price(x) <=20*. The idea is to define preferences associated to data types that are valuable and for which there exists an order relation.

Enumerated preferences are interpreted by a set of property values or class instances imported from the ontology instances (Table 7). It corresponds to the enumeration of individuals taken in an ontology that interprets a given preference. For example, we could define 'cheap' hotels as being {*Hotel(Formule1), Hotel(PremiereClasse)*}. This set, expresses that the 'cheap' preference corresponds to two hotels in the ontology and corresponds to #40 in Table 7.

Numeric preferences are interpreted by numeric values. For example, the rating of a hotel can be defined according to the numbers of stars the hotel is associated to (e.g., *1, 2, 3, or 4 stars*).

Table 7. Definition and instantiation of ENUMERATED_PREFERENCE

ENUMERATED_PREFERENCE
ENTITY ENUMERATED_PREFERENCE SUBTYPE OF (INTERPRETED_PREFERENCE); interpreted_by: LIST [1:?] PROPERTY_OR_CLASS_INSTANCE; pref_attributes: LIST[1:?] OF PREFERENCE_URI; END ENTITY;

Table 8. Definition of NUMERIC_PREFERENCE and its instantiation.

NUMERIC_PREFERENCE
ENTITY NUMERIC_PREFERENCE SUBTYPE OF (INTERPRETED_PREFERENCE); interpreted_by: NUMBER_VALUE pref_attributes: LIST[1:?] OF PREFERENCE_URI; END ENTITY;

The relation order is the one defined on numbers. It is specified on Table 8, and #27 is an instance that expresses that the value 2 is associated to the *cheap* preference.

Boolean preferences correspond to a list of Boolean properties which value is preferred to be true. For example, we can define a preference on hotels having air conditioning and providing wifi and swimming pool facilities. In this case, the list of considered properties is (*'aircondi-tioner'*, *'wifi'*, *'swimming pool'*). This type of preference is defined in EXPRESS according to the Table 9 and #22 is an example of instance. The PROPERTY_VALUE of *tv, airconditioner* and *wifi* correspond respectively to #p7, #p8, #p6 of the Figure 7.

Interval preferences are used when a preference is interpreted by a minimal and a maximal values. For example, costs of goods can be associated with the *cheap* or *expensive* prefer-ence. In this case, one can decide that a price is considered as *cheap* when its value belongs to the interval [45..60] and as *expensive* when it belongs to [90..100]. The EXPRESS code for this type of preferences is expressed in Table 10 and Table 11.

#100 and #110 show that a value is cheap (#2) when it belongs to the interval [45, 60] of #12 and expensive (#3) when it belongs to the interval [90, 100] of #17.

Fuzzy preferences associate probability values to a given preference. If we take the previous example, we get (*'air conditioning'* 0.3, *'wifi'* 0.6, *'swimming pool'* 0.1) meaning that a strongest preference is allowed to having wifi while having a swimming pool is a weak preference. This type of preferences is useful for processing ontological data with fuzzy logic approaches. Their formal definition is specified in Table 12.

Table 9. Definition of BOOLEAN_PREFERENCE and its instantiation

BOOLEAN_PREFERENCE
ENTITY BOOLEAN_PREFERENCE SUBTYPE OF (INTERPRETED_PREFERENCE); interpreted_by: LIST[1:?] OF PROPERTY_VALUE; pref_attributes: LIST[1:?] OF PREFERENCE_URI; END ENTITY;

Table 10. Definition of INTERVAL_VALUE ENTITY and its instantiation

INTERVAL_VALUE ENTITY
ENTITY INTERVAL_VALUE min_value: REAL; max_value: REAL; WHERE min_value < max_value; END_ENTITY;

Table 11. Definition of INTERVAL PREFERENCE and its instantiation

INTERVAL_PREFERENCE
ENTITY INTERVAL_PREFERENCE SUBTYPE OF (INTERPRETED_PREFERENCE); interpreted_by: LIST[1:?] INTERVAL_VALUE; pref_attributes: LIST[1:?] OF PREFERENCE_URI; END ENTITY;

Figure 5. Ontology preference relationship

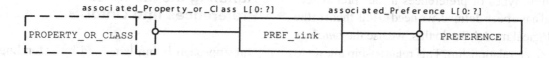

#26 instance states that a probability of 0.1 is associated to the cheap preference. PROB_VALUE is a redefinition of the REAL data type of EXPRESS.

Uninterpreted Preferences

Uninterpreted preferences correspond to a set of ontology's properties or classes instances which are considered as preferred. There is no any rationale for choosing these instances. For example, *HotelIBIS, SwimmingPool, pizza,* and *coffee* can be the different preferences that one can have in the tourism domain. The EXPRESS code defining such preferences and the instance #47 corresponding to *HotelIBIS, SwimmingPool* instances are given in Table 13.

Context Based Preferences

The definition of preferences may depend on the context in which they can be interpreted. For example, someone may interpret differently the *cheap* preference attached to the price of a hotel depending on whether the hotel is localised in Paris, London, or Poitiers. In this case, the interpretation of a preference depends on the value of another property (*localisation* in our example). To handle these kinds of preferences, we have introduced the notion of context preferences defined in EXPRESS as indicated in Table 14. The PROPERTY_VALUE of *price* correspond to the instance property #p2 presented in Figure 7.

Table 12. Definition of FUZZY_PREFERENCE and its instantiation

FUZZY_PREFERENCE
ENTITY FUZZY_PREFERENCE SUBTYPE OF (INTERPRETED_PREFERENCE); interpreted_by: LIST [1:?] OF PROB_VALUE; pref_attributes: LIST[1:?] OF PREFERENCE_URI; END ENTITY;

Table 13. Definition of UNINTERPRETED_PREFERENCE and its instantiation

UNINTERPRETED_PREFERENCE
ENTITY UNINTERPRETED_PREFERENCE SUBTYPE OF (PREFERENCEDEFINITION); interpreted_by: SET [1:?] OF PROPERTY_OR_CLASS_INSTANCE; pref_attributes: LIST[1:?] OF PREFERENCE_URI; END ENTITY;

Ontology Preference Link

When all types of preferences in our preferences model have been defined, we need to link them to the ontological model. To do this, we use the *ontology preference* relationship. This relationship allows to attaching a particular preference to a given ontological entity, being either a class or a property.

The PROPERTY_OR_CLASS resource represents data elements of the model of the ontology that we refer to. It represents both the data and the domain knowledge (described in an ontology) independently of any implementation model. Moreover, it is modelled independently from any specific model of ontology (e.g. OWL, F-Logic (Kifer et al., 1995), PLIB). The EXPRESS-G representation of the *Preference_Link* is represented in Figure 5.

Once our preference model is formally defined,

we need to handle it into the OntoDB system.

Handling the Model of Preferences into OntoDB

Our approach is implemented by extending the OntoDB system. OntoDB offers the necessary facilities to store in the same infrastructure both ontologies and the preference model. Thanks to the use of the OntoQL language, the manipulation of these different components becomes easier.

OntoDB Extension with Preferences

The extension of OntoDB handling preferences consists first in creating the entity PREFERENCE using the CREATE clause of the OntoQL language as schematised in the following expression

Table 14. Definition of CONTEXT_BASED PREFERENCE and its instantiation

Context_Based_PREFERENCE
ENTITY Context_Based_PREFERENCE SUBTYPE OF (PREFERENCE); context_value: PROPERTY_OR_CLASS_INSTANCE; preference: PREFERENCE_ DEFINITION; pref_attributes: LIST[1:?] OF PREFERENCE_URI; END ENTITY

```
CREATE ENTITY #Preference (
#oid int,
...
);
```

We note that the created entity is *#Preference*, prefixed by the (#) symbol to precise that the creation is at the entity meta-model level. Table 15 presents the creation of 4 entities of the preference model using the OntoQL language. In the first column, we give the syntax of the creation of the root entity of the model, Preference. In the second column, the creation of the entity Preference_URI, attached to a preference, is given. Finally, in the last columns the creation of interval and numeric preferences is given.

Associating the Ontology and the Preferences Model

Once the preferences containers are defined at the meta-schema level, they need to be linked to their corresponding ontological entity at the meta-schema as well. This link has been previously illustrated in Figure 4 by the Pref_Link class. Practically, in order to encode composition, the preference link is absorbed by the entity Property_or_Class of the ontology model by becoming its attribute. The following OntoQL statement is used to create such a link into OntoDB.

```
ALTER ENTITY #Property_Or_Class
ADD ATTRIBUTE #PREF_Link REF
(#Preference) ARRAY
```

It expresses that an aggregate of preference elements is associated to a class or a property through the *PREF_Link* attribute.

Querying OntoDB by Integrating Preferences Facility

In order to handle the preferences in the OntoQL queries, a preference interpreter has been developed on top of the OntoQL engine. This is materialized by adding a PREFERRING subclause to OntoQL SELECT clause. An interpretation function is associated to each type of preference available in our preference model and is associated to this subclause. The syntax of the SELECT clause becomes as follows.

```
SELECT 'selection'
FROM 'tableReference'
PREFERRING 'preferenceIdentifer'
```

For example, assuming the tourism domain, the cheap hotels can be retrieved using the following SELECT clause.

```
SELECT name
FROM Hotel
PREFERRING 'CHEAP'
```

The whole model and operational resources associated to preferences are defined. Now it is possible to show how our approach works on a case study. The following section illustrates it with an example taken from the tourism domain and specifically an online holiday booking domain.

Table 15. Creating the main entities of the model and 2 types of preferences (Interval and Numeric) with the OntoQL Create clause at the meta-schema level

CREATE ENTITY #Preference(#oid int, #uri REF(#Preference_Uri));	CREATE ENTITY #Preference_URI(#code int, #name string, #classification String);	CREATE ENTITY #Interval_Preference UNDER #Preference (#min_value int, #max_value int);	CREATE ENTITY #Numeric_Preference UNDER #Preference (#number_value int)

Figure 6. A fragment of the tourism ontology

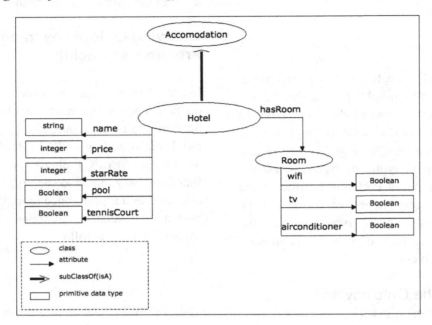

IMPLEMENTING THE MODEL: THE HOLLIDAY BOOKING CASE STUDY

In order to illustrate our approach, let us consider a research scientist, Marc, wants to book a hotel room for his summer holidays. To do this, he uses his favorite online holidays booking system. This booking system manages a set of hotels disseminated over the world. These hotels offer various leisure facilities and are rated according to the international hotels rating standard ranging from 1 star hotels to 5 stars hotels. The number of stars depends on various characteristics including the level of comfort and the leisure facilities offered by the hotel. The price of a room depends on the category of the hotel and of the period. The booking system uses an ontology about the tourism domain. This ontology formally describes the knowledge about the domain.

Marc would like to minimise the budget he will spend for his holidays. He prefers living in cheap hotels and he has a preference for standard room facilities.

Regarding this situation, the objective is to satisfy Marc making sure that his preferences are considered. Two preferences are identified here: the room facilities '*standard*' and the cost description '*cheap*'.

The instantiation of our preference model for this case study is described below. Firstly we give a fragment of the tourism ontology corresponding to the case study. Then we describe how we express the preferences. Finally, the querying process is outlined.

The Domain Ontology: A Tourism Ontology

The Tourism Ontology defines the entities describing the accommodation and complementary services usually offered by hotels. It defines entities such as rooms (categorised in single, double and suite rooms), reservation, room facilities (e.g., TV, wifi), provision of meals (e.g., half board), etc. Figure 6 gives a graphical representation of a fragment of this ontology and Figure 7 describes a set of its instances.

The ontology described previously is defined

Figure 7. Instantiation of the tourism ontology

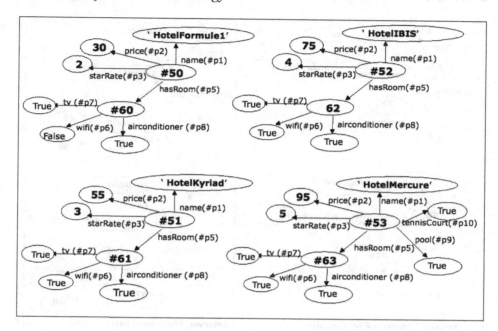

in the OntoDB system by populating its different entities. Table 16 gives the ONTOQL fragment that instantiates into OntoDB the previously defined Hotel class with the hotel Kyriad.

The Preference Model Instantiation

The preference model defines different type of preferences. In our case study, it is instantiated for numeric and interval preference types to encode respectively the *standard* and *cheap* preferences like they are graphically represented on Figure 8.

For our illustration, we focus on defining the preferences attached to the star rating and to the price attributes.

- *star rating* means that a hotel has 1, 2, etc.

stars according to the star rating quality classification. The OntoQL statement that defines a three star rating is described as:

```
INSERT INTO #Numeric_
Preference(#number_Value, #code,
#name, #classification) VALUES(3,
51,'standard','starRate');
```

- *very cheap, cheap, expensive, very expensive* are preferences associated to a price in the cost quality classification.

The following OntoQL statement describes the cheap quality as being any price belonging

Table 16. Instantiating The Class Hotel With The Hotel Kyriad

```
INSERT INTO Hotel (id, name, starRating, price,
airCond, tv, wifi, pool, jakuzi, tennisCourt, casino)
VALUES (51, 'HotelKyriad', 3, 55, True, True, True, False, False, False, False);
```

Figure 8. Numeric and interval preferences instantiation

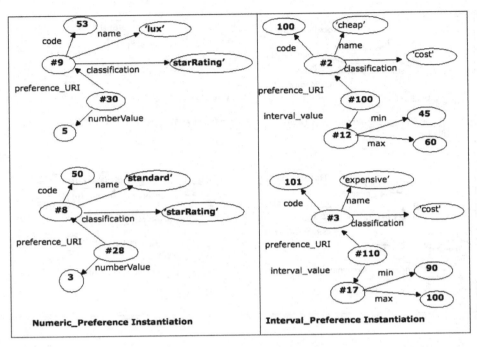

to the interval [45, 60] and the expensive quality any price between 90 and 100.

```
INSERT INTO Interval_
Preference(#label, #min_value,
#max_value)
VALUES('cheap',45, 60);
INSERT INTO Interval_
Preference(#label, #min_value,
#max_value)
VALUES('expensive',90, 100);
```

Attaching Preferences to the Ontology of the Tourism Domain

When the preferences and the ontology have been defined, the next step is to link ontology entities to the preferences that are expressed on these entities. In our case, a preference is attached to the price and to the star rating property. We update the *Property_Or_Class* entity accordingly. The first instruction below link the property price to the interval preferences defined previously.

```
UPDATE #Property_Or_Class set
#Pref_link=ARRAY ['cheap', 'expen-
sive'] where #name='price';
UPDATE #Property_Or_Class set
#Pref_link=ARRAY ['standard'] where
#name='starRate';
```

When the preferences are linked to the ontology concepts, the database can be queried.

Querying OntoDB with Preferences

Once the three previous steps are realised, it becomes possible to query the implemented model. We give below two examples of queries with an asserted quality on the data thanks to the PREFERRING clause.

1.   A query that gives only the 3 stars hotels is written as follows.

Table 17. Query Result for the Preference Standard

name	starRate
Kyriad	3

Table 18. Query Result for the Preference Cheap

name	price
Kyriad	55

```
SELECT name, starRate
FROM Hotel
PREFERRING 'Standard';
```

As *standard* is defined as a numeric preference attached to the property *starRate* having the value 3, when the PREFERRING clause is interpreted, the query is automatically rewritten as follows (cf. Table 17).

```
SELECT name, starRate
From Hotel
WHERE starRate = 3;
```

2.   A query retrieving cheap hotels is written as follows.

```
SELECT name, price
FROM hotel
PREFERRING 'cheap ';
```

As in the previous example, the query has to be rewritten according to type of preference in the PREFERRING clause. In this case, the preference *cheap* has been defined as an interval preference attached to the property *price*. It takes its values in the interval [45, 60] which can be interpreted by the clause BETWEEN. Thus, the query is automatically rewritten as follows (cf. Table 18).

```
SELECT name, price
From Hotel
WHERE price BETWEEN 45 and 60;
```

Notice that all the authorised subclauses of the

SELECT OntoQL clause can be used in building the query. The last clause is the PREFERRING clause used for rewriting the queries into standard OntoQL queries. This extension preserves upward compatibility with the classical SELECT clause.

CONCLUSION AND FUTURE WORK

We have proposed in this chapter a formal and generic model to handle users' preferences. We have described how the OntoDB ontology based database framework has been extended in order to handle preferences at the semantic level instead of handling them on the logical level of the data like it is supported in most existing preference models. Our model is composed of several types of preferences usually addressed in the literature in a separate way. These preferences are independent of any logical model of data. The model is generic thanks to its ability to define a relationship with any ontology model.

Our preference model fulfils the following three main requirements to ensure its flexibility. Firstly, the explicit representation of the ontology into the database. As a consequence, we have been able to attach the preferences to the entities of the ontology and not to the columns of the logical model of the database in the opposite of the other approaches. Then, the possibility to access and to manipulate the ontology model through accessing and manipulating directly its meta-model. Finally, the availability of an exploitation language which allows manipulating the instances, their classes and the meta-model of the considered ontology.

The extension of the ontology model with the preference model permitted to attach various types of preferences to the entities of the ontology. We have been able then to describe semantic queries that handle preferences expressed in the semantic level, and thus abstracting from the logical model. The possibility to access the meta-model level is well adapted for defining some model extensions that preserve upward compatibility with the extended model.

This work has opened several new directions and perspectives. Indeed, in a future work a significant evaluation of the approach in a broader area is planned in order to better understand its possible limitations. From the Data Warehousing perspective, a possible improvement is to extend the preference model in order to take aggregation into account. This will allow users expressing their preferences directly at the query aggregation level too (Rizzi, 2007). From a performance point of view, the evaluation and optimisation of preference queries (e.g. cost based optimisation) and the complexity implications of introducing preferences into queries would be beneficial.

REFERENCES

Abadi, D. J., Marcus, A., Madden, S. R., & Hollenbach, K. (2007). Scalable Semantic Web data management using vertical partitioning. In *Proceedings of the 33rd International Conference on Very Large Data Bases (VLDB'07)* (pp. 411-422).

Agrawal, R., Somani, A., & Xu, Y. (2001). Storage and querying of e-commerce data. In *Proceedings of the 27th International Conference on Very Large Data Bases (VLDB'01)* (pp. 149-158).

Agrawal, R., & Wimmers, E. L. (2000). A framework for expressing and combining preferences. In *SIGMOD Conference* (pp. 297-306).

Alexaki, S., Christophides, V., Karvounarakis, G., Plexousakis, D., & Tolle, K. (2001). The ICS-FORTH RDFSuite: Managing voluminous RDF description bases. In *Proceedings of the 2nd International Workshop on the Semantic Web (SemWeb'01)* (pp. 1-13).

Bellatreche, L., Giacometti, A., Marcel, P., Mouloudi, H., & Laurent, D. (2005). A personalization framework for OLAP queries. In *DOLAP '05: Proceedings of the 8th ACM International Workshop on Data Warehousing and OLAP* (pp. 9-18). New York: ACM.

Berners-Lee, T., Hendler, J., & Lassila, O. (2001). The Semantic Web. *Scientific American, 284*(5), 34–43.

Brickley, D., & Guha, R. V. (2004). Rdf schema (Technical Report, W3C). Retrieved from, http://www.w3.org/TR/2004/REC-rdfschema-20040210

Broekstra, J., Kampman, A., & van Harmelen, F. (2002). Sesame: A generic architecture for storing and querying RDF and RDF schema. In *Proceedings of the 1st International Semantic Web Conference (ISWC'02)* (pp. 54-68).

Brzsnyi, S., Kossmann, D., & Stocker, K. (2001). The skyline operator. In *Proceedings of 17th International Conference of Data Engineering (ICDE'01)* (pp. 421-430).

Cherniack, M., Galvez, E. F., Franklin, M. J., & Zdonik, S. B. (2003). Profile-driven cache management. In *Proceedings of 19th International Conference of Data Engineering (ICDE'03)* (pp. 645-656). IEEE Computer Society.

Chomicki, J. (2003). Preference formulas in relations queries. [TODS]. *ACM Transactions on Database Systems, 28*(4), 427–466. doi:10.1145/958942.958946

Chong, E. I., Das, S., Eadon, G., & Srinivasan, J. (2005). An efficient SQL-based RDF querying scheme. In *Proceedings of the 31st international conference on Very Large Data Bases (VLDB'05)* (pp. 1216-1227).

Daoud, M., Tamine, L., Boughanem, M., & Chebaro, B. (2007). Learning implicit user interests using ontology and search history for personalization. *International Web Information Systems Engineering - International Workshop on Personalized Access to Web Information* (WISE-PAWI 2007).

Das, G., Hristidis, V., Kapoor, N., & Sudarshan, S. (2006). Ordering the attributes of query results. In S. Chaudhuri, V. Hristidis, & N. Polyzotis (Eds.), *SIGMOD Conference* (pp. 395-406). ACM.

Dehainsala, H., Pierra, G., & Bellatreche, L. (2007). OntoDB: An ontology-based database for data intensive applications. In *Proceedings of the 12th International Conference on Database Systems for Advanced Applications (DASFAA'07)* (pp. 497-508).

Gruber, T. R. (1993). A translation approach to portable ontology specifications. *Knowledge Acquisition*, 5(2), 199–220. doi:10.1006/knac.1993.1008

Gurský, P., Horváth T., Jirásek J., Krajči S., Novotný R., Pribolová J.,Vaneková V., & Vojtáš P. (2008). User preference Web search – Experiments with a system connecting Web and user. *Computing and Informatics Journal*, 25-32.

Harris, S., & Gibbins, N. (2003). 3store: Efficient bulk RDF storage. In *Proceedings of the 1st International Workshop on Practical and Scalable Semantic Systems (PSSS'03)* (pp. 1-15).

IS010303.02 (1994). *Product data representation and exchange Part 2: Express reference manual*. ISO-055.

Jean, S., Aït-Ameur, Y., & Pierra, G. (2006). Querying ontology based database using OntoQL (an Ontology Query Language). In *Proceedings of On the Move to Meaningful Internet Systems 2006: CoopIS, DOA, GADA, and ODBASE, OTM Confederated International Conferences (OD-BASE'06)*, (LNCS 4275, pp. 704-721).

Jean, S., Pierra, G., & Ait-ameur, Y. (2005). OntoQL: An exploitation language for OBDBS. In *VLDB Ph.D. Workshop* (pp. 41-45).

Kießling, W. (2002). Foundations of preferences in database systems. In N. J. I. Mars (Ed.), *Knowledge and data engineering* (pp. 311-322). Amsterdam: IOS Press.

Kießling, W., & Kostler, G. (2000). Preference sql -design, implementation, experience. In N. J. I. Mars (Ed.), *Knowledge and data engineering* (pp. 778-789). Amsterdam: IOS Press.

Kifer, M., Lausen, G., & Wu, J. (1995). Logical foundations of object-oriented and frame-based languages. *Journal of the ACM, 42*(4), 741–843. doi:10.1145/210332.210335

Koutrika, G., & Ioannidis, Y. E. (2004). Personalization of queries in database systems. In *Proceedings of 20th International Conference of Data Engineering (ICDE'04)* (pp. 597-608).

Lassila, O., Swick, R. R. (1999, February 22). Resource description framework (RDF) model and syntax specification. *World Wide Web Consortium W3C Recommendation.*

Ma, L., Su, Z., Pan, Y., Zhang, L., & Liu, T. (2004). RStar: An RDF storage and query system for enterprise resource management. In *Proceedings of the 30th International Conference on Information and Knowledge Management (CIKM'04)* (pp. 484-491).

McGuinness, D., Fikes, R., Hendler, J., & Stein, L. A. (2002). DAML+OIL: An ontology language for the Semantic Web. *IEEE Intelligent Systems*, *17*(5), 72–80. doi:10.1109/MIS.2002.1039835

McGuinness, D. L., van Harmelen, F. (2004). Owl web ontology language overview. *World Wide Web Consortium, Recommendation* REC-owlfeatures-20040210.

Mouloudi, H., Bellatreche, L., Giacometti, A., & Marcel, P. (2006). Personalization of MDX queries. In *Actes Bases de Données Avancées (BDA 2006)*, Informal Proceedings.

Pan, Z., & Heflin, J. (2003). DLDB: Extending relational databases to support Semantic Web queries. In *Proceedings of the 1st International Workshop on Practical and Scalable Semantic Systems (PSSS'03)* (pp. 109-113).

Park, M. J., Lee, J. H., Lee, C. H., Lin, J., Serres, O., & Chung, C. W. (2007). An efficient and scalable management of ontology. In *Proceedings of the 12th International Conference on Database Systems for Advanced Applications (DASFAA'07)* (pp. 975-980).

Petrini, J., & Risch, T. (2007). SWARD: Semantic Web abridged relational databases. In *Proceedings of the 18th International Conference on Database and Expert Systems Applications (DEXA'07)* (pp. 455- 459).

Pierra, G., Dehainsala, H., Aït-Ameur, Y., & Bellatreche, L. (2005). Base de Données à Base Ontologique: Principes et mise en oeuvre. *Ingénierie des Systèmes d'Information*, *10*(2), 91–115. doi:10.3166/isi.10.2.91-115

Rizzi, S. (2007). OLAP Preferences: A research agenda. In *Proceedings of the ACM tenth international workshop on Data warehousing and OLAP DOLAP'07*. Lisboa, Portugal.

Schenck, D., & Wilson, P. (1994). *Information modelling the EXPRESS way*. New York: Oxford University Press.

Siberski, W., Pan, J. Z., & Thaden, U. (2006). Querying the Semantic Web with preferences. In *Proceedings of the 5th International Semantic Web Conference ISWC* (pp. 612-624).

Sieg, A., Mobasher, B., & Burke, R. (2007). Ontological user profiles for representing context in Web search. In *Proceedings of the 2007 IEEE/WIC/ACM International Conferences on Web Intelligence and Intelligent Agent Technology – Workshops* (pp. 91-94).

SPARQL Query Language for RDF. (January 2008). *SPARQL*. Retrieved from http://www.w3.org/TR/rdf-sparql-query

Theobald, M., Weikum, G., & Schenkel, R. (2004). Top-k query evaluation with probabilistic guarantees. In *Proceedings of the 13th International Conference on Very Large Database VLDB'04* (pp. 648-659).

Theoharis, Y., Christophides, V., & Karvounarakis, G. (2005). Benchmarking database representations of RDF/S stores. In *Proceedings of the 4th International Semantic Web Conference (ISWC'05)* (pp. 685-701).

Toninelli, A., Corradi, A., & Montanari, R. (2008). Semantic-based discovery to support mobile context aware service access. *Computer Communications*, *31*(5), 935–949. doi:10.1016/j.comcom.2007.12.026

Viappiani, P., Faltings, B., & Pu, P. (2006). Preference based search using example-critiquing with suggestions. *Journal of Artificial Intelligence Research*, 27.

KEY TERMS AND DEFINITIONS

Ontology-Based Database (OBDB): is a data source which contains i) a (local) ontology, ii) possibly some references from this ontology to external (shared) ontologies, iii) a set of data, iv) and finally a relationship between each data and the ontological notion which explicit its meaning. An OBDB has two main characteristics: i) both ontologies and data are represented in a unique database and the same processing can be applied on them (Insert, Update, Querying, Versioning, etc.); ii) any data is associated to an ontological element which defines it meaning and vice versa (Dehainsala et al., 2007).

EXPRESS Language: defined in ISO 10303 Part 11, is a data modelling language that provides a rich set of facilities for defining complex data types. It combines ideas from the entity-attribute and the Object-Oriented modelling approaches.

Personalisation: is tailoring a consumer product, electronic or written medium to a user based on personal details or characteristics they provide. More recently, it has especially been applied in the context of the World Wide Web (Wikipedia).

Ontology: a formal and consensual dictionary of categories and properties of entities of a domain and the relationships that hold among them.

User Preferences: a set of criterions allowing for a specific user to measure the relevance of given information and to evaluate whether a given information is more relevant that another

Chapter 15
Security in Data Warehouses

Edgar R. Weippl
Secure Business Austria, Austria

ABSTRACT

The last several years have been characterized by global companies building up massive databases containing computer users' search queries and sites visited; government agencies accruing sensitive data and extrapolating knowledge from uncertain data with little incentive to provide citizens ways of correcting false data; and individuals who can easily combine publicly available data to derive information that – in former times – was not so readily accessible. Security in data warehouses becomes more important as reliable and appropriate security mechanisms are required to achieve the desired level of privacy protection.

INTRODUCTION

Landwehr (2001) defines how the etymological roots of the term "secure" are found in "se" which means "without," or "apart from," and "cure," i.e. "to care for," or "to be concerned about".

While there are many definitions of the primary requirements of security, the classical requirements are summarized by the acronym CIA. CIA is the acronym for confidentiality, integrity, and availability. All other security requirements such as non-repudiation can be traced back to these three basic properties.

Avizienis (2004) defines *confidentiality* as the absence of unauthorized disclosure of information, *integrity* as the absence of improper system alterations and *availability* as readiness for correct service.

- *Dependability* is a broader concept that encompasses all primary aspects of security save confidentiality, and, in addition.
- *Reliability*, which refers to the continuity of correct service.
- *Safety*, defined as the absence of catastrophic consequences for user(s) and environment.

DOI: 10.4018/978-1-60566-756-0.ch015

- *Maintainability,* which is the ability to undergo modifications and repairs.

BACKGROUND

While security obviously encompasses the requirements of the CIA triad this article will focus on the mechanism of access control (AC) as this addresses both confidentiality and—to some extent—integrity. Database security was addressed in the 1960s by introducing *mandatory access control* (MAC), driven mainly by military requirements. Today, *role-based access control* (RBAC) is the commonly used access control model in commercial databases.

There is a difference between trusting a person and trusting a program. For instance, Alice gives Bob a program that Alice trusts. Since Bob trusts Alice he trusts the program. However neither of them is aware that the program contains a Trojan. This security threat leads to the introduction of MAC. In MAC, the system itself imposes an access control policy and object owners cannot change that policy. MAC is often implemented in systems with mulitlevel security (MLS). In MLS information objects are classified in different levels and subjects are cleared for levels.

The *need-to-know* principle, also known from the military, stipulates that every subject receives only the information required to perform its task. To comply with this principle, it is not sufficient to use sensitivity labels to classify objects. Every object is associated with a set of compartments. Subjects are classified according to their security clearance for each given area/compartment.

Classification labels are of the form (Ss, Sc) where Sr is a sensitivity and Sc a set of compartments. (Os, Oc) dominates (Ss, Sc) if $(Ss, Sc) <= (Os, Oc)$.

This $<=$ relation is true when

- $Ss <= Os$ where the $<=$ relationship here is with respect to the classified $<$ sensitive

$<$ secret $<$ top secret sensitivity classification, and
- $Sc <= Oc$ where the $<=$ relationship is a subset relation of sets.

The Bell LaPadula (BLP) model (1975) forms the fundamental architectural idea behind guarantee of secrecy in MLS. The Biba model by the Mitre Corporation (1997) is used to protect integrity: BLP's no-read-up and no-write-down properties are inverted to the no-write-up and no-read-down rules. Today, Oracle's Label Security and DB2's Label Access Control are contemporary examples of this security model.

The most widely used access control model is the role-based access control (RBAC) model. This section will briefly summarize various properties of NIST's RBAC model as pointed out by Sandhu et al. (2000). The notion of *scalability* is multi-dimensional. RBAC does not define the degree of scalability implemented in a system with respect to the number of roles, number of permissions, size of role hierarchy, or limits on user-role assignments, etc.

As RBAC is based on permissions that confer the ability to do something on holders of the permission, it does not contain *negative authorizations* (prohibitions). The *nature of permissions* is not specified in the RBAC model itself. Permissions can be either fine-grained or coarse-grained and may also be customized. The exact nature of permissions is determined by the application.

Moreover, RBAC does not specify the ability of a user to select which roles are activated in a particular session. The only requirement is that it should be possible to allow a user to activate multiple roles simultaneously. It does not matter if the user is able to explicitly activate roles or if all roles are automatically activated by the system.

RBAC Constraints

Since permissions are organized into tasks by using roles, conflicts of interests are more evident than if dealing with permissions on a per-user basis. In fact, a conflict of interest among permissions on an individual basis is hard if not impossible to determine. Separation of duties among roles (i.e., defining mutually exclusive roles) provides the administrator with enhanced capabilities to specify and enforce enterprise policies. Since RBAC has static (user-role membership) and dynamic (role activation) aspects, the following two possibilities can be distinguished accordingly.

First, *Static Separation of Duties* (SSD) is based on user-role membership. It enforces constraints on the assignment of users to roles. This means that if a user is authorized as a member of one role, the user is prohibited from being a member of a second role. Constraints are inherited within a role hierarchy.

Second, *Dynamic Separation of Duties* (DSD) is based on role activation. It is employed when a user is authorized for more roles that must not be activated simultaneously. DSD is necessary to prohibit a user from circumventing a policy requirement by activating another role.

Administrating RBAC

Definition of roles and constraints, assigning permissions to roles, and granting membership to roles are the most common administrative tasks in RBAC. When a new employee enters the company, the administrator simply adds this person to one or more existing roles according to the users tasks and needs. Similarly, users can be removed from a role when they leave the company or added to new roles when their functions change.

It is commonly agreed that one of RBAC's biggest advantages is its easy administration. Nonetheless, managing a large number of roles can still be a difficult task. However, Sandhu and Coyne (1996) present an intriguing concept that shows how RBAC might be used to manage itself. An administrative role hierarchy is introduced, which is mapped to a subset of the role hierarchy it manages.

Coexistence with MAC / DAC

Mandatory access control is based on distinct levels of security to which subjects and objects are assigned. Discretionary access control (DAC) controls access to an object on the basis of an individual user's permissions and/or prohibitions. RBAC, however, is an independent component of these access controls and can coexist with MAC and DAC. RBAC can be used to enforce MAC and DAC policies as shown in (2000). The authors point out the possibilities and configurations necessary to use RBAC in the sense of MAC or DAC. For a detailed discussion on defining and organizing roles please refer to Nyanchama and Osborn (1994), who introduce a formal role graph to facilitate role administration. Ferraiolo and Kuhn (1992), for example, published fundamental concepts on granting and revoking membership to the set of specified named roles.

SCIENTIFIC CONCEPTS

Classic access control is still the mechanism of choice to protect not only databases but also data warehouses. The difference between a database and a data warehouse is that database is designed and optimized to process individual tuples and the data warehouse is optimized to respond to queries that analyze aggregated data. OLTP (On-Line Transaction Processing) systems are secured by controlling access to individual tuples but for data warehouses the issue of data protection is more complex. For typical access control there are several shortcomings. First and foremost, users can do anything with the data once they have access to it; Second, even if access to fine grained detail data is not permitted, querying different similar datasets can reveal fine details; this is also known as inference attacks. The first issue can be addressed—in theory—by usage control as described by Park and Sandhu (2004), the second by several methods of statistical database security.

Figure 1. The UCONABC usage control model from Park and Sandhu (2004)

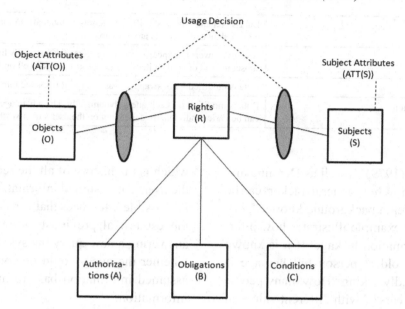

Usage Control

The main problem with data collection is that people might allow companies to use data for specific reasons (such as recommending related products) but do not consent to other uses of the same data. Usage control byPark and Sandhu (2004) is a concept that makes it possible to enforce pre- and postconditions when using data. It is similar to a traditional reference monitor, only that the restrictions are enforced during the entire access, as proposed by Thuraisingham (2005): The privacy control would "limit and watch access to the DBMS (that access the data in the database) (cf. Figure 1)."

Statistical Database Security

A statistical database contains information about individuals, but allows only aggregate queries (such as asking for the average age and not an individual's age). Nonetheless, inference can be used to infer some secret information. Data warehouses are built to support data mining. If a data mining tool can be used to derive sensitive information from unclassified information legitimately obtained, there is an inference problem, as discussed by Bertino et al. (2006).

Well-established protection concepts for statistical database security, such as: restriction-based techniques, query set size control, expanded query set size control-audit based (assumed information base), perturbation-based techniques, data swapping (distribution unchanged), random-sample queries, fixed perturbation (modify data), and query-based perturbation. For an in-depth description Castano et al. (1994) and Willenborg and De Waal (1996) are excellent sources.

Query set size control Enforcing a minimum set size for returned information does not offer adequate protection. Denning (1982) described trackers that are sequences of queries all within the size limits allowed by the database; when combined with AND statements and negations, information on individuals can be inferred. While simple trackers require some background infor-

Table 1. Different perturbation-based techniques

Data swapping	Data is exchanged between different records; individual information is thus protected while calculated statistics are not impacted.
Random sample queries	A set of answers to a specific query are created dynamically by selecting a random subset instead of all data item. This approach works well only for large datasets.
Fixed perturbation	Data is modified—not swapped—as soon as it is loaded into the data warehouse.
Query-based perturbation	Data is modified for each query dynamically. The advantage is that the accuracy can be varied individually depending on the user's trustworthiness.

mation, Denning (1979) as well as Denning and Schlorer (1983) show how general trackers can be used without in-depth background knowledge.

A very simple example illustrates how inference causes information leakage. If it is known that Alice is the oldest person but her age is unknown, repeatedly asking "How many people are older than X years?" with different values of X until the database returns the value 1, allows inference of Alice's age. By enforcing that each query returns aggregated data of more than one rows will not solve the problem. Repeatedly querying "How many employees are older than X? " until the system rejects the query because the query would return less than N rows, identifies a minimum set. This set includes $N+1$ employees, including Alice, w are older than X; let $X=66$ at this point. Subsequently, a query "Retrieve the sum of ages of all employees who are older than X? " will return a result $R1$. The last query "Retrieve the sum of ages of all employees who are not called Alice and are older than X? " will return $R2$. Finally, subtract $R2$ from $R1$ to obtain Alice's age. The example includes a query "not called Alice" that excludes a single item. If the "not equal" operation would not be allowed, a binary search could still be used to exclude a single item with a comparison operator. Simple control of result sizes as described here are not designed to prevent such an exclusion.

In *audit-based expanded query set size control* aka. Nabil and Worthmann's (1989) 'query set overlap control' the system decided whether to grant access to an "assumed information base,"

which is the history of all the requests issued by the user. The assumed information base contains all possible inferences that can be generated with the results of all previously issued queries; before answering a new query the system has to decide whether the query could be combined with the assumed information base to infer confidential information.

Perturbation-based techniques (cf. Table 1) are characterized by modifying the data so that the privacy of individuals can still be guaranteed even if more detailed data is returned than in restriction-based techniques. Data can be modified in the original data or in the results returned.

According to Samarati and Sweeney (1998) k-anonymity refers to a concept that guarantees that data of an individual will remain indistinguishable from that of at least k-1 others. The basic idea to protect privacy is centered on quasi-identifiers. Quasi-identifiers are usually a combination of data items that probably allow an identification of a person such as birth date, ZIP code, and gender. The idea, explained by Sweeney (2002), is that the data provider knows which data is externally available, for example a list of people with their names, birth date, ZIP code and gender. High dimensionality, however, may cause problems. Charu (2005) points out that once the number of dimensions increases to about 20, even 2-anonymity cannot be preserved in most cases without losing too much original information.

K-anonymity can be attacked using the homogeneity attack or the background knowledge attack. The homogeneity attack is very simple. If all *k* datasets have the same values in the field with sensitive data, privacy is not protected. For instance, if 5-anonymity is guaranteed and all patients suffer the same illness, there is no longer privacy. The background knowledge attack uses background knowledge to exclude impossible or unlikely datasets, as shown by Loukides and Shao (2007). Machanavajjhala et al. (2006) state that l-diversity is a measure that even the attacker needs *l*-1 relevant pieces of background knowledge to infer a (positive) disclosure.

APPLICATIONS

The previous sections focused on security concepts that are relevant for databases in general and—as data warehouses are databases optimized for a certain type of queries—for data warehouses. When implementing a data warehouse it is, however, essential that security is considered in an end-to-end way. The real goal is to protect the data and not only the data in the data warehouse. Before data is loaded into the DWH, it needs to be extracted from the source systems and is subsequently transformed, cleansed and prepared for loading. During this process the data has to be secured to the same standard as in the data warehouse. When clients query data, client security also becomes an issue. The data may be well protected in the DWH but a compromised client with full access to the DWH will certainly compromise all of the data. Security considerations need to consider all layers of the system involved. A DWH is not secure unless the underlying operating system is well secured and network security is adequately addressed.

DWH security and privacy is an active research area and is also relevant for industrial projects. Oracle, for instance, provides a detailed white paper on this topic. In industry, the challenge is mainly securing an entire and complex system, whereas academia strives to establish methods to preserve privacy of individuals and yet allow for the computation of meaningful statistics and detection of patterns.

FUTURE TRENDS AND OUTLOOK

Future research in data warehouse security will address several issues. First, with the increasing size of DWHs containing very personal information, privacy-preserving techniques will become more important. This area of research has also received more attention because nation-wide data gathering programs for national security are established. Second, while this theoretical research is certainly important, there are many more aspects to security that need to be considered. A nationwide DWH needs to be secured as an entire system including the mechanisms of data delivery, data querying, and usage. Security in DWH rests on three tiers: (1) technical infrastructure such as firewalls, encryption, (2) security in data gathering, privacy preserving techniques, and (3) secure applications including authentication, access control, authorization and auditing[20].

With the increasing number of DWH applications, incorporating security into training and education are important. Guimaraes (2006) describes a curriculum that addresses both database security and data warehouse security. Fernández-Medina et al. (2006) propose a model for access control and audit in DWHs. This approach is promising because it supports the specification of security requirements in early stages of establishing a DWH.

REFERENCES

Adam, N. R., & Worthmann, J. C. (1989). Security-control methods for statistical databases: A comparative study. *ACM Computing Surveys, 21*(4), 515–556. doi:10.1145/76894.76895

Aggarwal, C. C. (2005). On k-anonymity and the curse of dimensionality. In *Proceedings of the 31st VLDB Conference*.

Avizienis, A., Laprie, J.-C., Randell, B., & Landwehr, C. (2004). Basic concepts and taxonomy of dependable and secure computing. *IEEE Transactions on Dependable and Secure Computing, 1*(1), 11–33. doi:10.1109/TDSC.2004.2

Bell, D., & La Padula, L. (1975). *Secure computer system: Unified exposition and multics interpretation* (Esd-tr-75-306, Technical Report mtr-2997). Bedford, MA: The MITRE Corporation.

Bertino, E., Khan, L. R., Sandhu, R., & Thuraisingham, B. (2006, May). Secure knowledge management: Confidentiality, trust, and privacy. *IEEE Transactions on Systems, Man, and Cybernetics. Part A, Systems and Humans, 36*(3), 429–438. doi:10.1109/TSMCA.2006.871796

Castano, S., Martella, G., Samarati, P., & Fugini, M. (1994). *Database Security*. Addison-Wesely, ACM Press.

Denning, D. E. (1982). *Cryptography and data security*. Reading, MA: Addison Wesley.

Denning, D. E., & Denning, P. J. (1979). Data security. *ACM Computing Surveys, 11*(3), 227–249. doi:10.1145/356778.356782

Denning, D. E., & Schlorer, J. (1983, July). Inference controls for statistical databases. *IEEE Computer*.

Fernández-Medina, E., Trujillo, J., Villarroel, R., & Piattini, M. (2006). Access control and audit model for the multidimensional modeling of data warehouses. *Decision Support Systems, 42*(3), 1270–1289. doi:10.1016/j.dss.2005.10.008

Ferraiolo, D. F., & Kuhn, R. (1992, October). Role-based access control (rbac). In *Proc. 15th NIST-NSA National Computer Security Conference*. Baltimore, MD.

Guimaraes, M. (2006). New challenges in teaching database security. In *InfoSecCD '06: Proceedings of the 3rd annual conference on Information security curriculum development* (pp. 64-67). New York: ACM.

Landwehr, C. E. (2001). Computer security. *International Journal of Information Security, 1*(1), 3–13.

Loukides, G., & Shao, J. (2007). Capturing data usefulness and privacy protection in k-anonymisation. In *SAC '07: Proceedings of the 2007 ACM symposium on Applied computing* (pp. 370-374). New York: ACM.

Machanavajjhala, A., Gehrke, J., Kifer, D., & Venkitasubramaniam, M. (2006). L-diversity: Privacy beyond k-anonymity. In *ICDE '06: Proceedings of the 22nd International Conference on Data Engineering (ICDE'06)*, 24, Washington, DC: IEEE Computer Society.

Mitre Corporation (1997, April). *Integrity considerations for secure computer systems*. (Technical Report esdtr-76-372, esd,/afsc, mtr 3153). Bedford, MA: Mitre Corporation.

Nyanchama, M., & Osborn, S. (1994). Ifip wg 11.3 working conf. on database security. database security viii: Status and prospects. In *Proc. 15th Annual Computer Security Applications Conference*. North-Holland.

Osborn, S., Sandhu, R. S., & Munawer, Q. (2000). Configuring role-based access control to enforce mandatory and discretionary access control policies. *ACM Transactions on Information and System Security, 3*(2), 85–206. doi:10.1145/354876.354878

Park, J., & Sandhu, R. (2004). The ucon-abc usage control model. *ACM Transactions on Information Security*, 7(1), 128–174. doi:10.1145/984334.984339

Priebe, T., & Pernul, G. (2004). Sicherheit in Data-Warehouse- und OLAP-Systemen. *Rundbrief der Fachgruppe Modellierung betrieblicher Informationssysteme (MobIS) der Gesellschaft für Informatik e.V. (GI)*.

Samarati, P., & Sweeney, L. (1998). Protecting privacy when disclosing information: k-anonymity and its through generalization and suppression. In *Proceedings of the IEEE Symposium on Research in Security and Privacy*.

Sandhu, R. S., Coyne, E. J., Feinstein, H. L., & Youman, C. E. (1996, February). Role-based access control models. *IEEE Computer, 29*(2), 38–47.

Sandhu, R. S., Ferraiolo, D., & Kuhn, R. (2000, July). The nist model for role-based access control: Towards a unified standard. In *Proc. of 5th ACM Workshop on Role-Based Access Control*, Berlin, Germany: ACM Press.

Sweeney, L. (2002). k-anonymity: a model for protecting privacy. *International Journal on Uncertainty, Fuzziness and Knowledge-based Systems, 10*(5), 557–570. doi:10.1142/S0218488502001648

Thuraisingham, B. (2005). Privacy constraint processing in a privacy-enhanced database management system. *Data & Knowledge Engineering, 55*, 159–188. doi:10.1016/j.datak.2005.03.001

Willenborg, L., & De Waal, T. (1996). *Statistical disclosure control in practice*. Berlin: Springer-Verlag.

Compilation of References

Abadi, D. J., Marcus, A., Madden, S. R., & Hollenbach, K. (2007). Scalable Semantic Web data management using vertical partitioning. In *Proceedings of the 33rd International Conference on Very Large Data Bases (VLDB'07)* (pp. 411-422).

Abello, A., Samos, J., & Saltor, F. (2006). YAM²: A multidimensional conceptual model extending UML. *Information Systems, 31*(6), 541–567. doi:10.1016/j.is.2004.12.002

Abiteboul, S., Cluet, S., & Milo, T. (1997). Correspondence and translation for heterogeneous data. In *Proceedings of the International Conference on DataBase Theory* (pp. 351-363).

Adam, N. R., & Worthmann, J. C. (1989). Security-control methods for statistical databases: A comparative study. *ACM Computing Surveys, 21*(4), 515–556. doi:10.1145/76894.76895

Aggarwal, C. C. (2005). On k-anonymity and the curse of dimensionality. In *Proceedings of the 31st VLDB Conference*.

Agrawal, R., & Wimmers, E. L. (2000). A framework for expressing and combining preferences. In *SIGMOD Conference* (pp. 297-306).

Agrawal, R., Gupta, A., & Sarawagi, S. (1997). Modeling multidimensional databases. In *Proceedings of the International Conference on Data Engineering*, Birmingham U.K. (pp. 232-243).

Agrawal, R., Somani, A., & Xu, Y. (2001). Storage and querying of e-commerce data. In *Proceedings of the 27th International Conference on Very Large Data Bases (VLDB'01)* (pp. 149-158).

Agrawal, S., Chaudhuri, S., & Narasayya, V. (2000). *Automated selection of materialized views and indexes for SQL database.* Paper presented at the International Conference on Very Large Databases (VLDB00), Cairo, Egypt.

Ahmed, T., & Miquel, M. (2005). Multidimensional structures dedicated to continuous spatiotemporal phenomena. In M. Jackson, D. Nelson, & S. Stirk (Eds.), *Proceedings of the 22nd British National Conference on Databases* (Vol. 3567, pp. 29-40). Berlin, Germany: Springer.

Akal, F., Böhm, K., & Schek, H.-J. (2002). OLAP Query Evaluation in a Database Cluster: A performance study on intra-query parallelism. East-European Conf. on Advances in Databases and Information Systems (ADBIS), Bratislava, Slovakia.

Akal, F., Türker, C., Schek, H., Breitbart, Y., Grabs, T., & Veen, L. (2005). Fine-grained replication and scheduling with freshness and correctness guarantees. In *Proceedings of the 31st international Conference on Very Large Data Bases* (pp. 565-576).

Akinde, M. O., Böhlen, M. H., Johnson, T., Lakshmanan, L. V., & Srivastava, D. (2002). Efficient OLAP query processing in distributed data warehouses. In *Proceedings of the 8th international Conference on Extending Database Technology: Advances in Database Technology.* (LNCS 2287, pp. 336-353.

Alexaki, S., Christophides, V., Karvounarakis, G., Plexousakis, D., & Tolle, K. (2001). The ICS-FORTH RDFSuite: Managing voluminous RDF description bases. In *Proceedings of the 2nd International Workshop on the Semantic Web (SemWeb'01)* (pp. 1-13).

Allcock, W., Bresnahan, J., Kettimuthu, R., & Link, M. (2005). The Globus striped GridFTP framework and server. In *Proceedings of the 2005 ACM/IEEE Conference on Supercomputing* (pp. 54-65).

Alpdemir, M., Mukherjee, A., Paton, N., Watson, P., Fernandes, A., Gounaris, A., & Smith, J. (2003). OGSA-DQP: A service-based distributed query processor for the Grid. In *Proceedings of UK e-Science All Hands Meeting*.

Avizienis, A., Laprie, J.-C., Randell, B., & Landwehr, C. (2004). Basic concepts and taxonomy of dependable and secure computing. *IEEE Transactions on Dependable and Secure Computing, 1*(1), 11–33. doi:10.1109/TDSC.2004.2

Badri, M. (2008). *Maintenance des entrepôts de données issus de sources hétérogènes*. PhD thesis, University Paris Descartes.

Badri, M., Boufarès, F., & Heiwy, V. (2007). Des critères pour choisir l'architecture physique d'un entrepôt de données hétérogènes. *In Workshop ASD Atelier des systèmes décisionnels*.

Badri, M., Boufarès, F., Ducateau, C. F., & Gargouri, F. (2005). Etat de l'art de la maintenance des entrepôts de données issus des systèmes d'information hétérogènes. *Cinquièmes Journées Scientifiques GEI* (pp. 13-18).

Badri, M., Boufarès, F., Ducateau, C. F., & Nefoussi, R. (2006). Maintenance des vues matérialisées hétérogènes sous oracle. *In Workshop SID Systèmes d Information Décisionnels . INFORSID, 2006*, 8–14.

Badri, M., Heiwy, V., & Boufarès, F. (2008). Mise à jour incrémentale des agrégats: Cas des indicateurs ROLAP dans les entrepôts de données. *In CNRIUT'08*.

Bailey, J., Bry, F., Furche, T., & Schaffert, S. (2005). Web and Semantic Web query languages: A survey. In *Reasoning Web, First International Summer School* (LNCS, pp. 35-133).

Baril, X., & Bellahsène, Z. (2003). Designing and managing an XML warehouse. In *XML Data Management: Native XML and XML-enabled Database Systems* (pp. 455-473). Reading, MA: Addison Wesley.

Baril, X., & Bellahsene, Z. (2003). *Selection of materialized views: A cost-based approach*. Paper presented at the International Conference on Advanced Information Systems Engineering.

Basili, V. R., Caldiera, G., & Rombaci, H. D. (1994). The goal question metric approach. In *Encyclopedia of software engineering* (pp. 528-532). New York: John Wiley & Sons, Inc.

Baumgartner, R., Flesca, S., & Gottlob, G. (2001). Visual Web information extraction with Lixto. In *Proceedings of the 27th International Conference on Very Large Data Bases* (pp. 119-128).

Baxter, R., Christen, P., & Churches, T. (2003). A comparison of fast blocking methods for record linkage. In *Proceedings of the ACM SIGKDD'03 Workshop on Data Cleaning Record Linkage and Object Consolidation*, Washington, DC, USA (pp. 25-27).

Baziz, M., Boughanem, M., Prade, H., & Pasi, G. (2006). A fuzzy logic approach to information retrieval using a ontology-based representation of documents. In E. Sanchez (Ed.), *Fuzzy logic and the Semantic Web* (pp. 363-377). Amsterdam: Elsevier.

Bębel, B., Eder, J., Koncilia, C., Morzy, T., & Wrembel, R. (2004). Creation and management of versions in multiversion data warehouse. In *Proc. of ACM Symposium on Applied Computing (SAC)* (pp. 717-723).

Bédard, Y. (1997). Spatial OLAP. In *Proceedings of the 2nd Forum annuel sur la R-D, Géomatique VI: Un monde accessible*, Montréal, Canada.

Bédard, Y., Merrett, T., & Han, J. (2001). Fundaments of spatial data warehousing for geographic knowledge discovery. In H. Miller & J. Han (Eds.), *Geographic data mining and knowledge discovery* (pp. 53-73). London: Taylor & Francis.

Bédard, Y., Proulx, M., & Rivest, S. (2005). Enrichissement du OLAP pour l'analyse géographique: Exemples de réalisation et différentes possibilités technologiques. In *Revue des Nouvelles Technologies de l Information, Entrepôts de données et l Analyse en ligne* (pp. 1-20).

Bell, D., & La Padula, L. (1975). *Secure computer system: Unified exposition and multics interpretation* (Esd-tr-75-306, Technical Report mtr-2997). Bedford, MA: The MITRE Corporation.

Bellahsene, Z. (2002). Schema evolution in data warehouses. *Knowledge and Information Systems, 4*(3), 283–304. doi:10.1007/s101150200008

Bellahsene, Z. (2004). View adaptation in the fragment-based approach. *IEEE Transactions on Knowledge and Data Engineering, 16*(11), 1441–1455. doi:10.1109/TKDE.2004.79

Bellatreche, L., & Boukhalfa, K. (2005). An evolutionary approach to schema partitioning selection in a data warehouse. *International Conference on Data Warehousing and Knowledge Discovery.*

Bellatreche, L., Giacometti, A., Laurent, D., & Mouloudi, H. (2005). A personalization framework for OLAP queries. In I. Y. Song & Y. Trujillo (Eds.), *Proceedings of the ACM 8th International Workshop on Data Warehousing and OLAP* (pp. 9-18). New York: AMC Press.

Ben Abdallah, M., Feki, J., & Ben-Abdallah, H. (2006). MPI-EDITOR: Un outil de spécification de besoins OLAP par réutilisation logique de patrons multidimensionnels. In *Proceedings of the Atelier des Systèmes Décisionnels (ASD 06)*, Agadir, Morocco.

Beneventano, D., Bergamaschi, S., Castano, S., Antonellis, V. D., Ferrara, A., Guerra, F., et al. (2002). Semantic integration and query optimization of heterogenous data sources. In *Proceedings of the workshops on advances in Object-Oriented Information Systems (OOIS)* (LNCS 2426).

BenMessaoud, R., Boussaïd, O., & Loudcher-Rabaséda, S. (2006). Efficient multidimensional data representation based on multiple correspondence analysis. In *Proceedings of the ACM SIGKDD International Conference on Knowledge Discovery and Data Mining (KDD'06)*, Philadelphia, USA (pp. 662-667) New York: ACM Press.

BenMessaoud, R., Boussaïd, O., & Loudcher-Rabaséda, S. (2007). A multiple correspondence analysis to organize data cubes. In *Vol. 155(1) of Databases and Information Systems IV – Frontiers in Artificial Intelligence and Applications* (pp. 133-146). Amsterdam: IOS Press.

BenMessaoud, R., Loudcher-Rabaséda, S., & Boussaïd, O. (2006a). A data mining-based OLAP aggregation of complex data: Application on XML DOCUMent. *International Journal of Data Warehousing and Mining, 2*(4), 1–26.

Berglund, A., Boag, S., Chamberlin, D., Fernandez, M. F., Kay, M., Robie, J., & Simeon, J. (2007). *XML path language (XPath) 2.0.* Retrieved from http://www.w3.org/TR/xpath20/

Berners-Lee, T., Hendler, J., & Lassila, O. (2001). The Semantic Web. *Scientific American, 284*(5), 34–43.

Bertin, J., & Bonin, S. (1992). *La graphique et le traitement graphique de l'information*. Paris: Flammarion.

Bertino, E., Khan, L. R., Sandhu, R., & Thuraisingham, B. (2006, May). Secure knowledge management: Confidentiality, trust, and privacy. *IEEE Transactions on Systems, Man, and Cybernetics. Part A, Systems and Humans, 36*(3), 429–438. doi:10.1109/TSMCA.2006.871796

Bertolotto, M., Di Martino, S., Ferrucci, F., & Kechadi, T. (2007). Towards a framework for mining and analyzing spatio-temporal datasets. *International Journal of Geographical Information Science, 21*(8), 1–12. doi:10.1080/13658810701349052

Beyer, K. S., Chamberlin, D. D., Colby, L. S., Ozcan, F., Pirahesh, H., & Xu, Y. (2005). Extending XQuery for analytics. In *Proceedings of the ACM SIGMOD International Conference on Management of Data (SIGMOD'05)*, Baltimore, USA (pp. 503-514). New York: ACM Press.

Beyer, K. S., Cochrane, R., Colby, L. S., Ozcan, F., & Pirahesh, H. (2004). XQuery for analytics: Challenges and requirements. In *Proceedings of the First International Workshop on XQuery Implementation, Experience and Perspectives <XIME-P/>*, Paris, France (pp. 3-8).

Bhattacharya, I., & Getoor, L. (2006). Entity resolution in graphs. In L. B. Holder & D. J. Cook (Eds.), *Mining graph data*. New York: John Wiley & Sons.

Bilke, A., & Naumann, F. (2005). Schema matching using duplicates. In *Proceedings of the International Conference on Data Engineering* (pp. 69-80).

Bimonte, S. (2007). *Vers l intégration de l information géographique dans les entrepôts de données et l analyse en ligne: De la modélisation à la visualization.* Unpublished doctoral dissertation, INSA Lyon, France.

Bimonte, S. (2008). Des entrepôts de données, l'analyse en ligne et l'information géographique. *Journal of Decision Systems.*

Bimonte, S., Tchounikine, A., & Miquel, M. (2007). Spatial OLAP: Open issues and a Web based prototype. In M. Wachowicz & L. Bodum (Eds.), *Proceedings of the 10th AGILE International Conference on Geographic Information Science.*

Bimonte, S., Tchounikine, A., Miquel, M., & Laurini, R. (2007). Vers l'intégration de l'analyse spatiale et multidimensionnelle. In M. Batton-Hubert, T. Joliveau, & S. Lardon (Eds.), *Proceedings of the Colloque International de GEOmatique et d'Analyse Spatiale.*

Bimonte, S., Wehrle, P., Tchounikine, A., & Miquel, M. (2006). GeWOlap: A Web based spatial OLAP proposal. In R. Meersman, Z. Tari, & P. Herrero (Eds.), *Proceedings of the Workshop on Semantic-Based Geographical Information Systems* (Vol. 4278, pp. 1596-1605). Berlin, Germany: Springer.

Bird, I. & The LCG Editorial Board (2005). LHC Computing Grid Technical Design Report [LCG-TDR-001, CERN-LHCC-2005-024].

Blaschka, M., Sapia, C., & Höfling, G. (1999). On schema evolution in multidimensional databases. In M. Mohania & A. M. Tjoa (Eds.), *Proceedings of the 1st International Conference on Data Warehousing and Knowledge Discovery* (pp. 153-164). Heidelberg: Springer.

Boag, S., Chamberlin, D., Fernandez, M. F., Florescu, D., Robie, J., & Simeon, J. (2007). *XQuery 1.0: An XML query language* (W3C Recommendation). Retrieved from http://www.w3.org/TR/xquery/

Boag, S., Chamberlin, D., Fernandez, M., Florescu, D., Robie, J., & Simeon, J. (2007). *XQuery 1.0: An XML query language* (W3C Recommendation). Retrieved from http://www.w3.org/TR/xquery/

Body, M., Miquel, M., Bédard, Y., & Tchounikine, A. (2002). A multidimensional and multiversion structure for OLAP applications. In *Proc. of ACM Int. Workshop on Data Warehousing and OLAP (DOLAP)* (pp. 1-6).

Body, M., Miquel, M., Bedard, Y., & Tchounikine, A. (2003) Handling evolutions in multidimensional structures. In U. Dayal, K. Ramamritham, & T.M. Vijayaraman (Eds.), *Proceedings of the 19th International Conference on Data Engineering* (pp. 581-591). New York: IEEE Computer Society.

Boehnlein, M., & Ulbrich vom Ende, A. (2000). Business process oriented development of data warehouse structures. In *Proceedings of Data Warehousing 2000.* Heidelberg, Germany: Physica Verlag.

Böhnlein, M., & Ulbrich-vom Ende, A. (1999). Deriving initial data warehouse structures from the conceptual data models of the underlying operational information systems. In *Proceedings of the 2nd ACM international workshop on Data warehousing and OLAP,* Kansas City, Missouri (pp. 15-21).

Bonifati, A., Cattaneo, F., Ceri, S., Fuggetta, A., & Paraboschi, S. (2001). Designing data marts for data warehouses. *ACM Transactions on Software Engineering and Methodology, 10*(4), 452–483. doi:10.1145/384189.384190

Boufares, F., & Hamdoun, S. (2005). Integration techniques to build a data warehouse using heterogeneous data sources. *Journal of Computer Science,* 48-55.

Boukraa, D., BenMessaoud, R., & Boussaïd, O. (2006). Proposition d'un modèle physique pour les entrepôts XML. In *Proceedings of the Atelier Systèmes Décisionnels (ASD 06), 9th Maghrebian Conference on Information Technologies (MCSEAI'06),* Agadir, Morocco.

Boussaïd, O., BenMessaoud, R., Choquet, R., & Anthoard, S. (2006). X-warehousing: An XML-based approach for warehousing complex data. In *Proceedings of the 10th East-European Conference on Advances in Databases and Information Systems (ADBIS'06),* Thessaloniki, Greece (LNCS 4152, pp. 39-54). Berlin, Germany: Springer.

Boussaïd, O., Bentayeb, F., & Darmont, J. (2003). A multi-agent system-based ETL approach for complex data. In *Proceedings of the 10th ISPE International Conference on Concurrent Engineering: Research and Applications (CE'03)*, Madeira, Portugal (pp. 49-52).

Boussaïd, O., Darmont, J., Bentayeb, F., & Loudcher-Rabaseda, S. (2008). Warehousing complex data from the Web. *International Journal of Web Engineering and Technology, 4*(4), 408–433. doi:10.1504/IJWET.2008.019942

Boussaïd, O., Darmont, J., Bentayeb, F., & Loudcher-Rabaseda, S. (2008). Warehousing complex data from the Web. [invited paper]. *International Journal of Web Engineering and Technology, 4*(4), 408–433. doi:10.1504/IJWET.2008.019942

Boussaïd, O., Tanasescu, A., Bentayeb, F., & Darmont, J. (2007). Integration and dimensional modelling approaches for complex data warehousing. *Journal of Global Optimization, 37*(4), 571–591. doi:10.1007/s10898-006-9064-6

Bray, T., Paoli, J., Sperberg-McQueen, C., Maler, E., Yergeau, F., & Cowan, J. (2006). *Extensible markup language (XML) 1.1* (W3C Recommendation). Retrieved from http://www.w3.org/TR/2006/REC-xml11-20060816/

Breitbart, Y., Komondoor, R., Rastogi, R., Seshadri, S., & Silberschatz, A. (1999). Update propagation protocols for replicated databases. *SIGMOD Record, 28*(2), 97–108. doi:10.1145/304181.304191

Bresciani, P., Giorgini, P., Giunchiglia, F., Mylopoulos, J., & Perini, A. (2004). Tropos: An agent-oriented software development methodology. *Journal of Autonomous Agents and Multi-Agent Systems, 8*(3), 203–236. doi:10.1023/B:AGNT.0000018806.20944.ef

Brickley, D., & Guha, R. V. (2004). Rdf schema (Technical Report, W3C). Retrieved from, http://www.w3.org/TR/2004/REC-rdfschema- 20040210

Brickley, D., & Guha, R. V. (2004). *RDF Vocabulary Description Language 1.0: RDF Schema*. World Wide Web Consortium. Retrieved from http://www.w3.org/TR/rdf-schema

Bright, M. W., Hurson, A. R., & Pakzad, S. (1994). Automated resolution of semantic heterogeneity in multidatabases. [TODS]. *ACM Transactions on Database Systems, 19*(2), 212–253. doi:10.1145/176567.176569

Broekstra, J., Kampman, A., & van Harmelen, F. (2002). Sesame: A generic architecture for storing and querying RDF and RDF schema. In *Proceedings of the 1st International Semantic Web Conference (ISWC'02)* (pp. 54-68).

Broeskstra, J., & Kampman, A. (2003). SeRQL: A second generation RDF query language. In *SWADEurope Workshop on Semantic Web Storage and Retrieval*.

Bruckner, R., & Tjoa, A. M. (2002). Capturing delays and valid times in data warehouses - towards timely consistent analyses. [JIIS]. *Journal of Intelligent Information Systems, 19*(2), 169–190. doi:10.1023/A:1016555410197

Bruckner, R., List, B., & Schiefer, J. (2001). Developing requirements for data warehouse systems with use cases. In *Proceedings of the 7th Americas Conf. on Information Systems* (pp. 329-335).

Brzsnyi, S., Kossmann, D., & Stocker, K. (2001). The skyline operator. In *Proceedings of 17th International Conference of Data Engineering (ICDE'01)* (pp. 421-430).

Buche, P., Dervin, C., Haemmerlé, O., & Thomopoulos, R. (2005). Fuzzy querying of incomplete, imprecise, and heterogeneously structured data in the relational model using ontologies and rules. *IEEE transactions on Fuzzy Systems, 13*(3), 373–383. doi:10.1109/TFUZZ.2004.841736

Buche, P., Dibie-Barthélemy, J., & Ibanescu, L. (2008). Ontology Mapping using fuzzy conceptual graphs and rules. In P. Eklund & O. Haemmerlé (Eds.), *Supplementary Proceedings of the 16th International Conference on Conceptual Structures* (pp. 17-24).

Buche, P., Soler, L., & Tressou, J. (2006). Le logiciel CARAT. In P. Bertail, M. Feinberg, J. Tressou. & P. Verger (Eds.), *Analyse des risques alimentaires* (pp. 305-333). Lavoisier Tech&Doc.

Cabibbo, L., & Torlone, R. (1998). A logical approach to multidimensional databases. In *Proceedings of the International Conference on Extending Database Technology*, Valencia, Spain (pp. 183-197).

Campi, A., Damiani, E., Guinea, S., Marrara, S., Pasi, G., & Spoletini, P. (2006). A fuzzy extension for the Xpath query language. In *Flexible Query Answering Systems* (LNCS 4027, pp. 210-221). Berlin, Germany: Springer.

Carroll, J. J., Bizer, C., Hayes, P., & Stickler, P. (2005). Named graphs, provenance and trust. In *Proceedings of the 14th international conference on World Wide Web (WWW'05)* (pp. 613-622). New York: ACM Press.

Castano, S., Ferrara, A., Montanelli, S., Hess, G. N., & Bruno, S. (2007). *BOEMIE (bootstrapping ontology evolution with multimedia information extraction). State of the art on ontology coordination and matching* (FP6-027538 Delivrable 4.4). Università degli Studi di Milano.

Castano, S., Martella, G., Samarati, P., & Fugini, M. (1994). *Database Security.* Addison-Wesely, ACM Press.

Cattell, R. G. G. (1993). *The object database standard: ODMG-93.* Morgan Kaufmann.

Ceri, S., & Widom, J. (1993). Managing semantic heterogeneity with production rules and persistent queues source. In *Proceedings of the 19ᵗʰ International Conference on Very Large Data Bases* (pp. 108-119).

Ceri, S., Fraternali, P., & Paraboschi, S. (2000). XML: Current developments and future challenges for the database community. In *Proceedings of the 7ᵗʰ Int. Conf. on Extending Database Technology (EDBT)*, (LNCS 1777). Berlin, Germany: Springer.

Chamoni, P., & Stock, S. (1999). Temporal structures in data warehousing. In Proc. of *Int. Conference on Data Warehousing and Knowledge Discovery (DaWaK)* (LNCS 1676, pp. 353-358).

Chang, C., & Lee, R. C. (1997). *Symbolic logic and mechanical theorem proving.* New York: Academic Press.

Chaudhuri, S., & Dayal, U. (1997). An overview of data warehousing and OLAP technology. *SIGMOD Record, 26*(1), 65–74. doi:10.1145/248603.248616

Chaudhuri, S., & Dayal, U. (1997). An overview of data warehousing and OLAP technology. *SIGMOD Record, 26*(1), 65–74. doi:10.1145/248603.248616

Chaudhuri, S., & Narasayya, V. (2007). Self-tuning database systems: A decade of progress. In *Proceedings of the 33rd International Conference on Very Large Databases (VLDB07)*, Vienna, Austria.

Chen, G., Pan, Y., Guo, M., & Lu, J. (2005). An asynchronous replica consistency model in data grid. In *Proceedings of Parallel and Distributed Processing and Applications - 2005 Workshops* (LNCS 3759, pp. 475-484).

Cherniack, M., Galvez, E. F., Franklin, M. J., & Zdonik, S. B. (2003). Profile-driven cache management. In *Proceedings of 19th International Conference of Data Engineering (ICDE'03)* (pp. 645-656). IEEE Computer Society.

Chervenak, A. L., Palavalli, N., Bharathi, S., Kesselman, C., & Schwartzkopf, R. (2004). Performance and scalability of a replica location service. In *Proceedings of the 13th IEEE international Symposium on High Performance Distributed Computing* (pp.182-191).

Chirkova, R., Halevy, A., & Suciu, D. (2001). *A formal perspective on the view selection problem.* Paper presented at the International Conference on Very Large Databases, Rome, Italy.

Chomicki, J. (2003). Preference formulas in relations queries. [TODS]. *ACM Transactions on Database Systems, 28*(4), 427–466. doi:10.1145/958942.958946

Chong, E. I., Das, S., Eadon, G., & Srinivasan, J. (2005). An efficient SQL based RDF querying scheme. In *Proceedings of the 31st International Conference on Very Large Data Bases (VLDB'05)* (pp. 1216-1227).

Chong, E. I., Das, S., Eadon, G., & Srinivasan, J. (2005). An efficient SQL-based RDF querying scheme. In *Proceedings of the 31st international conference on Very Large Data Bases (VLDB'05)* (pp. 1216-1227).

Chou, P. L., & Zhang, X. (2004). Computing complex iceberg cubes by multiway aggregation and bounding. In *DaWaK* (pp.108-117).

Chung, L., Nixon, B. A., Yu, E., & Mylopoulos, J. (1999). *Non-functional requirements in software*. Berlin, Germany: Springer.

Cluet, S., Delobel, C., Simeon, J., & Smaga, K. (1998). Your mediators need data conversion! In *Proceedings of the SIGMOD'98*, Seattle, USA (pp. 177-188).

Codd, E. F. (1970). A relational model of data for large data banks. *ACM Communications, 13*(6), 377–387. doi:10.1145/362384.362685

Codd, E., Codd, S., & Salley, C. (1994). *Providing OLAP (on-line analytical processing) to user-analysts: An IT mandate* [white paper]. E.F. Codd Associates.

Cohen, P., & Levesque, H. (1990). Intention is choice with commitment. *Artificial Intelligence, 42*(2-3), 213–261. doi:10.1016/0004-3702(90)90055-5

Cohen, W. W. (2000). Data integration using similarity joins and a word-based information representation language. *ACM Transactions on Information Systems, 18*(3), 288–321. doi:10.1145/352595.352598

Cohen, W. W., Ravikumar, P., & Fienberg, S. E. (2003). A comparison of string distance metrics for name-matching tasks. In *Proceedings of the Workshop on Information Integration on the Web* (pp. 73-78).

Colonese, G., Manhaes, R., Montenegro, S., Carvalho, R., & Tanaka, A. (2005). PostGeoOlap: an open-source tool for decision support. In *Proceedings of the 2nd Simpósio Brasileiro de Sistemas de Informação*.

Corby, O., Dieng-Kuntz, R., & Faron-Zucker, C. (2004). Querying the Semantic Web with corese search engine. In *Proceedings of the 16th European Conference on Artificial Intelligence. Subconference PAIS'2004* (pp. 705-709). Amsterdam: IOS Press.

Costa, R. L. C., & Furtado, P. (2008). QoS-oriented reputation-aware query scheduling in data grids. In *Proceedings of the 14th European Conference on Parallel and Distributed Computing (Euro-Par)*.

Costa, R. L. C., & Furtado, P. (2008). Scheduling in Grid databases. In *Proceedings of the 22nd international Conference on Advanced information Networking and Applications – Workshops* (pp. 696-701).

Costa, R. L. C., & Furtado, P. 2008. A QoS-oriented external scheduler. In *Proceedings of the 2008 ACM Symposium on Applied Computing* (pp. 1029-1033). New York: ACM Press.

Cysneiros, L. M., & Sampaio do Prado Leite, J. C. (2004). Nonfunctional requirements: From elicitation to conceptual models. *IEEE Transactions on Software Engineering, 30*(5), 328–350. doi:10.1109/TSE.2004.10

Da Silva, A. S., Filha, I. M. R. E., Laender, A. H. F., & Embley, D. W. (2002). Representing and querying semistructured Web data using nested tables with structural variants. In *Proceedings of the 21st International Conference on Conceptual Modeling* (LNCS 2503, pp. 135-151).

Daoud, M., Tamine, L., Boughanem, M., & Chebaro, B. (2007). Learning implicit user interests using ontology and search history for personalization. *International Web Information Systems Engineering - International Workshop on Personalized Access to Web Information* (WISE-PAWI 2007).

Darmont, J., & Boussaïd, O. (Eds.). (2006). *Managing and processing complex data for decision support*. Hershey, PA: Idea Group Publishing.

Darmont, J., & Olivier, E. (2006). A complex data warehouse for personalized, anticipative medicine. In *Proceedings of the 17th Information Resources Management Association International Conference (IRMA'06)*, Washington, USA (pp. 685-687). Hershey, PA: Idea Group Publishing.

Darmont, J., & Olivier, E. (2008). Biomedical data warehouses. In *Encyclopaedia of healthcare information systems*. Hershey, PA: IGI Global.

Darmont, J., Boussaïd, O., Bentayeb, F., & Sabine Loudcher-Rabaseda, Y. Z. (2003). Web multiform data structuring for warehousing. In *Vol. 22 of Multimedia Systems and Applications* (pp. 179-194). Amsterdam: Kluwer Academic Publishers.

Darmont, J., Boussaïd, O., Ralaivao, J.-C., & Aouiche, K. (2005). An architecture framework for complex data warehouses. In *Proceedings of the 7th International Conference on Enterprise Information Systems (ICEIS'05)*, Miami, USA (pp. 370-373).

Das, G., Hristidis, V., Kapoor, N., & Sudarshan, S. (2006). Ordering the attributes of query results. In S. Chaudhuri, V. Hristidis, & N. Polyzotis (Eds.), *SIGMOD Conference* (pp. 395-406). ACM.

Databasedev.co.uk. (2008). *Sample data models for relational database design*. Retrieved July 30, 2008, from http://www.databasedev.co.uk/data_models.html

Dean, M., & Schreiber, G. (2004). *OWL Web ontology language reference*. World Wide Web Consortium. Retrieved from http://www.w3.org/TR/owl-ref

Dehainsala, H., Pierra, G., & Bellatreche, L. (2007). OntoDB: An ontology-based database for data intensive applications. In *Proceedings of the 12th International Conference on Database Systems for Advanced Applications (DASFAA'07)* (LNCS 4443, pp. 497-508).

Dehainsala, H., Pierra, G., & Bellatreche, L. (2007). OntoDB: An ontology-based database for data intensive applications. In *Proceedings of the 12th International Conference on Database Systems for Advanced Applications (DASFAA'07)* (pp. 497-508).

Demarest, M. (1997). *The politics of data warehousing*. Retrieved August 2008, from http://www.noumenal.com/marc/dwpoly.html

Denning, D. E. (1982). *Cryptography and data security*. Reading, MA: Addison Wesley.

Denning, D. E., & Denning, P. J. (1979). Data security. *ACM Computing Surveys*, *11*(3), 227–249. doi:10.1145/356778.356782

Denning, D. E., & Schlorer, J. (1983, July). Inference controls for statistical databases. *IEEE Computer*.

Deshpande, P. M., Ramasamy, K., Shukla, A., & Naughton, J. F. (1998). Caching multidimensional queries using chunks. In A. Tiwary & M. Franklin (Eds.), *Proceedings of the 1998 ACM SIGMOD international Conference on Management of Data (Seattle, Washington, United States, June 01 - 04, 1998)* (pp. 259-270). New York: ACM Press.

Deshpande, P., & Naughton, J. F. (2000). Aggregate aware caching for multi-dimensional queries. In *Proceedings of the 7th international Conference on Extending Database Technology: Advances in Database Technology vol. 1777* (pp. 167-182).

Deutsch, A., Fernandez, M., & Suciu, D. (1999). Storing semi structured data in relations. In *Proceedings of the Workshop on Query Processing for Semi structured Data and Non-Standard Data Formats*.

Dey, D., Sarkar, S., & De, P. (1998). A probabilistic decision model for entity matching in heterogeneous databases. *Management Science*, *44*(10), 1379–1395. doi:10.1287/mnsc.44.10.1379

Dey, D., Sarkar, S., & De, P. (1998). Entity matching in heterogeneous databases: A distance based decision model. In *Proceedings of the Thirty-First Hawaii International Conference on System Sciences* (pp. 305-313). Washington, DC: IEEE Computer Society.

Doan, A., Domingos, P., & Halevy, A. Y. (2003). Learning to match the schemas of data sources: A multi-strategy approach. *Machine Learning*, *50*(3), 279–301. doi:10.1023/A:1021765902788

Dong, X., Halevy, A., & Madhavan, J. (2005). Reference reconciliation in complex information spaces, In *Proceedings of the ACM SIGMOD International Conference on Management of Data* (pp. 85-96). New York: ACM Press.

Dubois, D., & Prade, H. (1988). *Possibility theory: An approach to computerized processing of uncertainty*. New York: Plenum Press.

Dynamic Information Warehouse, K. A. L. I. D. O. (2004). *A technical overview*. Retrieved May 8, 2007 from http://www.kalido.com

Eder, J., & Koncilia, C. (2001). Changes of dimension data in temporal data warehouses. In Y. Kambayashi, M. Mohania, & W. Wöß (Eds.), *Proceedings of the*

3rd International Conference on Data Warehousing and Knowledge Discovery (pp. 284-293). Heidelberg: Springer.

Eder, J., & Koncilia, C. (2001). Changes of dimension data in temporal data warehouses. In *Proc. of Int. Conference on Data Warehousing and Knowledge Discovery (DaWaK)* (LNCS 2114, pp. 284-293).

Eder, J., & Wiggisser, K. (2008). Modeling transformations between versions of a temporal data warehouse. In *Proceedings of ER 2008 Workshops.* Heidelberg: Springer.

Eder, J., & Wiggisser, K. (2009). Data warehouse maintenance, evolution and versioning. In L. Liu & T. Özsu (Ed.), *Encyclopedia of Database Systems.* Heidelberg: Springer.

Eder, J., Koncilia, C., & Morzy, T. (2002). The COMET metamodel for temporal data warehouses. In A. Pidduck, et al. (Eds.), *Proceedings of the 14th International Conference on Advanced Information Systems Engineering* (pp. 83-99). Heidelberg: Springer

Eder, J., Koncilia, C., & Morzy, T. (2002). The COMET metamodel for temporal data warehouses. In *Proc. of Conference on Advanced Information Systems Engineering (CAiSE)* (LNCS 2348, pp. 83-99).

Eder, J., Koncilia, C., & Wiggisser, K. (2006). Maintaining temporal warehouse models. In L. Xu & A. M. Tjoa (Eds.), *Proceedings of the IFIP International Conference on Research and Practical Issues of Enterprise Information Systems* (pp. 21-30). Heidelberg: Springer.

Engstrom, H., Chakravarthy, S., & Lings, B. (2003). Maintenance policy selection in heterogeneous data warehouse environments: A heuristics-based approach. In *DOLAP Proceedings* (pp. 71-78).

Escribano, A., Gomez, L., Kuijpers, B., & Vaisman, A. (2007). Piet: A GIS-OLAP implementation. In I. Y. Song & T. B. Pedersen (Eds.), *Proceedings of the ACM 10th International Workshop on Data Warehousing and OLAP* (pp. 73-80). New York: ACM Press.

Euzenat, J., & Shvaiko, P. (2007). *Ontology matching.* Berlin, Germany: Springer.

Fankam, C., Jean, S., Bellatreche, L., & Ameur, Y. A. (2008). Extending the ANSI/SPARC architecture database with explicit data semantics: An ontology-based approach. In R. Morrison, D. Balasubramaniam, & K. E. Falkner (Eds.), *Proceedings of the 2nd European Conference on Software Architecture (ECSA'08)* (LNCS 5292, pp.318-321).

Feki, J., & Ben-Abdallah, H. (2007). Multidimensional pattern construction and logical reuse for the design of data marts. *International Review on Computers and Software, 2*(2), 124–134.

Feki, J., & Hachaichi, Y. (2007). Conception assistée de MD: Une démarche et un outil. *Journal of Decision Systems, 16*(3), 303–333. doi:10.3166/jds.16.303-333

Feki, J., & Hachaichi, Y. (2007). Constellation discovery from OLTP parallel-relations. In *Proceedings of the 8th International Arab Conference on Information Technology ACIT 07,* Lattakia, Syria.

Feki, J., & Hachaichi, Y. (2007). Du relationnel au multidimensionnel: Conception de magasins de données. In *Proceedings of the Revue des Nouvelles Technologies de l'Information: Entrepôts de données et analyse en ligne (EDA 2007)* (Vol. B-3, pp. 5-19).

Feki, J., Nabli, A., Ben-Abdallah, H., & Gargouri, F. (2008). An automatic data warehouse conceptual design approach. In *Encyclopedia of data warehousing and mining* (2nd ed.). Hershey, PA: IGI Global.

Fellegi, I. P., & Sunter, A. B. (1969). A theory for record linkage. *Journal of the American Statistical Association, 64*(328), 1183–1210. doi:10.2307/2286061

Fernández-Medina, E., Trujillo, J., Villarroel, R., & Piattini, M. (2006). Access control and audit model for the multidimensional modeling of data warehouses. *Decision Support Systems, 42*(3), 1270–1289. doi:10.1016/j.dss.2005.10.008

Fernández-Medina, E., Trujillo, J., Villarroel, R., & Piattini, M. (2006). Access control and audit model for the multidimensional modeling of data warehouses. *Decision Support Systems, 42*(3), 1270–1289. doi:10.1016/j.dss.2005.10.008

Ferraiolo, D. F., & Kuhn, R. (1992, October). Role-based access control (rbac). In *Proc. 15th NIST-NSA National Computer Security Conference*. Baltimore, MD.

Forbus, K. D., & De Kleer, J. (1993). *Building problem solvers*. Cambridge, MA: MIT Press.

Foster, I. Kesselman, C. Nick, J., & Tuecke, S. (2002). *The physiology of the grid: An open grid services architecture for distributed systems integration* (Globus Project Tech Report).

Foster, I. T. (2001). The anatomy of the grid: Enabling scalable virtual organizations. In *Proceedings of the 7th international Euro-Par Conference on Parallel Processing* (LNCS 2150, pp. 1-4).

Foster, I., Kesselman, C., Tsudik, G., & Tuecke, S. (1998). A security architecture for computational grids. In *Proceedings of the 5th ACM Conference on Computer and Communications Security. CCS '98* (pp. 83-92).

Franconi, E., & Kamble, A. (2004). A data warehouse conceptual data model. In *Proceedings of the International Conference on Statistical and Scientific Database Management*, Santorini Island, Greece (pp. 435-436).

Franklin, C. (1992). An introduction to geographic information systems: Linking maps to databases. *Database, 15*(2), 13–21.

Freitag, D., & Kushmerick, N. (2000). Boosted wrapper induction. In *Proceedings of the 17th National Conference on Artificial Intelligence and 20th Conference on Innovative Applications of Artificial Intelligence* (pp. 577-583). Menlo Park, CA: AAAI Press.

Froeschl, K., Yamada, T., & Kudrna, R. (2002). Industrial statistics revisited: From footnotes to meta-information management. *Österreichische Zeitschrift für Statistik, 31*(1), 9-34.

Furtado, P. (2004). Experimental evidence on partitioning in parallel data warehouses. In *Proceedings of the ACM DOLAP 04 - Workshop of the International Conference on Information and Knowledge Management*, Washington USA.

Furtado, P. (2004). Experimental evidence on partitioning in parallel data warehouses. In *Proceedings of the 7th ACM international Workshop on Data Warehousing and OLAP* (pp. 23-30).

Furtado, P. (2004). Workload-based placement and join processing in node-partitioned data warehouses. In *Proceedings of the International Conference on Data Warehousing and Knowledge Discovery* (pp. 38-47), Zaragoza, Spain.

Furtado, P. (2004). Workload-based placement and join processing in node-partitioned data warehouses. In *Proceedings of the 6th International Conference on Data Warehousing and Knowledge Discovery* (LNCS 3181, pp. 38-47).

Furtado, P. (2005). Efficiently processing query-intensive databases over a non-dedicated local network. In *Proceedings of the 19th International Parallel and Distributed Processing Symposium*.

Furtado, P. (2005). Replication in node-partitioned data warehouses. *DDIDR2005 Workshop of VLDB 2005*.

Furtado, P. (2007). Efficient and robust node-partitioned data warehouses. In R. Wrembel and C. Koncilia (Eds.), *Data warehouses and OLAP: Concepts, architectures and solutions* (pp. 203-229). Hershey, PA: IGI Global.

Gardarin, G. (2002). *Des bases de données aux services Web*. Edition Dunod - Paris.

Ghozzi, F., Ravat, F., Teste, O., & Zurfluh, G. (2003). *Constraints and multidimensional databases*. In *Proceedings of the International Conference Enterprise CEIS* (pp. 104-111).

Giorgini, P., Rizzi, S., & Garzetti, M. (2008). GRAnD: A goal-oriented approach to requirement analysis in data warehouses. *Decision Support Systems, 45*(1), 4–21. doi:10.1016/j.dss.2006.12.001

Giorgini, P., Rizzi, S., & Maddalena, G. (2005). Goal-oriented requirement analysis for data warehouse design. In *Proceedings of the ACM Eighth International Workshop on Data Warehousing and OLAP*, Bremen, Germany (pp 47-56).

Golfarelli, M. (2008). The DFM: A conceptual model for data warehouse. In J. Wang (Ed.), *Encyclopedia of data warehousing and mining* (2nd ed.). Hershey, PA: IGI Global.

Golfarelli, M., & Rizzi, S. (2001). WanD: A CASE tool for data warehouse design. In *Demo Proceedings of the 17th International Conference on Data Engineering (ICDE 2001)*, Heidelberg, Germany (pp. 7-9).

Golfarelli, M., & Rizzi, S. (2009). A survey on temporal data warehousing. [IJDWM]. *International Journal of Data Warehousing and Mining, 5*(1), 1–17.

Golfarelli, M., Lechtenbörger, J., Rizzi, S., & Vossen, G. (2004). Schema versioning in data warehouses. In S. Wang et al. (Eds.), *Conceptual Modeling for Advanced Application Domains, ER 2004 Workshops* (pp. 415-428). Heidelberg: Springer.

Golfarelli, M., Lechtenbörger, J., Rizzi, S., & Vossen, G. (2004). Schema versioning in data warehouses. In *Proc. of ER Workshops* (LNCS 3289, pp. 415-428).

Golfarelli, M., Lechtenbörger, J., Rizzi, S., & Vossen, G. (2006). Schema versioning in data warehouses: Enabling cross-version querying via schema augmentation. *Data & Knowledge Engineering, 59*(2), 435–459. doi:10.1016/j.datak.2005.09.004

Golfarelli, M., Maio, D., & Rizzi, S. (1998). Conceptual design of data warehouses from E/R schemas. In *Proceedings of the Conference on System Sciences*, Kona, Hawaii. Washington, DC, USA: IEEE Computer Society.

Golfarelli, M., Maio, D., & Rizzi, S. (1998). The dimensional fact model: A conceptual model for data warehouses. *International Journal of Cooperative Information Systems, 7*(2-3), 215–247. doi:10.1142/S0218843098000118

Golfarelli, M., Rizzi, S., & Vrdoljak, B. (2001). Data warehouse design from XML sources. In *Proceedings of the 4th International Workshop on Data Warehousing and OLAP (DOLAP'01)*, Atlanta, USA (pp. 40-47). New York: ACM Press.

Golfarelli, M., Rizzi, S., & Vrdoljak, B. (2001). Data warehouse design from XML sources. In *Proceedings of the Fourth ACM International Workshop on Data Warehousing and OLAP* Atlanta, GA, USA (pp. 40-47).

Golub, G. H., & Loan, C. F. V. (1996). *Matrix computations* (3rd ed.). Baltimore, MD, USA: Johns Hopkins University Press.

Gruber, T. R. (1993). A translation approach to portable ontology specifications. *Knowledge Acquisition, 5*(2), 199–220. doi:10.1006/knac.1993.1008

Guarino, N. (1998). Formal ontology and information systems. In N. Guarino (Ed.), *Proceedings of the 1st International Conference on Formal Ontologies in Information Systems (FOIS'98)* (pp. 315). IOS Press.

Guimaraes, M. (2006). New challenges in teaching database security. In *InfoSecCD '06: Proceedings of the 3rd annual conference on Information security curriculum development* (pp. 64-67). New York: ACM.

Guo, Y., Tang, S., Tong, Y., & Yang, D. (2006). Triple-driven data modeling methodology in data warehousing: A case study. In *Proceedings of the ACM International Workshop on Data Warehousing and OLAP* (pp. 59-66).

Gupta, A., & Mumick, I. (1995). Maintenance of materialized views: Problems, techniques, and applications. *Data Engineering Bulletin, 18*(2), 3–18.

Gupta, H., & Mumick, I. S. (1999). *Selection of views to materialize under a maintenance cost constraint.* Paper presented at the 7th International Conference on Database Theory.

Gurský, P., Horváth T., Jirásek J., Krajči S., Novotný R., Pribolová J.,Vaneková V., & Vojtáš P. (2008). User preference Web search – Experiments with a system connecting Web and user. *Computing and Informatics Journal*, 25-32.

Gyssens, M., & Lakshmanan, L. V. S. (1997). A foundation for multidimensional databases. In *Proc. of Int. Conference on Very Large Data Bases (VLDB)* (pp. 106-115).

Haase, P., Broekstra, J., Eberhart, A., & Volz, R. (2004). A comparison of RDF Query languages. In *Proceedings of the 3nd International Semantic Web Conference (ISWC'04)* (pp. 502-517).

Hachaichi, Y., & Feki, J. (2007). Patron multidimensionnel et MDA pour les entrepôts de données. In *Proceedings of the 2ⁿᵈ Workshop on Decisional Systems*, Sousse-Tunisia.

Hachaichi, Y., Feki, J., & Ben-Abdallah, H. (2008). Du XML au multidimensionnel: Conception de magasins de données. In *Proceedings of the 4èmes journées francophones sur les Entrepôts de Données et l Analyse en ligne (EDA 2008), Toulouse, RNTI*, Toulouse, France (Vol. B-4. pp. 45-59).

Hachaichi, Y., Feki, J., & Ben-Abdallah, H. (2008). XML source preparation for building data warehouses. In *Proceedings of the International Conference on Enterprise Information Systems and Web Technologies EISWT-08*, Orlando, Florida, USA (pp. 61-67).

Haddad, C., & Slimani, Y. (2007). Economic model for replicated database placement in Grid. In *Proceedings of the Seventh IEEE international Symposium on Cluster Computing and the Grid* (pp. 283-292). IEEE Computer Society.

Halevy, A. (2001). Answering queries using views: A survey. *The VLDB Journal, 10*(4), 270–294. doi:10.1007/s007780100054

Hamdoun S., Boufarès F. & Badri M. (2007). Construction et maintenance des entrepôts de données hétérogènes. *Revue e-TI, (4)*.

Hamdoun, S. (2006). *Construction d entrepôts de données par intégration de sources hétérogènes*. PhD thesis, University Paris Nord.

Han, J., Kopersky, K., & Stefanovic, N. (1997). GeoMiner: A system prototype for spatial data mining. In J. Peckham (Ed.), *Proceedings of the ACM SIGMOD International Conference on Management of Data* (pp. 553-556). New York: ACM Press.

Harris, S., & Gibbins, N. (2003). 3store: Efficient bulk RDF storage. In *Proceedings of the 1st International Workshop on Practical and Scalable Semantic Systems (PSSS'03)* (pp. 1-15).

Hayes, P. (2004). *RDF semantics*. Retrieved from http://www.w3.org/TR/rdf-mt/

Henschen, L. J., & Wos, L. (1974). Unit refutations and horn sets. [ACM]. *Journal of the Association for Computing Machinery, 21*(4), 590–605.

Hignette, G., Buche, P., Dibie-Barthélemy, J., & Haemmerlé, O. (2007). An ontology-driven annotation of data tables. In *Proceedings of the Web Information Systems Engineering – WISE 2007 Workshops* (LNCS 4832, pp. 29-40). Berlin, Germany: Springer.

Horrocks, I., Patel-Schneider, P. F., Boley, H., Tabet, S., Grosof, B., & Dean, M. (2004). *SWRL: A Semantic Web rule language combining OWL and RuleML* (W3C Member Submission). Retrieved from http://www.w3.org/Submission/SWRL

Hsiao, H., & DeWitt, D. (1990). Chained declustering: A new availability strategy for multi-processor database machines. *Intl. Conf. on Data Engineering*.

Hsiao, H., & DeWitt, D. (1990). Replicated data management in the gamma database machine. *Workshop on the Management of Replicated Data*.

Hsiao, H., & DeWitt, D. J. (1991). A performance study of three high availability data replication strategies. In *Proceedings of the Parallel and Distributed Systems*.

Hull, R. (1997). Managing semantic heterogeneity in databases: A theoretical prospective. In *Proceedings of the sixteenth ACM SIGACT-SIGMOD-SIGART symposium on Principles of database systems*, Tucson, AZ, USA (pp. 51-61).

Hümmer, W., Bauer, A., & Harde, G. (2003). XCube: XML for data warehouses. In *Proceedings of the 6ᵗʰ International Workshop on Data Warehousing and OLAP (DOLAP'03)*, New Orleans, USA (pp. 33-40). New York: ACM Press.

Hurtado, C., Mendelzon, A., & Vaisman, A. (1999). Updating OLAP Dimensions. In *Proceedings of the ACM Second International Workshop on Data Warehousing and OLAP* (pp. 60-66), New York: ACM Press.

Hüsemann, B., Lechtenbörger, J., & Vossen, G. (2000). Conceptual data warehouse design. In *Proceedings of the International Workshop on Design and Management of Data Warehouses*. Stockholm, Sweden (pp. 3-9).

Hutardo, C. A., Poulovassilis, A., & Wood, P. T. (2006). A relaxed approach to RDF querying. In *Proceedings of the 5th International Semantic Web Conference* (LNCS 4273, pp. 314-328). Berlin, Germany: Springer.

Huynh, T. D., Jennings, N. R., & Shadbolt, N. R. (2006). An integrated trust and reputation model for open multi-agent systems. *Autonomous Agents and Multi-Agent Systems*, *13*(2), 119–154. doi:10.1007/s10458-005-6825-4

Hwang, K., Jin, H., & Ho, R. S. C. (2002). Orthogonal striping and mirroring in distributed RAID for I/O-centric cluster computing. *IEEE Transactions on Parallel and Distributed Systems*, *13*(1), 26–44. doi:10.1109/71.980025

IBM. (2008). IBM DB2 Server. Retrieved from http://www.ibm.com/db2.

IEC61360-4 (1999). *Standard data element types with associated classification scheme for electric components - Part 4: IEC reference collection of standard data element types, component classes and terms* (Tech. Rep., International Standards Organization).

Inmon, W. (2005) *Building the data warehouse* (4th ed.) New York: John Wiley & Sons.

Inmon, W. (2005). *Building the data warehouse* (4th ed.). New York: John Wiley & Sons.

Inmon, W. H. (1995). Multidimensional databases and data warehousing. *Data Management Review*.

Inmon, W. H. (1996). *Building the data warehouse* (2nd ed.). New York: John Wiley & Sons.

Inmon, W. H. (1996). *Building the data warehouse*. New York: John Wiley & Sons.

Ireland, J. D., & Moller, A. (2000). Review of international food classification and description. *Journal of food composition and analysis*, *13*, 529-538.

IS010303.02 (1994). *Product data representation and exchange Part 2: Express reference manual*. ISO-055.

Jarke, M., Lenzerini, M., Vassiliou, Y., & Vassiliadis, P. (2003). *Fundamentals of data warehouses*. Springer-Verlag.

Jean, S. (2007). *OntoQL, un langage d'exploitation des bases de donnes base ontologique*. PhD thesis, LISI/ENSMA and University of Poitiers.

Jean, S., Aït-Ameur, Y., & Pierra, G. (2006). Querying ontology based database using OntoQL (an Ontology Query Language). In *Proceedings of On the Move to Meaningful Internet Systems 2006: CoopIS, DOA, GADA, and ODBASE, OTM Confederated International Conferences (ODBASE'06)* (LNCS 4275, pp. 704-721).

Jean, S., Aït-Ameur, Y., & Pierra, G. (2006). Querying ontology based database using OntoQL (an Ontology Query Language). In *Proceedings of On the Move to Meaningful Internet Systems 2006: CoopIS, DOA, GADA, and ODBASE, OTM Confederated International Conferences (ODBASE'06)*, (LNCS 4275, pp. 704-721).

Jean, S., Aït-Ameur, Y., & Pierra, G. (2007). An object-oriented based algebra for ontologies and their instances. In *Proceedings of the 11th East European Conference in Advances in Databases and Information Systems (ADBIS'07)* (LNCS 4690, pp. 141-156).

Jean, S., Pierra, G., & Ait-ameur, Y. (2005). OntoQL: An exploitation language for OBDBS. In *VLDB Ph.D. Workshop* (pp. 41-45).

Jean, S., Pierra, G., & Aït-Ameur, Y. (2007). Domain ontologies: A database-oriented analysis, *Lecture Notes in Business Information Processing: Volume 1* (pp. 238-254). Berlin: Springer.

Jensen, M., Holmgren, T., & Pedersen, T. (2004). Discovering multidimensional structure in relational data. In *Proceedings of the International Conference on Data Warehousing and Knowledge Discovery*, Zaragoza, Spain (pp. 138-148).

Jensen, M., Møller, T., & Pedersen, T. B. (2001). Specifying OLAP cubes on XML data. *Journal of Intelligent Information Systems.*

Kaas, C., Pedersen, T. B., & Rasmussen, B. (2004). Schema evolution for stars and snowflakes. In *Proceedings of the 6th International Conference on Enterprise Information Systems* (pp. 425-433).

Kalfoglou, Y., & Schorlemmer, M. (2003). Ontology mapping: The state of the art. *The Knowledge Engineering Review, 18*(1), 1–31. doi:10.1017/S0269888903000651

Kappel, G., Kapsammer, E., & Retschitzegger, W. (2001). XML and relational database systems - a comparison of concepts. In *Proceedings of the International Conference on Internet Computing (1)* (pp. 199-205).

Kappel, G., Kapsammer, E., Rausch-Schott, S., & Retschitzegger, W. (2000). X-ray - towards integrating XML and relational database systems. In *Proceedings of the 19th Int. Conf. on Conceptual Modeling (ER)*, Salt Lake City, USA (LNCS 1920). Berlin, Germany: Springer.

Karvounarakis, G., Magkanaraki, A., Alexaki, S., Christophides, V., Plexousakis, D., Scholl, M., & Tolle, K. (2004). RQL: A functional query language for RDF. In P. M. D. Gray, L. Kerschberg, P. J. H.King, & A. Poulovassilis (Eds.), *The functional approach to data management: Modelling, analyzing and integrating heterogeneous data.* (LNCS, pp. 435-465).

Kießling, W. (2002). Foundations of preferences in database systems. In N. J. I. Mars (Ed.), *Knowledge and data engineering* (pp. 311-322). Amsterdam: IOS Press.

Kießling, W., & Kostler, G. (2000). Preference sql -design, implementation, experience. In N. J. I. Mars (Ed.), *Knowledge and data engineering* (pp. 778-789). Amsterdam: IOS Press.

Kifer, M., Lausen, G., & Wu, J. (1995). Logical foundations of object-oriented and frame-based languages. *Journal of the ACM, 42*(4), 741–843. doi:10.1145/210332.210335

Kim, H. H., & Park, S. S. (2003). Building a Web-enabled multimedia data warehouse. *In Proceedings of the Web Communication Technologies and Internet-Related Social Issues (HSI2003)* (LNCS 2713, pp. 594-600).

Kimbal, R., Reeves, L., Ross, M., & Thornthwaite, W. (1998). *The data warehouse lifecycle toolkit.* New York: John Wiley and Sons, Inc

Kimball, R. (1996). Slowly changing dimensions. *DBMS Magazine, 9*(4), 14.

Kimball, R., & Ross, M. (2002). *The data warehouse toolkit* (2nd ed.). New York: John Wiley & Sons.

Kimball, R., Reeves, L., Ross, M., & Thornthwaite, W. (1998). *The data warehouse lifecycle toolkit.* New York: John Wiley & Sons.

Koffina, I., Serfiotis, G., & Christophides, V. (2006). Mediating RDF/S queries to relational and XML sources. *International Journal on Semantic Web and Information Systems, 2*(4), 78–91.

Kotidis, Y., & Roussopoulos, N. (1999). DynaMat: *A dynamic view management system for data warehouses.* Paper presented at the ACM SIGMOD International Conference on Management of Data, Philadelphia, United States.

Kouba, Z., Matousek, K., & Miksovsky, P. (2000). On data warehouse and GIS integration. In M. Ibrahim, J. Kung, & N. Revell (Eds.), *Proceedings of the 11th International Conference on Database and Expert Systems Applications* (Vol. 1873, pp. 604-613). London: Springer.

Koutrika, G., & Ioannidis, Y. E. (2004). Personalization of queries in database systems. In *Proceedings of 20th International Conference of Data Engineering (ICDE'04)* (pp. 597-608).

Krauter, K., Buyya, R., & Maheswaran, M. (2002). A taxonomy and survey of grid resource management systems for distributed computing. *Software, Practice & Experience, 32*(2), 135–164. doi:10.1002/spe.432

Landwehr, C. E. (2001). Computer security. *International Journal of Information Security, 1*(1), 3–13.

Lassila, O., Swick, R. R. (1999, February 22). Resource description framework (RDF) model and syntax specification. *World Wide Web Consortium W3C Recommendation.*

Laurent, D., Lechtenborger, J., Spyratos, N., & Vossen, G. (2001). Monotonic complements for independent data warehouses. *The VLDB Journal, 10*(4), 295–315. doi:10.1007/s007780100055

Lawrence, M., & Rau-Chaplin, A. (2006). The OLAP-Enabled Grid: Model and query processing algorithms. In *Proc. of the 20th international Symposium on High-Performance Computing in An Advanced Collaborative Environment (HPCS)*.

Lechtenboerger, J., & Vossen, G. (2003). Multidimensional normal forms for data warehouse design. *Information Systems, 28*(5), 415–434. doi:10.1016/S0306-4379(02)00024-8

Lee, D., & Chu, W. (2000). Constraints-preserving transformation from XML document type definition to relational schema. In *Proceedings of the 19th Int. Conf. on Conceptual Modeling (ER)*, Salt Lake City, USA (LNCS 1920). Berlin, Germany: Springer.

Lee, E. K., & Chandramohan, A. Thekkath, P. (1996). Distributed virtual disks. In *Proceedings of the Seventh International Conference on Architectural Support for Programming Languages and Operating Systems*.

Lellahi, S. K. (2002). Modelling data and objects: An algebraic viewpoint. *Theoretical aspects of computer science, advanced lectures (First summer school on theoretical aspects of computer science) (. LNCS, 2292*, 113–147.

Lerner, A. (1998). *An architecture for the load-balanced parallel join operation in shared-nothing environments* (in Portuguese). M.Sc. Dissertation, Computer Science Department, Pontificia Univ. Catolica do Rio de Janeiro.

Lerner, A., & Lifschitz, S. (1998). A study of workload balancing techniques on parallel join algorithms. In *Proceedings of the International Conference on Parallel and Distributed Processing Techniques and Applications (PDPTA)* (pp. 966-973).

Letz, C., Henn, E. T., & Vossen, G. (2002). Consistency in data warehouse dimensions. In *Proc. of Int. Database Engineering and Application Symposium (IDEAS)* (pp. 224-232).

Lima, A. A. B., Mattoso, M., & Valduriez, P. (2004). OLAP query processing in a database cluster. In *Proc. 10th Euro-Par Conf.*

Lima, A. A., Mattoso, M., & Valduriez, P. (2004). *Adaptive virtual partitioning for OLAP query processing in a database cluster*. Paper presented at the 19th Brasilian Simposium on Databases SBBD, Brasília, Brasil.

Lima, A., Mattoso, M., & Valduriez, P. (2004). Adaptive virtual partitioning for OLAP query processing in a database cluster. In *Proceedings of the Brazilian Symposium on Databases (SBBD)* (pp. 92-105).

Lin, Y., Liu, P., & Wu, J. (2006). Optimal placement of replicas in data grid environments with locality assurance. In *Proceedings of the 12th international Conference on Parallel and Distributed Systems - Vol 1 (2006)* (pp. 465-474).

List, B., Bruckner, R. M., Machacze, K., & Schiefer, J. (2002). A comparison of data warehouse development methodologies case study of the process warehouse. In *Proceedings of the International Conference on Database and Expert Systems Applications DEXA*

List, B., Bruckner, R., Machaczek, K., & Schiefer, J. (2002). A comparison of data warehouse development methodologies: Case study of the process warehouse. In *Proceedings of the International Conference on Database and Expert Systems Applications* (pp. 203-215).

Longley, P., Goodchild, M., Maguire, D., & Rhind, D. (2001). *Geographic information systems and science*. New York: John Wiley & Sons.

Loukides, G., & Shao, J. (2007). Capturing data usefulness and privacy protection in k-anonymisation. In *SAC '07: Proceedings of the 2007 ACM symposium on Applied computing* (pp. 370-374). New York: ACM.

Loukopoulos, T., & Ahmad, I. (2000). Static and adaptive data replication algorithms for fast information access in large distributed systems. In *Proc. of the 20th Intern. Conference on Distributed Computing Systems (ICDCS)*.

Luján-Mora, S., Trujillo, J., & Song, I. Y. (2006). A UML profile for multidimensional modeling in data warehouses. *Data & Knowledge Engineering, 59*(3), 725–769. doi:10.1016/j.datak.2005.11.004

Ma, L., Su, Z., Pan, Y., Zhang, L., & Liu, T. (2004). RStar: An RDF storage and query system for enterprise resource management. In *Proceedings of the 30th International Conference on Information and Knowledge Management (CIKM'04)* (pp. 484-491).

MacEachren, A., & Kraak, M. (1997). Exploratory cartographic visualization: Advancing the agenda. *Computers & Geosciences, 23*(4), 335–343. doi:10.1016/S0098-3004(97)00018-6

MacEachren, A., Gahegan, M., Pike, W., Brewer, I., Cai, G., Lengerich, E., & Hardisty, F. (2004). Geovisualization for knowledge construction and decision support. *IEEE Computer graphics and application, 24*(1) 13-17.

Machanavajjhala, A., Gehrke, J., Kifer, D., & Venkitasubramaniam, M. (2006). L-diversity: Privacy beyond k-anonymity. In *ICDE '06: Proceedings of the 22nd International Conference on Data Engineering (ICDE'06)*, 24, Washington, DC: IEEE Computer Society.

Magiridou, M., Sahtouris, S., Christophides, V., & Koubarakis, M. (2005). RUL: A declarative update language for RDF. In *Proceedings of the 4th International Semantic Web Conference (ISWC'05)* (pp. 506-521).

Magkanaraki, A., Tannen, V., Christophides, V., & Plexousakis, D. (2004). Viewing the Semantic Web through RVL lenses. *Journal of Web Semantics, 1*(4), 359–375. doi:10.1016/j.websem.2004.06.004

Mahboubi, H., & Darmont, J. (2007). Indices in XML databases. In *Encyclopedia of database technologies and applications, second edition*. Hershey, PA: IGI Global.

Mahboubi, H., Aouiche, K., & Darmont, J. (2006). Materialized view selection by query clustering in XML data warehouses. In *Proceedings of the 4th International Multiconference on Computer Science and Information Technology (CSIT'06)*, Amman, Jordan (pp. 68-77).

Mahboubi, H., Aouiche, K., & Darmont, J. (2008). A join index for XML data warehouses. In *Proceedings of the*

2008 *International Conference on Information Resources Management (Conf-IRM'08)*, Niagara Falls, Canada.

Malinowski, E., & Zimányi, E. (2004). OLAP hierarchies: A conceptual perspective. In J. Persson & J. Stirna (Eds.), *Proceedings of the 16th International Conference on Advanced Information Systems Engineering* (pp. 477-491). Heidelberg: Springer.

Malinowski, E., & Zimányi, E. (2006). A conceptual solution for representing time in data warehouse dimensions. In M. Stumptner, S. Hartmann, & Y. Kiyoki (Eds.), *Proceedings of the 3rd Asia-Pacific Conference on Conceptual Modelling* (pp 45-54). Newcastle: CRPIT

Malinowski, E., & Zimányi, E. (2008). *Advanced data warehouse design: from conventional to spatial and temporal applications*. Springer.

Malinowsky, E., & Zimányi, E. (2004). Representing spatiality in a conceptual multidimensional model. In D. Pfoser, I. Cruz, & M. Ronthaler (Eds.), *Proceedings of the 12th ACM International Workshop on Geographic Information Systems* (pp. 12-22). New York: ACM Press.

Malinowsky, E., & Zimányi, E. (2005). Spatial hierarchies and topological relationships in SpatialMultiDimER model. In M. Jackson, D. Nelson, & S. Stirk (Eds.), *Proceedings of the 22nd British National Conference on Databases* (Vol. 3567, pp. 17-28). Berlin, Germany: Springer.

Malinowsky, E., & Zimányi, E. (2007). Logical representation of a conceptual model for spatial data warehouses. *Geoinformatica*.

Marchand, P., Brisebois, A., Bédad, Y., & Edwards, G. (2003). Implementation and evaluation of a hypercube-based method for spatio-temporal exploration and analysis. *Journal of the International Society of Photogrammetry and Remote Sensing, 59*(1), 6–20. doi:10.1016/j.isprsjprs.2003.12.002

Matias, R., & Moura-Pires, J. (2005). Spatial on-line analytical processing: A tool to analyze the emission of pollutants in industrial installations. In C. Bento, A. Cardoso, & G. Dias (Eds.), *Proceedings of the 5th International Workshop on Extraction of Knowledge from Databases and Warehouses*.

Mazon, J. N., & Trujillo, J. (2008). An MDA approach for the development of data warehouses. *Decision Support Systems, 45*(1), 41–58. doi:10.1016/j.dss.2006.12.003

Mazon, J. N., Trujillo, J., & Lechtenboerger, J. (2007). Reconciling requirement-driven data warehouses with data sources via multidimensional normal forms. *Data & Knowledge Engineering, 63*, 725–751. doi:10.1016/j.datak.2007.04.004

Mazón, J.-N., & Trujillo, J. (2008). An MDA approach for the development of data warehouses. *Decision Support Systems, 45*(1), 41–58. doi:10.1016/j.dss.2006.12.003

Mc Meekin, T. A., Baranyi, J., Bowman, J., Dalgaard, P., Kirk, M., & Ross, T. (2006). Information systems in food safety management. *International Journal of Food Microbiology, 112*(3), 181–194. doi:10.1016/j.ijfoodmicro.2006.04.048

McBride, B. (2004). The resource description framework (RDF) and its vocabulary description language RDFS. In S. Staab & R. Studer (Eds.), *Handbook on ontologies* (pp. 51-66). Berlin, Germany: Springer.

McGuinness, D. L., & Van Harmelen, F. (2004). *OWL: Web ontology language overview* (W3C recommendation). Retrieved from http://www.w3.org/TR/owl-features

McGuinness, D., Fikes, R., Hendler, J., & Stein, L. A. (2002). DAML+OIL: An ontology language for the Semantic Web. *IEEE Intelligent Systems, 17*(5), 72–80. doi:10.1109/MIS.2002.1039835

Meier, W. (2002). eXist: An open source native XML database. In *Proceedings of the Web, Web-services, and database systems, NODe 2002 Web and Database-Related Workshops*, Erfurt, Germany (LNCS 2593, pp. 169-183). Berlin, Germany: Springer.

Mendelzon, A. O., & Vaisman, A. A. (2000). Temporal queries in OLAP. In *Proc. of Int. Conference on Very Large Data Bases (VLDB)* (pp. 242-253).

Miller, L., Seaborne, A., & Reggiori, A. (2002). Three implementations of SquishQL, a simple RDF query language. In *Proceedings of the 1st International Semantic Web Conference (ISWC'02)* (pp. 423-435).

Mitre Corporation (1997, April). *Integrity considerations for secure computer systems.* (Technical Report esdtr-76-372, esd,/afsc, mtr 3153). Bedford, MA: Mitre Corporation.

Mizoguchi-Shimogori, Y., Murayama, H., & Minamino, N. (2002). Class query language and its application to ISO13584 parts library standard. In *Proceedings of the 9th European Concurrent Engineering Conference (ECEC'02)* (pp. 128-135).

Mohraz, K. (2000). Geographical analysis in SAP business information warehouse. In K. Li, K. Makki, N. Pissinou, & S. Ravada (Eds.), *Proceedings of the 8th ACM Symposium on Advances in Geographic Information Systems* (pp. 191-193). Washington: ACM Press.

Moody, D., & Kortnik, M. (2000). From enterprise models to dimensional models: A methodology for data warehouse and data mart design. In *Proceedings of the DMDW'00*, Suede.

Morzy, T., & Wrembel, R. (2004). On querying versions of multiversion data warehouse. In *Proc. of ACM Int. Workshop on Data Warehousing and OLAP (DOLAP)* (pp. 92-101).

Mouloudi, H., Bellatreche, L., Giacometti, A., & Marcel, P. (2006). Personalization of MDX queries. In *Actes Bases de Données Avancées (BDA 2006)*, Informal Proceedings.

Mylopoulos, J., Chung, L., & Nixon, B. (1992). Representing and using non-functional requirements: A process-oriented approach. *IEEE Transactions on Software Engineering, 18*(6), 483–497. doi:10.1109/32.142871

Nassis, V., Rajugan, R., Dillon, T. S., & Rahayu, J. W. (2004). Conceptual design of XML document warehouses. In *Proceedings of the 6th International Conference on Data Warehousing and Knowledge Discovery (DaWaK'04)*, Zaragoza, Spain (LNCS 3181, pp. 1-14). Berlin, Germany: Springer.

Nassis, V., Rajugan, R., Dillon, T. S., & Rahayu, J. W. (2005). A requirement engineering approach for designing XML-view driven, XML document warehouses. In *Proceedings of the 29th International Conference on*

Computer Software and Applications (COMPSAC '05), Edinburgh, UK (pp. 388-395). Washington, DC: IEEE Computer Society.

Nassis, V., Rajugan, R., Dillon, T. S., & Rahayu, J. W. (2005). Conceptual and systematic design approach for XML document warehouses. *International Journal of Data Warehousing and Mining, 1*(3), 63–86.

Newcombe, H. B., & Kennedy, J. M. (1962). Record linkage: Making maximum use of the discriminating power of identifying information. *Communications of the ACM, 5*(11), 563–566. doi:10.1145/368996.369026

Newcombe, H. B., Kennedy, J. M., Axford, S. J., & James, A. P. (1959). Automatic linkage of vital records. *Science, 130*, 954–959. doi:10.1126/science.130.3381.954

Nieto-Santisteban, M. A., Gray, J., Szalay, A., Annis, J., Thakar, A. R., & O'Mullane, W. (2005). When database systems meet the grid. In *CIDR* (pp. 154-161).

Noy, N. F. (2004). Semantic integration: A survey of ontology-based approaches. *SIGMOD Record, 33*(4), 65–70. doi:10.1145/1041410.1041421

Nyanchama, M., & Osborn, S. (1994). Ifip wg 11.3 working conf. on database security. database security viii: Status and prospects. In *Proc. 15th Annual Computer Security Applications Conference*. North-Holland.

O'Gorman, K., Agrawal, D., & El Abbadi, A. (1999). Posse: A framework for optimizing incremental view maintenance at data warehouse. In *DaWaK '99, London, UK* (pp. 106-115). Springer-Verlag.

Orlando, S., Orsini, R., Raffaetà, A., Roncato, A., & Silvestri, C. (2007). Spatio-temporal aggregations in trajectory data warehouses. In I. Y. Song, J. Eder, & T. M. Nguyen (Eds.), *Proceedings of the 9th International Conference Data Warehousing and Knowledge Discovery* (Vol. 4654, pp. 66-77). Berlin, Germany: Springer.

Osborn, S., Sandhu, R. S., & Munawer, Q. (2000). Configuring role-based access control to enforce mandatory and discretionary access control policies. *ACM Transactions on Information and System Security, 3*(2), 85–206. doi:10.1145/354876.354878

Ouaret, Z., Bellatreche, L., & Boussaid, O. (2007). XUML star: Conception d'un entrepôt de données XML. In *Proceedings of the Atelier des Systèmes d Information Décisionnels*, Sousse, Tunisie (pp. 19-20).

Paim, F. R. S., & Castro, J. (2002). Enhancing data warehouse design with the NFR framework. In *Proceedings of the Workshop em Engenharia de Requisitos*, Valencia, Spain (pp. 40-57).

Paim, F. R. S., & Castro, J. (2003). DWARF: An approach for requirements definition and management of data warehouse systems. In *Proceedings of the 11th IEEE International Conference on Requirements Engineering*, Monterey Bay, CA, USA (pp. 75-84).

Paim, F. R. S., & Castro, J. B. (2003). DWARF: An approach for requirements definition and management of data warehouse systems. In *Proceedings of the Int. Conf. on Requirements Engineering*, Monterey Bay, CA.

Palpanas, T., Sidle, R., Cochrane, R., & Pirahesh, H. (2002). Incremental maintenance for non-distributive aggregate functions. In *VLDB* (pp. 802-813).

Pan, Z., & Heflin, J. (2003). DLDB: Extending relational databases to support Semantic Web queries. In *Proceedings of the 1st International Workshop on Practical and Scalable Semantic Systems (PSSS'03)* (pp. 109-113).

Pang, A. (2008). Visualizing uncertainty in natural hazards. In A. Bostrom, S. French, & S. Gottlieb (Eds.), *Risk assessment, modeling and decision support: Strategic directions series: Risk, governance and society* (pp. 261-294). Berlin, Germany: Springer.

Papadias, D., Tao, Y., Kalnis, P., & Zhang, J. (2002). Indexing spatio-temporal data warehouses. In *Proceedings of the 18th International Conference on Data Engineering* (pp. 166-175). Los Alamitos, CA, USA: IEEE Computer Society.

Parag, S., & Pedro, D. (2004). Multi-relational record linkage. In *Proceedings of the ACM SIGKDD Workshop on Multi-Relational Data Mining* (pp. 31-48).

Park, B.-K., Han, H., & Song, I.-Y. (2005). XML-OLAP: A multidimensional analysis framework for XML warehouses. In *Proceedings of the 7th International Conference on Data Warehousing and Knowledge Discovery (DaWaK'05)*, Copenhagen, Denmark (LNCS 3589, pp. 32-42). Berlin, Germany: Springer.

Park, J., & Sandhu, R. (2004). The uconabc usage control model. *ACM Transactions on Information Security, 7*(1), 128–174. doi:10.1145/984334.984339

Park, M. J., Lee, J. H., Lee, C. H., Lin, J., Serres, O., & Chung, C. W. (2007). An efficient and scalable management of ontology. In *Proceedings of the 12th International Conference on Database Systems for Advanced Applications (DASFAA'07)* (pp. 975-980).

Park, S., & Kim, J. (2003). Chameleon: A resource scheduler in a data grid environment. In *Proceedings of the 3st international Symposium on Cluster Computing and the Grid*. IEEE Computer Society.

Patel-Schneider, P. F., & Motik, B. (2008). OWL2 Web ontology language: Mapping to RDF graphs. *W3C Working Draft 08 October 2008*. Retrieved from http://www.w3.org/TR/owl-ref

Patterson, D. A., Gibson, G., & Katz, R. H. (1998). A case for redundant arrays of inexpensive disks (raid). In *Proceedings of the International Conference on Management of Data* (pp. 109-116).

Pedersen, T. B., & Jensen, C. (1999). Multidimensional data modeling for complex data. In *Proceedings of the International Conference on Data Engineering*, Sydney, Australia (pp. 336-345).

Peralta, V., Illarze, A., & Ruggia, R. (2003). On the applicability of rules to automate data warehouse logical design. In *Proceedings of the Decision Systems Engineering Workshop*, Klagenfurt, Austria (pp. 317-328).

Petrini, J., & Risch, T. (2007). SWARD: Semantic Web abridged relational databases. In *Proceedings of the 18th International Conference on Database and Expert Systems Applications (DEXA'07)* (pp. 455- 459).

Phipps, C., & Davis, K. (2002). Automating data warehouse conceptual schema design and evaluation. *In Proceedings of the 4th Int. Workshop on Design and Management of Data Warehouses* (Vol. 58, pp. 23-32).

Pierra, G. (2008). Context representation in domain ontologies and its use for Semantic integration of data. [JODS]. *Journal of Data Semantics, X*, 173–210.

Pierra, G., Dehainsala, H., Aït-Ameur, Y., & Bellatreche, L. (2005). Base de Données à Base Ontologique: Principes et mise en oeuvre. *Ingénierie des Systèmes d Information, 10*(2), 91–115. doi:10.3166/isi.10.2.91-115

Pivk, A., Cimiano, P., & Sure, Y. (2004). From tables to frames. In *Proceedings of the International Semantic Web Conference* (LNCS 3298, pp. 116-181). Berlin, Germany: Springer.

Poess, M., & Othayoth, R. K. (2005). Large scale data warehouses on grid: Oracle database 10g and HP proliant servers. In *Proc. of the 31st international Conference on Very Large Data Bases* (pp. 1055-1066).

Pokorný, J. (2002). XML data warehouse: Modelling and querying. In *Proceedings of the 5th International Baltic Conference (BalticDB&IS'06)*, Tallin, Estonia (pp. 267-280). Institute of Cybernetics at Tallin Technical University.

Popa, L., Velegrakis, Y., Miller, R. J., Hernadez, M. A., & Fagin, R. (2002). Translating Web data. In *Proceedings of the VLDB Conference* (pp. 598-609).

Pourabbas, E., & Rafanelli, M. (2002). A pictorial query language for querying geographic databases using positional and OLAP operators. *SIGMOD Record, 31*(2), 22–27. doi:10.1145/565117.565121

Prakash, N., & Gosain, A. (2003). Requirements driven data warehouse development. In *Proceedings of the 15th Conference on Advanced Information Systems Engineering Short Paper Proc.*, Velden, Austria.

Prat, N., Akoka, J., & Comyn-Wattiau, I. (2006). A UML-based data warehouse design method. *Decision Support Systems, 42*, 1449–1473. doi:10.1016/j.dss.2005.12.001

Priebe, T., & Pernul, G. (2004). Sicherheit in Data-Warehouse- und OLAP-Systemen. *Rundbrief der Fachgruppe Modellierung betrieblicher Informationssysteme (MobIS) der Gesellschaft für Informatik e.V. (GI)*.

Prud'hommeaux, E., & Seaborne, A. (2008). SPARQL query language for RDF. W3C *Candidate Recommendation 15 January 2008*. Retrieved from http://www.w3.org/TR/rdf-sparql-query

Quix, C. (1999). Repository support for data warehouse evolution. In S. Gatziu et al. (Eds.), *Proceedings of the 1st International Workshop on Design and Management of Data Warehouses* (p. 4). CEUS-WS.org

Rajugan, R., Chang, E., & Dillon, T. S. (2005). Conceptual design of an XML FACT repository for dispersed XML document warehouses and XML marts. In *Proceedings of the 20th International Conference on Computer and Information Technology (CIT'05)*, Shanghai, China (pp. 141-149). Washington, DC: IEEE Computer Society.

Ranganathan, K., & Foster, I. (2004). Computation scheduling and data replication algorithms for data Grids. In *Grid resource management: State of the art and future trends* (pp. 359-373). Norwell, MA: Kluwer Academic Publishers.

Rantzau, R., Constantinescu, C., Heinkel, U., & Meinecke, H. (2002). Champagne: Data change propagation for heterogeneous information systems. In *VLDB '02, VLDB Endowment* (pp. 1099-1102).

Rao, J., Zhang, C., Megiddo, N., & Lohman, G. (2002). Automating physical database design in a parallel database. Proceedings of the ACM International Conference on Management of Data, 558-569, Madison, Wisconsin, USA, June 2002.

Ravat, F., & Teste, O. (2000). A temporal object-oriented data warehouse model. In M. Ibrahim, J. Küng, & N. Revell (Eds.), *Proceedings of the International conference on Database and Expert Systems Applications* (pp. 583-592). Heidelberg: Springer.

Ravat, F., Teste, O., & Zurfluh, G. (2006). A multiversion-based multidimensional model. In *Proc. of Int. Conference on Data Warehousing and Knowledge Discovery (DaWaK)* (LNCS 4081, pp. 65-74).

Reed, M. (2007). A definition of data warehousing. *Intranet Journal*. Retrieved from http://www.intranetjournal.com/features/datawarehousing.html

Reynaud, C., & Safar, B. (2009). Construction automatique d'adaptateurs guidée par une ontologie pour l'intégration de sources et de données XML. *Technique et Science Informatiques. Numéro spécial Web Sémantique, 28*(2).

Rivest, S., Bédard, Y., & Marcand, P. (2001). Towards better support for spatial decision-making: Defining the characteristics of spatial on-line analytical processing. *Journal of the Canadian Institute of Geomatics, 55*(4), 539–555.

Rivest, S., Bédard, Y., Proulx, M., Nadeaum, M., Hubert, F., & Pastor, J. (2005). SOLAP: Merging business intelligence with geospatial technology for interactive spatio-temporal exploration and analysis of data. *Journal of International Society for Photogrammetry and Remote Sensing, 60*(1), 17–33. doi:10.1016/j.isprsjprs.2005.10.002

Rizzi, S. (2007). OLAP Preferences: A research agenda. In *Proceedings of the ACM tenth international workshop on Data warehousing and OLAP DOLAP '07*. Lisboa, Portugal.

Rizzi, S., & Golfarelli, M. (2006). What time is it in the data warehouse? In A. Tjoa & J. Trujillo (Eds.), *Proceedings of the 8th International Conference on Data Warehousing and Knwoledge Discovery, DaWaK 2006* (pp. 134-144). Heidelberg: Springer.

Rizzi, S., & Golfarelli, M. (2007). X-time: Schema versioning and cross-version querying in data warehouses. In *Proc. of Int. Conference on Data Engineering (ICDE)* (pp. 1471-1472).

Robinson, A. (1965). A machine-oriented logic based on the resolution principle. *Journal of Association for Computing Machinery, 12*(1), 23–41.

Rousset, M.-C., & Reynaud, C. (2003). Picsel and Xyleme: Two illustrative information integration agents. In M. Klusch, S. Bergamaschi, P. Petta, & P. Edwards (Eds.), *Intelligent information agents research and development in Europe: An AgentLink perspective* (LNCS State of the Art Surveys, pp. 50-78). Berlin, Germany: Springer Verlag.

Rousset, M.-C., Bidault, A., Froidevaux, C., Gagliardi, H., Goasdoué, F., Reynaud, C., & Safar, B. (2002). Construction de médiateurs pour intégrer des sources d'information multiples et hétérogènes: Le projet PICSEL. *Revue 13, 2*(1), 9-59.

Roy, A., & Sander, V. (2004). GARA: A uniform quality of service architecture. In Grid resource management: State of the art and future trends (pp. 377-394). Norwell, MA: Kluwer Academic Publishers.

Roy, P. Seshadri, S., Sudarshan, S., & Bhobe, S. (2000). *Efficient and extensible algorithms for multiquery optimization.* Paper presented at the International Conference on Management of Data SIGMOD, San Diego, USA.

Rundensteiner, E., Koeller, A., & Zhang, X. (2000). Maintaining data warehouses over changing information sources. *Communications of the ACM, 43*(6), 57–62. doi:10.1145/336460.336475

Rusu, L. I., Rahayu, J. W., & Taniar, D. (2005). A methodology for building XML data warehouse. *International Journal of Data Warehousing and Mining, 1*(2), 67–92.

Rusu, L. I., Rahayu, W., & Taniar, D. (2004). On data cleaning in building XML data warehouses. In *Proceedings of the 6th Intl. Conference on Information Integration and Web-based Applications & Services (iiWAS2004),* Jakarta, Indonesia (pp. 797-807).

Rusu, L. I., Rahayu, W., & Taniar, D. (2005). A methodology for building XML data warehouses. *International Journal of Data Warehousing and Mining, 1*(2), 67–92.

Saccol, D. B., & Heuser, C. A. (2002). Integration of XML Data. In *Proceedings of VLDB workshop on Efficiency and Effectiveness of XML Tools and Techniques (EEXTT) and of the international Conference on Advanced Information System Engineering (CAISE) workshop on Databases in Telecommunications and Web (DTWeb2002) Revised papers* (LNCS 2590, pp. 68-80).

Sahuguet, A. (2000). Everything you ever wanted to know about DTDs, but were afraid to ask. In *Proceedings of the International Workshop on the Web and Databases WebDB 2000* (pp. 171-183).

Saïs, F., Pernelle, N., & Rousset, M. C. (2007). L2R: A logical method for reference reconciliation. In [Menlo Park, CA: AAAI Press.]. *Proceedings of the AAAI, 2007,* 329–334.

Saïs, F., Pernelle, N., & Rousset, M.-C. (2007). L2R: A logical method for reference reconciliation. In *Proceedings of the Twenty-Second AAAI Conference on Artificial Intelligence* (pp. 329-334).

Saïs, F., Pernelle, N., & Rousset, M.-C. (2009). Combining a logical and a numerical method for data reconciliation. *Journal of Data Semantics, LNCS 5480, 12,* 66-94.

Salem, A., Ghozzi, F., & Ben-Abdallah, H. (2008). Multi-dimensional modeling - formal specification and verification of the hierarchy concept. In . *Proceedings of the ICEIS, 2008*(1), 317–322.

Samarati, P., & Sweeney, L. (1998). Protecting privacy when disclosing information: k-anonymity and its through generalization and suppression. In *Proceedings of the IEEE Symposium on Research in Security and Privacy.*

Sampaio, M., Sousa, A., & Baptista, C. (2006). Towards a logical multidimensional model for spatial data warehousing and OLAP. In Y. Song & P. Vassiliadis (Eds.), *Proceedings of the 9th ACM International Workshop on Data Warehousing and OLAP* (pp. 83-90). New York: ACM Press.

Sandhu, R. S., Coyne, E. J., Feinstein, H. L., & Youman, C. E. (1996, February). Role-based access control models. *IEEE Computer, 29*(2), 38–47.

Sandhu, R. S., Ferraiolo, D., & Kuhn, R. (2000, July). The nist model for role-based access control: Towards a unified standard. In *Proc. of 5th ACM Workshop on Role-Based Access Control*, Berlin, Germany: ACM Press.

SAP. (2000). *Multi-dimensional Modeling with BW: ASAP for BW Accelerator.* Retrieved May 8, 2007 from http://sap.com

Sapia, C., Blaschka, M., Hofling, G., & Dinter, B. (1999). *Extending the E/R model for the multidimensional paradigm* (. *LNCS, 1552,* 105–116.

Sarda, N. (1999). Temporal issues in data warehouse systems. In *Proceedings of the International Symposium on Database Applications in Non-traditional Environments* (pp. 27-34). New York: IEEE Computer Society.

Schenck, D., & Wilson, P. (1994). *Information modelling the EXPRESS way*. New York: Oxford University Press.

Schlesinger, L., Bauer, A., Lehner, W., Ediberidze, G., & Gutzman, M. (2001). Efficiently synchronizing multidimensional schema data. In *Proc. of ACM Int. Workshop on Data Warehousing and OLAP (DOLAP)* (pp. 69-76).

Schmidt, A. R., Kersten, M. L., Windhouwer, M. A., & Waas, F. (2000). Efficient relational storage and retrieval of XML documents. In *Proceedings of the Workshop on the Web and Databases (WebDB)*, Dallas, USA.

Schnaitter, K., Abiteboul, S., Milo, T., & Polyzotis, N. N. (2006). *COLT – Continuous Online Database Tuning*. Paper presented at the ACM SIGMOD Conference on Data Management, SIGMOD'06

Schneider, M. (2003). Well-formed data warehouse structures. In *Proceedings of the 5th International Workshop at VLDB'03 on Design and Management of Data Warehouses (DMDW'2003)*, Berlin, Germany.

Scotch, M., & Parmanto, B. (2006). Development of SOVAT: A numerical-spatial decision support system for community health assessment research. *International Journal of Medical Informatics*, 75(10-11), 771–784. doi:10.1016/j.ijmedinf.2005.10.008

Seaborne, A. (2004). RDQL – A query language for RDF. *W3C Member Submission 9 January 2004*. Retrieved from http://www.w3.org/Submission/2004/SUBM-RDQL-20040109

Seaborne, A., & Manjunath, G. (2008). SPARQL/Update: A language for updating RDF graphs. Retrieved from http://jena.hpl.hp.com/~afs/SPARQL-Update.html

Seba, D. (2003). *Merise - concepts et mise en œuvre*. France: Eni.

Sen, A., & Sinha, A. P. (2005). A comparison of data warehousing methodologies. *Communications of the ACM, 48*(3), 79–84. doi:10.1145/1047671.1047673

Shahzad, M. K., Nasir, J. A., & Pasha, M. A. (2005). CEV-DW: Creation and evolution of versions in data warehouse. *Asian Journal of Information Technology, 4*(10), 910–917.

Shanmugasundarma, J., Tufte, K., He, G., Zhang, C., DeWitt, D., & Naughton, J. (1999). Relational database for querying XML documents: Limitation and opportunities. *Proceedings of the 25th VLDB Conferences*, Scotland.

Shekar, S., Lu, C., Tan, X., Chawla, S., & Vatsavai, R. (2001). Map cube: A visualization tool for spatial data warehouses. In H. Miller & J. Han (Eds.), *Geographic data mining and knowledge discovery* (pp. 74-109). London: Taylor & Francis.

Sheth, A. P., & Larson, J. A. (1990). Federated database systems for managing distributed, heterogeneous, and autonoumous databases. *ACM Computing Surveys, 22*(3), 183–236. doi:10.1145/96602.96604

Siberski, W., Pan, J. Z., & Thaden, U. (2006). Querying the Semantic Web with preferences. In *Proceedings of the 5th International SemanticWeb Conference ISWC* (pp. 612-624).

Sieg, A., Mobasher, B., & Burke, R. (2007). Ontological user profiles for representing context in Web search. In *Proceedings of the 2007 IEEE/WIC/ACM International Conferences on Web Intelligence and Intelligent Agent Technology – Workshops* (pp. 91-94).

Silva, J., Times, V., & Salgado, A. (2006). An open source and Web based framework for geographic and multidimensional processing. In H. Haddad (Ed.), *Proceedings of the ACM Symposium on Applied Computing* (pp. 63-67). New York: ACM Press.

Siva Sathya, S., Kuppuswami, S., & Ragupathi, R. (2006). Replication strategies for data grids. *International Conference on Advanced Computing and Communications. ADCOM 2006* (pp 123-128).

Soergel, D., Lauser, B., Liang, A., Fisseha, F., Keizer, J., & Katz, S. (2004). Reengineering thesauri for new applications: The AGROVOC example. *Journal of Digital Information, 4*(4). Retrieved from http://www.informatik.uni-trier.de/~ley/db/journals/jodi/jodi4.html

Soler, E., Stefanov, V., Mazon, J. N., Trujillo, J., Fernandez-Medina, E., & Piattini, M. (2008). Towards comprehensive requirement analysis for data warehouses: Considering security requirements. In *Proceedings of the Third International Conference on Availability, Reliability and Security - ARES 2008*, Barcelona, Spain (pp. 4-7).

SPARQL Query Language for RDF. (January 2008). *SPARQL*. Retrieved from http://www.w3.org/TR/rdf-sparql-query

Stefanovic, N., Han, J., & Kopersky, K. (2000). Object-based selective materialization for efficient implementation of spatial data cubes. *IEEE Transactions on Knowledge and Data Engineering, 12*(6), 938–958. doi:10.1109/69.895803

Stöhr et al, 2000 Stöhr, T., Märtens, H., & Rahm, E. 2000. Multi-Dimensional Database Allocation for Parallel Data Warehouses. In Proceedings of the 26th international Conference on Very Large Data Bases. 273-284.

Stöhr, T., & Märtens, H. Rahm, E. (2000). Multi-dimensional database allocation for parallel data warehouses, In *Proc. 26th Intl. Conf. on Very Large Databases (VLDB)*.

Stolte, C., Tang, D., & Hanrahan, P. (2003). Multiscale visualization using data cubes. *IEEE Transactions on Visualization and Computer Graphics, 9*(2), 176–187. doi:10.1109/TVCG.2003.1196005

Stonebraker, M., & Schloss, G. A. (1990). Distributed RAID - A new multiple copy algorithm. *International Conference on Data Engineering* (pp. 430-437).

Sweeney, L. (2002). k-anonymity: a model for protecting privacy. *International Journal on Uncertainty, Fuzziness and Knowledge-based Systems, 10*(5), 557–570. doi:10.1142/S0218488502001648

Tandem (1987). *NonStop SQL, A distributed, high-performance, high-reliability implementation of SQL.* Paper presented at the Workshop on High Performance Transactional Systems.

TCP(2005). TCP Benchmark H Standard Specification Revision 2.3.0.

Theobald, M., Weikum, G., & Schenkel, R. (2004). Top-k query evaluation with probabilistic guarantees. In *Proceedings of the 13th International Conference on Very Large Database VLDB'04* (pp. 648-659).

Theodoratos, D., Ligoudistianos, S., & Sellis, T. (2001). View selection for designing the global data warehouse. *Data and Knowledge Engineering Journal, 39*, 219–240. doi:10.1016/S0169-023X(01)00041-6

Theoharis, Y., Christophides, V., & Karvounarakis, G. (2005). Benchmarking database representations of RDF/S stores. In *Proceedings of the 4th International Semantic Web Conference (ISWC'05)* (pp. 685-701).

Thomopoulos, R., Buche, B., & Haemmerle, O. (2006). Fuzzy sets defined on a hierarchical domain. *IEEE Transactions on Knowledge and Data Engineering, 18*(10), 1397–1410. doi:10.1109/TKDE.2006.161

Thuraisingham, B. (2005). Privacy constraint processing in a privacy-enhanced database management system. *Data & Knowledge Engineering, 55*, 159–188. doi:10.1016/j.datak.2005.03.001

Tolle, K., & Wleklinski, F. (2004). *Easy RDF query language (eRQL).* Retrieved from http://www.dbis.informatik.uni-frankfurt.de/~tolle/RDF/eRQL

Tomlin, D. (1990). *Geographic information systems and cartographic modeling.* Upper Saddle River, NJ: Prentice Hall.

Toninelli, A., Corradi, A., & Montanari, R. (2008). Semantic-based discovery to support mobile context aware service access. *Computer Communications, 31*(5), 935–949. doi:10.1016/j.comcom.2007.12.026

Transaction processing council benchmarks (2008). Retrieved from http://www.tpc.org

Trujillo, J., Luján-Mora, S., & Medina, E. (2002). The gold model case tool: An environment for designing OLAP applications. In *Proceedings of the International Conference on Enterprise Information Systems*, Ciutad Real, Spain (pp. 699-707).

Tryfona, N., Busborg, F., & Borch Christiansen, J. G. (1999). starER: A conceptual model for data warehouse design. In *Proceedings of the ACM International Workshop on Data Warehousing and OLAP*, Kansas City, USA (pp. 3-8).

Tsois, A., Karayannidis, N., & Sellis, T. (2001). MAC: Conceptual data modeling for OLAP. In *Proceedings of the International Workshop on Design and Management of Data Warehouses*. Interlaken, Switzerland (pp. 5.1-5.11).

Vaisman, A., & Mendelzon, A. (2001). A temporal query language for OLAP: Implementation and case study. In G. Ghelli & G. Grahne (Eds.), *Proceedings of the 8th International Workshop on Database Programing Languages* (pp. 78-96). Heidelberg: Springer.

Vaisman, A., & Mendelzon, A. (2001). A temporal query language for OLAP: Implementation and case study. In *Proc. of Int. Workshop on Database Programming Languages (DBPL)* (LNCS 2397, pp. 78-96).

Van Rijsbergen, C. J. (1979). *Information retrieval* (2nd ed.)., Department of computer science, University of Glasgow, Scotland: Butterworth-Heinemann.

Vangenot, C. (2001). Supporting decision-making with alternative data representations. *Journal of Geographic Information and Decision Analysis, 5*(2), 66–82.

Vassiliadis, P., Bouzeghoub, M., & Quix, C. (1999). Towards quality-oriented data warehouse usage and evolution. In *Proceedings of the International Conference on Advanced Information Systems Engineering*, Heidelberg, Germany (pp. 149-163).

Venugopal, S., Buyya, R., & Ramamohanarao, K. (2006). A taxonomy of Data Grids for distributed data sharing, management, and processing. *ACM Computing Surveys, 38*(1), 3. doi:10.1145/1132952.1132955

Viappiani, P., Faltings, B., & Pu, P. (2006). Preference based search using example-critiquing with suggestions. *Journal of Artificial Intelligence Research, 27*.

Voss, A., Hernandez, V., Voss, H., & Scheider, S. (2004). Interactive Visual exploration of multidimensional data: Requirements for CommonGIS with OLAP. In *Proceedings of the 15th International Workshop on Database and Expert Systems Applications* (pp. 883-887). Los Alamitos, CA: IEEE Computer Society.

Vrdoljak, B., Banek, M., & Rizzi, S. (2003). Designing Web warehouses from XML schema. In *Proceedings of the 5th International Conference Data Warehousing and Knowledge Discovery: DaWak*, Prague Czech.

Vrdoljak, B., Banek, M., & Rizzi, S. (2003). DesigningWebwarehouses from XML schemas. In *Proceedings of the 5th International Conference on DataWarehousing and Knowledge Discovery (DaWaK'03)*, Prague, Czech Republic (LNCS 2737, pp. 89-98). Berlin Germany: Springer.

Wan, T., Zeitouni, K., & Meng, X. (2007). An OLAP system for network-constrained moving objects. In Y. Cho, R. Wainwright, H. Haddad, S. Shin, & Y. Koo (Eds.), *Proceedings of the ACM symposium on Applied computing* (pp. 13-18). New York: ACM Press.

Wang, H., Li, J., He, Z., & Gao, H. (2005). OLAP for XML data. In *Proceedings of the 1st International Conference on Computer and Information Technology (CIT'05)*, Shanghai, China (pp. 233-237). Washington, DC: IEEE Computer Society.

Watson, P. (2001). *Databases and the grid*. UK e-Science Technical Report Series.

Wehrle, P., Miquel, M., & Tchounikine, A. (2007). A grid services-oriented architecture for efficient operation of distributed data warehouses on Globus. In *Proceedings of the 21st international Conference on Advanced Networking and Applications (AINA)* (pp. 994-999).

Weibel, R., & Dutton, G. (2001). Generalizing spatial data and dealing with multiple representations. In P. Longley, M. Goodchild, D. Maguire, & D. Rhind (Eds.),

Geographic Information systems and science (pp. 125-155). New York: John Wiley & Sons.

Widom, J. (1995). Research problems in data warehousing. In *Proc. of ACM Conference on Information and Knowledge Management (CIKM)* (pp. 25-30).

Widom, J. (1999). Data management for XML - research directions. *IEEE Data Engineering Bulletin, Special Issue on XML, 22*(3).

Wikipedia Encyclopedia. (2008). *Database*. Retrieved August 1, 2008, from http://en.wikipedia.org/wiki/Database

Willenborg, L., & De Waal, T. (1996). *Statistical disclosure control in practice*. Berlin: Springer-Verlag.

Winter, R., & Strauch, B. (2003). A method for demand-driven information requirements analysis in data warehousing. In *Proceedings of the Hawaii International Conference on System Sciences*, Hawaii (pp. 1359-1365).

Wolski, R. (1997). Forecasting network performance to support dynamicscheduling using the network weather service. In *Proceedings of the 6th IEEE international Symposium on High Performance Distributed Computing (August 05 - 08, 1997)* (pp. 316). IEEE.

World Wide Web Consortium XML Schema. (2008). *W3C candidate recommendation*. Retrieved August 1, 2008, from http://www.w3.org/XML/Schema.html

Wrembel, R. (2009). A survey on managing the evolution of data warehouses. [IGI Global.]. *International Journal of Data Warehousing and Mining, 5*(2), 24–56.

Wrembel, R., & Bebel, B. (2007). Metadata management in a multiversion data warehouse. *Journal on Data Semantics, 8*, 118–157.

Wrembel, R., & Bębel, B. (2007). Metadata management in a multiversion data warehouse. *Journal on Data Semantics (JODS), 8*, 118-157. LNCS 4380.

Wrembel, R., & Morzy, T. (2006). Managing and querying versions of multiversion data warehouse. In *Proc. of Int. Conference on Extending Database Technology (EDBT)* (LNCS 3896, pp. 1121-1124).

Wu, Z., Eadon, G., Das, S., Chong, E. I., Kolovski, V., Annamalai, M., & Srinivasan, J. (2008). Implementing an inference engine for RDFS/OWL constructs and user-defined rules in Oracle. In *Proceedings of the 24th International Conference on Data Engineering (ICDE'08)* (pp. 1239-1248).

Xuan, D. N., Bellatreche, L., & Pierra, G. (2006). A versioning management model for ontology-based data warehouses. In *Proceedings of the 8th International Conference on Data Warehousing and Knowledge Discovery (DaWak'06)* (pp. 195-206).

Xyleme, L. (2001). Xyleme: A dynamic warehouse for XML data of the Web. In *Proceedings of the International Database Engineering & Applications Symposium (IDEAS'01)*, Grenoble, France (pp. 3-7). Washington, DC: IEEE Computer Society.

Yan, M. H., & Ada, W. C. F. (2001). From XML to relational database. In *Proceedings of the CEUR Workshop.*

Yang, J., & Widom, J. (1998). Maintaining temporal views over non-temporal information sources for data warehousing. In H-J. Schenk, F. Saltor, I. Ramos, & G. Alonso (Eds.), *Proceedings of the 1998 International Conference on Extending Database Technology* (pp. 389-403). Heidelberg: Springer.

Yang, J., Karlapalem, K., & Li, Q. (1997). Algorithm for materialized view design in data warehousing environment. *23rd International Conf. on Very Large Data Bases, VLDB'97, Athens, Greece* (pp. 136-145.

Yu, E. (1993). Modeling organizations for information systems requirements engineering. In *Proceedings of the First IEEE International Symposium on Requirements Engineering*, San Jose, USA (pp. 34-41).

Yu, E. (1995). *Modelling strategic relationships for process reengineering*. Unpublished doctoral dissertation, Department of Computer Science, University of Toronto.

Yu, E. (1997). Towards modeling and reasoning support for early-phase requirements engineering. In *Proceedings of the 3ʳᵈ IEEE International Symposium on Requirements Engineering*, Annapolis, USA.

Yu, E., & Mylopoulos, J. (1994). Understanding 'why' in software process modeling, analysis and design. In *Proceedings of the Sixteenth International Conference on Software Engineering*, Sorrento, Italy.

Yu, E., & Mylopoulos, J. (1996). Using goals, rules, and methods to support reasoning in business process reengineering. *International Journal of Intelligent Systems in Accounting Finance & Management, 5*(1), 1–13. doi:10.1002/(SICI)1099-1174(199603)5:1<1::AID-ISAF99>3.0.CO;2-C

Zadeh, L. A. (1965). Fuzzy sets. *Information and Control, 8*, 338–353. doi:10.1016/S0019-9958(65)90241-X

Zhang, J., Wang, W., Liu, H., & Zhang, S. (2005). X-warehouse: Building query pattern-driven data. In *Proceedings of the 14ᵗʰ international conference on World Wide Web (WWW'05)*, Chiba, Japan (pp. 896-897). New York: ACM Press.

Zhang, L., & Yang, X. (2008). An approach to semantic annotation for metadata in relational databases. In *Proceedings of the International Symposiums on Information Processing (ISIP)* (pp. 635-639).

Zhang, X., & Rundensteiner, E. A. (2000). Dyda: Dynamic data warehouse maintenance in a fully concurrent environment. In *DaWaK 2000: Proceedings of the Second International Conference on Data Warehousing and Knowledge Discovery, London, UK* (pp. 94-103). Springer-Verlag.

Zhou, J., Larson, P., Goldstein, J., & Ding, L. (2007). *Dynamic materialized views.* Paper presented at the International Conference of Data Engineering (ICDE'07).

Zhuge, Y., Garcia-Molina, H., Hamer, J., & Widom, J. (1995). View maintenance in a warehousing environment. In M. Carey & D. Schreider (Eds.), *Proceedings of SIGMOD* (pp. 316-327). New York: ACM Press.

Ziegler, P., Sturm, C., & Dittrich, K. R. (2005). Unified querying of ontology languages with the SIRUP Ontology Query API. In *Datenbanksysteme in Business, Technologie und Web (BTW'05)* (pp. 325-344).

About the Contributors

Ladjel Bellatreche received his PhD in computer science from the Clermont Ferrand University (France, 2000). He is an Assistant Professor in Computer Science at Poitiers University, France since 2002. Before joining Poitiers University, he has been a visiting researcher at Hong Kong University of Science and Technology (HKUST) from 1997 to 1999 and also has been a visiting researcher in the Computer Science Department at Purdue University, USA during the summer of 2001. He has worked extensively in the areas: heterogeneous data integration using formal ontologies, distributed databases, data warehousing, and data mining. He has published more than 75 research papers in these areas in leading international journal and conferences. Ladjel has been associated with many conferences and journals as program committee members.

* * *

Yamine Ait Ameur is full professor at the National School of Engineers in Mechanics and Aeronautics (ENSMA). He is the director of the laboratory of computing (LISI) at ENSMA and head of the data engineering research team. Formal methods, ontology based data modeling and database are his main topics of interest. He has written several research papers and supervised several PhD thesis. His research results have been applied in various engineering areas like aeronautics, embedded systems and petroleum industry.

Mohamed Badri defended his Phd in computer science at the Paris Descartes University in 2008. Since 2007 he has worked as an adjunct assistant professor in the Department of Computer Science. His interests include maintenance of heterogeneous data warehouses. He also worked in the OLAP area trying to find a new OLAP structure.

Hanene Ben-Abdallah received a BS in computer science and a BS in mathematics from the University of Minnesota, MPLS, MN, USA in 1989, a Master's degree (in 1991) and a PhD in Computer and Information Science from the University of Pennsylvania, Philadelphia, PA, USA in 1996. She joined the Electrical and Computer Engineering Department of the University of Waterloo, CA for a postdoctoral fellowship in 1996. Since 1997, she has been in the Computer Science department in the Faculty of Economics and Management at the University of Sfax, Tunisia, where she is now an associate professor. Hanene's research interests include the application of formal methods and reuse techniques in software engineering, and graphical specification languages.

Zohra Bellahsene is Professor in computer science, at the University of Montpellier 2, France. She has devoted her recent research and publications on various aspects of data integration, and Database view mechanisms, organizing database summer schools, and serving on the committees of several French and international conferences. She has organized or chaired several international conferences and workshops, including being the PC chair of 20th International Conference on Advanced Information Systems Engineering (CAiSE'08), the general chair of the XML Database Symposium (XSym2006), the PC co-chair of the International conference on Object-Oriented Information Systems (OOIS'02) and the local chair of OTM'06 the confederated conferences (400 participants). She was the editor of the special issue of the DKE Journal on Data Integration over the Web in 2003. She is a founding member of the XML Database Symposium a co-event of VLDB since 2003. She has published in the following topics: object-oriented database views, meta-modelling, human genome databases, schema evolution, distributed database systems, view adaptation in data warehousing systems, data warehouse design, data integration, XML views management and P2P data sharing and schema matching. She is a member of the IEEE and Specif. She has been expert for Science Foundation Ireland (2004), ACI grande masse de données (2003) et ARA grande masse de données, 2005. She is currently the scientific responsible of the funded ARA masses de données project FORUM and the PICS project (CNRS-Ireland). PC member of international conferences in 2009: ER 2009, CoopIS2009, CAiSE 09, ESWC 2009, DATAX 2009 PC member of national conferences: BDA 2009 and EDA 09 Recent publications (2008):

- Khalid Saleem, Zohra Bellahsene, Ela Hunt PORSCHE: Performance ORiented SCHEma Mediation Information Systems Journal, Elsevier, to appear in 2008
- Duchateau Fabien, Zohra Bellahsene, Rémi Coletta. A Flexible Approach for Planning Schema Matching Algorithms, CoopIS'08, LNCS, Springer Verlag, Mexico, 2008, To appear
- Khalid Saleem and Zohra Bellahsene. Automatic Extraction of Structurally Coherent Mini-Taxonomies. In 27th International Conference on Conceptual Modeling (ER'08), LNCS, Barcelona, October 2008.

Fadila Bentayeb has been an associate professor at the University of Lyon 2, France since 2001. She is a member of the Decision Support Databases research group within the ERIC laboratory. She received her PhD degree in computer science from the University of Orléans, France in 1998. Her current research interests regard database management systems, including the integration of data mining techniques into DBMSs and data warehouse design, with a special interest for schema evolution, analysis personalization, XML and complex data warehousing, benchmarking and optimisation techniques.

Born in 1978, **Sandro Bimonte** is researcher at CEMAGREF, and more exactly he is at TSCF. He speaks fluently French, English, and Italian. Previously, he carried out researches at the University of Salerno, Italy (2002-2003), INSA-Lyon, French (2004-2007), IMAG, French 2007-2008. He is Managing Editor de Journal of Decision Systems, Editorial Board member of International Journal of Decision Support System Technology, and International Journal of Data Mining, Modelling and Management and member of the Commission on GeoVisualization of the International Cartographic Association. His research activities concern Spatial Data Warehouses and Spatial OLAP, Visual Languages, Geographic Information Systems, Spatio-temporal Databases and GeoVisualization.

Faouzi Boufarès has presented his Phd in 1986 at University Paris 11. He works as an associate professor in Paris Nord University. His research focus on database, data warehouse, integrity constraints in databases and integration of heterogeneous data sources.

Omar Boussaid is a full professor in computer science at the School of Economics and Management of the University of Lyon 2, France. He received his PhD degree in computer science from the University of Lyon 1, France in 1988. Since 1995, he is the director of the Master Computer Science Engineering for Decision and Economic Evaluation of the University of Lyon 2. He is a head of the Decision Support Databases research group within the ERIC Laboratory. His main research subjects are data warehousing, multidimensional databases and OLAP. His current research concerns complex data warehousing and mining, XML warehousing, combining OLAP and data mining, and the use of ontologies within complex data warehousing.

Patrice Buche received the Ph.D degree in computer science from the University of Rennes (France) in 1990. He was an assistant professor at INA P-G (Institut National Agronomique Paris-Grignon) from 1992 to 2002. He has been a research engineer at the Applied Mathematical and Computer Science department of INRA (Institut National de la Recherche Agronomique) since 2002. His research works mainly concern data integration and fuzzy querying in structured and weakly-structured databases. Dr Buche has published papers in these areas in several international conferences and journals.

Sandrine Contenot received the vocational training certificate taken at end of 2-year higher education course from the high school of Bar le Duc (France) in 1999. She was research computer technician at GEVES (Group for studies and controls on varieties and seeds) of INRA (Institut National de la Recherche Agronomique) from 2000 to 2007. She has been assistant engineer in computer science at the Applied Mathematical and Computer Science department of INRA since 2007.

Rogério Luís de Carvalho Costa is a PhD student at the University of Coimbra □ Portugal and aggregate professor at the Pontifícia Universidade Católica do Rio de Janeiro (PUC-Rio) - Brazil, where he teaches undergraduate curricula. His research interests include data warehousing, parallel and distributed database systems, database self-tuning and bioinformatics.

Jérôme Darmont received his Ph.D. in computer science from the University of Clermont-Ferrand II, France in 1999. He joined the University of Lyon 2, France in 1999 as an associate professor, and became full professor in 2008. He was head of the Decision Support Databases research group within the ERIC laboratory from 2000 to 2008, and has been director of the Computer Science and Statistics Department of the School of Economics and Management since 2003. His current research interests mainly relate to performance in database management systems and data warehouses (performance optimization, auto-administration, benchmarking...), but also include XML and complex data warehousing and mining, and medical or health-related applications.

Gayo Diallo is a member of the LISI/ENSMA Laboratory of Futuroscope Poitiers (data engineering research team). Prior to join LISI he was working as a postdoctoral researcher at City University of London on the EU funded project SeaLife (Semantic Web Browser for the Life Science). Gayo Diallo completed his PhD thesis in Computer Science in 2006 at University of Joseph Fourier Grenoble 1. He was also a part time Lecturer at University Pierre Mendes France Grenoble 2. His research interests include DB&IR integration, Semantic Web technologies and Ontologies, Information Personalisation, Knowledge Representation and Reasoning.

Juliette Dibie-Barthélemy received the Ph.D degree in computer science from the University of Paris-Dauphine (France) in 2000. She has been an assistant professor at AgroParisTech since 2000. Her research works mainly concern ontology-based data integration and flexible querying. He has published papers in these areas in several international conferences and journals.

David Doussot received an engineer degree in agronomy (computer science specialization) from the top French agronomy school (INA P-G) in 1997. He has been working as a developer and as a consultant in major banks and Telecom Company during 6 years. He specialized in web and Java technologies and participated to a book called « Technologies et Architectures Internet » published in 2000. He joined AgroParisTech as an assistant professor in 2003. Since then, he has been working in prototyping and implementing software concerning data integration and fuzzy querying.

Johann Eder is full professor for Information and Communication Systems at the University of Klagenfurt, Austria. Since 2005 he serves as vice president of the Austrian Science Funds (FWF). The research interests of Prof. Eder are databases, information systems and knowledge engineering. He successfully directed several funded research projects e.g. on workflow management systems, temporal data warehousing, application interoperability, self-healing web services, etc. He authored one book, edited 19 books/proceedings/special issues of journals and published more than 120 papers in international journals, edited books, and peer-reviewed conference proceedings. He served in numerous program committees for international conferences (including CAiSE, ER, CoopIS, ICDE, BPM, DEXA, DAWAK, ADBIS, etc) and as referee or editorial board member for international journals and conferences (including ACM TODS, ACM TOIS, IEEE TKDE, Information Systems, DKE, Computer Journal, JCSE, JUCS, etc.). Johann Eder received the degrees of Diplom-Ingenieur and Doctor of technical sciences from the University Linz, Austria. He held positions at the Universities of Vienna and Klagenfurt and visiting positions at the University of Hamburg, Germany, and with AT&T Research Shannon Labs, USA.

Jamel Feki received a BS in Computer and Information Systems from the University of Sfax, Tunisia in 1980, a Master's degree (in 1981) and a thèse troisième cycle in Computer Science (database field) from the University Paul SABATIER, Toulouse, France in 1984. He worked as a project manager at the Tunisian Petroleum company ETAP. Since 1986, he has been an assistant professor in the computer science department in the Faculty of Economics and Management at the University of Sfax, Tunisia. He was a visiting professor at the University of Qatar from 1993 until 1999. Jamel's research interests cover decision support systems domain: OLAP requirements specification, data warehouse design methods, and active data warehouses.

Pedro Furtado is assistant professor and senior researcher at the University of Coimbra, where he teaches both undergraduate and postgraduate curricula. His research interests include data warehousing, parallel and distributed database systems, performance and scalability, distributed data intensive systems. He received a PhD in computer science from the University of Coimbra - Portugal in 2000.

Matteo Golfarelli received his Ph.D. for his work on autonomous agents in 1998. In 2000 he joined the University of Bologna as a researcher. Since 2005 he is Associate Professor, teaching Information Systems, Database Systems and Data Mining. He has published over 60 papers in refereed journals and international conferences in the fields of data warehousing, pattern recognition, mobile robotics, multi-agent systems. He is co-author of the book **Data Warehouse Design: Modern Principles and Methodologies.** He served in the PC of several international conferences and as a reviewer in journals. Matteo Golfarelli is co-chair of the Business Information System conference; he is member of the editorial board of the International Journal of Data Mining, Modelling and Management (IJDMMM). His current research interests include all the aspects related to business intelligence and data warehousing, in particular multidimensional modeling, what-if analysis and BPM.

Yasser Hachaichi is a PhD student from the University of Sfax (Tunisia). He is currently a researcher at Multimedia, InfoRmation systems and Advanced Computing Laboratory (MIR@CL) .He received a Master in Computer Science in 2007 from the University of Sfax. He has published several papers about data warehouses in national and international workshops and conferences, such as EISWT, EDA, ASD, JDS, SIIE and so on. His research interests are: conceptual design of data warehouses, database modeling, multidimensional databases, and decision support systems.

Sana Hamdoun received her Phd in computer science at Paris Nord University at 2006. She works as an adjunct assistant professor at Paris Descartes University. His interests include construction of heterogeneous data warehouses.

Veronique Heiwy defended her PhD in Computer Science at the Sorbonne in 1996. Since then, she has worked as an associate professor. Her research focused on Information Systems, Process Modeling, Requirements Engineering. She also worked in the Data Mining area- more specifically to find similarities between times series. She took part as an active member in several European research Esprit projects. She defended her "ability to direct researches" at the Paris Descartes university in 2006. She is currently interested in the Data warehouses and Agent-oriented Software Engineering methods.

Gaëlle Hignette received an engineer degree in agronomy (computer science specialization) from the agronomy school INA P-G (Institut National Agronomique Paris-Grignon) in 2003. She received a master's degree in artificial intelligence from the Paris XI University (also known as Orsay) in 2004. She received a Ph.D degree in computer science from AgroParisTech in 2007. Her research work is focused on semantic annotation.

Liliana Ibanescu received a BSc/MSc degree in Computer Science in 1993 from the 'Alexandru Ioan Cuza' University, Iasi, Romania and a Ph.D degree in Computer Science in 2004 from 'Institut National Polytechnique de Lorraine', Nancy, France. She worked as an Assistant Professor at 'Alexandru Ioan Cuza' University during 6 years and she joined AgroParisTech in 2006. Her current research interest is in the mapping process of ontologies, with application to risk assessment in food.

Stephane Jean is assistant professor at the University of Poitiers. He is a member of the data engineering research team of the laboratory of computing (LISI) at the National School of Engineers in Mechanics and Aeronautics (ENSMA). He conducts research in the area of ontologies management especially in the context of databases. During his PhD thesis he has designed the OntoQL exploitation language for databases that store ontologies and the data they describe. This language is currently used in several projects in the engineering area.

Kazem Lellahi is Professor at Paris Nord University. He worked for many years in object database area. His research focus on theoretical aspects of computer science for modeling data and objects.

Wojciech Leja (MSc) and **Robert Ziembicki** (MSc) are graduate students from the Faculty of Computing and Management at Poznań University of Technology.

Sabine Loudcher (sabine.loudcher@univ-lyon2.fr) is an associate professor in computer science at the Department of Statistics and Computer Science of University of Lyon 2, France. She received her PhD degree in computer science from the University of Lyon 1, France in 1996. Since 2000, she has been a member of the Decision Support Databases research group within the ERIC Laboratory. Her main research subjects are data mining, multi-dimensional databases, OLAP, and complex data. Since 2003, she has been the assistant director of the ERIC Laboratory.

Hadj Mahboubi was born on 17 March 1981 in Tlemcen Algeria. Since December 2008, he holds a PhD in computer science from the University of Lyon 2, France. He received his master degree from INSA Lyon in 2005 and his engineering degree in computer science in 2003 from the University of Tlemcen, Algeria. He is a research assistant in the University of Lyon 2, France. He teaches relational and XML databases and programming languages. His research interests lie in the field of XML data warehouse design and performance optimization. He has published and presented his work in known database and data warehouse conferences such as DOLAP 2008.

Nathalie Pernelle is an assistant professor of Computer Science in the Laboratory ofComputer Science (LRI) at the University of Paris-Sud and member of the Gemo INRIA-Saclay team. Her research interest was first Natural Language Processing, then multi-valued data clustering using Galois lattices (ZOOM system), and finally information integration of heterogeneous sources. She works now on ontology-based reference reconciliation of RDF Data (LN2R), semantic annotation of more or less structured data (HTML or XML documents, tables), and query reformulation. These works are realized in the settings of several projects and various application domains such as food risk assessment, tourism domain, scientific publication citations or geographical data.

Guy Pierra is professor of computer science at ENSMA, Poitiers. He funded the Laboratory of computing (LISI) in Poitiers in 1992 as a laboratory common to ENSMA and Poitiers University. His main interests are data engineering, software engineering, ontology-based modeling, CAD/CAM and human-computer interaction. He published one book and more than hundred papers on these topics. Since the late 80's, G. Pierra and his colleagues of the LISI data engineering team have developed an ontology model, and an ontology-based approach, providing for modeling technical knowledge and industrial products. This approach, known as PLIB, has also been published as a series of international standard identified as ISO 13584. The PLIB ontology model and approach are now largely used in the engineering domain both for exchanging electronic catalogues and for developing ontology-based database of industrial components.

Jean-Christian Ralaivao is a PhD student in computer at ERIC laboratory, University of Lyon 2. He is actually an associate professor in computer science at Ecole Nationale d'Informatique, Madagascar. He received his master degree from University of Laval Québec Canada in 1995 and his engineering degree in computer science in 1990 from the Ecole Nationale d'Informatique, Madagascar. His research interests lie in the field of XML data warehouse design, decision support databases and performance optimisation.

Chantal Reynaud is a professor of Computer Science in the Laboratory of Computer Science (LRI) at the University of Paris-Sud. Her areas of research are Ontology Engineering and Information Integration. In particular, she works on the following topics: Information extraction from semi-structured data (e.g. XML documents), mappings between ontologies, discovery of mappings in peer to peer data management systems, ontology evolution. She is involved in several projects combining artificial intelligence and database techniques for information integration. She is the head of the Artificial Intelligence and Inference Systems Group in LRI and member of the INRIA-Saclay Île-de-France group called Gemo. She is the author of more than 70 refereed journal articles and conference papers.

Marie-Christine Rousset is a Professor of Computer Science at the University of Grenoble. Her areas of research are Knowledge Representation, Information Integration, and the Semantic Web. In particular, she works on the following topics: logic-based mediation between distributed data sources, automatic classification and clustering of semistructured data (e.g., XML documents), distributed reasoning, semantic dataspaces, semantic social networks. She has published over 80 refereed international journal articles and conference papers, and participated in several cooperative industry-university projects. She received a best paper award from AAAI in 1996, and has been nominated ECCAI fellow in 2005. She has served in many program committees of international conferences and workshops and in editorial boards of several journals.

Brigitte Safar is an Assistant Professor of Computer Science at the University of Paris-Sud 11. Her areas of research are Knowledge Representation, Information Integration, and the Semantic Web. In particular, she works on the following topics: logic-based mediation between distributed data sources, representation of ontology, cooperative query answering using ontology (query relaxation and refinement), ontology mapping.

Fatiha Saïs is an Assistant Professor of Computer Science in the Laboratory of Computer Science (LRI) at the University Paris-Sud. Her research interests are Semantic Data Integration and Semantic Web. More specifically, she works on Semantic Annotation of structured information, Reference Reconciliation and Reference Fusion. After graduating as a Master 1 from the University of Provence in 2003, she joined the University of Paris-Sud for a Master 2 Research and a PhD of Computer Science. In 2007, she graduated as a PhD with a thesis on "Semantic Data Integration guided by an Ontology". In 2008, she joined the Knowledge Representation and Reasoning group of Montpellier 2 University for a post-doc on the topic of Knowledge Representation of real world entities in the Conceptual Graph formalism.

Lydie Soler received the Professional Master's degree in Computer Sciences from the University of Versailles Saint Quentin en Yvelines (France) in 2003. She has been an engineer at the Applied Mathematical and Computer Science department of INRA (Institut National de la Recherche Agronomique) since 2004. She is a Java/J2EE analyst and software developer.

Dilek Tapucu was born in Izmir, Turkey. She received her B.S. degree in Chemical Engineering Department of Ege University in 1998. In Fall 1999, she joined the Izmir Institute of Technology (IZTECH) as a Research Assistant. She received her M.Sc. degree in 2002 from Computer Engineering Department of IZTECH. During her master degree she worked on Intrusion Detection Systems. She is currently working toward the Ph.D. degree with the LISI/ENSMA University of Poitiers, France and University of Ege, Turkey. Her PhD research is carried out under a joint supervision of Prof. Yamine Ait AMEUR (LISI/ENSMA) and Asst. Prof. Osman UNALIR (Ege University). Her research is focused on Ontology based Preference Modeling and Querying.

Murat Osman Ünalir was born in 1971. He received his Masters Degree from the Computer Engineering Department of Ege University in 1995. His M.Sc. thesis was "Declustering and Reorganization Methods in Parallel Databases". In 2001, he received his Ph.D. from the same Institution with a dissertation thesis of "Design of an Object-Oriented and Distributed Architecture for Reusable Component Libraries". He is currently working in the Computer Engineering Department as an Assistant Professor. He has experience in teaching Databases, Metadata Management, Semantic Web and .NET related courses, namely Windows Programming and Web Based Windows Programming. He was the project manager of the projects, AEGONT and DB.NET which were supported by Microsoft Research Cambridge. His research interests are Semantic Web and Distributed Knowledge Management.

Edgar R. Weippl (CISSP, CISA, CISM) is Science Director of Secure Business Austria and university assistant at the Vienna University of Technology. His research focuses on applied concepts of IT-security and e-learning. Edgar has taught several tutorials on security issues in e-learning at international conferences, including ED-MEDIA 2003-2007 and E-Learn 2005. In 2005, he published Security in E-Learning with Springer. After graduating with a Ph.D. from the Vienna University of Technology, Edgar worked for two years in a research startup. He then spent one year teaching as an assistant professor at Beloit College, WI. From 2002 to 2004, while with the software vendor ISIS Papyrus, he worked as a consultant for an HMO (Empire BlueCross BlueShield) in New York, NY and Albany, NY, and for Deutsche Bank (PWM) in Frankfurt, Germany.

From 2004 to 2008 **Karl Wiggisser** was a member of the Information- and Commounication Systems group at the Institute of Informatics-Systems at Klagenfurt University. He received his DI and PhD in Computer Science from Klagenfurt University in 2004 and 2008 respectively. His main research interest lies in Data Warehouse Maintenance. In this area he mainly worked on methods for change detection in data warehouse structures and meaningful data transformation between different versions of a data warehouse. Since 2008 Karl Wiggisser is a software developer at WINTERHELLER software.

Robert Wrembel (PhD, DSc) works in the Institute of Computing Science, at the Poznań University of Technology, Poland. In 2008 he received the post-doctoral degree in computer science, specializing in database systems and data warehouses. He was elected a deputy dean of the Faculty of Computing Science and Management, at the Poznań University of Technology for the period Sept. 2008 - Aug. 2012. Since 1996 he has been actively involved in 6 research projects on databases and 5 industrial projects in the field of information technologies. He has paid a number of visits to research and education centers, including the INRIA Paris-Rocquencourt (France), the Paris Dauphine University (France), the Klagenfurt University (Austria), and the Loyola University (USA). His main research interests encompass data warehouse technologies (temporal, multiversion, object-relational) and object-oriented systems (views, data access optimization, methods and views materialization).

Index